Reorienting the East

JEWISH CULTURE AND CONTEXTS

Published in association with the
Herbert D. Katz Center for Advanced Judaic Studies
of the University of Pennsylvania

A complete list of books in the series is available from the publisher.

Reorienting the East

Jewish Travelers to the Medieval Muslim World

Martin Jacobs

PENN

UNIVERSITY OF PENNSYLVANIA PRESS

PHILADELPHIA

Publication of this volume was assisted by a grant from the Herbert D. Katz Publications Fund of the Center for Advanced Judaic Studies.

Published by
University of Pennsylvania Press
Philadelphia, Pennsylvania 19104-4112
www.upenn.edu/pennpress

Printed in the United States of America on acid-free paper
10 9 8 7 6 5 4 3 2 1

Library of Congress Cataloging-in-Publication Data
Jacobs, Martin.
Reorienting the East : Jewish travelers to the medieval Muslim world / Martin Jacobs. — 1st ed.
p. cm. — (Jewish culture and contexts)
Includes bibliographical references and index.
ISBN 978-0-8122-4622-3 (hardcover : alk. paper)
1. Jews—Travel—History—Early works to 1800. 2. Jewish travelers—History—Early works to 1800. 3. Travelers' writings, Hebrew—Early works to 1800—History and criticism. 4. Travel, Medieval—Early works to 1800—History and criticism. 5. Jews—Islamic Empire—History. 6. Palestine—Description and travel—Early works to 1800. 7. Middle East—Description and travel—Early works to 1800. 8. Judaism—Relations—Islam—History. 9. Islam—Relations—Judaism—History. 10. Judaism—Relations—Christianity—History. 11. Christianity and other religions—Judaism—History. I. Title. II. Series: Jewish culture and contexts.
G277.J34 2014
915.604'14089924—dc23

2014004169

Contents

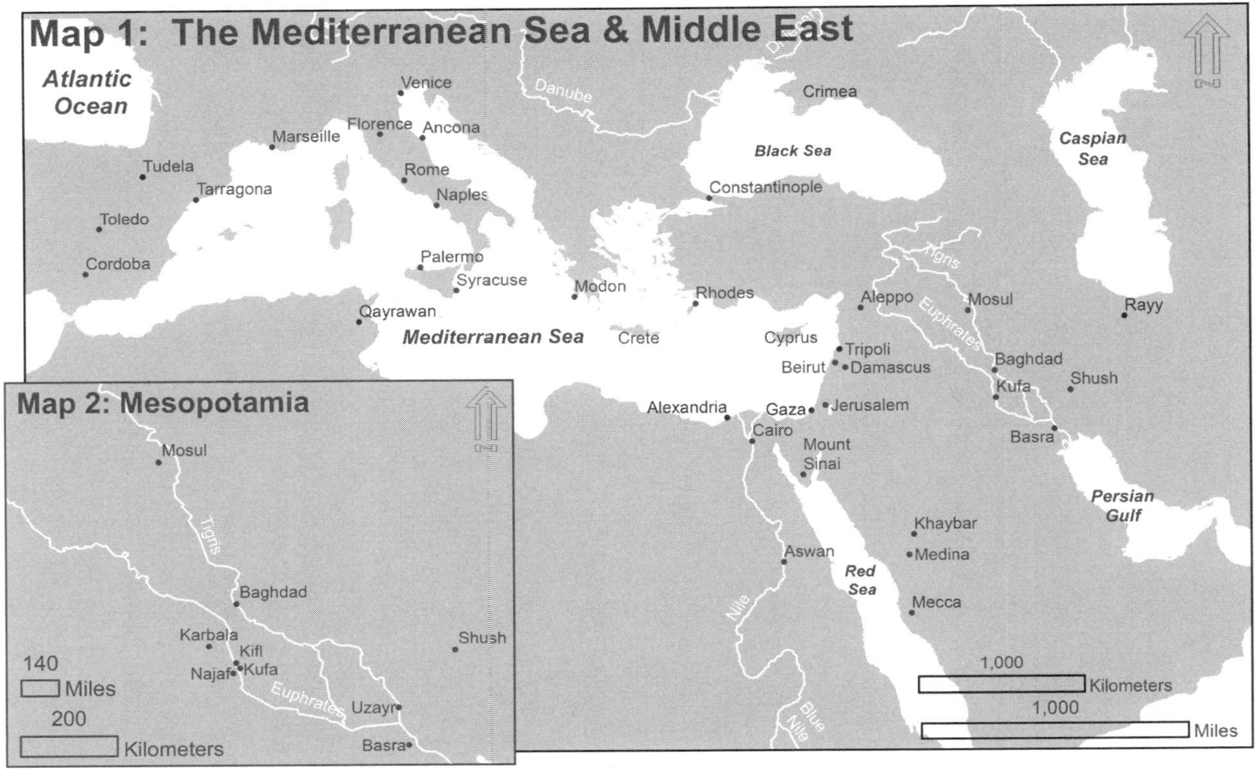

Map 1. The Mediterranean Sea and Middle East.

Map 2. Mesopotamia. Maps by Jennifer Moore, GIS Librarian at Washington University in St. Louis.

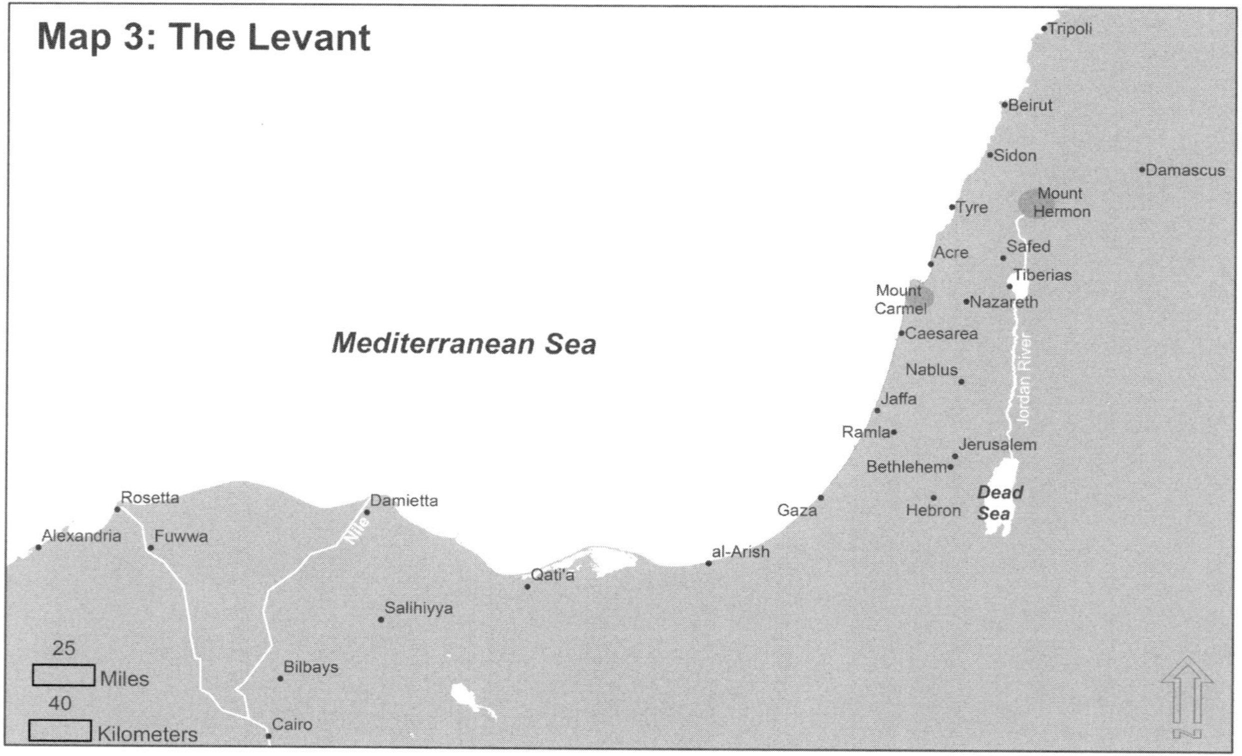

Map 3. The Levant. Map by Jennifer Moore, GIS Librarian at Washington University in St. Louis.

A Note on Translations and Transliterations

All translations of primary sources are mine, if not stated otherwise. When using other translations, I sometimes have made cuts or silently changed spellings, for the sake of uniformity. At times, I have translated technical terms differently, and added in brackets transliterated words in the original language. Modifications are always acknowledged in the notes.

Quotations from the Hebrew Bible generally follow the Jewish Publication Society's translation but are sometimes adapted to the context in which they are cited.

Hebrew terms and names are transliterated as in the *Encyclopaedia Judaica*, second edition, with the exception that the letter *ṣade* is transliterated as ṣ (instead of ẓ); an *'ayin* is (always) represented by ', and *alef* as ' when occurring in the middle of a word. Biblical names and biblical place names are rendered according to the aforementioned translation. Some well-known postbiblical names and Hebrew words that have entered common English usage are given in that form as well.

Arabic terms and names are transliterated as in the *Encyclopedia of Islam*, second edition, except that instead of *dj* (for the letter *jīm*) and *ḳ* (for *qūf*) I use *j* and *q*, respectively. Well-known Arabic place names, dynasties, certain proper names (e.g., Baghdad, Abbasids, and Muhammad), and other widely used terms (such as Qur'an, or Ramadan) are printed without diacritical marks.

Abbreviations

AJS Review	*Association for Jewish Studies Review*
b.	Babylonian Talmud, followed by tractate title
CCCM	Corpus Christianorum, Continuatio Mediaevalis
EI	*Encyclopedia of Islam.* 2nd ed., ed. P. J. Bearman et al. 12 vols. Leiden: Brill, 1960–2005
EJ	*Encyclopaedia Judaica.* 2nd ed., ed. Fred Skolnik et al. 22 vols. Detroit: Macmillan Reference USA, 2007
m.	Mishnah, followed by tractate title
JQR	*Jewish Quarterly Review*
r.	reigned
R.	Rabbi, sometimes used as an honorific in the sources
t.	Tosefta, followed by tractate title
y.	Talmud Yerushalmi (Jerusalem Talmud), followed by tractate title
ZDPV	*Zeitschrift des Deutschen Palästinavereins*

Introduction

> The coward who chooses the stay-at-home life
> must drink of the cup of vexation.
> The sluggard, a tent-peg thrust deep in the earth,
> is a study in want and frustration. . . .
> But the man who is wise travels eastward and west,
> till he topple Ill Luck's domination.
> The adventurer, spurning the gifts of repose,
> wins Wandering's high consummation:
> The splendor of mountain, of ocean, and plain:
> gold-illumination.
> —Judah Alḥarizi, *Taḥkemoni*, Gate 26

Curiosity, material gain, spiritual quest, and simple wanderlust have propelled people on long-distance journeys ever since travels were recorded. These motives were also invoked by Judah Alḥarizi (1165–1225), author of the poem quoted in the epigraph. Born in Toledo and buried in Aleppo, Alḥarizi bridges East and West in both his itinerant life and literary oeuvre. The theme of the journey frequently serves this Jewish poet as a means to comment on the virtues and vices of his adopted and childhood homes. As illustrated by Alḥarizi's case, travel narratives offer unique outlets for reflecting on the alien and the familiar, the other and the self—both of which are commonly depicted as in a mirror.

From this standpoint, the accounts of medieval Christians who visited or conjured up imaginary journeys to the Muslim world have been widely discussed for their role in the construction and dissemination of the European image of the "Orient."[1] Marco Polo, the thirteenth-century Venetian globetrotter, today is arguably the most frequently evoked eastbound voyager. Even more popular among premodern audiences was the fourteenth-century *Book of Mandeville*, despite (or perhaps because of) the often fantastic nature of the journeys it describes.[2] Both works are counted among the classics of Western travel literature and have attracted considerable scholarly work from such varied disciplines as history, literature, anthropology, and postcolonial studies. However, Jewish travel writing from this same period (including Alḥarizi's work) has yet to receive a similarly broad or critically intense investigation.

To this end, *Reorienting the East* explores what constitutes and informs medieval Jewish travel literature about the Islamic world. At the same time, this book appraises travel writing's role in corroborating and challenging any sense of a clearly defined "East" and "West" at the heart of Jewish constructions of identity and difference.

It seems fitting to broach this study's topic by way of a medieval Hebrew classic, the *Book of Travels* (*Sefer ha-Massa'ot*), by Benjamin of Tudela, and its modern interpretation. In the introduction to his critical edition and translation of this twelfth-century itinerary—which was published more than a hundred years ago but remains largely unquestioned—Marcus Nathan Adler (1837–1911) contextualized Benjamin's journey to the Middle East within the history of the Crusades, or what Adler considered a far longer "struggle between Cross and Crescent."[3] However, Adler (a British actuary and not a historian by training) failed to ask what particular view a Navarran Jew might take on this historical struggle, even though the political and cultural landscape of the Iberian Peninsula had shifted several times during Benjamin's lifetime. Nor did Adler contemplate whether the Tudelan's engagement with Islam differed appreciably from that of other European authors.

Like Benjamin and Alḥarizi, most premodern Jews who left accounts of their peregrinations hailed from Christian-ruled lands, and many traveled to the Levant aboard Christian-owned vessels. Moreover, the emergence of Jewish travel literature is tied to the Crusades, when the increase in maritime traffic between western Europe and the eastern Mediterranean included Jewish pilgrims and merchants. If European Jews traveled to the same regions as Christians, did they describe them through the same lenses and for the same reasons? Did these Jewish authors share certain "Western" perceptions of the Islamic world with their Christian counterparts? Or did looking at the Near East through a medieval Jewish prism fracture the myth of home and abroad in unexpected ways? For instance, did the existence of Jewish communities throughout the then-known world allow Jewish travelers to see sameness within the otherness of foreign lands?[4] Where did they locate exile (Hebrew: *galut*) and domicile, where were the center and the periphery of their universe:

in Europe, or in Palestine, the ancestral homeland of the Jewish people?[5] How did they use travel writing to negotiate an identity between East and West, their countries of origin and what they considered the Land of Israel (*ereṣ yisra'el*)? To what extent were European Jewish perspectives on the Middle East predicated on the fact that Occidental Christians viewed their Jewish neighbors as aliens (and later as Orientals)?

In challenging a facile coupling of Europe with domicile and Middle East with exile—as I argue in this book—medieval Jewish travelers deliberately reoriented the East and decentered Europe.[6] Medieval Christian travel accounts and world maps (*mappae mundi*) similarly depict Jerusalem as the navel of the universe.[7] However, Jewish descriptions of Palestine do not embrace a Christian vision of the Holy Land but frequently disturb such dominant worldviews (much as they subvert the theology of supersession). In yet another sense, the narratives discussed in this study reorient common (modern) perceptions of the East: they complicate simplified models of interpretation that regard all Western travel writing as representing an "Orientalist" (to use Edward Said's term) gaze on an utterly different, exotic rest of the world.[8] Namely, these works resist a binarism that characterizes some early forms of postcolonial theory and instead ask historians to pay careful attention to the social and cultural contexts that generated their sources.

The above-noted example of Marco Polo serves as a stepping-stone to several related issues. It has been said that his *Description of the World* already "registers the full range of the tropes of othering that shaped the Western sense of identity and difference."[9] In her classical survey of premodern travel literature, Mary Baine Campbell portrays Polo as the first to look at the East through "the eye of a merchant."[10] However, the writings of Benjamin of Tudela, whose voyage preceded that of his Venetian counterpart by about a century, similarly provide a full dossier of Near Eastern products and colorful portraits of "exotic" peoples. As a result, should not Benjamin also be considered among the first Europeans to "sell" the East to the West, thereby heralding the exploitative or colonialist attitude of the Occident that would inform later generations?

I seriously doubt that reading premodern travel accounts as mere antecedents of nineteenth-century Orientalism does these works justice (Said's arguments are strongest when applied to the imperial age). Before the Occident's ascendancy, the encounter between a Western traveler (Christian or Jewish) and a non-European other was hardly based on "highly asymmetrical relations of domination and subordination," as Mary Louise Pratt describes such encounters from the mid-eighteenth century onward.[11] As a result, medieval travel writings did not inevitably give rise to visions of European hegemony and empire. While the narratives of Polo and "Mandeville" have been referred to as an "imaginative preparation" for later European explorers such as Christopher Columbus,[12] they were written without such purpose. Whatever the case, Jewish travel writers certainly did not inspire any conquests.[13] Still, it seems difficult today to embark on any analysis of travel literature without consideration of Said's highly influential theory or the ensuing (and partly more nuanced) discussions about the historical relationships among travel, trade, and imperialism.[14]

Since such notions as East and West are contingent constructs and their invocation may unintentionally perpetuate the very cultural dichotomies and academic boundaries that I question, the scope of this book needs further definition. I use these quasi-geographic (east and west) concepts mainly for taxonomic convenience; but these terms—*mizraḥ* and *ma'arav* in Hebrew, *mashriq* and *maghrib* in Arabic—are not employed in my sources in the sense of the modern Occident-versus-Orient binary.[15] (That some quattrocento Jewish travelers reveal proto-Orientalist attitudes is a point to be addressed later.) Even so, most of the Jewish travelers whose Near Eastern journeys I discuss originated from Latin Europe and hence engaged with a Christian view of the Levant, even after the end of the crusader period. In reclaiming a Christian *terra sancta* for their Jewish audience, they symbolically subverted—or reoriented—medieval European constructions of the world; in this critical sense, a specific Jewish notion of the East seems stable enough to serve as a schema across the roughly four centuries (ca. 1150-1520; see below) covered in this book. In terms of physical geography, this study is limited to what is otherwise known as the Middle (or Near) East, which, for present purposes, refers to the swath of land that extends from Egypt to Iran.[16]

Travel is rarely one-directional; hence the focus on yet another group of eastbound Europeans (Jews, in this case) may inadvertently reinscribe an Orientalist perspective.[17] (Recognizing this argument, the point will be made that most of my authors do not portray the West as epicenter). Of course, there were also Levantine Jews, such as merchants, rabbis, and communal emissaries, who went to Christian Europe. However, during the period under discussion, none of them seem to have left a significant account of their westward journeys.[18] In fact, Hebrew travel narratives, a rather protean and middlebrow literary genre, emerged as a direct result of the growing Jewish pilgrimage movement to the area of Palestine in the wake of the Crusades.[19]

Just as premodern Christian travel literature about the Near East divides roughly into two categories—the period of the Crusades and the subsequent European encounter with Mamluks, Ayyubids, and Ottomans—a similar classification system befits the corresponding Jewish corpus. Consequently, this book analyzes more than two dozen (mostly) Hebrew and Judeo-Arabic travel accounts, letters, and poetic works that were written between the mid-twelfth and the early sixteenth centuries.

Most Jewish travel texts from that period describe pious journeys to the Levant, as the pilgrimage account was the main medieval mode for narrating a recollected travel. However, a few authors, such as Benjamin of Tudela and his Ashkenazi contemporary Petaḥyah of Regensburg, dealt with the Middle East at large and extended their purview to Egypt and Mesopotamia. Given their historical context (the Crusades), these travel accounts harbor numerous polemical remarks about Christians, rather than Muslims. (This polemical language has often been sanitized by the available translations, including Adler's aforementioned one.) Conversely, some of these same writers depicted Muslim rulers as benevolent monarchs who respected the wide-ranging autonomy of their Jewish subjects in general and granted considerable authority to Jewish representatives in particular. In light of this spectrum, the hypothesis of this study is that these Jewish authors viewed the lands of Islam as an alternative world—one in contradistinction to their actual lived experiences in Europe. Painting idealized portraits of the Islamic realm, in other words, was part of these Jewish writers' attempts (besides challenging Christian claims to the Holy Land) to reorient a Western-cum-Christian vision of the Levant.

Letters penned by fifteenth- and sixteenth-century Italian Jewish pilgrims and merchants sailing to the eastern Mediterranean constitute the second major category of travel writings that I discuss. These texts seem to echo a period of intensified trade between Europe and the Mamluk Empire, which was dominated by Venice and other Italian centers of commerce. In contrast with the first category (the crusader-period accounts), some of these works are informed by a more condescending attitude toward the Islamicate world.[20] In this sense, they reflect the participation of Jewish merchants in early modern trade as well as their integration into Italian society, limited though it may have been.

Against this backdrop, I contrast the travel report of Meshullam of Volterra, a Tuscan businessman, with the letters of the renowned rabbi Obadiah of Bertinoro. Specifically, I demonstrate how the former echoed stereotypes of Orientals held by some of his Christian compatriots, whereas the latter offered an ostensibly unbiased depiction of Muslim, Jewish, and other communities in the lands of Islam. However, on what terms can Meshullam's travel diary be considered an early example of Orientalism? As I argue, Meshullam is incapable of being pegged to any artificial classification because his dual identity as a (self-assured) Tuscan and a (vulnerable) Jew is in constant flux. Obadiah's nonjudgmental tableau of the people he met in the Levant can be interpreted as a conscious revision of some of the clichés that were expressed by Meshullam, whose account he may well have read. In other words, a careful study of medieval and early modern Jewish accounts of the Muslim world does not offer a simple answer to such questions as when pro-Islamic attitudes gave way to Orientalism among Jewish travel writers.[21]

This study could easily have been extended beyond the turn of the sixteenth century. Travels in the Ottoman Empire continued to capture the imagination of early modern Christian and Jewish readers,[22] while news about the European discoveries in Africa, the Indian Ocean, and the Americas only slowly altered common conceptions of geography.[23] Also, the Spanish expulsion of 1492 set off major waves of Jewish migration from the western to the eastern Mediterranean.[24] Even so, the generations of travelers who wrote after the parameters set for this book often reiterated, confirmed, or qualified what was already known or expected. The Italian Jewish merchant David dei Rossi apparently alluded to this fact in a letter he sent from Ottoman Palestine in 1535: "What news shall I tell you about this country, as so many people before me have reported its character and greatness in writing and orally?"[25] By then, a number of texts provided a template for later writers, who relied on their predecessors' legacy of images to create their own travel records.[26] In addition, many reports of journeys to the Levant are—at least, in part—pilgrimage accounts, and the ritualized nature of the underlying experience is one reason that they resemble one another so closely. In light of the redundant character of many subsequent works, the time frame of this book tapers off shortly after the Ottoman conquest of the Near East (1516–17)—an event that contributed immensely to Europe's conceptual homogenization of the "Orient" into a self-contained cultural entity. This study's relatively broad time span of about four centuries—from around 1150 to 1520—enables the reader to discern the shifting and mutually transforming boundaries between imagined cultural and geographical spheres through the unique lens of premodern Jewish travelers.

Methodological Considerations

Medieval Jewish travel literature has been attracting modern audiences, popular and scholarly, for some time. Nevertheless, this body of work has been largely underestimated, and the critical scholarship on it has been relatively meager. This reflects the questionable view that travel writing, with its poorly defined literary genres and forms, constitutes a peripheral topic in the Jewish system of knowledge. It has rarely merited the same rigorous analysis as, say, rabbinic literature or medieval Jewish philosophy, both of which have become established parts of the academic canon.

A number of the existing studies on Hebrew travel writing have been arguably shaped by apologetic considerations. This is best exemplified by Leopold Zunz (1794–1886), a founder of the *Wissenschaft des Judentums* (Science of Judaism) school of thought. In his classic "An Essay on the Geographical Literature of the Jews," Zunz begins by admitting that the marginalized political and social status of most medieval Jews prevented these writers from enjoying the same conditions as Greek and Roman authors about geography and foreign lands.[27] This does not deter him from producing a long list of Jewish "geographical literature" from antiquity to his own day (1841)—a list that includes some of the sources discussed in this book. At the same time, he stresses that none of these works was interested in "geography" in the sense of a "real and precise knowledge of the earth and its inhabitants."[28] In all likelihood, the implicit motivation behind Zunz's eighty-five-page bibliography was to prove that, despite the aforementioned limitations, Jewish travel writing contains an impressive amount of data valuable for the study of historical geography; and this was part of the efforts of the *Wissenschaft des Judentums* to introduce the study of Jewish sources into Europe's academic institutions, alongside comparable Greek, Roman, Muslim, and Christian works.

Motives aside, Zunz established paradigms of research that dominate the field to this day. Consequently, Hebrew travel accounts have primarily been mined as a quarry of information and data for a Jewish historical geography, such as population centers, pilgrimage sites, and travel routes. Since many of the texts describe journeys to Jerusalem, they have become the domain of choice for a school of historians focusing on the annals of Jewish settlement in and immigration to premodern Palestine (the Old Yishuv).[29] Most scholars have read these medieval sources largely as reliable reports of factual peregrinations consisting of the personal testimonies of eyewitnesses.

Whenever possible, these scholars have sought to corroborate the assertions made in the travel account with external evidence. For instance, they have endeavored to clarify obscure geographical names and have occasionally filled in missing information, such as historical events, that the author may have taken for granted. Whatever does not make sense in the narrative has either been attributed to hearsay, which the traveler may have incorporated in cases where he was unable to visit a certain place, or dismissed as the later addition of an ignorant copyist. Thus, much of this scholarly effort has been dedicated to producing a rational reconstruction of a text that had been mutilated by meddling copyists.[30] As Zunz put it: "As we find . . . the historical and geographical data [in Benjamin of Tudela's work] to be fully authenticated, and as the fables must be charged, not to his own account, but to that of his time, a sound critique has rejected with justice all those suspicions and attempts at derogation, which have been directed against this, *our* first traveller."[31]

A more recent, though related, approach views medieval Hebrew travel writings as unique repositories of information for the study of local Jewish identities, cultures, and popular religion in areas beyond Palestine. In his discussion on Obadiah of Bertinoro's portrait of the Jewish community in Palermo, Elliott Horowitz offers a poignant example of "how the evidence of travel accounts may enrich our understanding of popular religious life."[32]

The late fifteenth-century rabbi's insights about other people (including other Jews) appear to be much more credible than earlier travel writings (such as Benjamin of Tudela's), largely on account of Obadiah's relatively objective tone. In noting specific eating habits, rituals, and social practices, he revealed what might be considered an early ethnographic curiosity.[33] But his often detailed and lifelike descriptions are not necessarily a sign of accuracy, given the limitations imposed on the foreigner's full understanding of what he saw by his own cultural, social, and linguistic background. This is still more evident in the case of his contemporary Meshullam of Volterra, whose observations frequently seem obscured by a "European veil of prejudice."[34] Yet even Obadiah's writings reflect both the growing importance attributed to empirical observations and the continued belief in legends and myth, which were equally characteristic of his time. For instance, the rabbi is skeptical about precisely locating the salt-turned image of Lot's wife near the Dead Sea ("for there are plenty of pillars of salt").[35] But he also gives credence to current rumors regarding the continued existence of the Lost Tribes of Israel, a topic of particular interest to European Jews during the age of exploration.[36]

As illustrated by the last-mentioned example, travel literature is directed at a specific readership whose worldview it is expected to expand and confirm in balanced measure. Hence, even the testimony of a presumed eyewitness may be shown to represent a misrecognition, stereotype, or literary topos that says more about the beholder and his intended audience than the object of his gaze. The numerous geographic and chronological inconsistencies, narrative leaps, miracle stories, and fantastic elements that inform the majority of medieval travel accounts ultimately undermine their capacity to serve as reliable records of events and observations and thus demand a more careful reading.

The pitfalls involved in many of the summarized approaches are aptly described in François Hartog's *Mirror of Herodotus*, a seminal work on classical representations of the other. Hartog opens his analysis of Herodotus's (fifth century BCE) depiction of the mysterious Scythians by asking, "[W]ho, in the first place, are Herodotus's Scythians?" He then outlines several possibilities for comparing the narrative to the archaeological evidence:

> Passing from the text to the archaeological remains and from the remains back to the text, it might be possible to seize upon the convergences and, above all, to ponder upon the divergences. This might lead to some conclusions regarding the accuracy of Herodotus's information: was his description good, or poor? His mistakes would probably be ascribed to misleading information, an insufficiently critical approach or naïveté. The "points of agreement," on the other hand, would be credited to his powers of observation and his freedom of preconceptions. If the debit side outweighed the credit side, he would be judged to have given a poor description; if conversely, his credit was high, he would be deemed a truthful witness.[37]

Mutatis mutandis, these methods also have been applied to medieval Jewish travel literature. While credits and debits may be variously assigned to each of the authors discussed in this book, every instance of premodern travel writing would have to be considered a mixture of actuality and myth. Indeed, components are amalgamated in varying proportions, often in a manner that makes it difficult to distinguish one from the other.

Since the dividing line between the real and the imagined appears to be vague in these accounts, literary critics and folklorists might question whether medieval travel writings should be approached as trustworthy records that provide the modern reader with at least a smattering of verifiable historical data. Indeed, the recognition of certain literary forms and motifs that inform these texts obligates us to place medieval Jewish travel writings in a literary (as well as an oral) tradition that goes beyond the Hebrew canon. A correlation must be drawn between the corpus discussed here and ancient Greek, medieval Latin, vernacular, and Arabic sources, among others. For example, since the time of Herodotus, every author of a description of the Middle and Far East felt compelled to enhance his narrative with entertaining descriptions of marvels and curiosities.[38] To postcolonial theorists, these exotic images are a constituent part of the rhetoric of otherness. Unlike historicist and empiricist approaches, the more recent reappraisals of the legendary elements have enabled scholars to acknowledge that medieval authors espoused a religious worldview that deemed wonders and miracles, no less than the mundane, to be integral parts of reality.[39]

The positivist and the literary approaches to premodern travel writings both come up short in answering why their authors mixed empirical and imagined elements in such an unrestrained fashion. In the case of travel literature on the Middle East, the answer lies, at least in part, in the fact that the medieval European perspective was predicated on biblical and classical literary traditions whereby the East was primarily a conceptual rather than a geographical realm. It is therefore the genre's ultimately rhetorical nature that renders it a precarious source of accurate information for scholars of geography and ethnography.

With this in mind, I try to confront assertions made in the travel accounts with evidence from outside their pages; similarly, I question where things were actually located in time and space. This allows me to ask how reality affects the traveler's perception and where generic conventions give contour to territory and experience in the texts under review. Where does the author apparently write against the grain of his own observations, and why? However, in the chapters that follow, the focus is not on the reliability of certain travel accounts as historical, geographical, or ethnographical sources; or hitherto overlooked information of that kind that they might contain; nor is the analysis of literary genres, forms, and motifs an aim of this study. Instead, my primary concern is the historical significance of the writings.[40]

I approach my sources seeking answers to the following critical questions: How did medieval European Jews engage with foreign cultures, particularly Near Eastern ones? To what extent did factual or fictive travel serve Jewish writers as a trope for cross-cultural encounters? What models and rhetoric did Jewish travelers use to describe people who were—geographically, religiously, or culturally—other to themselves? What differences in viewpoint and cultural sensibility do the selected authors reveal toward the Islamicate world? How did the theme of easterly peregrinations facilitate Jewish reflections on identity, community, and home?

Postcolonial Middle Ages?[41]

In reading travel literature primarily, though not exclusively, as a discursive revelation of the other and the collective self, I am obviously drawing inspiration from postcolonial studies. Over the past two decades, postcolonial studies and its "innovative models of reading" have, in the words of Steve Clark, "made the question of travel inseparable from that of power and desire."[42] However, Clark's statement was made regarding English and French travel writers from the eighteenth and nineteenth centuries. The issue that needs to be raised here once more is: Can the interpretative models of postcolonial studies, with their emphasis on constructions of power, be applied to medieval Jewish travel texts?[43]

I doubt that all medieval Christian narratives of journeys in the Levant should be viewed as mere links in a genealogy of Orientalist representation.[44] As noted, a simplistic reduction of cross-cultural encounters into the categories of domination and subordination is problematic for travel writings that predate the age of European imperialism. Given that it ignores the reciprocity of human relationships and makes them appear static, such an approach may in any case be questionable. When characterizing certain positions taken by premodern authors, it seems more appropriate to speak of "proto-Orientalism" (Richmond Barbour), by which I mean a salient construction of the East, whose rhetoric appears to foreshadow later imperialism without necessarily enabling it.[45] This study investigates whether medieval and early modern Jewish travelers were also inclined toward "othering" the Islamic world and, if so, in what sense, to what degree, and for what purposes.[46] Beyond being simplifications, what role do stereotypes play in the attempts of European Jewish authors to articulate their visions of the Middle East? And are these exclusively negative stereotypes? Did Jews, in spite of their own marginality or because of it, take part in creating a larger Western discourse that imposes a set of prejudices on an alien world? Or did they potentially subvert such positions, since their own multifaceted identities were neither exclusively Western nor Eastern but included elements of both?

The Jewishness of Jewish Travel Writing

Having repeatedly compared Jewish travel writings with their Christian counterparts, I would like to reflect on what characterizes these texts as Jewish. It is not only the fact that all of them were authored by Jewish men (there are no records of medieval Jewish women reporting their travels)[47] but also that they were directed at an exclusively Jewish readership and hence much of their subject matter possesses at least a modicum of Jewish significance. Because many of them consist of pilgrimage accounts, they focus on the description of places central to the Jewish collective memory.[48] Even if the sites had been converted into Christian or Islamic places of worship—most notably, the Temple Mount in Jerusalem or Hebron's Tomb of the Patriarchs—the Jewish authors reappropriated them for their intended audience. Additionally, they structured their journey according to the rabbinic calendar, with mandatory breaks on Shabbat and the Jewish holidays, and diaries were often dated in accordance with the Jewish year (sometimes in conjunction with Christian dates). Most important, when traveling in the Islamicate world, Jews did not journey through an entirely alien environment but through a Jewish diaspora—or overlapping diasporas—that was simultaneously foreign and familiar: they stopped off at Jewish communities and homes, relied on kinship networks and support systems linking their communities throughout Europe and into the Middle East, and met fellow pilgrims at Jewish places of worship.

While Jewish travel writings display a certain fascination with the foreign and exotic, they do not systematically focus on the Islamic world. As in much of premodern Jewish literature, references to other religious practices, cultures, and ethnicities are generally made for the purpose of enhancing Jewish self-understanding. This is due in no small part to the language of most of these accounts, which is Hebrew. Through myriad biblical phrases and allusions to rabbinic literature, they engage in a dialogue with a literary heritage that insists on intertextuality rather than mere mimesis. The authors describe their world through the lens of rabbinic Judaism and tend to reconfirm and validate the authority of earlier Jewish literature, thus giving testimony to the priority of established texts over subjective experience. That said, was traveling to Palestine only a confirmation of previously built convictions, or did the concrete experience lead these travelers to revise some of their preconceptions?

Insofar as medieval Christian travel writings are concerned, the extent to which they cite from the Bible, allude to earlier Christian works, and reconfirm preconceived values is on a par with their Jewish counterparts.[49] Furthermore, medieval Christian representations of the non-European are neither monolithic nor uniformly hostile.[50] In essence, the multiple differences and nuances within each of the above-mentioned categories of travel literature impinge upon any artificial dichotomy between Christian and Jewish encounters with the Middle East. With this in mind, I attempt to broaden the context by providing selected comparisons between specific passages from Jewish travel accounts and those from analogous Christian or Muslim-authored texts. Nonetheless, the underlying objective of *Reorienting the East* is to reconstruct the efforts of Jewish authors in late medieval Europe to use travel writing as a narrative strategy to comprehend the world, themselves, and others.

Book Outline

Framed by an introduction and a conclusion, this book is organized around three larger parts that proceed roughly from the historical and factual to the perceptual aspects of Jewish travel writing on the medieval Muslim world. The first part is devoted to a discussion of the travelers, their works, and the conditions under which they set out from Europe to the Middle East; the second part examines the description of territory and place in the texts that form the basis of this study; and the third part looks at the way people are portrayed in these writings. Each of these three parts is further divided into three or four thematic chapters on selected topics. For the purpose of tracing possible continuities or shifts in perception within the works, my discussion in every chapter largely adheres to a chronological progression (from the earliest to the latest texts), except where this proves too unwieldy. This allows me to investigate travel accounts both as responses to historical circumstances and as expressions of Jewish identity in its changing relationship to the non-Jewish other.

As a cultural historian, I find it necessary to open the book with an introduction to my authors' works and the literary forms and rhetorical conventions according to which they operated (Part I, Chapter 1), since it is easy to misinterpret these texts if one approaches them with expectations formed by modern travelogues.[51] For this reason, I begin by providing a concise survey of Jewish medieval travel writing's various genres and forms: itineraries, epistolary accounts, imaginary voyages, and travel poetry. While I can offer only brief summaries of the authors' biographies and works here, this opening chapter constitutes a first step toward a post-positivist discussion of medieval Jewish travel writing. (Readers less interested in the history of the Jewish travel account may want to skip the first chapter and start reading this book with Chapter 2.)

This book's emphasis is on literary representations of Islamicate culture and society; but given the chosen platform of travel literature, it would be odd to overlook the topic of actual travel in time and space. I begin my reading of the texts in Chapter 2 with a brief look at the two major impulses behind premodern Jewish journeys from Europe to the Middle East: trade and pilgrimage. In this context, I pick up on some of the points raised above: Are medieval Jewish travel accounts inhered by a mercantile worldview? Do they betray fledgling attitudes that would eventually inform later colonialist adventures?

In Chapter 3, I showcase a handful of texts that describe the aids and impediments to premodern travel, such as means of transportation and dangers on the road, so as to shed historical light on the social, political, and economic context of Levantine travel during the period under discussion—or how it reverberates in the sources. This chapter also explores aspects of what might be characterized as a Jewish travel experience. I investigate how Jewish religious observance impacted the journey and what it meant for a Jew to traverse Christian- or Muslim-ruled lands and board Christian-manned ships that were destined for the Levant.

Space and place are the focus of Part II,[52] in which the construct of the Muslim world is divided into several geographic and thematic categories. Chapter 4, which constitutes a linchpin of the present study, discusses the ways in which Palestine—the primary destination of premodern Jewish travelers—was conceptualized in their accounts. The main paradox with which these authors contended was the fact that the Land of Israel they visited had an exceedingly non-Jewish character. To begin with, it lacked a substantial Jewish population and was ruled by either Christians (crusaders) or Muslims (Ayyubids, Mamluks, and Ottomans). In addition, the most important Jewish holy places, the Temple Mount and the Tomb of the Patriarchs, were under the control of whichever of the two larger religious communities happened to be ascendant. Consequently, these writers were forced to adopt certain rhetorical strategies, such as denying the reality on the ground or projecting an alternative Jewish map onto the Christian or Muslim stratum, in order to reappropriate Christian *terra sancta* or Muslim *arḍ al-muqaddasa* ("holy land" in Latin and Arabic, respectively) for their own religious tradition.

Similarly, the relationship of Ḥaram al-Sharīf (the Noble Sanctuary, the

Islamic term for the Temple Mount) to the Jewish Temple is often ambiguous in the travel writings. The Dome of the Rock is unmistakably of Islamic origin and was retrofitted into a Christian church by the crusaders, but Jewish travelers usually identified it with the (destroyed) Temple or endowed it with miraculous powers that emanated from the site's Jewish past. Among the questions to be considered is whether it made a difference to Jewish travelers if the Temple Mount was a Muslim or a Christian sanctuary at any given time.

Chapter 5 continues the exploration of places that were sacred to members of different communities but addresses additional aspects of this phenomenon. In Jerusalem and Hebron, the dominant religion frequently barred followers of a rival faith from the most significant *loci sancti*, while secondary pilgrimage places such as Samuel's tomb (Nabī Ṣamwīl, on the road to Jerusalem) appear to have seen some intermingling of pilgrims from different backgrounds—Muslims and Jews, in particular. Do these travel accounts evince any notion of partaking in the sanctity of a specific place with the religious other? Are these multi-faith venues depicted as "liminal" spaces (Victor and Edith Turner) where religious boundaries relax, or do they, too, emerge as contested places in the writings?[53] The first half of Chapter 5 is devoted to holy tombs in the Palestinian countryside; the discussion moves in the second half to southern Iraq and western Iran, where the reputed graves of the prophets Ezekiel and Daniel attracted throngs of Jewish and Muslim devotees. In this context, the question begs to be asked: How do Iraqi Jewish shrines compare with Palestinian holy sites in the travel narratives, given that a competition with Latin Christianity had never been part of Mesopotamia's religious discourse?

Some of the Muslim world's most famous urban centers are the subject of Chapter 6. Long after its halcyon days, Baghdad still served as a repository of potent memories of Muslim and Jewish past glory, as evidenced by the eclectic accounts of Benjamin of Tudela and Petaḥyah of Regensburg. Against the backdrop of the Muslim metropolis and its marvels, both travelers offered glowing—yet anachronistic—portraits of the local Jewish community. Here I raise the possibility that their narratives use the Jewish community of Baghdad, under the leadership of the so-called exilarch (Hebrew: *rosh ha-golah*), as a negative mirror of the Jewish experience in Europe. As a Jewish metropolis, Baghdad embodied all that, in the eyes of the visitors, European Jews lacked: powerful representatives, far-reaching autonomy, and scholarly erudition.

Along with Baghdad, the metropolises of Damascus and Alexandria figure prominently in the accounts. These cities, in particular, are described by the authors as sites of urban marvels, which was a popular theme of medieval travel writing in general. Chapter 6 further explores the manner in which architectural wonders, such as the Umayyad Mosque of Damascus and the Pharos of Alexandria, were disseminated by medieval Jewish travelers, whose descriptions owe more to cross-cultural lore than to any personal on-site explorations. Still, what seems significant in these Jewish portraits of Near Eastern cityscapes is the way they depict Islam as a highly refined civilization that is deeply rooted in the region's Hellenistic-Roman heritage.

Part III of this study turns to the representation of other people in the sources, be they directly or indirectly motivated by a traveler's experiences in foreign lands. Chapter 7 opens this topic with a look at how the Jewish writers portrayed Muslims and Christians, who, based on biblical typologies, are traditionally labeled Ishmaelites and Edomites in Hebrew literature. Not unlike medieval historiography's emphasis on royal histories, the Muslim ruler assumes a leading role in premodern Jewish constructions of the Middle East. Depending on the particular author and the period in which he lived, these literary portraits range from the benign monarch to the Oriental despot. I also examine how the later travelers—foremost among them Meshullam of Volterra—stereotyped Muslim ways of life. For instance, Meshullam considered Near Eastern table manners to be uncivilized in comparison with the emerging norms of a European elite.

Notwithstanding their relatively meager number, the references to Christians (both European and Near Eastern) in Jewish accounts of the Levant play a prominent role in my effort to gauge the authors' perception of the foreign lands to which they traveled. Their European background was the reason that they frequently engaged in a conversation with Christianity when encountering the Muslim world. In addition, I examine the sometimes tense meetings between Jewish and Christian pilgrims in the Holy Land. These episodes raise the question of the extent to which quattrocento Jews identified with their Gentile neighbors.

Because of their heightened interest in other Jewish communities, the travel writers went into considerable detail about the Jews of Islamic lands, which is the topic of Chapter 8. The earlier sources depict them as exemplary Jews and compare them favorably with their own communities back home, whereas some of the more recent texts highlight the cultural differences between the Italian Jewish visitor and his rather distant and occasionally Orientalized kin. Chapter 8 sheds light on the minority (*dhimmī*) status of Jews in Muslim society—or how it was perceived by Jewish visitors from

Christian Europe. Did the travelers—-specifically, the more recent ones—depict their Levantine coreligionists as being discriminated against by their Muslim compatriots?

Karaites and Samaritans in the Near East also drew the attention of the writers. These groups' significant differences from rabbinic Judaism in practices and doctrines raised further questions of Jewish identity in the authors' minds (discussed in Chapter 9). That chapter also touches upon legends concerning the Lost Tribes, which were believed to be living in remote parts of the Middle East. Imagining the Islamic world as the home of Jewish warrior tribes, these stories portray the region (or distant areas of it) as a kind of Jewish utopia.

Like premodern travel literature in general, the texts under review display an abiding curiosity in the outlandish and the strange. The authors' reports on exotic—or exoticized—people, such as Assassins, Druze, or blacks, drew on motifs familiar to us from classical literature, mythology, and folktales. Chapter 10 opens with an investigation of the ways in which ethnic and religious communities on the margins of the Muslim world (in the geographical or the social sense) were pictured by medieval Jewish travelers. In this context, I explore the extent to which ethnic and racial classification practices mirrored the repertoire of self-conceptualizations that were available to the authors.

An important element in the cultural mapping of the Islamic realm is the representation of "Oriental" women (Muslim and Jewish) in male-authored travel narratives that were likewise written for a mainly male readership. Hence Chapter 10 addresses also the gender aspect of the representational power (the "male gaze") that was wielded by a Jewish author against the depicted female object. Some of the most prevalent stereotypes about the Muslim world, such as the invisibility of veiled women, are to be found in the accounts by Jewish travelers analyzed herein. In fact, they speak in conflicting voices, for female veiling may be either criticized or praised, depending on whether the foreigner considered it to be a form of modesty (to be emulated) or subversive disguise.

In sum, one of this book's principal aims is to understand how premodern Jewish travelers utilized their representations of the Islamicate world as part of their search for definitions of identity, community, and home. In this respect, categories such as East and West, or exile and domicile, did not constitute distinct poles. Instead, they were versatile referents that frequently challenged a Western-cum-Christian notion of the Middle East and the world at large, as the ensuing chapters will show.

PART I

Travels and Travel Narratives

Chapter 1

Medieval Jewish Travelers and Their Writings

Spanning ages and cultures, travel has served as a nearly universal literary motif and subject matter in manifold forms and modes, poetic and pedestrian, mimetic and imaginative.[1] Throughout this work, the terms medieval Jewish *travel literature* and *travel writing* are used interchangeably to encompass a rather disparate corpus of about two dozen Hebrew and several Judeo-Arabic texts that originated between the mid-twelfth and early sixteenth centuries. All are the product of travel or about travel—but they hardly constitute a discrete genre, as defined by common literary techniques, linguistic properties, and styles. Because my interest in these texts lies in their cultural functions and representational practices, I have chosen to avoid narrow definitions and instead have adopted a general understanding of travel literature that Joan-Pau Rubiés has described as "that varied body of writing which . . . takes travel as an *essential* condition of its production."[2] For the purposes of this work, Jewish travel writing includes the following: itineraries, lists of holy places, and pilgrims' reference books; diaries and letters; poetic evocations of travel;[3] and a wide range of hybrid forms.

Although there is little material that has not attracted a scholar's eye, many known examples of premodern Jewish travel writing still await their publication in critical editions. Even the critical editions are assailable, as they reflect specific choices and ephemeral paradigms of scholarship going back to the time of initial publication. Until recently, these editions offered what was considered the most reliable texts, usually the earliest manuscript available that was believed to be as close as possible to that of the putative author and his urtext—which may be irretrievable. However, variant traditions are difficult to write off as textual corruptions, especially in the case of travel writing:

they may represent different recensions, which offer glimpses into the worldviews of particular readership communities (or of those who listened to the account read aloud).[4] While the history of textual transmission is merely a side issue of this research, I refer to manuscripts and early print versions that contribute to the topic at hand.

Some of the texts analyzed herein have never been translated into European languages. In contrast, many of the English renderings that are cited on an almost exclusive basis to this day are antiquated. Although they substantially recast the travel accounts in the spirit of the Victorian age and were cleansed of all content that was then deemed to be offensive (such as religious polemics or references to sexual practices), they are rarely scrutinized against the original language, even by present-day scholars.[5] Therefore I offer my own translations of most of the numerous quotations from primary sources that are cited throughout this book. Given the fact that medieval Jewish travel writing has so far received scant critical and theoretical attention, the overview that I provide constitutes the first critical, posthistoricist introduction to these sources.

Itineraries, Reference Books, and Lists of Holy Places

The quintessential medieval form of travel writing (with roots in late antiquity) is the *itinerarium* (travel log), a Latin term that has no real Hebrew equivalent.[6] This form ranges from brief notations of stopping places on a given route and the distances in between, which were once considered subliterary, to more elaborate narratives. In their most abbreviated or skeletal form, medieval Jewish itineraries are short lists of the traditional burial sites in Palestine and Iraq of biblical figures and revered rabbis.[7] Since most of these lists contain only rudimentary data about the location of venerated tombs, they may be likened to road maps through otherwise empty space, so they are less important to my discussion. (Given the lack of reliable graphic maps, most topographical descriptions of the Near East were verbal during the time under consideration.)[8] In other cases, the genre of the itinerary seems to burst forth: the sequence of place descriptions is a grid on which various narratives about faraway countries and their people are loosely connected. It is these, of course, that promise to be most relevant to this study.

Given the routes that were mapped out, one likely purpose of these itineraries was pragmatic: to help would-be travelers plan trips of their own.

However, the sometimes substantial number of narrative interludes that are only vaguely related to the travel route confirms that another goal of these texts was to allow the reader to participate vicariously in the author's real or imagined journey to distant lands. This is especially true of the pilgrimage account (known in Latin as *peregrinatio*), a subgenre of the itinerary, which was arguably the paradigm of most medieval travel literature.[9] The experience of reading or listening to a pilgrimage narrative not only whets the audience's appetite for a visit of their own; it often seems to provide the alternative of a mental pilgrimage in lieu of an actual journey.

Besides edification or pure entertainment, a major impulse behind medieval travel books in general and the pilgrimage account in particular is apparently the desire to give expression to the relative mobility and wanderlust that informed this period, within the framework of accepted forms of knowledge, belief systems, and cultural attitudes. Though the reader is repeatedly reminded that the information was obtained by dint of the author's own efforts, or intermittently from other reliable eyewitnesses, the travel account adheres to the conservative guideline of providing a narrative that corresponds with the time's fundamental worldviews as stated, inter alia, in earlier authoritative texts. Medieval Jewish travel literature constitutes a paradigm of intertextuality[10]—namely, the sources feature numerous quotations from and allusions to the Hebrew Bible and classical rabbinic literature that serve the traveler as a kind of mental map.[11]

The intertextuality of travel writing is already evidenced by the classic Christian pilgrimage account that was penned in the late fourth century by a woman author known as Egeria, whose identity remains the subject of scholarly debate (save for the fact that she was one of the few female travelers to premodern Palestine who wrote about her experiences).[12] Like many of the Jewish-authored texts that are discussed below, Egeria's *Peregrinatio* endeavors to establish the location of biblical sites. Although the historical accuracy of these identifications is questionable, the author clearly felt compelled to map out these sites for the simple reason that they are mentioned in the scriptures. Mary B. Campbell describes Egeria's attitude: "She went to see a diorama of the Scriptures, and she found it. . . . The logic of her universe allows her to infer the authenticity of what she sees (for example, the grave of Adam) from the theological necessity of its being there. For Egeria, significance precedes existence, and in the overwhelming earnestness of this attitude there is no room for lying and no room for personality."[13] Jewish accounts likewise tend to portray the Near East as a biblical (or rabbinic) diorama and similarly express little doubt about the authenticity of the holy places they depict. In fact, every report of an *'aliyyah le-regel* (the Hebrew term for a Holy Land pilgrimage) echoed and reinforced a collective memory of the Land of Israel as consisting of a panoply of sacred places.[14]

Campbell's remark regarding the lack of a personal or subjective element in Egeria's account leads to another attribute of Hebrew itineraries. In general, their authors were rather self-effacing, as individual experience was considered too incidental to be a concern of premodern travel writing—be it Latin, Hebrew, Arabic, or otherwise. Following the literary and cultural conventions of the time, these works rarely deal with the physical conditions, perils, and privations of the trek or the happenstance chronology of the journey. More important to the topic at hand, they seldom describe the traveler's personal encounter with foreign people. But as Carl Thompson has observed, the "encounter itself will only be implicit in the writing, as it offers an account not of the actual travelling but of just . . . the new information acquired through travel."[15]

The absence of circumstantial descriptions and the scarcity of references to specific historical events make it extremely difficult to determine the approximate date of many Jewish itineraries and related texts; and their original layer is often barely distinguishable from later additions and interpolations. The propinquity between certain travel accounts (for example, their description of Hebron; see Chapter 4) suggests some form of textual interdependence. Given the complexity of these similarities, this topic is beyond the scope of this book. Earlier scholarship sought to separate "authentic" itineraries by identifiable authors from so-called forgeries.[16] This attempt to unfrock frauds seems to have been misplaced in all that concerns medieval literature: during this period, it was commonplace for writers to inconspicuously incorporate unacknowledged sources into their own work, so the distinction among author, copyist, and compiler tends to be blurred. (A "bona fide" forgery was perpetrated by the nineteenth-century scholar Eliakim Carmoly in the still-quoted pilgrims' guide of Isaac Chelo.)[17]

I will now introduce the Hebrew itineraries and pilgrimage guides that are explored in the chapters to come. As stated, Jewish itineraries emerged in the wake of the Crusades, when an increase in traffic and commerce between Europe and the Levant gave rise to a new wave of Jewish pilgrims to Frankish-ruled Palestine. The *Sitz im Leben* of this fledgling genre of travel literature was the medieval European pilgrimage movement, which is why most of the authors turned to Hebrew instead of Judeo-Arabic, which was the written language of Jews in the Islamicate world. Early Hebrew travel texts echo the contemporaneous Christian itineraries in structure and style and may thus be considered a case of transculturation.[18] The comparable Arabic *riḥla* ("journey") genre flourished at about the same time; its outstanding examples—the works of Ibn Jubayr (twelfth century) and Ibn Baṭṭūṭa (fourteenth century)—similarly recount voyages-cum-pilgrimages from the West (in this case, the Muslim *maghrib*) to the East (*mashriq*).[19] However, with the possible, albeit unlikely, exception of Benjamin of Tudela (see below), Arabic literature apparently had no influence on medieval Hebrew travel accounts.

In his classic *The History of the Jews in the Latin Kingdom of Jerusalem* (1988), Joshua Prawer counts ten surviving Hebrew itineraries from the crusader period, which almost exclusively derived from Christian Europe.[20] (Only eight of them prove relevant to this study's topic.) Based on the internal evidence, these works may have originated in the twelfth and thirteenth centuries. Given the historical backdrop, the majority of them confine themselves to Palestine. Only a few of the travelers—notably, Benjamin of Tudela and Petaḥyah of Regensburg—appear to have reached Iraq and Iran, so these two itineraries merit most of the attention in this book. Even so, I shall first survey the shorter examples, listed (more or less) in chronological order; with their background, the unique character of Benjamin's and Petaḥyah's works becomes evident.

Jacob ben Nathanel ha-Kohen

Scholars have dated the itinerary of Jacob ben Nathanel ha-Kohen to sometime between the mid-twelfth century and 1187, the year of Saladin's decisive victory over the crusaders.[21] Since it includes two references to Provence, the "author" was probably of southern French descent.[22] Following a copyist's introduction, the text opens in the first person: "I, Jacob ben R. Nathanel [ha]-Kohen, traveled under [many] hardships; but God helped me enter the Land of Israel; and I saw the tombs of our righteous patriarchs in Hebron."[23] Although the work starts out in the first person, this voice rarely crops up again. Instead, the text sticks to enumerating places and holy tombs and providing the distances between them, which are given in travel time or in parasangs—a measure of Persian origin.[24] The order of the places in this itinerary does not constitute an actual travel route. For example, the text sporadically alternates between descriptions of Palestine and Egypt, which indicates that the text draws on an assortment of previous material. Thus its opening with a first-person narration serves a rhetorical function, marking the following information as based on the testimony of someone supposedly present at the localities described.

Samuel ben Samson

The itinerary of Samuel ben Samson recounts a Jewish pilgrimage to the Holy Land in 1210—a generation after most of Palestine had come under Ayyubid rule.[25] This date is cited by an anonymous copyist in his introduction to the manuscript. The account is mostly in the first-person plural but occasionally switches to the first-person singular. Unlike the previously discussed case, this itinerary provides a bit more information about the actual journey. Samuel ben Samson, the otherwise unknown author, traveled with a culturally diverse group of Jewish pilgrims, which included R. Jonathan ha-Kohen of Lunel—a famous scholar and Maimonidean philosopher from southern France—and an anonymous exilarch (*rosh ha-golah*), probably from Mosul.[26] At the outset, Samuel ben Samson and Jonathan ha-Kohen apparently embarked on a sea voyage to Egypt, and evidently proceeded to Palestine via the Sinai Peninsula (see Map 3). Like other examples of this genre, the itinerary of Samuel ben Samson focuses on what the copyist described as the "tombs of our ancestors on account of which the world exists."[27]

Elleh ha-Massaʿot

In the next two sections, I introduce a pair of textually interrelated sources: *Elleh ha-Massaʿot* and *Toṣʾot Ereṣ Yisraʾel*. Some question whether the second work is an elaboration of the first (the more likely option), or whether the first is an abridged version of the second, but a detailed discussion of this issue is beyond the scope of the present survey.[28] Similarly, their dates of origin are speculative, but the conditions reflected in both sources appear to relate to the second crusader kingdom (1191–1291), whose capital was Acre (following the loss of Jerusalem).

Elleh ha-Massaʿot, which goes by its incipit, "These Are the Travel Routes," clearly does not convey the personal travel experiences of its anonymous author but has to be considered a pilgrimage guidebook.[29] Like the itinerary of Jacob ben Nathanel ha-Kohen, it primarily consists of information on travel routes, distances between certain towns, and sites of Jewish interest in their vicinity; but these technical data are enriched by brief descriptions of religious rituals. Most relevant to our topic, there is frequent mention of Islamic shrines at Jewish holy places or Muslims praying at the same sites as Jewish pilgrims.

Another noteworthy aspect of *Elleh ha-Massa'ot* is that it delineates a number of alternative trail maps to the major holy places in the region. While most of them are shorter excursions to tombs of saints in Galilee, the largest of these circuits reaches farther south to include Jerusalem and Hebron. Because all the tours have their starting point in Acre, the port of arrival for most European Jews during the thirteenth century, *Elleh ha-Massa'ot* reflects the particular pilgrimage patterns that developed during that era.[30] Following its account of Jewish sites in Palestine, the second, much shorter, part of *Elleh ha-Massa'ot* surveys holy tombs in Syria and Iraq.

Toṣ'ot Ereṣ Yisra'el

As Elchanan Reiner has compellingly argued, *Toṣ'ot Ereṣ Yisra'el*, whose Hebrew title translates as "Extremities of the Land of Israel,"[31] represents an expanded version of *Elleh ha-Massa'ot* and may have been composed a decade or two before the Mamluk conquest of Acre (1291), but a slightly later date is not to be excluded.[32] The text's widespread attribution to an "anonymous pupil of Naḥmanides," who, like his teacher, had come to Palestine from abroad, is dubious because the text provides no tangible information about its author.[33] He turned the guidebook (*Elleh ha-Massa'ot*) into a personal pilgrimage account: he frequently inserted into his template passages in the first-person singular and plural (for example, "I saw," or "we went from there"), thereby bolstering the claim that *Toṣ'ot* is a firsthand report of what its writer actually saw while in the company of other Jewish pilgrims.

Yitgaddal the Scribe

This incomplete list of pilgrimage sites was compiled from earlier inventories by an Egyptian Jew named Yitgaddal, the scribe of a certain Sar Shalom whose title *nasi* marks him as a Jewish dignitary of Davidic descent.[34] Sar Shalom Nasi ben Pinḥas is known to have lived in fourteenth-century Cairo,[35] so the list's date of origin can be roughly estimated to this period. I have included this work in my study because it sheds light on Jewish-Muslim relations in both Palestine and Egypt during the Mamluk period. The single surviving manuscript (sixteenth century) includes a handful of rather crude ink sketches of some of the holy places featured. These illustrations may constitute the earliest extant examples of this pictorial genre that was later to be popularized, as will become clear.

Yiḥus ha-Ṣaddiqim and Yiḥus Avot

In the late fifteenth and sixteenth centuries, medieval Jewish traditions of pilgrimage sites were standardized in lists such as *Yiḥus ha-Ṣaddiqim*[36] (Lineage of the Righteous) and the related *Yiḥus Avot* (Lineage of the Ancestors).[37] The primary objective of these lists was, in all likelihood, to provide an exhaustive catalog of all the Jewish holy tombs that were mentioned in previous compendia. My interest in these works stems from the fact that they frequently allude to Muslim worship at the same localities.

A number of copies of *Yiḥus Avot* come with colored sketches of the sacred places that constitute a kind of "paratext" supplementary to the written descriptions.[38] Some of these illustrated copies were produced in the holy cities of Safed and Jerusalem and then acquired by Italian pilgrims,[39] who took them home as souvenirs, pilgrimage advertisements, or fund-raising material for the Jewish community in Palestine. The earliest print edition of *Yiḥus Avot*, titled *Cippi Hebraici* (Hebrew Funerary Monuments, in Latin), was published in Heidelberg in 1659 by Johann Heinrich Hottinger, a German theologian and Hebraist.[40] Its bilingual, Hebrew-Latin text bears testimony to the growing interest taken by an early modern Christian reading public in Jewish Holy Land traditions. Like some of the earlier manuscript versions, *Cippi Hebraici* includes two pages with copperplate representations of some of the holy places mentioned in the text (see Figures 3 and 4). A number of these illustrations—such as those depicting lamps suspended from arches—echo an Islamicate material culture. By dint of these illustrated versions of *Yiḥus Avot*, a visual image of the Holy Land was distributed, hinting that many of its sacred venues held significance for both Judaism and Islam.[41]

Unlike the itineraries and lists surveyed above, the eclectic accounts of Benjamin of Tudela and Petaḥyah of Regensburg stand out for their length and geographical scope. The amount of social commentary added to mere place-specific information distinguishes these two from the aforementioned texts and makes them extremely relevant sources for this study. Questions of Jewish identity, place within society, and power pervade their narratives, as will be demonstrated in the ensuing chapters.

Benjamin of Tudela

As stated in the anonymous preface to his *Sefer ha-Massa'ot* (Book of Travels; henceforth *Massa'ot*), the famous—if ultimately elusive—traveler Benjamin bar (or ben, son of) Jonah hailed from the Iberian city of Tudela (see Map 1), on the Ebro River. According to the same prologue, he returned from his peregrinations in 1173—the only firm date that is known for him.[42] In 1119, the Christian Kingdom of Navarre captured Tudela (Arabic: al-Tuṭīla), which had been ruled by Muslims since the eighth century. This relatively recent change of power allows for the assumption that Benjamin had a hybrid cultural background.[43] As suggested by the numerous terms in *Massa'ot* that are of non-Hebrew origin, he must have known some Arabic (on this more below) and Romance vernacular—knowledge that would have proved helpful on his journey. In the absence of external sources that refer to him, this is almost all that can be known for certain about the Jewish globetrotter.

Even the exact duration of Benjamin's far-flung peregrinations and their detailed chronology are not entirely clear, as *Massa'ot* does not provide further dates (besides 1173). But this lack has not deterred scholars from trying to determine the time frame of his travels. While Marcus N. Adler believed that the Tudelan's voyage fell into the period 1166–73, David Jacoby has recently argued that he set out on his journey as early as 1159/60.[44] Both scholars assume that *Massa'ot* offers identifiable historical references (such as names of rulers and other prominent persons mentioned) from which they derive precise dates for Benjamin's various stations along the way—an approach that seems questionable on account of the rhetorical character of many of the relevant passages. (What is more, some of this information may have been added to the account after the traveler's return.) The handful of other available details about his voyage and its relation to *Massa'ot* are to be gleaned from the preface to the work, which was clearly penned by a secondary source. Before turning to the preface, I will take a brief look at the text itself and the history of its transmission, for its major textual witnesses come with varying prologues.

Massa'ot has been passed down in several manuscript versions and early print editions, as well as more than twenty modern reprints and translations. The repeated publication of Benjamin's work in the early modern period attests to its popularity among Jewish (and later also Christian) readers as a recreational pursuit.[45] Here I mention only the most influential editions: the editio princeps (of which few copies survive) was brought to press in Constantinople (Istanbul) by Eli'ezer ben Gershon Soncino in 1543, followed by Abraham Usque's Ferrara edition (Figure 1) only thirteen years later (1556); the next print (Freiburg im Breisgau) dates to 1582/83 (Figure 2).[46]

Usque's text (which significantly differs from the editio princeps) was to serve as the basis for the first modern critical edition (and English translation)

Figure 1. Title page of the second printed edition of Benjamin of Tudela's itinerary, *Massa'ot shel Rabbi Binyamin* (Ferrara: Abraham Usque, 1556). As evidenced on this and other title pages from his Ferrara print shop, the Portuguese-born Usque adopted as his printer's mark an armillary sphere with Isa. 40:31 as the legend. Given Usque's own background, this quotation seems to speak to a readership of former conversos (Jewish converts to Christianity) but here also underscores the consoling message of *Massa'ot*: "They who trust in the Lord shall renew their strength as eagles grow new plumes: They shall run and not grow weary, they shall march and not grow faint." © The British Library Board; C. 50.a.8.

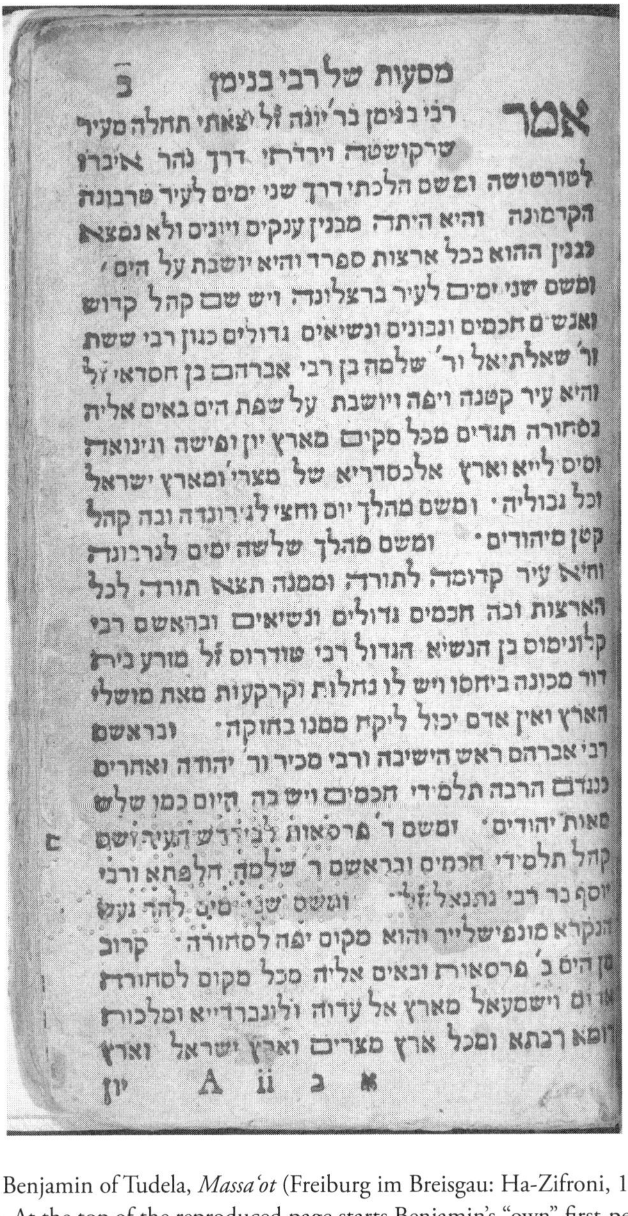

מסעות של רבי בנימן   ב
אמר רבי בנימן בר' יונה ז"ל יצאתי תחלה מעיר
שרקושטה וירדתי דרך נהר איברו
לטורטושה ומשם הלכתי דרך שני ימים לעיר טרבונה
הקדמונה והיא היתה מבנין ענקים ויונים ולא נמצא
כבנין ההוא בכל ארצות ספרד והיא יושבת על הים׳
ומשם שני ימים לעיר ברצלונה ויש שם קהל קדוש
ואנשים חכמים ונבונים ונשיאים גדולים כגון רבי ששת
ור' שאלתיאל ור' שלמה בן רבי אברהם בן חסדאי ז"ל
והיא עיר קטנה ויפה ויושבת על שפת הים באים אליה
בסחורה תגרים מכל מקום מארץ יון ומפישה וגינואה
וסיס לייא וארץ אלכסדריא של מצרי' ומארץ ישראל
וכל גבוליה׳ ומשם מהלך יום וחצי לגירונדה ובה קהל
קטן מיהודים׳ ומשם מהלך שלשה ימים לנרבונה
והיא עיר קדומה לתורה וממנה תצא תורה לכל
הארצות ובה חכמים גדולים ונשיאים ובראשם רבי
קלונימוס בן הנשיא הגדול רבי טודרוס ז"ל מזרע בית
דוד מכונה ביחסו ויש לו נחלות וקרקעות מאת מושלי
הארץ ואין אדם יכול ליקח ממנו בחזקה׳ ובראשם
רבי אברהם ראש הישיבה ורבי מכיר ור' יהודה ואחרים
כנגדם הרבה תלמידי חכמים ויש בה היום כמו שלש
מאות יהודים׳ ומשם ד' פרסאות לביזרש העיר ושם ב
קהל תלמידי חכמים ובראשם ר' שלמה חלפתא ורבי
יוסף בר רבי נתנאל ז"ל׳ ומשם שני ימים להר געש
הנקרא מונפישליר והוא מקום יפה לסחורה׳ קרוב
מן הים ב' פרסאות ובאים אליה מכל מקום לסחורה
אדום וישמעאל מארץ אלגרבה ולונברדייא ומלכות
רומא רבתא ומכל ארץ מצרים וארץ ישראל וארץ
יון   A ii   ב   א

Figure 2. Benjamin of Tudela, *Massa'ot* (Freiburg im Breisgau: Ha-Zifroni, 1582/83), p. 2 recto. At the top of the reproduced page starts Benjamin's "own" first-person account that follows the anonymous preface: "R. Benjamin ben R. Jonah—his memory be blessed—said: First, I set out from the city of Saragossa and then I went down the River Ebro to Tortosa. . . ." Courtesy of the Library at the Herbert D. Katz Center for Advanced Judaic Studies, University of Pennsylvania.

of *Massa'ot*, which was rendered by the German bibliographer Adolf Asher in 1840.[47] More than half a century later, Adler took the unprecedented step to base a new critical edition (which, together with his antiquated English translation, is still quoted on an almost exclusive basis) on several medieval manuscripts; foremost among them is a fourteenth-century Ashkenazi manuscript (now housed at the British Library; henceforth MS London).[48] Adler, inter alia, compared this witness of the text with a fifteenth-century manuscript in Italian handwriting (from the Casanatense Library of Rome; henceforth MS Rome).[49]

As evidenced by the disparate prologues that turn up in manuscript and print versions, *Massa'ot* was edited by several copyists. The discrepancies between the textual versions go well beyond the mere slip of a scribe. A closer investigation of the manuscript tradition (which demands new studies that go beyond the purposes of this monograph) would probably lead to the conclusion that there are several redactions of the work, each of which addresses a different audience (for example, an Ashkenazi and Italian Jewish readership, respectively). A brief perusal of the anonymous prefaces to the book in Asher's and Adler's modern editions suffices to demonstrate that the extant text is a multilayered document rather than an unmediated transcription of the Tudelan's travel journal—which raises a host of historiographic questions.

The Ashkenazi London manuscript that served as the base text for the Adler edition contains the following preface: "This is the book of travels [*sefer ha-massa'ot*] that was compiled [*she-ḥibber*] by R. Benjamin bar Jonah of the land of Navarre—[may] his repose be in paradise. The said R. Benjamin set forth from Tudela, his place of origin, and passed through many remote countries, as related in his book. In every place he visited, he wrote down all the things that he saw or *heard* from trustworthy persons [*anshe emet*]—[matters] not [previously] heard of in the land of *sefarad* [Iberia]."[50]

According to this introduction, Benjamin compiled the book from notes that he took on the road. In contrast to the previously discussed itineraries, the prologue distinguishes between things that Benjamin witnessed with his own eyes and those based on secondary oral sources. To strengthen the credibility of the secondhand accounts and defend them against charges of hearsay, the preface attributes the information to "trustworthy persons." But the inherently unverifiable nature of this commonplace medieval seal of approval inevitably leads the modern reader to inquire about the extent of the author's reliance on other sources. The prologue's third-person narration indicates that this section is a later addition (apparently after Benjamin's death) by an anonymous editor who endeavored to guarantee the truthfulness of the book, which raises the question of whether this editor revised, embellished, or abbreviated Benjamin's words—and if so, to what extent. To understand the implications of this question, it is worth taking a look at the preface according to Usque's Ferrara print of 1556 (the basis of Asher's edition): "This story [*sippur*] is compiled from the words *told* [*meḥubbar mi-devarim she-sipper*] by a certain man from the land of Navarre whose name is R. Benjamin bar Jonah, from Tudela. He went and passed through many remote countries, as will be related in these *his words*."[51]

Again, a modern critical reader is bound to ponder the meaning of the phrase "compiled from the words *told*." Could this possibly mean that Benjamin, at least according to this version, did not author his *Massaʿot*, in the modern sense, but was assisted by a ghost writer who composed the book as it is known? This sort of modus operandi informed the rendering of Petaḥyah of Regensburg's itinerary discussed below. Likewise, Marco Polo's work (which postdated Benjamin's by about a century) is known to have been heavily influenced by his collaborator Rustichello of Pisa, an author of Arthurian romance. He evidently wrote the foreword to *Divisament dou Monde* (Description of the World), which shares certain features with the Ferrara prologue to *Massaʿot*. Accordingly, Rustichello promised his readers that he would describe "the great wonders and curiosities" of the world "as they were *related* by Messer Marco Polo . . . who has seen them with his own eyes. There is also much here that he has not seen but has *heard* from men of credit and veracity [*persone degne de fede*]."[52] According to this passage, Marco Polo clearly produced an oral account, while the literary work was rendered by Rustichello. Like Benjamin's editor, Rustichello differentiates between the authority of an eyewitness and that of secondary sources. In both cases, the editor tried to establish the validity and significance of the following information with the help of a prologue.

Following the preface to *Massaʿot*, the anonymous editor (Ferrara edition) introduces the Tudelan's "own" words with "R. Benjamin bar Jonah said," after which comes a first-person account: "First, I set out from the city of Saragossa, and then I went down the River Ebro to Tortosa. From there, it took me two days [of travel] to the ancient city of Tarragona."[53] At this early point in his trip through northeastern Iberia (see Map 1), the first-person narration already comes to an abrupt end to give way to an impersonal mode: "From [Tarragona], it is [a journey of] two days to Barcelona."[54] The text continues to note the distances between destinations but eschews mentioning whether

Benjamin actually went there. While the practical itinerary seems to offer objectivity, its reliability varies greatly. Even Prawer, who believes that these measures provide a rough estimate of the time that Benjamin spent in certain regions, concedes that "some distances are simply absurd" and "how Benjamin actually calculated the distances ... remains a mystery."[55] In any case, the first-person narrative almost never resumes (a phenomenon observed in the itinerary of Jacob ben Nathanel ha-Kohen), which suggests that Benjamin's "own" report has been significantly edited by others.[56] Against this backdrop, my references to Benjamin or his book must be understood as the *received* text (as represented by Adler's edition, if not indicated otherwise), rather than the literary creation of an individual author in the modern sense of the word.[57]

In *Massa'ot*, the initial sequence of places gives the impression of a contiguous route from Navarre, through Catalonia, southern France, by way of Rome, Constantinople, Rhodes, and Cyprus, to Syria and Palestine.[58] Then Benjamin appears to have lost his compass, as it were, as there are several geographical inconsistencies in this part of the book. After being led on a circuitous route through Syria and northern and southern Mesopotamia, readers find themselves on ever more wayward routes featuring exceedingly dubious scenes. As early as a century ago, Adler questioned whether the Tudelan "went far into Persia" and ascribed his brief accounts of the Arabian Peninsula, India, and the China Sea to hearsay.[59] From Basra, at the mouth of the Persian Gulf, the traveler could have taken a sea passage to Egypt and then made his homeward journey via Italy. (Egypt and Sicily are portrayed in some detail toward the end of the book.) Instead of describing the Tudelan's return to Spain, *Massa'ot* concludes with brief references to Jewish communities in Germany, Prague, Kiev, and France—which seem to be later additions aimed at an Ashkenazi readership.[60] In any event, attempting to sort out which of the places Benjamin actually visited does not substantially contribute to the understanding of a work that appears to canvas the entire geographical trajectory existing up to his time.

If *Massa'ot* does not narrate Benjamin's personal experiences on the road, how is it to be understood? What may be characterized as a plotless itemization of place descriptions along a circuitous route demonstrates that the medieval itinerary genre served, inter alia, as a system for organizing diverse stores of information—both empirical and imaginary—about foreign lands. As Benjamin notes Jewish communities in places ranging from Tudela to Tibet—frequently offering population estimates and naming the communities' leaders—one of his work's major purposes seems to be documenting the physical existence of far-flung Jewish diasporas. While the historical reliability of this documentation is up for debate, it was clearly meant to deliver a consoling message to the traveler's home audience.[61] By its very nature, this sort of compendium of the Jewish world was open to additions and emendations by later generations.

Another encyclopedic quality of *Massa'ot* is that its toponyms often correspond to a variety of usages. Specifically, place names are simultaneously or alternatively given in adherence to biblical convention, contemporary crusader terminology (of Romance origin), or Arab tradition.[62] Although the book includes a fair number of Arabic terms and toponyms (transcribed in Hebrew characters), that does not necessarily mean that Benjamin was proficient in Arabic.[63] Given *Massa'ot*'s rather pedestrian style, it seems doubtful that much of the literary legacy of al-Andalus was bequeathed to the traveler. Notwithstanding a certain geographical overlap and the fact that some of the book's narrative motifs also turn up in Muslim-authored works, it would be quite a stretch to claim that *Massa'ot* was influenced by the *riḥla* literature noted above. Such resemblances indicate only a common store of cross-cultural oral traditions, some of which Benjamin would have picked up on his extended travels and some of which may have circulated in twelfth-century Iberia, beyond the porous boundaries of Muslim-held regions.

Petaḥyah of Regensburg

A nearly contemporaneous itinerary that shares much of Benjamin's geographical and cultural purview is R. Petaḥyah of Regensburg's *Sibbuv* (lit., "circuit" or "circular journey"). In contrast to the Sephardic traveler's *Massa'ot*, it offers an Ashkenazi perspective on the Middle East. According to both the work's secondary introduction and colophon,[64] Petaḥyah's brother was R. Isaac ha-Lavan (the White-Haired)—a student of Rabbenu Tam (Jacob ben Meir, the grandson of Rashi)—who authored Tosafot (commentaries) on several tractates of the Babylonian Talmud. After studying in France, Petaḥyah—the lesser known of the two brothers—lived in Prague and later Regensburg (Ratisbon, on the Danube), where he served as a *dayyan* (rabbinic judge). His residency in both cities places him in the cultural context of twelfth-century Ashkenazi scholars, as will be seen shortly.

From its starting point in Prague, Petaḥyah's extraordinary journey traced a wide arc via Kiev, Crimea, the Caucasus, Black Sea region, Mesopotamia, Syria, and finally down to Palestine. One characteristic it has in common with Benjamin's book is the complete lack of dates. Despite this shortcoming, the historical backdrop of the text suggests that the journey took place prior to the crusaders' defeat at the hands of Saladin (1187). It is commonly assumed that Petaḥyah set out for the Middle East about a decade after Benjamin.[65]

Whereas *Massa'ot* rarely states whether Benjamin personally visited a given place, *Sibbuv* leaves no room for doubt that Petaḥyah traveled through certain regions and towns. This is often expressed by verbs of movement, such as the Hebrew *halakh* ("he went"): "from Russia he went for six days on the River Dnieper";[66] or (a little later) "R. Petaḥyah crossed [*'avar*] through the whole land of Kedar [modern-day Ukraine] in sixteen days."[67] In another contrast to the Tudelan's book, *Sibbuv* does offer some intimate details. On one occasion, for example, the reader is informed that the voyager fell ill;[68] and on another, that Petaḥyah used river-craft to travel from Mosul to Baghdad "in fifteen days."[69]

Despite these glimpses at the traveler's experiences on the road, Petaḥyah's *Circuit* takes one step further the questions of authorship and editing that I raised with respect to Benjamin's *Massa'ot*; the reader gets the impression that *Sibbuv* was constructed in a haphazard fashion and then underwent several rounds of revision that only exacerbated the lack of consistency. The narration frequently oscillates from topic to topic, and the order of sites is devoid of geographical logic. As noted, the account was not put down into writing by its protagonist but seems to be based on the oral reports that Petaḥyah delivered before an unspecified audience back home.[70] Consequently, the narrative is composed entirely in the third person, as evidenced in the opening paragraph: "These are the words told by the master, R. Petaḥyah, who journeyed through [lit., 'circuited'] all countries, then returned, and told what he saw and heard."[71] In fact, a distinction between Petaḥyah as the *Circuit*'s persona and author seems important, as the traveler turns out to be a narrative construction.[72] In fact, the reader is often left wondering whose voice speaks in the final product: the traveler's, the writer's, or the collective voice of a whole community of recipients.[73]

Among those who apparently influenced *Sibbuv*'s received text was the famed Ashkenazi mystic R. Judah he-Ḥasid (the Pious) of Regensburg (d. 1217). A later voice comments that R. Judah intentionally deleted a passage from the *Circuit* about a messianic prediction by an astrologer whom Petaḥyah reportedly met in Mosul. R. Judah "would not write down" its content lest he be suspected of believing this prediction.[74] Though many *Ḥaside Ashkenaz* (medieval Ashkenazi mystics) harbored eschatological hopes, R. Judah is known for his fierce opposition to messianic prognostics.[75] The existence of a certain ideological affinity to *Ḥaside Ashkenaz*, for whom Regensburg was a center, may also explain the moralist tone of much of *Sibbuv* and its assortment of anecdotes on miraculous occurrences.[76] In any event, Petaḥyah's oral account seems to have been alternately condensed and expanded on the basis of other traditions. These redactions significantly altered the original—whatever it may have looked like.

While *Sibbuv*'s manuscript trail extends no further back than the late fifteenth century, the first print edition (Prague) dates to 1595.[77] Like the editio princeps of Benjamin's book (1543), the *Circuit*'s debut reflects a renewed interest in medieval travel literature among sixteenth-century Jews. Moreover, it managed to attract the attention of modern scholars at about the same time as *Massa'ot.* A few years earlier than Adler's version of Benjamin's work (1907), Lazar Grünhut, a Hungarian rabbi and midrash scholar, published the first critical edition of Petaḥyah's itinerary (1904–5), which is largely based on the aforementioned Prague imprint; this is also the textual version that will be discussed here.

Letters, Epistolary Travel Accounts, and Travel Diaries

In addition to the itineraries, I have analyzed the correspondence of about a dozen Jewish travelers from the eleventh to the early sixteenth centuries. While a few of them were penned by such renowned scholars as Naḥmanides (Moses ben Naḥman, also known as the Ramban, 1194–1270),[78] who does not need to be introduced here, other letter writers are known to us almost exclusively on account of their correspondence and therefore deserve a more detailed discussion. Some of their missives provide highly personalized travel accounts that were addressed to the author's kith and kin. The earliest example cited herein, a letter from the beginning of the eleventh century, was not meant for mass circulation and ended up on a scrap heap in the Cairo Genizah (a repository of discarded texts at the Ben Ezra Synagogue of Old Cairo). Though the document predates the time frame set for this book (ca. 1150–1520), I quote from it because it vividly illustrates a perilous sea journey from Italy to the Levant.[79]

Most letters relevant to the topic of this study were penned by northern Italian Jewish pilgrims, merchants, and immigrants to Palestine from the mid-fifteenth century onward. While those who settled in Jerusalem for good were no longer travelers per se, they still wished to be heard by readers in the "old country" and thus expressed views that accorded with the norms of

Italian Jewish culture. Though their immediate addressees were often family members, friends, or business partners back home, another objective of these expatriates (to use a modern category) was to reach a larger Italian Jewish readership wishing to visit the Land of Israel, whether in the imagination or in actuality. Some authors explicitly urge their addressees to distribute copies of their letters to other Jewish communities. This dual audience explains the documents' semiprivate-semipublic character. What distinguishes some of these letters from many earlier sources discussed herein is that their authors emerge as individualistic and partly self-conscious observers.

In the ensuing paragraphs, I offer a brief overview of some of the shorter epistolary accounts that I quote throughout this book, to be followed by a more detailed introduction to the elaborate narratives of Meshullam of Volterra, Obadiah of Bertinoro, and Moses Basola, which are among the most relevant sources for the topic at hand.

Among the writings dispatched from Mamluk Jerusalem to Italy is the pilgrimage account of Elijah of La Massa. Dated 1438, it was addressed to the notables of the Ferrara Jewish community (the author was apparently from the nearby town of Massa Fiscaglia), with a request that it be forwarded to Elijah's sons.[80] Another mid-fifteenth-century Italian pilgrim whose letter (from about 1455) I elaborate on is R. Isaac ben Meir Latif, whose surname hints at a Sephardic background.[81] Since the author seems to have been from Ancona, his unspecified addressees were likely in the same city or its vicinity. Lombardy was the home of R. Joseph of Montagna and his wife, who embarked on a voyage to Jerusalem in 1480.[82] Upon arriving safely at their destination, he described his experiences in a missive to his sons and daughters.[83]

The corpus also includes a letter (dated November 6, 1495) penned by an anonymous Italian Jew who, together with his brother Yequti'el, journeyed to Jerusalem to study with R. Obadiah of Bertinoro (whose own correspondence I discuss below); this letter helps contextualize another document:[84] having immigrated to Jerusalem with some other members of his prominent Sephardic family, Samuel ben Joseph Ibn Picho wrote to Don Judah ben Moses Ibn Picho, another relative living abroad (perhaps in Italy), whom the author encourages to follow their example and settle in the Holy Land.[85] Although the letter, which is attached to a Sephardic manuscript from approximately the mid-fifteenth century, bears no date, it appears to echo historical circumstances reminiscent of those described by Obadiah's aforesaid student. It may have been penned about the same time (1495) or, at the very latest, in the opening decades of the sixteenth century.[86] Another letter by an Italian Jewish expatriate is that of R. Israel ben Yeḥiel Ashkenazi, written shortly after the Ottoman conquest of Palestine (1516). Before relocating to Jerusalem in 1520, the author held rabbinical posts in Padua, Perugia, Bologna, and Rome. Upon his arrival in Jerusalem, R. Israel presided there over the Ashkenazi yeshiva, during a period in which the community was dominated by Sephardic Jews. His epistle, which was written about 1522,[87] was addressed to R. Abraham of Perugia, an important fund-raiser on behalf of the Jewish community in Palestine.

A number of the above-mentioned letter writers, such as Elijah of La Massa, were engaged in (limited) banking activities—a fact that reflects the social background of Italian Jewish pilgrims who left an account of their travels. Unlike their crusader-period predecessors, some of them recall their sea passage to the Levant in detail and even survey the ports of call that they visited along the way. Almost all of them describe sacred places and the Jewish community of the Mamluk- or Ottoman-ruled Levant. Those letters written by immigrants to Palestine tend to extol the virtues of living in the Holy Land. Many take stock of the relations between Jews and the local Muslims, which makes them especially valuable to the present discussion.

Meshullam of Volterra

The sociocultural profile of Meshullam ben Menaḥem mi-Volṭera (born before 1443, died after 1507) is already hinted at by the different names he used: besides the above-noted Hebrew one, he was known by the Italian name Bonaventura di Emanuele da Volterra. Like other members of his distinguished family, a dynasty of Tuscan *banchieri* (bankers), Meshullam was engaged in moneylending in Volterra and Florence; in addition, he traded in gemstones, pearls, wine, oil, grain, wool, and cloth.[88] As documented by two letters he wrote in the Tuscan vernacular to Lorenzo de' Medici (in 1471 and 1472), the Jewish merchant-banker embraced elements of an Italian upper-class lifestyle. He sent these letters to Lorenzo, together with some choice cuts of game, which Meshullam hunted in the Volterrean countryside—a pastime that was unusual for a Jew and attests to his desire to cultivate an aristocratic persona.[89] Not too surprisingly, in writing about his encounters in the Near East, he reveals a strongly developed class-consciousness, as to be evidenced in the chapters that follow.

In 1481, Meshullam made a pilgrimage to Jerusalem in fulfillment of a vow; at the same time, traveling to Egypt on the first leg of his trip, he combined the spiritual journey with mercantile interests.[90] This, his first tour of the Near East (in 1487, he made another sea voyage to the Eastern Mediterranean, probably for business reasons), is the topic of the travel account to be discussed here. In his later years, Meshullam coped with a decline in his family's fortunes and his children's conversion to Christianity.[91]

Unfortunately, the lone surviving manuscript of his travel diary, which appears to be a copy that was made by a professional scribe during the author's lifetime, is incomplete.[92] In the absence of a preface, one can only speculate as to whom the truncated document was addressed, for it includes several references to the reader (in the second-person singular or plural). Writing in a Hebrew loaded with Italian loanwords (on this, more later), the author seems to have an audience in mind, consisting of family members and other readers of similar socioreligious background. In part, Meshullam's account may have been intended as a guidebook providing future travelers with detailed advice about customs inspections, equipment for a desert trek, and potential dangers on the road. (As argued below, Obadiah of Bertinoro may have read it.) Besides this practical aspect, the text constitutes a rather enjoyable travelogue that is interlaced with themes of bravery and adventure, thereby dramatizing what would otherwise be a more generic pilgrimage account. Anecdotes and personal observations are juxtaposed with references to classical sources (such as Pliny) and Italian etymology. Meshullam's journal is a conscious literary creation that indicates the author's desire to commemorate his journey for posterity's sake and to establish himself as an accomplished diarist, in the spirit of his time.[93] Be they Christian or Jewish, quite a few fifteenth-century Italian merchants traveled to the Levant in pursuit of both riches and renown.[94]

Another sign of the author's interwoven Jewish and Italian identities is his manner of recording arrival and departure dates at each stop on his journey (that he records them at all differentiates his diary from the earlier accounts reviewed): the month is given according to the Christian calendar, but the year according to the Jewish one (that is, the years since creation). For example, Meshullam arrives in Rhodes on "Wednesday, the 30th of May [*maggio*] [5]241" (1481).[95] The use of Christian months seems to accord with the needs of a businessman who had to have his finger on the pulse of society at large, whereas the Christian anno Domini calculation had religious implications that a medieval Jew would have wished to avoid.

Obadiah of Bertinoro

R. Obadiah Yare of Bertinoro (ca. 1450–ca. 1515), the eminent Italian Jewish scholar and a contemporary of Meshullam, is best known for his Mishnah commentary.[96] Since first being published in Venice in 1549, his commentary has graced the margins of every traditional edition of the Mishnah. His family's place of origin is Bertinoro, a town in Romagna (southeast of Bologna), which at the time belonged to the Papal States.[97] In the 1480s, Obadiah resided in Città di Castello, a town in northern Umbria (a region also under papal control), where he served as a rabbi. Archival sources shine additional light on the rabbi's life, for an Italian version of his name (Maestro Servadio di Abramo da Bertinoro) appears at the top of a document from 1485 listing the Jewish moneylenders who were officially sanctioned by the city;[98] but Obadiah probably did not own one of the big banking houses of the day.

In autumn 1486, the Bertinorean set out for Jerusalem, where he was to settle for good (his grave is still shown to visitors at the foot of the Mount of Olives).[99] Because of protracted detours and delays along a complicated sea route, he would only arrive in Jerusalem a year and a half later, on the day before Passover eve. Soon after his arrival, Obadiah became the dominant spiritual figure of the local Jewish community and assumed an active role in its public affairs.

There are three extant texts of letters that Obadiah sent from Mamluk-ruled Palestine to Italy between 1488 and 1492. The first and longest of the three was composed about five months after his arrival in Jerusalem and is dated 8 Elul 5248 (August 15, 1488)—unlike Meshullam, the rabbi only cited Jewish dates. Though addressed to his father, Abraham, back in Città di Castello, the letter seems to have been written with a larger audience in mind. The dates of Obadiah's arrival and departure at the various venues that he passed through provide the structure of this epistolary diary, which chronicles his journey to the Holy Land. The author focuses on the Jewish communities that he visited along the way. Specifically, Obadiah describes their rituals and "their relations with the Gentiles [*goyim*] among whom they live."[100]

There are a number of striking similarities between Obadiah's first letter and Meshullam of Volterra's travel account,[101] which the latter penned seven years earlier. Though the dependence of Obadiah's epistle upon Meshullam's cannot be proved conclusively, it is a distinct probability, for the latter's report was apparently meant to be circulated among future travelers to the Levant (as stated earlier). Also, by the time Obadiah wrote *his* letter, the two Italians had already crossed paths during Meshullam's second journey to the eastern Mediterranean.[102] It is my hypothesis—to be substantiated in the ensuing chapters—that Obadiah had indeed read the Volterrean's travel journal.

Written in the late summer of 1489, Obadiah's second and much shorter letter is addressed to his brother, whose name is unknown.[103] This document is more private in character than the first and responds to certain inquiries that his brother had made. While it does not provide a diaristic account of the eminent rabbi's travels, it does shed light on Jewish-Muslim relations in Mamluk Palestine. Obadiah's third letter was dispatched from Hebron sometime after December 1491.[104] The anonymous recipient is probably Emanuel Ḥay of Camerino, a Florentine Jewish banker, with whom Obadiah had invested considerable sums of money—the proceeds of which he was now living off.[105]

Moses Basola

Elleh Mas'ay (These Are My Travels) is a gem of late medieval and early modern Hebrew travel writing. The text was transmitted anonymously in both the single extant manuscript and its editio princeps (Livorno, 1785). However, based on a reference by the Jewish polymath 'Azaryah de' Rossi (see below), Isaac Ben-Zvi (the scholar and later president of Israel, 1884–1963) determined conclusively that its author is the renowned Italian rabbi and kabbalist Moses Basola (ca. 1480–1560).[106] Like Obadiah of Bertinoro and other Italian Jewish travelers to the Levant, Basola (whose family may have originated in Basel; hence the name) was engaged in finance, owning a bank in the city of Rocca in the Marches (northeast of Rome). What is more, Basola set out on multiple trips to the eastern Mediterranean, as did Meshullam of Volterra. In the account of his first Levantine journey that is analyzed herein, he writes that he embarked from Venice to Beirut in the late summer of 1521 and returned to Italy in spring 1523. Having served in the rabbinate of Ancona in the intervening period, Basola, in his old age, headed east yet again and was to die in the Palestinian city of Safed the same year (1560).[107]

While there is no hint as to the original addressees of Basola's narration (strictly speaking, this is not an epistolary account), it resembles the travel journals by Meshullam and Obadiah in structure and content. It soon caught the attention of a wider circle of Italian Jewish intellectuals, as evidenced by the fact that 'Azaryah de' Rossi (ca. 1511–77), shortly after its author's death, perused the "actual autograph of the itinerary to the Holy Land written by R. Moses Basola of blessed memory."[108]

Basola's work includes one of the most comprehensive accounts of holy tombs in the Land of Israel, which he enumerated in the order in which he visited them. That said, the author, like many of his predecessors, appears to have made use of earlier lists, among them the above-mentioned *Yiḥus Avot* (which seems to have been popular among Italian Jewry of the time).[109] An appendix to *Elleh Mas'ay* contains prayers to be recited by the pilgrim at various holy places. It also offers detailed advice on the sea passage from Venice to the Levant, including information on money exchange, prices, provisions, contracts with patrons of vessels, and the best places to lodge on cargo ships. In this sense, the rabbi's travel account (much like Christian pilgrim books of the time) may have been intended as a vade mecum to provide future travelers with ready reference and to be carried on the trip.

Imaginary Travel

Though the letters and diaries from the fifteenth and sixteenth centuries offer more realistic descriptions than the crusader-period accounts, they, too, include miracle stories or legends about the Lost Tribes—a staple of Jewish travel writing that continued to be very popular among quattrocento Jews.[110] While the distinction between fact, imagination, and fiction (to use a modern literary term) was less important to a premodern audience, there is also a subgenre of travel narratives that has to be considered purely, or at least overwhelmingly, imaginary; it is obvious that the author opined about most, if not all, of the places without ever having personally seen them.

Eldad ha-Dani

Among these imaginary accounts has to be counted that of Eldad ha-Dani, who is said to have appeared in the North African city of Qayrawān (Cairouan, in present-day Tunisia; Map 1) in the last quarter of the ninth century. Eldad, as his epithet ha-Dani suggests, claimed to be a member of the biblical tribe of Dan. Likewise, he stated that four of the Lost Tribes were living as independent warriors in the ancient "Havilah, where the gold is" (Gen. 2:11). Some of these stories were transmitted in a letter by the Jews of Qayrawān to one *ga'on* R. Ṣemaḥ (perhaps R. Ṣemaḥ ben Ḥayyim of Sura) in Baghdad. In that same letter, they asked the sage for an authoritative opinion on the credibility of Eldad's contentions. Though the epistle to R. Ṣemaḥ only survived in much later manuscripts and early prints (editio princeps: Mantua, ca. 1480),[111] this correspondence is considered the keystone of Eldad's historicity and the authenticity of much of the other material that is associated with him—including his soon-to-be discussed travel book. However, both the date of the correspondence (883) and the identification of the rabbinic addressee are far from certain.[112] Furthermore, Eldad's self-purported tribal affiliation weakens his credibility because tribal distinctions had long ceased to be significant in Judaism. Last, the question as to his possible country of origin (Yemen or Ethiopia) seems to be moot, as the legends about his provenance appear to have overshadowed any detectable kernel of historical truth, if there was one to begin with.[113]

Another alleged source on this mysterious figure is the so-called *Book of Eldad* (*Sefer Eldad*), which purports to be Eldad's first-person account of his adventures "beyond the rivers of Cush" and includes additional stories about the Lost Tribes.[114] It shares numerous folkloristic motifs with the medieval letters of Prester John, whose legendary Christian kingdom was thought to have been in India or Ethiopia.[115] Although a comprehensive analysis of these legends is beyond the scope of this study, I discuss a few of the themes and motifs that turn up in the *Book of Eldad*; above all, this work narrates an imaginary journey. The book clearly existed in the mid-twelfth century,[116] but there are doubts as to whether there was a complete and intelligible version before its editio princeps (Constantinople, 1519)—the version that is cited herein.

David Re'uveni

No less enigmatic than the figure of Eldad is that of David (ha)-Re'uveni. Although Re'uveni is a bona fide historical figure (something that cannot be ascertained in the case of the former), he may be considered a self-styled, sixteenth-century reincarnation of Eldad or a Jewish "impersonation" of Prester John. In his travel tale, Re'uveni introduces himself as David, son of King Solomon and younger brother of King Joseph, who ruled over two and a half Lost Tribes of Israel (Gad, Reuben, and half of Manasseh) living in the "wilderness of Ḥabor," somewhere on the Arabian Peninsula.[117] Later Jewish chroniclers would add to his name the epithet "ha-Re'uveni" (from the tribe of Reuben), which henceforth accompanies the references to him in the literature.[118] Re'uveni's protestations concerning his provenance are apparently predicated on the Eldad traditions and Benjamin of Tudela's account of the Jews of Khaybar.[119] The view that Re'uveni was from Yemen or Ethiopia lacks a firm basis.[120] If his story were to be believed, he would have advanced from the Near Eastern "periphery" to the European "center," unlike most of the other travelers discussed herein.

As outlandish as Re'uveni's claims may seem to the modern reader, many of his contemporaries did not summarily dismiss them. He even managed to secure audiences with Pope Clement VII and the Portuguese king João III. The relative seriousness with which Re'uveni was taken has to be understood in the context of the age of European expansion, when rumors about hitherto unknown or rediscovered "ancient" peoples were given far more credence than might be expected today.[121] Re'uveni's vague references to the Arabian Peninsula and East Africa, whence he purportedly set out for Europe, must have attracted the attention of the Portuguese monarchy on account of its strategic interests in the Red Sea region (through which much of the spice trade was directed).[122]

As suggested in the colophon of his work, Re'uveni apparently composed the account of his travels from a jail cell in Provence, with the help of his servant-cum-secretary Solomon ha-Kohen of Prato.[123] This collaboration is reminiscent of the aforementioned one between Marco Polo and Rustichello of Pisa and thus casts further doubt on the narrative's authenticity. The book, moreover, has both a historical and an imaginary dimension that roughly correspond to its two parts.

The first (imaginary) part of Re'uveni's "diary" traces his peregrinations from the "wilderness of Ḥabor," through the Land of Cush, Palestine, and on to Alexandria. Despite its rather crude language, this part of Re'uveni's narrative contains elements of a chivalric romance, an adventure story, and a utopian travel tale. For instance, in the early chapters, which are vaguely set on both sides of the Red Sea, the protagonist roams among "savage" peoples and faces every last threat to his life with admirable courage.

The second part covers his subsequent diplomatic odyssey through Europe. From his debarkation in Venice in 1523 to his incarceration in Provence four years later, Re'uveni sought to promote a military alliance between Christian forces and "his" Jewish warriors from Ḥabor against the Ottoman Empire, with the aim to "liberate" the Holy Land. His narration of this fantastic tour, which was frequently interrupted by frustrating delays and numerous plots against him, may have been a personal attempt to explain why he ultimately failed to bring to fruition his military plan that seems to have been motivated by millenarian expectations.[124]

Notwithstanding the litany of far-fetched claims that dot Re'uveni's narrative, the second part of his account is partially corroborated by several firsthand accounts, official documents, and other contemporaneous references.[125] As fascinating as this still-insufficiently understood affair may be, I here concentrate entirely on the first (Near Eastern) part of Re'uveni's travel narrative on account of the images of the East that it conjures up.

Travel Poems

Beyond the common boundaries of culture and epoch, travel has consistently served as one of poetry's most prevalent themes and motifs. Like imaginary voyages, travel poems seem to blend the metaphorical with the author's personal experiences to such an extent that they become virtually indistinguishable. The vivid and highly stylized travel poems of Judah Halevi epitomize this sort of blend.

Judah Halevi

Yehudah ha-Levi (ca. 1075–1141), or Abū l-Ḥasan Ibn al-Lawī (as he was known in Arabic), long harbored personal qualms regarding the privileged existence that he led in both al-Andalus (Muslim Iberia) and Castile as a member of the intellectual urban elite. He fervently desired to go on a pilgrimage to Palestine, but it was only in 1040, when he was well into his sixties, that Halevi finally took the decisive step toward fulfilling his vow and ventured to the Near East.

Like many travelers of that period, Halevi set out for crusader-ruled Jerusalem along the well-established Mediterranean sea route to Alexandria (see the following chapter), where he arrived in autumn 1140. Subsequently, Halevi encountered a series of delays that prevented him from embarking on the considerably shorter, second leg of his journey to Palestine. During this time, Halevi apparently produced some of the travel-themed Hebrew poems that were compiled posthumously in a *dīwān*, as such collections of poems are commonly called in Arabic. Notwithstanding the realistic background of the poems, the Iberian intellectual employed a metaphorical language that far transcended his actual itinerary. While scholars have derived the biographic context of these compositions partly based on the Hebrew poems' (Judeo-Arabic) headings, this interpretation is complicated by the fact that the superscriptions have been added by compilers and edited in subsequent collections.[126]

To understand the relationship between Halevi's authentic voyage and his poetry, I juxtapose these poetic enactments of travel with some data that have emerged from a Judeo-Arabic correspondence involving his circle of friends, most prominent among them Ḥalfon ben Nathanel, a well-connected Jewish businessman and scholar from Cairo who had been to Spain several times.[127] In fact, Halevi met Ḥalfon over a decade before his trip to Fatimid Egypt; and the Cairo Genizah has yielded the autograph of a letter that Halevi wrote to the Egyptian in which he already refers to his travel plans: "I have no other wish than to go to the East as soon as I can, if I am so enabled by [divine] decree [Arabic: *qadr*]."[128]

Judah Alḥarizi

Another Iberian Jewish poet whose Near Eastern travels are echoed in his creative work is Judah ben Solomon Alḥarizi (Yaḥyā Ibn Sulaymān al-Ḥarīzī, 1165–1225). In his literary oeuvre, Alḥarizi spans and fuses Jewish and Arab cultural identities in a unique fashion. He was reared in Toledo, where he must have been deeply immersed in the Arabic culture that still suffused the city two generations after its incorporation into Christian Castile (in 1085). Alḥarizi later moved to northern Spain and Provence, where he helped disseminate (in Hebrew translation) Arabic sources of philosophy and science to Jewish communities that had never been part of the Islamicate orbit. Among his patrons from southern France was the acclaimed R. Jonathan ha-Kohen of Lunel, who was the travel companion of Samuel ben Samson, the abovementioned author of a Holy Land itinerary.

Emulating Judah Halevi, Alḥarizi chose to forsake an accomplished career by moving to the *mashriq* when he was in his early fifties. His decision to travel to the Levant also must be understood in the context of a wider movement of primarily French Jewish intellectuals (among them Jonathan ha-Kohen of Lunel) who flocked to Palestine during the late crusader period.[129] Following a sea journey from Marseille to Alexandria in roughly 1215, Alḥarizi proceeded to Cairo and then took the land route to Jerusalem. Thereupon he embarked on a long and meandering journey through the Fertile Crescent. Extending his pilgrimage circuit to the tomb shrines of southern Iraq, he visited Jewish communities and holy places in Damascus, Aleppo, Mosul, Baghdad, and Basra, before settling down in Aleppo, where he died in 1225.

Alḥarizi's literary fame stems from his successful Hebrew adaptation of the *maqāma* (pl., *maqāmāt*), a prolific genre of Arabic elite prose (called *maḥberet* in Hebrew). As opposed to high-style metric verse, the *maqāma* is characterized by a rhymed and rhythmic prose narrative that is skillfully embellished with rhetorical figures and eloquent wordplays. At key junctures, it may be interlaced with metric verse.[130] While he does not offer a description of his journeys per se, Alḥarizi's peregrinations through the Near East come to expression in numerous poetic and prose compositions about the Jewish communities that he visited on multiple trips between Syria and southern Iraq. Within the framework of either panegyric or satirical poems, he passed judgment on many of the communal leaders, patrons, and poets whom he met, on the basis of the generosity and hospitality that he had received—or frequently the lack thereof. These accounts have survived in several Hebrew and Judeo-Arabic manuscript versions, whose intricate relationship only recently has been mapped.[131]

The shortest rendition of Alḥarizi's portraits of Near Eastern Jewish notables is known as the Hebrew *Maqāma* of the Patrons (*maḥberet ha-nedivim*),[132] while his fullest recollection of local Jewish communities is found in his Judeo-Arabic *Book of Pearls* (*Kitāb al-Durar*), a collection of about a hundred poems that the author arranged according to the various cities he had passed through.[133] Yet another version of these literary portraits has been incorporated into Alḥarizi's *Taḥkemoni*, the most famous collection of his Hebrew *maqāmāt* (which has been preserved in both a shorter and an expanded edition by the author).[134] The travel motif serves as the *Taḥkemoni*'s ballast, as the book is loosely structured around the Near Eastern journeys of its narrator, Heman the Ezraḥite, and a trickster-cum-poet named Ḥever the Qenite, who happen to cross paths in various locations. Despite its fictional character, *Taḥkemoni* contains not a few thinly veiled references to Alḥarizi's own travels, and, at times, Heman or Ḥever appears as the author's alter ego.

I examine only a handful of these literary sketches, as a comprehensive analysis of the references or allusions to people and events in the different versions of Alḥarizi's oeuvre is beyond the scope of this study. That said, the fact that he revised his poetic representations several times, to the extent that he sometimes altered the meaning from parody to praise, hints at the shifting character of human relationships—such as the one between poet and patron.[135] A biographical analysis only partly explains the fluctuations in Alḥarizi's expressed opinions, as his sometimes radical revisions of specific portraits must also be viewed as a means for the poet to channel his representational acumen and versatility.

A Final Note on the Language

Reflecting the diverse array of literary genres and forms that are here subsumed under the broad category of travel literature, the texts discussed feature various levels of sophistication (a fact that does not always come across in their commonly quoted English renditions). The two Iberian poets, Judah Halevi and Judah Alḥarizi, not only availed themselves of metric verse or rhymed prose (*maqāma*) but employed a rich language and eloquent style that abounds with textual allusions, wordplay, and witticisms. In contrast, the book of another Sephardic Jew, Benjamin of Tudela's *Massaʿot*, is characterized by unadorned prose and a rather modest vocabulary; Benjamin's formulaic style is informed by phrases that recur with monotonous frequency. Similarly, the language of Petaḥyah of Regensburg, whose *Circuit* appears to have been significantly compromised over the course of the transmission process, seems like a patched-up fabric to the modern Hebrew reader.

The mediocre quality of these itineraries may reflect the plebeian character of medieval travel writing, which was held in relatively low esteem by the era's custodians of Jewish (as well as Christian) culture. Even though Hebrew was not a spoken language during the Middle Ages, the "low" prose that characterizes several Hebrew travel accounts is reminiscent of the vernacular language of some of their Romance counterparts. For example, *The Book of Mandeville* was one of the most popular and widely circulated late medieval texts, thanks to its use of the vernacular instead of Latin.[136] The Jewish itineraries discussed herein appear to have been targeting an audience that was socially differentiated from the readers of Halevi's and Alḥarizi's highbrow poetry. While the former were written for the ordinary Jewish breadwinner (or head of household; *baʿal bayit*), whose Hebrew was rather limited, the poetry was clearly earmarked for a cultural elite.

The highly stylized language of Elijah of La Massa and Obadiah of Bertinoro attests to the superb education of fifteenth-century Italian rabbis. Like other quattrocento Jewish authors, Meshullam of Volterra sprinkled his travel diary with an assortment of Italian loanwords, given the absence of classical Hebrew expressions for certain current terms. For example, he transliterated Italian terms for sea vessels (*galea* for a galley) and weapons (*bonbardelle* for small cannons). At times, even his usage of bona fide Hebrew words seems to echo specific Italian idioms and hence bears witness to his extensive acculturation.[137]

Chapter 2

Travel Motivations: Pilgrimage and Trade

As noted in the Introduction, this is not a book on Jewish mobility, pilgrimage, or trade per se, nor am I foregrounding the mechanisms of medieval journeys.[1] However, because travel literature reflects a historically evolving practice, it is impossible to examine this topic without referring to the cultural, social, and political contexts that inform the facts and fictions of travel. As a prelude to my examination of the modes of representation employed by medieval Jewish travel writers, this chapter explicates some of the religious and economic motives that European Jews had upon taking off for the Levant. Having addressed the question of why they took to the roads and seas, the next chapter turns to practical facets of their journeys.

While people travel for many reasons, the main catalysts behind the medieval voyages of European Jews to the Middle East—as expressed in literary artifacts—were pilgrimage and trade.[2] Quests for knowledge and religious studies were also among the objectives, but these appear less frequently in the texts under review than, say, comparable works of Arabic literature.[3] This discrepancy probably stems from the fact that Palestine and Iraq (Jewish "Babylonia"), the regions where rabbinic Judaism took form, had lost much of their prestige as centers of Jewish learning before the emergence of the Hebrew travel account (during the twelfth century);[4] concomitantly, a number of reputable Talmudic academies sprouted up in Europe and North Africa.[5] I focus on trade and pilgrimage as the major impulses behind my authors' travels; by extension, the ensuing discussion is meant to shed light on their motives for travel writing.

Travel and Trade

Against the spotlight that postcolonial studies have cast on the ways in which travel literature paints the East as an object of mercantile desire,[6] the major topic that I explore in the following pages is the stress on commerce in the sources under review. To what extent were the Jewish authors' trips motivated by financial gain? Specifically, was Benjamin of Tudela a merchant?

As is evident from a brief perusal of his *Itinerary*, Benjamin's work contains numerous references to centers of trade (to which I will turn in a moment), commodities, and their regions of production. For instance, he mentions glass manufacturing and sugar works in Antioch and Tyre, pearl diving in the Persian Gulf, and pepper production along the south Indian coast of Malabar.[7] However, remarks on local products and ways of doing business had been an integral part of travel writing since the times of Herodotus.[8] In the Tudelan's case, one can only speculate as to whether commerce was a reason for his far-flung peregrinations, since *Massa'ot* proves to be more of a lexicon of foreign places than a personal travel narrative. Because of the literary conventions of the twelfth-century Hebrew itinerary, this text does not offer insight into the writer's own activities, commercial or otherwise.[9]

The main motivation behind most of the travelers' Near Eastern journeys was apparently religious—the focus of the second half of this chapter. Intent as they were on making the pilgrimage to Zion, a few nevertheless engaged in limited trade along the way to defray some of their travel expenses. The most prominent example of a traveler who mixed business with pious motives was the poet Judah Halevi. In a letter sent from Alexandria to Ḥalfon ben Nathanel, the aforenoted Cairo merchant, Halevi mentions silk and other merchandise that he appears to have purchased after his arrival in Egypt (in autumn 1140).[10] Over three centuries later, Meshullam of Volterra similarly ventured to the Nile on the first leg of his own pilgrimage. In Cairo, he obtained pearls and precious stones, which he probably intended to sell back in Italy.[11] Thanks to their diminutive size, these items did not weigh the Tuscan down on his subsequent desert trek to Palestine.[12] For Halevi and Meshullam, pilgrimage and business interests clearly went hand in hand; but from the majority of the accounts, there is little evidence for profit being made. Beyond mercantile activities during the journey, do the travelers discussed in this book view the Near East through the "eye of a merchant" (to use once more Mary Baine Campbell's phrase)?[13] In traveling to foreing lands and writing about their travels, was one of their aims to canvass new markets and offer advice on commercial opportunities? If so, to what extent?

Among the Mediterranean basin's key trade hubs, Alexandria receives much attention in Benjamin's account. It was from this port city that importers and exporters stocked up on spices, aromatics, pearls, and other products that were transported to Egypt from the Indian Ocean region via the Red Sea. In the Tudelan's words: "The merchants from India bring all kinds of spices there, and the merchants of Edom [Christendom] buy them."[14] Describing the city as a vibrant crossroads, he provides a long list of nations trading in Alexandria, including various Italian cities and states; merchants from the Black Sea region, Russia, and Germany; from Scotland, England, Normandy, Flanders, Burgundy, France, and several Iberian states; and from North Africa, Arabia, Ethiopia, and India.[15] Since this list appreciably varies from one manuscript version of *Massa'ot* to the next, Benjamin's account should be mined not only for its concrete information (which nations traded in Alexandria during the twelfth century) but also for a late-medieval Jewish perception of economic networks connecting Africa, Asia, and Europe.

The continued influx of international merchants had led to the establishment of special hostelries and commercial spaces in Alexandria that were leased to the Christian states that had a predominant position among the buyers of eastern commodities. Hence Benjamin notes that "each nation has its own hostelry,"[16] using the appropriate Arabic term, *funduq*, for such a merchants' inn. Known to have flourished in many Muslim cities since the eleventh century, *funduqs* typically consisted of buildings constructed on a square plan around a central courtyard, the lower stories containing warehouses and the upper ones functioning as lodging places,[17] as reflected in Meshullam's colorful canvas of such a facility at Cairo:

> In Cairo, there are big *funduqs* [Meshullam transliterates an Italianized form: *fonnachi*] with a courtyard in the center that is surrounded by the houses, namely the stores [Italian: *magazzini*], and two, three, or four gates, which are closed every night; and there are always guards standing there. Within the mentioned *funduqs* are all kinds of merchandise, and the merchants and craftsmen sit in front of their shops, which are very small, and they display only a small amount of all of their merchandise. If you want to buy from them a large item or a certain amount, they bring you into their store, and within the store, you will see such marvelous goods of theirs that it is unbelievable. Within each *funduq* are a

thousand stores and more, even in the smaller ones. And there is nothing that is not to be found in Egypt.[18]

Grossly exaggerating the number of stores contained in each *funduq*, Meshullam paints Cairo as an emporium of hidden treasures. In a similar vein, he claims to have received a list of 3,600 different commodities that were imported to Egypt twice a year and then shipped to Venice and other "Christian lands."[19] While the volume of spices and other exotic goods that were plied through Egypt to European markets was certainly huge,[20] this number seems to be inflated. Hence one may rightly say that Meshullam let his mercantile fantasies roam freely. (However, mercantile fantasies are not to be confused with colonialist desires.) Impressed as he was with Cairo's abundance in exotic goods, the Tuscan Jew purchased only a small number of pearls and gemstones (as will be remembered), for the Jerusalem pilgrimage was the major purpose of his journey.

In addition to Cairo and Alexandria, other cities also played a role in the bustling trade between the Mamluk Empire and the maritime cities of Italy. Particularly Damascus's primary outlet to the sea, Beirut, grew in commercial significance during the late fifteenth century. Even Obadiah's student to be, who seems to have had no mercantile interests of his own, offers his readers a glimpse of the Venice-Beirut-Damascus trade. Possibly, he gained this information from merchants traveling on his ship: "To Beirut and Damascus, the Venetians export silver, gold, tin, copper, refined [metal], and thick soft clothes. On their way back, they carry pepper, ginger, and all sorts of spices, silks, and Cordovan fabrics and sometimes precious stones and pearls, if any are to be found; and according to what I have heard, there are few precious stones [for sale] in Damascus."[21]

In the early sixteenth century, Moses Basola, a rabbi-cum-banker, similarly cataloged some of the goods that made their way from Beirut to the Most Serene Republic: "The commodities taken on there for export to Venice include large quantities of silk, which constitute the bulk of the goods, along with many spices, scammony, and spun cotton. Unspun cotton, however, is transported by cargo ships and not by the galleys due to the lack of space."[22] During a stopover in Beirut, on his homeward journey, Meshullam took a detour to Damascus. The Tuscan was particularly impressed by the city's bazaars, not least their silk (the top-quality fabric was imported from the Far East, whereas the relatively inferior variety was produced locally). "Inlaid with gold and silver," the famed Damascene brassware, which was highly valued in Europe, also struck his fancy.[23] Yet again, Meshullam seems to have made inquiries only, for he does not mention the purchase of any of these goods.

Since most of the authors spent time in Jerusalem, there are many descriptions of the city's economy, modest as it was. Even anonymous guidebooks, such as *Yiḥus ha-Ṣaddiqim* and *Yiḥus Avot* (originating from the late fifteenth and sixteenth centuries, respectively) refer to the covered commercial streets of Jerusalem. Most notably, *Yiḥus ha-Ṣaddiqim* documents that vendors of manufactured goods and food products tended to gravitate to different areas: "At the first market, the merchants sell garments of silk, purple and other clothes. At the middle market, they sell all kinds of foodstuffs. At the third market, they sell dates, weapons, earthenware, and [the products of] silver- and goldsmiths."[24] While *Yiḥus Avot* reports of similar goods in the first two locations, it mentions "scent powder" only in the third, as this was apparently a product that caught the fancy of the manuscript's copyist.[25] Evidently, pilgrims (with the necessary funds) were not only interested in local food supplies but also in luxury items for sale in the Holy City.

According to Isaac ben Meir Latif (mid-fifteenth century), shiploads of goods from the Mediterranean islands arrived in Jaffa on a daily basis, from where they were hauled to Jerusalem by caravans of "asses, mules, and many camels."[26] His letter also mentions a flourishing trade between Jerusalem and Damascus. However, these accounts of bustling commerce in the Holy City should probably be taken with a grain of salt, as the economic sway of Mamluk Jerusalem was minor. To wit, all the major trade routes bypassed the hillside town, and it lacked a fertile hinterland.[27] R. Isaac's testimony as to the brisk trade in Jerusalem may have to be attributed to the religious ardor of a pilgrim.

Land of Opportunity?

In stark contrast to some of the aforementioned sources, Obadiah paints a bleak portrait of Jerusalem's economy. This state of affairs should not be blamed exclusively on the famine that had ravaged the city the year before the rabbi's arrival (in spring 1488) but also on the fact that he had settled in Palestine for good. Whereas the majority of the other accounts are based on short pilgrimages, Obadiah acquired a more realistic picture of the situation. A case in point is his rather candid assessment of a Jewish immigrant's chances of making a living in the Promised Land: "The land is still good, wide, and fertile. However, no profit is to be made there. No one should hope to make a profit by any skill or trade, save for a cobbler, weaver, or [gold]-smith—even they will barely earn a living—or someone who buys some merchandise in the city and goes to sell it in the villages."[28]

A generation later, Israel Ashkenazi and Moses Basola echo their predecessor's words (which they may well have read). Basola notes that one should not count on living off charity, for there were many indigent Jews in the land. "Therefore, he who possesses neither craft nor funds should not leave Italy, lest he regret his actions and return, and a word to the wise is sufficient."[29]

The situation was reportedly different in other parts of the Levant. For instance, Obadiah writes about business opportunities in the Syrian port of Tripoli (now part of modern Lebanon), although he did not visit there: "Many told me that if there was an intelligent and suitable [Jewish] man from Italy [residing in Tripoli], he would become extremely wealthy in a short time [by trading] with the Italian merchants who are always passing through the area."[30] According to Obadiah's student, polyglot Jewish merchants were ideal middlemen in the east-west exchange: "In Damascus, Cairo, Alexandria, and Aleppo . . . , in all these places a Jew may make as much profit as he desires; especially if he knows Arabic as well as our language [Italian], he will reap a harvest as plentiful as dust—so I have heard."[31] Basola, by contrast, who was a moneylender and thus may have gained comparatively reliable information, offers a more realistic picture of the earning potential of an enterprising Jew who took up residence in Damascus:

> One can start a clothing shop with but a hundred [Venetian gold] ducats. The Venetians provide clothing on consignment, and he then pockets the difference. Another sells haberdashery [Italian: *merceria*] or spices. Others take goods from the shops [*botteghe*] and peddle them in the city, for the daily business traffic and the number of people assembled outnumber the largest fair in Italy. Therefore, he who has a little capital and is trustworthy can obtain *credito* from the Ishmaelites [Muslims or Arabs] and the Venetians and profit in any venture. A wealthy person can buy large amounts of merchandise when it is cheap and store it in a warehouse [*magazzino*] until prices go up. There are also [Jewish] moneylenders who lend to the Venetian traders who pay [interest rates of] at least 2 percent monthly, and, if necessary, they pay more.[32]

While all the Italian Jewish travelers comment on business opportunities in the fifteenth- and sixteenth-century Levant, it would be a stretch to peg any of them (Meshullam included) with "aspirations of economic expansion and empire"—Mary Louise Pratt's characterization of eighteenth-century English travel and exploration writers.[33] Instead, Obadiah and Basola observed that

Italian Jewish residents of the region were well suited to fill the relatively modest role of brokers between Venetian importers and local wholesalers. They saw Jewish merchants as part of a Mediterranean web of trade partners, rather than as agents of commercial monopolies and empires. Such a colonialist outlook on the Near East was practically inconceivable during the period in question.[34]

Still, a few quattrocento travelers articulated inchoate notions of European preeminence in trade and science. For example, in his account of Mamluk Jerusalem, Elijah of La Massa (1438) writes that the city's merchants lacked expertise in the goods they plied. Furthermore, the locals "are no mavens in drugs and pharmaceuticals . . . much less medicine, for they are all asses."[35] While Mamluk Jerusalem was indeed a backwater town from an economic standpoint, Elijah's disparaging remark may constitute an early example of a European tendency to depict Middle Eastern populations as ignorant and incapable of scientific thinking.[36]

A similar outlook appears to inform the following case: like other inventions, paper had originated in the East (the Abbasids adopted papermaking from the Chinese). By the late fifteenth century, Italian paper mills were turning out refined products of their own. Joseph of Montagna (1480) preferred Italian writing material to the stock that he found in Mamluk Palestine. Consequently, he ends a letter with this remark: "I have no paper left, for I do not know how to write on the paper [produced] here. If you don't send me paper, I will not be able to write [to you] again."[37] Elijah and Joseph both undoubtedly thought that their home Italian culture outshined that of the Middle East. Nonetheless, one would be hard-pressed to argue that they perceived the Levant as an expanse ripe for Western economic penetration and dominance.

Pilgrimage

While trade will have provided a major impulse for travel, the principal type of journey that merited literary attention during the Middle Ages would appear to be the pilgrimage. The authors discussed here are no exception to this rule: for most of them, the trade motive apparently took a backseat to the devotional one.

In its capacity as ritualized travel to sacred territory beyond the everyday world, pilgrimage is a universal and time-honored motivation for taking to the road. Until the destruction of the Second Temple by the Romans (in 70 CE), Jewish pilgrimage to Jerusalem (Hebrew: *'aliyyah le-regel*)—the site of the only officially sanctioned sacrificial cult—was considered a scriptural obligation during the three pilgrimage festivals (*shalosh regalim*): Sukkot (the Feast of Booths) in the fall; and the springtime festivals of Pesaḥ (Passover) and Shavu'ot (Festival of Weeks).[38] For practical reasons, this obligation could never be fulfilled by all Palestinian and diaspora Jews even when the Temple stood. After its destruction, the primacy of Jerusalem and the Land of Israel still came to expression in prayers (be it daily, Shabbat, or holiday liturgies) and other rituals. These practices ensured that Zion would retain its special place in the Jewish collective memory. However, unlike the Islamic *ḥajj* to Mecca that every Muslim is enjoined to make at least once, Jewish pilgrimage to Jerusalem—meritorious as it may be—was downgraded to a voluntary act and hence performed by relatively few.

Besides (and often instead of) the canonical or central pilgrimages, medieval Jews, Christians, and Muslims traveled to a host of local sacred places, especially the tombs of holy men and women that were considered loci of power with special access to the divine.[39] This widespread custom, which the learned elite did not always approve of, is known as *ziyāra* in medieval Arabic sources (or *ziyārat al-qubūr*, "visitation of tombs," in a more specific sense).[40] The corresponding Hebrew terminology (*hishtaṭḥut 'al qivre ṣaddiqim*, "prostration on the tombs of the righteous")[41] is of relatively late provenance and is less entrenched in the texts that concern me here than their counterparts in the Arabic literature. Since Jewish tomb visitations in the Middle East appear to have closely resembled Islamic customs—Jews and Muslims frequently flocked to the same venerated sites—the Arabic term *ziyāra* is used herein also for Jewish pilgrimages to the shrines of biblical figures and Talmudic sages. Many of these holy tombs were located in the historical centers of rabbinic Judaism: Palestine and Iraq.[42] In his Judeo-Arabic *Book of Pearls*, Judah Alḥarizi explains his far-flung journey (first quarter of the thirteenth century) with the desire to combine a *ziyāra* to "noble Jerusalem" (*al-Quds al-Sharīf*) with a pilgrimage to the "venerable shrines" (*al-maqām al-karīm*) of Ezekiel and Ezra in Mesopotamia; the Arabic terminology that he employs in this case strikingly resembles Islamic pilgrimage literature.[43]

While Jewish visits to the Holy City probably never ceased, Fatimid-ruled Jerusalem seems to have attracted comparatively large numbers of Jews from the Maghreb and the Levant—but, to some extent, also from Christian Europe.[44] Their devotional visits largely fell during the autumn holy days, a phenomenon that is widely attested by personal letters preserved in the Cairo Genizah. What seems unique about this eleventh-century pilgrimage is that it attests to a largely peaceful division of sacred space between Muslims, who controlled the Ḥaram al-Sharīf, and Jews, who gathered on the Mount of Olives facing the former Temple's site. There the festivities culminated in a solemn prayer service on Hoshana Rabbah (the seventh day of Sukkot). Other rituals included prayers at the gates to the Temple Mount. However, this form of Jewish *ziyāra* to Jerusalem and its particular rituals came to an abrupt end with the crusader conquest of the city in 1099.

After the First Crusade, as travel and commerce between Europe and the Latin states of the Levant expanded, new forms of Christian and Jewish pilgrimage to Palestine took shape—and here is where this study picks up the historical narrative. Differing from those of the Fatimid period, most of the surviving accounts stem from European Jews who took advantage of the greatly improved transportation between their countries of origin and outre-mer. After they arrived in the Holy Land, these Jewish pious developed devotional itineraries that frequently paralleled or intersected with Christian pilgrimage routes in the region.[45] However, their major destinations were sites embedded in the Jewish cultural memory, most of which were located in and around Jerusalem, as well as holy tombs in Galilee. From thereon, these venues became standard fixtures in Hebrew travel accounts (as will be seen in Chapter 4). By combining (so to speak) a *peregrinatio* to Jerusalem with a *ziyāra* to assorted grave sites, late-medieval Jewish pilgrimage incorporated aspects of both Latin Christian and Levantine (Muslim and Jewish) religious praxis.[46]

In another contrast to the Fatimid period, crusader Jerusalem lacked any infrastructure to accommodate Jewish pilgrims, for Jews were forbidden to permanently reside in the city throughout the Frankish era (1099–1187).[47] The only hospitality that Jewish visitors apparently received in Jerusalem was at the home of a few Jewish dyers who were granted special permission to establish a business within the Christian-dominated city.[48] In consequence, only a small number of Jews could visit Jerusalem for a few days.[49] It bears noting that subsequent Ayyubid, Mamluk, and Ottoman administrations did not impose similar restrictions on Jewish residency in the Holy City. Even so, the local community never exceeded a few hundred members, largely depended on external funding, and lacked the means and institutions that could support significant numbers of Jewish pilgrims.

After becoming the economic and administrative center of the second crusader kingdom in 1191, Acre served as the logistical base from where Jewish pilgrims from Europe embarked on excursions to the holy places, including those that, by this juncture, were already under Muslim rule. The number of Jewish visitors to Palestine appears to have reached its peak in the early thirteenth century, with the arrival of the Tosafists (a distinguished school of Ashkenazi commentators on the Babylonian Talmud) to Acre, some of whom settled in what was then a bustling port city. This influx of mainly French Jews, among them some of the travelers whose accounts are the subject of this book, continued until the Mamluk capture of Acre in 1291, but its extent should not be overestimated, given the limited local support system.[50]

As noted for Alḥarizi, Palestine was not the only destination of medieval Jewish pilgrims in the Middle East. Even the Ashkenazi rabbi Petaḥyah of Regensburg included in his extended circuit the Jewish tomb shrines of Iraq. *Sibbuv* attests that foreign pilgrims in Iraq (as in other places) depended on the local Jewish community to gain access to the region's venerated sites: "R. Samuel [ben 'Eli], the head of academy [*rosh yeshiva*, in Baghdad], gave R. Petaḥyah a letter with his seal so that in every place he would arrive, they would take him around and show him the burial places of [the] scholars [*talmide ḥakhamim*] and the righteous [*ṣaddiqim*]."[51] As a result, travelers' perspectives on the Middle East were frequently shaped by their local hosts and guides.

Judah Halevi: Pilgrimage and the Mystical Quest

Aside from visiting and praying at specific sites (some of which are highlighted in Chapters 4 and 5), pilgrimages often represent a greater spiritual quest. This allegorical aspect of the journey was most saliently expressed by Judah Halevi. Though vastly different from the more pedestrian itineraries and letters that constitute the majority of the corpus, it seems fitting to include some of his poems in my discussion of medieval Jewish pilgrimage.[52] The philosophical and mystical ideas that underpin Halevi's conceptualizations of the East are largely absent from most of the works under review. The poet-philosopher's uniqueness notwithstanding, his outlook exemplifies that other travelers also considered the Levantine voyage to be more than a mere ritual performance.

In a late turn to piety and asceticism (with parallels to Muslim biographies),[53] it was only after enjoying the life of the Andalusian elite to its fullest that the aged poet Halevi set out for the Near East. In doing so, his intention was to live out the remainder of his days in the Holy Land. Thanks to the Genizah findings, some details of Halevi's factual travels can now be reconstructed. Upon arriving in Alexandria on September 8, 1140 (a week before Rosh Hashanah), he spent about eight months in Egypt, where he was received with great honor.[54] In Cairo, Halevi soon became engrossed in the intellectual circles of an Arab metropolis that were highly reminiscent of the cosmopolitan culture of Iberia that he had just forsaken. Consequently, the first leg of his journey took longer than planned. From the correspondence of his aforementioned friend, Ḥalfon ben Nathanel, it is known that, after some failed attempts to complete his pilgrimage, Halevi was finally ready to set sail to Palestine in May 1141. However, unfavorable weather kept his ship from leaving Alexandria's port for a week.[55] Another letter from within the Halevi-Ḥalfon circle, which is dated roughly four months later, mentions the poet's passing, the circumstances of which are unknown.[56] While this interval would have given Halevi enough time to complete his trip to Jerusalem, there is no conclusive evidence that he ever reached his coveted destination.[57]

Although the final chapter of his voyage remains obscure, his anticipatory imagination is reflected and refracted in his writings. Many years before he left the Iberian Peninsula, Halevi envisioned the journey in this poem, which voices his unique understanding of pilgrimage:

> Can dead bodies be closed rooms
> For hearts bound fast to eagles' wings—
> For a life-weary man whose sole desire
> Is to roll his cheeks in the chosen dust?
> Yet he fears and trembles with falling tears,
> To cast Spain from him and travel beyond;
> To ride upon ships, to tread through deserts,
> "Dens of lions, mountains of leopards"—
> He rebukes his loved ones and chooses wandering,
> Forsakes shelter and inhabits sun-scorched places.[58]

What makes the protagonist so eager to set out on his journey? Is it an aged, "life-weary" man's desire for eternal rest "in the chosen dust"—as generations of Jews wished to be buried in the Holy Land? Is it the pilgrimage vow that causes him to disregard the dangers lurking along the way: "dens of lions, mountains of leopards" (Song of Songs 4:8)? Does he also possess a streak of adventure that compels him to rebuke "his loved ones" and choose "wandering"? Why does Halevi's alter ego feel the urge "to cast Spain from him and travel beyond"?

Among other devices, this poem consists of allegorical language that demands multiple levels of interpretation. The opening lines feature a pair of interconnected metaphors: living "hearts" inside "dead bodies" (lit., "corpses" or "carcasses") and a bird caged up in a closed room. As heart and bird are equated, the former is "bound fast to eagles' wings." The heart desiring to escape its imprisonment in the body is clearly a Neoplatonic or mystical motif. The citation from Song of Songs provides yet another hint, for the very next verse reads: "You have captured my *heart*, my own, my bride, you have captured my heart" (Song of Songs 4:9). To a medieval reader with mystical leanings, Song of Songs is about a person's love relationship with the divine. Against this backdrop, the desire expressed in this poem is more than just the pilgrim's wish to reach Jerusalem; it also serves as a metaphor for a flight from the sentient world to a vision of God. The poet's yearning for Zion and mystical pursuits are here closely connected, if not interchangeable.[59]

In another poem, Halevi adopts slightly different, though related, imagery. He speaks of a quest for a divine vision "within" the heart,[60] a quest that he compares to a "run toward the fountain of true life," which is clearly a metaphor for God.[61] Such an inward-looking mysticism does not seem to depend on any pilgrimage in time and place; the vision "within" the heart appears to render an actual trip to Jerusalem superfluous.[62] That said, as a movement, this "run" echoes the ship voyage and desert trek that were the topic of the above-quoted work. Similarly, the inward-looking poem expresses the author's weariness "with a life of vanity," which is reminiscent of his previously voiced desire "to cast Spain from him." As Halevi otherwise alluded to his wish to be buried in the Holy Land, the visionary poem also hints at death as an "everlasting sleep." Clearly, the following three images overlap and complement one another in his poetry: the physical journey to Zion; the spiritual process by which the mystic draws near to God; and death, which enables the ultimate union between the soul and its divine provenance.

While the two mystical poems predate Halevi's actual pilgrimage, Shlomo Dov Goitein (1900–1985), the first to reconstruct the poet's journey in some detail, has linked his so-called Sea Poems to the aforementioned delay in Alexandria.[63] In a poem to the westerly wind, for example, the pilgrim greets a sudden change in weather that will allow his vessel to finally lift anchor. As suggestive as Goitein's reading may be, this work transcends the narrow limits of biographical interpretation and sheds further light on Halevi's understanding of pilgrimage:

This is your wind, o West [*ma'arav*],
perfumed with nards and apples in its wings.
From the vaults of the spice merchants is your source,
you are not from the vaults of the wind.[64]

> Let the wings of the swallow [*dror*] spread and set me free [*ve-tiqra-li dror*]—like "pure myrrh" [*mar-dror*, Exod. 30:23] taken from the bundle of spices.[65]

Though the opening line obviously refers to a westerly wind, the West—in the Arabic sense of the word (*maghrib*)—also signifies the Iberian Peninsula.[66] The westerly is the traveler's ("your") wind, as it apparently evokes certain memories of al-Andalus.[67] Has the pilgrim succumbed to a bout of homesickness after having been away for so many months?

The metaphor of the freed swallow (*dror*) expresses his desire to be liberated from everything holding him back: in Hebrew, *dror* means both "songbird" and "freedom" (Lev. 25:10).[68] It is also an image of the soul that longs to be reunited with the divine.[69] The "bundle of spices" echoes once more the Song of Songs (1:12–13): "While the king was on his couch, my nard gave forth its fragrance. My beloved to me is a *bag of myrrh* lodged between my breasts." As noted, Halevi reads this biblical work as an allegory for the love between the soul and God. On one level, the poem to the wind is about a favorable change in the weather, allowing him to complete his journey to Palestine; but it also seems to celebrate a much anticipated mystical union.

In sum, the East, in Halevi's poetry, is more than a geographic dichotomy of Iberia; it also emerges as its cultural and spiritual antithesis. The distinction between the two, moreover, is one of lifestyle—between the material abundance of the sedentary life (home) and the insecurities of a traveler (abroad). The West represents the savor of food and all the "good things of Spain," and the westerly wind bears the fragrance of "spices"—all of which convey the notion of Andalusian riches and cultural sophistication. Nevertheless, it is Palestine that is Halevi's destiny, as he invisions Zion as the place in which the mystical love between the individual and God comes to fruition. Underscoring the essential introspection of the travel or quest motif, Halevi's pilgrimage from the margin (Iberia) to the center (Jerusalem) parallels a spiritual and allegorical journey out of the phenomenal world and into the mystical landscape of the self.

Chapter 3

Levantine Journeys: Choices and Challenges

Having ventured into the mystical realms of pilgrimage, the discussion now turns to the mundane facets of medieval peregrinations. Under what conditions did the authors travel?[1] Were most of them solitary wayfarers in search of a distinctly individualistic experience—as one might assume in the case of Judah Halevi? While the poet appears to have been on his own throughout the final leg of his journey, he arrived in Egypt in the company of two other Iberian Jews (one of whom was apparently Isaac, the son of Abraham Ibn Ezra).[2] In fact, most Jewish pilgrims seem to have banded together into small groups. For both men and women, these associations not only improved their security but allowed them to pool their resources in order to cut costs. Furthermore, the traveler's companions were likely to share and affirm his or her religious perceptions, thereby collectivizing the experience and pilgrim identity (some of the accounts are written in the first-person plural).

Most shared journeys are documented for the fifteenth century, when the well-established maritime route between Venice and the eastern shores of the Mediterranean induced numerous Christian and Jewish pilgrims to visit Palestine.[3] Ever class-conscious, Meshullam of Volterra, for instance, was joined by his Jewish servant Raphael during the entire trip. On his arduous tour through the Sinai wilderness, Meshullam also hired an Egyptian Jew named Joseph ben Hezekiah to serve as an interpreter and guide.[4]

Obadiah of Bertinoro apparently set out for the Levant on his own, but ran into Meshullam (who was then on his second trip to the eastern Mediterranean) along the way: "On the eve of Sukkot, 5248 [the Jewish year; 1487], a large galley [Italian: *galeazza*] from France came to Palermo, en route to Alexandria. On it were the formidable R. Meshullam of Volterra and his servant.

I was glad to meet him and joined his company."[5] Eleven more Jews boarded the ship at Messina: "A sugar merchant with his servant and three Jewish cobblers from Syracuse [Sicily] and a Sephardic Jew with his wife and two sons and two daughters."[6] Upon reaching Alexandria, Obadiah met a Jewish family of four that was on a pilgrimage to Jerusalem and accompanied them to Cairo.[7] In the Mamluk capital, the small party of Jews was augmented by two men and two women.[8] Mounted on five camels, this band of coreligionists then joined a caravan traversing the northern Sinai.

Travel Routes and Transport Services

Medieval Jewish travelers rarely described the overland roads that some of them took from Christian Europe. During the crusader period, the most frequented land route to Jerusalem went through the Balkans to Constantinople and then south. Only Petaḥyah of Regensburg offers a glimpse of his extraordinary trek (the details of which I do not try to chart here) from Prague to Palestine via eastern Europe, the Caucasus, Mesopotamia, and Syria. The sequence of places mentioned by Benjamin of Tudela suggests that he followed the trunk roads connecting northern Iberia by way of Provence to southern Italy; from there, he apparently continued by land and sea to the crusader states of the Levant, with stops in Constantinople, Rhodes, and Cyprus. Henceforth, the route he took seems hazy, and it is far from certain that he actually visited all the sites cataloged in his *Massa'ot*.[9] Likewise, twelfth-century Hebrew writers did not consider it worthwhile to provide much information about the modes of transportation they used. What is known, however, is that beasts of burden, ox wagons, river craft, and walking were the most common forms of premodern overland transit, when travel time was measured in days or weeks rather than in hours. One of the few exceptions is Petaḥyah, who mentions his trip down the Tigris River on a raft that took him fifteen days from Mosul to Baghdad instead of a month on foot.[10] It was only in the late fifteenth and sixteenth centuries that Italian Jewish voyagers started giving detailed accounts of their experiences along the way—a significant shift in Hebrew travel literature. Their accounts offer us insights into both the practice and narrativization of early modern travel. For example, Meshullam painted a colorful canvas of his trek through the Sinai as a paying passenger in a caravan of approximately 120 Arabs and Turks.[11]

The physical and political obstructions inherent in premodern overland travel seem to have been the reason that all the travelers from Italy discussed in this book chose a shorter and less time-consuming sea passage to the eastern Mediterranean. It typically took four to six weeks, depending on weather—the sailing season lasted from April to October—and the number of ports of call, where provisions and freshwater were replenished. In fact, most sea lanes hugged coastlines or linked islands, such as Sicily, Crete, Rhodes, and Cyprus (see Map 1).[12] Much like the political and economic circumstances, this route underwent certain changes between the twelfth and the early sixteenth century. However, the major port of embarkation to the Levant continued to be Venice (the next most important hubs were Ancona and Naples); since its involvement in the Fourth Crusade (1204), the Lagoon City had provided fairly reliable transport to the Holy Land.[13] Until the fall of Acre (1291) and the destruction of its port by the Mamluks, it was here that most Jerusalem-bound pilgrims (Christian and Jewish) made landfall. Even after the demise of the Latin kingdom, Venice retained its predominant position in the traffic between Italy and the Levant, thanks to commercial and diplomatic ties between the Mamluks and the Most Serene Republic. During the second half of the fifteenth century, one or two pilgrim galleys departed for Jaffa annually. But because of the Christian character of this expedition, Jews seem to have preferred passage on merchant galleys that sailed to Tripoli, Beirut, or Alexandria,[14] whence one could continue by ship to Palestine or take the overland road.

Fifteenth-century Jews interested in going to Jerusalem were likely to run into a serious political obstacle. In 1428, the Franciscans made the local Jews responsible for having been evicted by the Mamluks from the tomb of King David and the adjacent monastery of Mount Zion.[15] Though the shrine was converted into an Islamic place of worship, the friars accused the Jews of having bribed the authorities to turn the structure into a synagogue—an attempt that, even if true, failed. As a result of the religious order's propaganda, Venice barred Jews from traveling on the republic's pilgrim or mercantile vessels.[16] However, it appears that sea captains often turned a blind eye to Jewish passengers, so long as they were not in large conspicuous groups.[17] Nevertheless, the edict affected Jewish travel until at least 1488; that year, Obadiah took a detour via Sicily and Egypt, instead of sailing directly to Palestine, to circumvent the ban. Ironically, the decree had already been abrogated, but the rabbi was unaware of this while planning his trip: "I wish I had known this while I was still in those parts [Italy], as I would not have tarried so long on the journey, for it takes no more than forty days for the galleys to arrive here [Palestine] from Venice."[18]

Drawing on the experience of his own voyage from Venice to Tripoli, Moses Basola explicitly advises seafarers to travel on Venetian galleys, "for they are safe from Corsairs and storms at sea."[19] In addition, he offers detailed advice concerning the best accommodations on a merchant ship: one should avoid renting a cheap place in the hold, where passengers slept on the floor amid the cargo. "But there is no place on a galley better than the cabin of the boatswain [Italian: *comito*]," which was located in the stern—if one could afford the steep rental fee of at least fifteen ducats.[20]

Perils and Privations of Travel

The hazards and discomforts of traveling are strikingly absent from most of the early texts analyzed herein, for the authors considered it self-indulgent to dwell on such matters. An exception to this rule is a private letter by an anonymous eleventh-century Jew who had set out from Palermo to Alexandria to study with some acclaimed Jewish teachers. The letter offers a vivid portrait of his perilous sea crossing during the tempestuous fall season, when, after a few days on the sea, a storm caused the ship (with about four hundred persons) to leak water. They tried to keep the vessel afloat by bailing out the water and throwing part of the cargo overboard—to no avail: "Finally, the ship touched ground and cracked asunder, like [an egg] when a man presses it with his two hands. Passengers began to drown here and [there, and pieces from] the ship floated above them."[21] The letter writer seems to have survived by catching a piece of wood and riding upon it until his eventual rescue.

Meshullam, another nonswimmer, did not endure such a harrowing experience but also had a brush with death: in the harbor of Candia (present-day Heraklion, Crete), in the final leg of his journey. On his return from a brief shore leave, he slipped into the sea while hurrying to climb from a skiff aboard his galley: "I sunk deep beneath the sea, more than ten cubits [fifteen feet (4.6 meters)] under water, with all my clothes on, [including] my silk coat [*giuppetto*]. And in my purse [*scarsella*], bound in some taffeta, were all the pearls and precious stones that I had procured in Egypt; the purse turned [upside-down], and some carats fell into the sea."[22]

Fortunately, the ship's master was present and ordered the sailors to rush to pull him out. However, five days after leaving Crete, Meshullam once again fell off a skiff (he may have been a little clumsy) while his vessel anchored at the port of Modon (Greek: Methóni; see Map 1), on the western Peloponnese.

This time around, he managed to grab on to the ship's ladder. But an expensive ring with a cameo that he had taken from the ship's dragoman as a guarantee for a loan (of six Venetian ducats) slipped off his finger and into the sea.[23] As in the previous case, the merchant's description places equal importance on both the rescue and the financial loss.

As mentioned, Meshullam also provides a detailed account of the Sinai expedition that he took on his way from Cairo to Jerusalem. He highlights the danger of raiders: "They ride on 'horses that are swift as leopards,' and they wield reed lances, all of which are topped with iron and are very hard. In their hands, they also carry iron maces [*mazze ferrate*] and bucklers [*buclieri*] made of parchment and pitch. They ride naked with only a tunic upon them and without stockings or shoes or spurs [*sproni*]. They take the caravan by surprise and carry off all [the travelers'] belongings, all their clothes, and also the horses. Sometimes [the bandits] kill [the travelers], but for the most part they don't kill but [just] rob them."[24]

Because of the brigands in the Sinai Desert, most travelers taking the Cairo-Gaza route joined reputable caravans, which were escorted by armed Mamluks. So did Meshullam, so he should have had little reason to worry. In fact, he does not even claim to have been waylaid; he saw only a single highwayman, who approached his caravan near Bilbays (see Map 3), northeast of Cairo, but who immediately withdrew when he became aware of the caravan's considerable size.[25] The merchant's picturesque portrayal of the unruly Bedouin and their exotic weaponry, which probably draws on others' stories, seems to reflect his own anxieties more than any real danger.

Meshullam's assertion that the route is lined with "heaps upon heaps of bones of camels, horses, and asses that have died in the desert" appears to be another device meant to underscore the arduous character of the journey. The same can be said for the following sequence: "Even if you escape all these [pitfalls], it often happens that the horses you ride die, or they are nearly dead upon reaching Jerusalem on account of the brackish water they drink, the great heat, the sand that gets into their mouths, and the sand that reaches up to their knees, for they go in great pain, and also there is a lack of food during the long journey."[26]

Aside from dispensing practical information to prospective travelers, Meshullam's dramatic account of his trek through an inhospitable wilderness was probably intended to cast the Tuscan as a seasoned traveler and an intrepid adventurer, rather than a mere pilgrim.[27]

Illness

Among the more onerous tribulations of the road are the prospects of falling ill in an alien land. The majority of early Jewish travel writers, such as Benjamin, are disembodied spectators who remained silent about the privations, boils, blisters, and maladies that they suffered along the way. However, *Sibbuv* relates that Petaḥyah fell severely ill in Mosul. Because he wore beautiful clothes, he was considered rich, and, according to the law of the land, "when a visiting Jew dies, half of his money is taken by the government."[28] The government's scribes were already waiting to collect the money, readers are told, as soon as Petaḥyah expired. However, what appears to be a rare glimpse at the traveler's perils in northern Mesopotamia ultimately has to be considered one of the miracle stories that this pilgrimage book is replete with. For, sick as he was, Petaḥyah ordered that he be carried on a raft over the River Tigris, and by dint of the water's healing powers, "he immediately recovered." The righteous rabbi survived against all odds, and the greedy government's plans were foiled.

Among the most heart-wrenching documents about the health risks of medieval travel is a letter that Elijah of La Massa penned in 1438. The writer mourns "all the hardships that have befallen me on the way and that have devoured me and overwhelmed me."[29] To begin with, his nephew Jacob died, perhaps on the sea voyage; and during a stopover in Egypt, his son Menaḥem and a friend apparently contracted the plague that had ravaged the Middle East (and much of Europe) that year, before perishing as well.[30] Elijah may have caught the same life-threatening disease: shortly afterward, the author was confined to a sickbed and feared that death was upon him. Despite these traumas, the pilgrim ultimately managed to reach Jerusalem, the city of his longing.

Half a century later, Meshullam was much more willing than his predecessors to describe the travails he encountered, including less serious health problems. For instance, while near the town of al-ʿArīsh (see Map 3) on the Mediterranean coast of the Sinai, he was afflicted by sand fleas as "big as two flies and slightly red; and there are many of them in the desert."[31] Having just left Egypt, he equates them with "the sort of lice that plagued Pharaoh."[32] They left big bite marks on his body, but "fortunately we had *limoni* [lemons, as they are called], in Italian. Upon leaving Cairo, we took them with us for that reason, since we knew that there is no remedy for [the flea] bite save the juice of the said lemons. This juice prevents the wound from spreading over a person's flesh. I swear that in all my life, I had never been in so much pain as that night."[33]

Meshullam spent almost an entire month in Jerusalem (July 29 to August 26, 1481). However, he did not get around much because of what appears to be a serious stomach ailment, so Zion—the center of the Jewish universe—is allotted only a few pages in his work. While Meshullam may have suffered from disagreeable food—he says that he was "on the verge of death"—the unfamiliar tastes and smells added to his sense of himself as an alien, for he says: "I could not [even] look at their cooked food, as it is foreign and strange to a healthy man, all the more so for a sick man like myself."[34] He slowly recovered in the care of some Ashkenazi Jews from Italy who prepared a diet for him that he was accustomed to. Nor did Meshullam's mood improve much upon leaving Jerusalem to begin his long-awaited homeward journey. On the ride to Jaffa, he once again complained about the intense heat, which gave him a fever as well as a severe headache.[35]

As usual, Meshullam's account sharply differs from that of Obadiah. Having chosen to make Jerusalem his home, Obadiah strikes a different tone: he was spared the tribulation of sickness in the Holy City, for which he praises God. He then adds, perhaps with Meshullam in mind, that "most people coming to Jerusalem from distant lands fall ill due to the change of climate and also because of the rapid change from cold to hot and from hot to cold," which was characteristic of the local weather.[36]

Border Hopping

Aside from the general dangers and discomforts of travel, crossing between Christian and Muslim dominions posed certain risks, which, during the crusader period, might require travelers to attain letters of safe-conduct from both sides of the frontier.[37] Obadiah attests that sea transit was just as vulnerable to the political tensions as crossing land borders.

After arriving at Rhodes from Sicily in autumn 1487, Obadiah's voyage was seriously delayed as a result of international machinations surrounding Jem (Cem) Sulṭān (1459–95). Jem, a son of the Ottoman sultan Meḥmed II (conqueror of Constantinople), vied with his brother Bāyezīd II (r. 1481–1512) over the throne after their father's death. Having been defeated on the battlefield, Jem first found refuge at the court of Qā'yt Bāy, the Mamluk sultan of Egypt (in 1481).[38] The following year, he left Egypt to take part in another military campaign against his brother in Anatolia. The effort failed, and Jem fled this time to Rhodes, where he was granted asylum by the Knights of Saint John (the Hospitalers). Now both the Christian powers and the Mamluks vied over the hapless prince as a potential bargaining chip in their respective conflicts with the Ottomans.

A peace treaty was hammered out between Bāyezīd and Pierre d'Aubusson, Grand Master of the Knights, whereby d'Aubusson pledged to detain the Turkish prince in France if the Ottomans refrained from all hostilities against Rhodes. On account of the war that broke out between the Ottomans and Mamluks in 1485, the Mamluk sultan, Qā'yt Bāy, entered diplomatic negotiations with the Hospitalers in the hope of regaining possession of Jem. Qā'yt Bāy even paid the knights 20,000 ducats in advance (a sum Obadiah was aware of), which they declared to be a precondition for facilitating the prince's passage to Egypt. However, the Hospitalers failed to fulfill their part of the bargain.[39]

Obadiah's detailed description of this intricate state of affairs indicates that he was well aware of the fraught political situation into which he was headed. In fact, the Alexandria-bound French galley that he boarded in Palermo remained docked in Rhodes for a month and a half because d'Aubusson thought it inadvisable to let it depart for Egypt, "since it contained great wealth and countless money,"[40] which the Mamluks, on the described background, might have been tempted to seize. When Obadiah's vessel finally lifted anchor, the journey to Egypt took all of six days. However, the shipmaster, who did not dare enter the port of Alexandria, berthed offshore east of the city in the bay of Abukir (Abū Qīr). Though the Mamluk governor of Alexandria vouched for the galley's safety, its *patrone* was willing to place his trust in an official guarantee only by the sultan himself and hence dispatched messengers all the way to Cairo.

In the meantime, the captain sent a smaller boat to Alexandria with a few people on board, including the ship's Jewish passengers, who hoped to spend Shabbat in the coastal city. However, the governor, who had ostensibly taken slight at the shipmaster's lack of trust in him, refused to permit the craft to enter the harbor. While the return of the captain's messengers from Cairo dragged on, both the galley and the smaller vessel with Obadiah on board remained in the bay of Abukir. Hours became days, and soon they ran out of food and water. To make matters worse, a violent storm tossed the moored boat around and almost drowned its passengers. In the meantime, the sultan vouched for their safety. On January 27, 1488, about a month after departing Rhodes, Obadiah finally reached the city of Alexandria "tired and weary."[41]

Immigration and Customs Procedures

At Alexandria, new arrivals had to pass through the city's Sea Gate (*bāb al-baḥr*), where they were subjected to intrusive searches for hidden valuables in their clothing. However, Meshullam's account of his disembarkation from a Genoese galley (in 1481) attests that these experiences were not always negative: "When we got to the gate, they searched us and found our money, even though it was [hidden] under [the soles of] my feet. They took 10 percent, but later gave me 9 percent back. For Jews pay [a duty of] only 1 percent, even if [the inspectors] find [the money] on you and you did not declare it. [Jews] do not pay so much as a trifle for all [their] merchandise, whereas the *goyim* [Christians] pay 10 percent. It is impossible to hide [your valuables] because they search up to the thighs, even women."[42]

Customs and import duties varied widely and were often stipulated in bilateral treaties between Mamluk Egypt and large European trading partners, but 10 percent was a fairly common levy on the goods of foreign merchants.[43] While Christians might be considered denizens of enemy territory (Arabic: *dār al-ḥarb*), Jewish merchants from Christian countries sometimes enjoyed preferential treatment, especially when the local customs officer happened to be a Jew.[44] In the case at hand, Meshullam seems to have been initially mistaken for a Christian—perhaps on account of his fashionable dress—and was charged the higher rate. However, after his identity was sorted out, the Volterrean was reimbursed. He also reports that foreign Christians arriving in Alexandria had to pay the considerable sum of thirteen gold ducats upon entering the city and could not leave without a receipt of payment, whereas Jews were exempt from this fee as well.[45]

Unlike Meshullam, Obadiah passed through customs at Alexandria without being inspected because he was greeted by Moses Grasso, a Jew who served as the Venetian dragoman in the city: "He came to meet us outside the city gate and saved us from the Ishmaelites who are sitting inside the gate. For they rob and plunder and do as they please with the foreign Jews that arrive."[46] Basola took a Venetian galley to Tripoli in 1521, and, in contrast to Meshullam and Obadiah, he writes that all passengers arriving at the Levantine port encountered the same, unbiased treatment.[47] This might indicate a change in the procedures following the region's conquest by the Ottomans five years earlier.

Conditions varied markedly, depending on place and time—or the luck of a Jewish person when passing through the customs station. It seems that affluent and well-connected Jews were able to bypass the controls or were spared the treatment that awaited their less fortunate coreligionists. Given that the customhouse was among the traveler's first impressions of a foreign country, it was highlighted in many travel reports.

Guides and Guards

Like modern tourists, medieval travelers often had to rely on locals to serve as facilitators. The changing dynamics of the Europeans' interactions with these strangers reflect their distinct personalities and cultural preconceptions. For instance, Meshullam's negative attitude toward guides, guards, shipowners, and other service providers seems to reflect his generally unfavorable disposition toward the Levant and its people. He often accuses these locals of trying to deceive travelers by inventing some excuse to raise the agreed-upon fee. He even describes incidents in which guides attempted to kill him and make off with his money.

Needless to say, robbery, financial extortion, and murder were very real dangers on premodern transit routes, even in Europe. However, in Meshullam's portrait, the Levant comes across as an especially dangerous and disorienting world, as illustrated by the account of his short trip from Alexandria to Rosetta (Arabic: Rashīd; see Map 3), near the western mouth of the Nile. The banker's social status is once more highlighted by the fact that he traveled in the company of one Messer Antonio (obviously a Christian), who served as *maestro di casa* (majordomo) to Catarina Cornaro, queen of Cyprus.[48] The distinguished group was escorted by a local Mamluk guard who, however, proved to offer little protection: "When we were about three miles away from Alexandria, the said Mamluk, who had a bow, arrows, and a sword, whereas we had no weapons, rose up to kill us, raising some false charges against us. And we were forced to give him eight ducats; I paid three for myself and my servant, and . . . Messer Antonio paid five for himself and his three servants. We were also accompanied by a camel driver with a camel that carried our belongings and clothes; he also played us false and was in cahoots with the *mamelucco*."[49]

In Fūwwa (see Map 3), a short distance upriver from Rosetta, the travelers planned to rent a boat and sail to Cairo. According to Meshullam, the local sailboat owners vied against one another over the transportation business, but the competition did not work to the customer's advantage: "It happened that we had rented a boat [Arabic: *jerma*] for a fee of thirty mu'ayyadīs [half-dirham silver coins][50] up to Cairo, and a contract was thus drawn up by an Ishmaelite scribe. One has to do so, for if you do not draw up a contract, they will demand more than twice as much when you arrive at the destination, and they will deny that you made an [oral] agreement. And after having done so and with the contract in our hands, the master of another boat came and hit the master whom we had hired and put all the movables in his boat and said, 'You are coming with me' and demanded ten [gold] ducats [a much higher amount]."[51] The two sides ultimately settled on forty mu'ayyadīs, instead of the original thirty.

A similar anecdote appears in the itinerary of Anselmo Adorno, a prominent Christian merchant and patrician of Genoese origin who resided in Bruges. In 1470, he and his son Giovanni went on a Holy Land pilgrimage via Egypt. After their debarkation at Alexandria, they followed the same route that Meshullam would take eleven years later. In Rosetta, they likewise rented a boat to sail up the Nile toward Cairo. At the same river port of Fūwwa, the Adornos were forced to abandon their vessel; their sailors were chased away by others. Before they could turn around, they were thrown into another boat, along with their luggage. Ignorant of the economics of the situation, the two newcomers initially believed that they had been abducted, until some Italian-speakers made clear to them that these sailors had been given a privilege by the sultan to load their boat before all others. A similar misunderstanding must be assumed in Meshullam's case. In both accounts, the authors were well-heeled merchants of Italian background. When the Adornos later had to give up their seats to some of the "most humble and wretched Moors" (*minimi atque miserrimi Mauri*), they felt that they had been treated like "beasts."[52]

For his trip from Hebron to Jerusalem, Meshullam hired two Mamluk guards and a guide named Ali, for the caravans under whose protection he otherwise traveled did not take this route. Ali promised to lead the small group of travelers over byways to circumvent the toll stations on the main road (throughout his journey, the thrifty Meshullam tried to avoid the numerous toll charges). Crafting a short, suspense-filled adventure story, the diarist relates how the covetous Ali purposely misled them and suddenly demanded immediate payment at twice the agreed-upon price. The company refused to accept the new terms, whereupon the "bastard" abandoned the pilgrims in the middle of the woods and summoned a few accomplices to rob them. Luckily, these two Mamluks stuck to their mission and protected the travelers, thereby enabling them to reach Jerusalem safe and sound.[53] In this instance, the Volterrean praises the "honorable" Mamluks for their trustworthiness; but his tendency to accuse locals of duplicity and treachery seems to further attest to an inherent bias toward Near Eastern people as well as his mounting frustration with the journey through strange lands.[54]

In fairness to Meshullam, similar exasperations and anxieties were voiced by other travelers, such as the aforementioned Adornos. The two patricians were on an excursion to Mount Sinai (Jabal Mūsa, a Christian pilgrimage site eschewed by medieval Jews; see Map 1) when their guide left the main road, ostensibly to avoid highwaymen. He likewise threatened his clients with abandonment in the middle of the desert if they did not increase his fee.[55] Also, Obadiah of Bertinoro's student tells that dishonest guides and toll collectors took advantage of foreigners along the Galilee-Jerusalem route, which was known to attract brigands. Appealing to local judges about undue charges was futile, "for in all these lands, there is no law and no judge, especially for Jews against Muslims."[56] Though a lump-sum payment to the muleteers usually covered the tolls, "it sometimes happened that the donkey drivers escape and leave the Jews with all their beasts at the toll collectors," so that they were forced to pay a second time.[57]

While I do not question the veracity of the student's account, it seems significant that, among the travelers discussed in this study, only Italian Jews voice such complaints. As I argue in the following chapters, certain quattrocento Jewish pilgrims shared an anti-Muslim bias with some of their Christian contemporaries.[58] As if to support this hypothesis, Obadiah's student writes that Jewish travelers in Palestine gradually developed a preference for Christian guides, whom he considers to be more reliable (though, using a traditional Jewish epithet for Christians, he calls them "uncircumcised ones").

Unlike the previously quoted pilgrims, Basola (early sixteenth century) offers a strikingly different picture of the Muslims in his small caravan. He recalls an incident where his cameleer eschewed the direct route from Sidon to Safed (see Map 3) in order to spend the night at his village. As will soon become clear, Basola's willingness to follow his guide without complaint may have paid off. Not without irony, he recalls an accident that he had while riding a camel. Preoccupied with his morning prayers, the rabbi struck a branch that knocked him flat on the ground. Whereas his Jewish travel companions heedlessly went on, two Muslims took care of Basola and transported him to Safed, where a Jewish widow bandaged him up and provided medicine. Basola's positive experiences caused him to heap praise on the "Ishmaelites" who "had it within their power to kill me and take my cash, saying that I had died from the force of the blow."[59] Ultimately, any traveler unfamiliar with these lands was entirely dependent on the goodwill and expertise of local guides.

"Jewish" Travel

While Christian-authored descriptions of travel conditions in the medieval Levant have much in common with those analyzed herein, all these texts reflect their authors' religious identity. That said, the dietary rules (kashrut) that Jewish travelers observed during their peregrinations are rarely mentioned, probably because these writers considered them to be self-evident, as most of them were pilgrims. On occasion, they were invited to Jewish homes, where they were sure to find a kosher kitchen; the rest of the time, they might simply have avoided meat.

Of all the accounts covered herein, only Obadiah, the rabbi, includes such details as that one could buy prepared kosher meals on Cairo's Jewish street.[60] Obadiah's anonymous student, for his part, specifies the provisions that he took on his maritime journey (*biscotti*, or biscuits) and the food that he purchased during stopovers (bread, cheese, grapes, and peaches).[61] Basola's advice to future travelers on a Venetian galley includes the information that for a tip, the cook would allow Jewish passengers to prepare their own meals and even make room for their (presumably kosher) pots.[62] David Re'uveni's travel account—however unreliable and partly spurious it may be—echoes the challenge of keeping kosher on a Christian-manned boat. He stocked up on foodstuffs in Alexandria before heading to the Lagoon City aboard a Venetian galley. The provisions were intended only for his servant Joseph, as Re'uveni meant to fast during the entire sea voyage (the author frequently boasts about observing lengthy fasts). But the food that he purchased got mixed up with the supplies for the Christian passengers, and Re'uveni accused Joseph of eating "from their utensils" (which would have rendered the meal nonpermissible, according to dietary laws).[63] In so doing, the eccentric diarist obviously intended to highlight his own abstinence.

It was commonly accepted that Jewish law did not require lengthy sea journeys to be interrupted for Shabbat and festivals.[64] In fact, Judah Halevi's ship left the Alexandrian harbor on the first day of Sukkot (1141). This in no way sullies the Jerusalem-bound poet's reputation as an observant Jew, for he had boarded the ship a week earlier; but it did not set sail because of unfavorable winds (as noted earlier).[65] On his way to Tripoli (see Map 3), Basola boarded a Venetian cargo vessel on a Tuesday (August 20, 1521), and the crew only lifted anchor on Friday night, after the onset of Shabbat.[66] The ship subsequently stopped in Corfu on the first night of Rosh Hashanah and resumed the journey on the Fast of Gedaliah (three days later), thereby allowing Jewish passengers to spend most of the holiday on firm ground. On Yom Kippur, the rabbi was back at sea, "when the wind was strong and the sea stormy."[67] The galley reached Tripoli on September 23, 1521, which happened to be Shemini Aṣeret (a holiday following the weeklong festival of Sukkot).[68]

In contrast to maritime journeys, Jews traveling by land were expected to rest during Shabbat and holy days. For example, in 1480, while traversing the land route from Beirut to Jerusalem, R. Joseph of Montagna and his wife stayed in Damascus from Yom Kippur until the end of Sukkot (about two weeks).[69] Meshullam and his companions, who took the caravan trail from Cairo to Gaza, spent the first Shabbat in Bilbays (see Map 3), northeast of Cairo. Hosted by the town's Jewish community, the pilgrims were housed near the local synagogue. Meshullam goes out of his way to praise "one honorable Jew, named R. Melamed Kohen and R. David, his son," for having invited his group to a Shabbat meal.[70]

At a similar stage in their own journey, Obadiah's small band of Jewish pilgrims stopped at Ṣāliḥiyya (see Map 3), where the desert route branched off from the Nile Delta, "to rest there on Shabbat and wait for a passing caravan, as from that point on, we would be entering the desert; and it would have been unsafe to travel with only five camels."[71]As Meshullam likewise notes, a small group of Jewish travelers could not risk setting up camp on the open plains without the protection of an armed caravan.[72] When the Tuscan's party reached a settlement or caravan post, such as the oasis town of Qaṭīʿa (see Map 3) in the northern Sinai, they would wait in its safe confines, even though it was still "five days until Shabbat." They could not proceed unescorted at the end of the rest day. However, this problem was easily solved: "Thanks to God, on Shabbat eve [Friday evening], around 6 P.M.,[73] a caravan of Turks arrived, all of whom were armed with bows."[74] On Sunday, this caravan resumed its trek to Gaza with Meshullam and company in tow.

Several accounts attest that Jews perceived themselves as more vulnerable than other medieval travelers. The abuse that some Jewish wayfarers absorbed started long before they reached foreign shores. It seems as though Jewish passengers on Venetian galleys were frequently harassed by crew members or Christian passengers. To avoid such harassment, they did better to promise a generous tip to the *comito*, the officer in charge of the crew, if he were to protect them. Basola remarks: "It is essential to make this promise at the beginning of the voyage and to keep one's word at its conclusion. A word to the wise is sufficient."[75]

Quarreling was not a rare phenomenon on cross-Mediterranean journeys, given the social and cultural differences among strangers who found themselves crammed together for weeks on the fickle high seas.[76] During his second maritime voyage to Alexandria, in autumn 1487, Meshullam was insulted by a Christian sailor. The incident was recorded by Obadiah, who happened to be on the same French galley:

> One of the seamen on the ship insulted the honorable R. Meshullam of Volterra, and R. Meshullam complained about him to the *patrone* of the ship. The master himself went down to seek [Meshullam's antagonist] out, and his companions tried to hide and save him, but were unable to do so. [The master] ordered [the crew] to tie [the offender] to the mast in the middle of the ship and lash him multiple times. And when [the master] noticed that the one flogging him was lax, he himself took the rope and flogged him for his insolence. He also wanted [the sailor] to apologize to the said R. Meshullam in front of everyone else. And the people were very upset about what the [ship's] lord had done to this man because of a few abusive words he had spoken against a Jew. From that day on, the sailors began to hate us and no longer treated us as before.[77]

This incident not only exemplifies the abuse that Jewish passengers might have suffered from Christian crew members but also echoes class distinction and related notions of honor; for the *patrone* apparently decided to severely punish the sailor for having crossed the line and offended an "honorable" (*ha-nikhbad*) merchant. Obadiah relates that the ordeal caused Meshullam to modify his travel plans: when another vessel crossed paths with the French galley, the Volterrean changed ships and went to Constantinople instead of Alexandria.

On his first sea journey to the Levant, the Genoese merchant galley carrying Meshullam was overtaken by two Venetian warships during its approach to Rhodes. This incident was symptomatic of the two maritime republics' long-standing rivalry over the eastern Mediterranean sea lanes. Despite their superior equipment, the Venetians failed to subdue the Genoese vessel and, according to Meshullam, looked for a way to withdraw without losing face: "Finally, they said that they had heard that [some] Jews were on the ship, [whom the Venetians] wanted together with their money—God forbid—and then they would let the ship, its merchants, and merchandise go their way in peace."[78] The Genoese captain, who felt equally obligated to all his passengers, refused to hand over Meshullam and his servant, for the release of whom the Venetians would probably have demanded a high ransom.[79] In the end, the steadfast shipmaster persuaded the assailants to make do with a barrel of Greek wine, a bag of nuts, and a block of cheese! Meshullam escaped with little more than a fright; but in this case, he did not fit the bill of a self-assured Tuscan banker but was exposed as a vulnerable Jew, at least in the eyes of the Venetians. Or he was a vulnerable Jew to the Venetian extortionist and an honorable fellow Italian to the Genoese captain.

On their return trip, the religious affiliation of Meshullam and his companions again constituted a potential problem. Upon boarding a Venetian pilgrims' galley at Jaffa, its master, Agostino Contarini, who in the late fifteenth century was one of the few licensed *patroni* serving the pilgrim traffic between Venice and Jaffa, thought it best to conceal the new arrivals' identity from the Christian passengers,[80] for having just returned from the sites most sacred to their faith, they may have been in a state of heightened religious fervor.[81]

In other circumstances, Meshullam took steps to mask his Italian Jewish identity. En route from Cairo to Gaza, he and his Jewish companions received the caravan master's permission to wear white turbans "like an Ishmaelite [here: Arab] or a Turk," in place of the yellow ones that were designated for Jews in Mamluk lands.[82] According to the Volterrean's account, the purpose of this disguise was to avoid the higher fees that foreign Jews and Christians were charged at certain stations along the way. Behaving as inconspicuously as possible, the Tuscan merchant claims to have been taken for a Turk: "Although the local people spoke to me and I did not understand their language, they still believed [that I was a Turk], for I would sit and eat on the ground and behaved as they do in every way. And while the Turks and the Ishmaelites all have the same faith, they do not understand each other's language."[83] Meshullam did look down on Near Eastern dress and habits, such as sitting on the ground;[84] but in this case, he assumed an Oriental identity for the sake of blending in with the others on the caravan. (Needless to say, this is not a case of cultural cross-dressing or "going native," which was quite common among later Romantic travelers to the Middle East.)

It will be recalled that Meshullam and his company joined another caravan at the northern Sinai town of Qaṭīʿa. This time, the leader of the new caravan explicitly advised them to don white turbans "according to the custom of the Turks and the Ishmaelites, for then we had nothing to fear from anyone."

Upon reaching a way station, Meshullam was approached by the toll master in Arabic, but "I did not know what to answer; however, the chief of the caravan quickly replied: 'Don't talk to him, for he does not understand your language because he is a Turk.' Hence the Ishmaelite did not notice that I am a Jew."[85] It bears noting that this is the only hint throughout the corpus of the difficulty of communicating in a foreign land.

Drawing on his own experiences, Meshullam offers detailed advice as to how caravan passengers should conduct themselves at toll stations or other encampments along the way in order to avoid being identified as foreigners from Christian lands. He basically tells his readers to carefully imitate local customs in every possible detail: "When you get to these places, you immediately have to take off your shoes and sit on the ground and bend your legs beneath yourself. Neither stretch out your legs nor stand on your legs at all."[86] Future (male) travelers are even told to urinate in a crouching position—from which it may be deduced that Meshullam wore a local tunic or robe on his desert trek instead of Italian "tights": "In addition, when you go to relieve yourself, make certain not to lift up your clothes. And when you urinate, crouch down to the ground so that your penis will be three fingers above the ground and [thus] relieve yourself."[87] Finally, he admonishes his addressees to "be very careful not to break any of these customs lest they find out, God forbid, that you are a Jew or a *franco* [foreigner from Christian lands], and *unlucky is he that falls into this trap*."[88]

The implications of Meshullam's closing remark are less than clear: Is he suggesting that a Western traveler whose identity was exposed in Islamic territory risked his life? Was he perhaps afraid of attracting bandits because his clothes gave him away as a wealthy merchant from Italy? Apparently, these were not his major considerations, for he repeatedly mentions his efforts to avoid the much higher tolls that were imposed on foreigners.[89] It is also possible that Meshullam took unnecessary precautions or exaggerated the risk that he had taken; in Obadiah's account of the same route, there is no indication that he was worried about being recognized as an Italian Jew. What is more, having passed twenty toll stations between Cairo and Jerusalem, Obadiah paid no more than a single ducat in total![90]

In advising travelers to adopt customs and behaviors that he normally ridicules, for the purpose of blending in with their surroundings, Meshullam unwittingly reveals the extent to which he perceived himself as a vulnerable alien in the Middle East. That said, his unpleasant encounters with

Christian pilgrims and seamen demonstrate that, on account of his Jewish identity, his home (Italy) and compatriots (European Christians) were likely to be no less threatening than the unknown Levant and its "strange" people. Oscillating between a number of potentially hostile worlds, the Tuscan Jew's account ultimately debunks the simplistic notions of dominant-inferior relations often associated with European descriptions of peregrinations in the Islamic world.

PART II

Territory and Place

Chapter 4

Facing a Gentile Land of Israel

Palestine was the focal point and ultimate destination of most travelers discussed here. However, in bringing the country to their readers, they had to contend with a paradox: during the late Middle Ages, not only was the Land of Israel ruled by Christians and/or Muslims, but the absence of a sizable Jewish community had rendered it virtually non-Jewish in character. While none of the demographic figures provided by Benjamin of Tudela or Petaḥyah of Regensburg is verifiable, a pattern seems to emerge with respect to Jewish communities. Both these twelfth-century travelers cite relatively large Jewish populations for cities outside the Land of Israel, such as Damascus (Benjamin estimates "about three thousand Jews" and Petaḥyah "ten thousand") and Aleppo ("five thousand," according to Benjamin), whereas the Jewish population within the country is small.[1] For instance, Petaḥyah admits that "there are no more than a hundred, two hundred, or three hundred" Jews in all of Palestine.[2] And there were other surprises in store for Jewish pilgrims of the crusader era: most disturbing must have been that many of the holy places that they had come to see—first and foremost the Temple Mount and Hebron's Tomb of the Patriarchs—were controlled by the Latin Church.

Medieval Jewish travelers and writers thus had to adopt certain mental and rhetorical strategies that were aimed at reclaiming a Gentile Land of Israel for their imagined audience. One measure, which is most evident in Benjamin's *Massa'ot*, was to reconcile a Christian present with a Jewish past by projecting a biblical landscape on the still-recognizable map of twelfth-century outremer. By fashioning a complex interplay of imagination and reality, Benjamin's description of crusader Palestine gives voice to two historical dimensions of geographical space: the first is a more or less reliable account of the contemporaneous political and religious landscape; the second is a critical interpretation of these realities on the basis of a Jewish cultural memory.[3]

The Tudelan introduces the Land of Israel via the major port cities of Tyre and Acre, both of which were part of the Latin Kingdom of Jerusalem in his days. Simultaneously, he reminds his readers that twelfth-century Acre is the same as biblical 'Akko, in whose hinterland the tribe of Asher had settled.[4] Following the biblical account, Asher was allotted the coastal areas of the western Galilee and the hinterland of Tyre and Sidon but the tribe never succeeded in occupying 'Akko.[5] From the perspective of rabbinic law, the coastal city was therefore considered to be on the border of (but strictly taken outside) *ereṣ yisra'el*—a territory of both halakhic and symbolic significance.[6] It seems to be in this sense that Benjamin refers to Acre as "the commencement of the Land of Israel."[7] To the Jewish pilgrim, the city was liminal space: from here onward, a Jew should observe certain religious laws (for example, those pertaining to prayer and festival observance) that do not apply in the same way in the diaspora—or the territory just north of Acre, in this case.

Benjamin acknowledges contemporaneous realities when he describes Acre as the most important port of arrival for Jerusalem-bound travelers: "There is the large port [serving] all the *errant ones* [Hebrew: *to'im*] who travel to Jerusalem by ship." In fact, *to'im* (singular: *to'eh*) is a polemical term for Christian pilgrims, as it seems to play on multiple connotations of the Hebrew root *t'h*: to err, go astray, deviate, or wander. With respect to the last sense, *to'eh* arguably echoes the Latin *peregrinus* (foreigner, wanderer, pilgrim).[8] Benjamin deems Christians to be deviant pilgrims, for their main destination—the Holy Sepulchre—was anathema to medieval Jews. Reflecting competing notions about the character of a true pilgrimage, Holy Land travel, in other words, emerges as a contested activity in *Massa'ot*.[9]

This distinction between righteous and deviant pilgrims has all the more meaning, given that Jewish pilgrimages from Europe took advantage of the indispensable infrastructure that the Kingdom of Jerusalem had established, such as regular cross-Mediterranean transportation, ports, improved road systems, and access to sacred venues.[10] Like their Christian counterparts, Jewish pilgrims profited from these innovations, which made overseas travel faster, cheaper, and safer. On the other hand, they were denied access to the services provided by monasteries and hostelries that were set up throughout the Latin Levant (if indeed they were asking for these services). The conflicting emotions that Jewish pilgrims to crusader Palestine must have harbored are given voice through Benjamin's account.

Clearly, the Iberian traveler felt the need to reconcile a Christian *terra sancta* with a Jewish Land of Israel, both of which appear to be intrinsically intertwined, from his perspective. This same sort of juxtaposition recurs in his account of Mount Carmel (south of Acre; see Map 3), where biblical sites, Jewish graves (some of which appear to be the final resting place of more recent arrivals), and a Christian church were in close proximity to one another: "Beneath Mount [Carmel] are many Jewish graves, and on the mountain is the Cave of Elijah, peace be upon him. The Edomites [Christians] have built there an [idolatrous] high place [Hebrew: *bamah*; here: church] that they call San Elias.[11] On top of the mountain, one can see the site of the destroyed altar that Elijah repaired in the days of Ahab."[12]

In keeping with biblical typologies, medieval Hebrew literature commonly refers to Christians as Edomites and Muslims as Ishmaelites. The word *bamah* chosen here for the Frankish church on Mount Carmel has further significance: in biblical Hebrew, the term denotes sites in which idolatry was practiced.[13] Castigating the Latins for having built a *bamah* on Mount Carmel, Benjamin appears to draw a parallel between these "Edomites" and those false prophets who erected an altar to Ba'al on that same site (1 Kings 18:26). While their prayer remained unanswered, Elijah "repaired the altar of the Lord that had been destroyed" (1 Kings 18:30), and his sacrifice—consumed by divine fire—was duly received. (It seems ironical that this idolatrous "high place" had been named "San Elias" by the Christians.) Contrasting in this way between true and false pilgrimage places, *Massa'ot* responds to the fact that through the construction of numerous new churches, the crusaders had significantly remade Palestine's sacred topography.

Non-Jewish Jerusalem: A Desolate City

Unlike Benjamin, other Jewish travel writers largely ignore the Christian or Muslim metamorphosis of the country. Collapsing time, they basically portray the land as though it were still in the state of ruin that the Romans had left it in, following their victory over the Jews and the destruction of the Second Temple in 70 CE.[14] Despite substantial changes to the urban and human landscape in the interim, many medieval Jewish visitors described Jerusalem and all of Palestine as a decimated land. For example, Meshullam of Volterra offers the following picture of Mamluk-ruled Jerusalem: "On Wednesday, 29 July [Italian: *luglio*] 5241 [1481], we arrived at Jerusalem, the Holy City. When I saw its ruins, full of bitterness, I rent my garments as long as a hand breadth and recited the appropriate prayer, which I had in a booklet.

Now Jerusalem has no walls, due to our sins. There is only a bit [of a wall] on the side where I entered. And though it was totally destroyed, due to our sins, there are ten thousand Ishmaelite householders [families] and about 250 Jewish householders."[15]Although the majority of fifteenth-century Jerusalem's defenses were down, this could no longer be attributed to the Roman conquest—an event that Jewish tradition considered a divine punishment for the people's sins. Instead, it was the Ayyubids who had demolished the city's fortifications in the early thirteenth century, so as to impair its defenses in the event that the Christians retook the city.[16] These historical details were of little concern (if not completely unknown) to Meshullam and many other Jewish pilgrims, as premodern Jews believed that the entire land would remain irreparably desolate until the coming of the Messiah.[17] At the same time, Meshullam challenges this belief by noting Jerusalem's significant population at the time of his visit.

Two centuries earlier, Naḥmanides had portrayed a city lying in waste. Toward the end of his life, the Spanish kabbalist and biblical commentator had settled in Acre, which was then the capital and commercial hub of the second crusader kingdom. In 1267, he went on pilgrimage to Mamluk-ruled Jerusalem, where the traces of the Mongolian invasion seven years earlier must still have been widely visible. However, in a letter to his son back in Spain, Naḥmanides' personal impressions are clearly suffused with religious interpretation: "What shall I tell you about the Land [of Israel]? For 'there are many deserted sites' [Isa. 6:12] and great is the desolation. As a rule, the more sacred a site is than another one, the more ruined it is. Jerusalem is more ruined than the rest [of the country] and Judah more than Galilee."[18]

A number of these impressions have also been woven into Naḥmanides' Prayer at the Ruins of Jerusalem. Before discussing this famous formula, let us look at the traditional mourning ritual in commemoration of the destruction of Jerusalem, which seems to have determined the mind-set with which many Jewish travelers approached the city. Meshullam's above-cited recollections sum up these customs: "When I saw [Jerusalem's] ruins, full of bitterness, I rent my garments as long as a hand breadth and recited the appropriate prayer."[19] According to *Toṣ'ot Ereṣ Yisra'el*, which was apparently compiled shortly after Naḥmanides' death in 1270, Jewish pilgrims first rent their clothes at a hilltop near Jerusalem that this text refers to as Ṣofim: "When one reaches Ṣofim, one beholds Jerusalem and rends his garment once on account of her [destruction]."[20] The hilltop in question is modern-day Nabī Ṣamwīl, a strategic site overlooking the roads from the coastal plain to Jerusalem. The crusaders named this observation point Montjoye (Latin: Mons Gaudii), as this was the spot from which in 1099 the advancing troops caught an initial glimpse of the coveted city. Like Montjoye, the Hebrew term "Ṣofim" alludes to the fact that "one beholds" Jerusalem for the first time when coming from the west.[21] According to the German Holy Land traveler Theoderic (1172), it was here that Christian "pilgrims have their first view of [Jerusalem] and, moved with great joy, put [on] their crosses."[22] Jewish travelers likely followed in the footsteps of Christian tour groups; in rending their garments at this same vantage point, Jews developed a ritual that apparently drew upon Christian praxis—a phenomenon that might best be described as transculturation.

Upon laying eyes on the Temple Mount, Jewish pilgrims would tear their clothes a second time.[23] Both rituals are depicted in Naḥmanides' aforementioned Prayer at the Ruins of Jerusalem (*tefillah 'al ḥorvot yerushalayim*). While drawing on his personal experience, it is also a literary piece that integrates a number of related scriptural quotations:

> I recited over [Jerusalem] as it is proper: "Zion has become a desert, Jerusalem a desolation" [Isa. 64:9]. Near the city, in front of the gate, I rent [my clothes] over her, and when I arrived opposite the Great and Sacred House [*ha-bayit ha-gadol ve-ha-qadosh*], we recited with great weeping, "Our Holy House, our pride, where our fathers praised You, has been consumed by fire, and all that was dear to us is ruined" [Isa. 64:10]. We then rent [our garments] a second time with "mourning and lament" [Isa. 29:2] and recited on the spot the psalm of lamentation, saying: "O God, heathens [*goyim*] have entered Your inheritance [they have defiled Your holy Temple and turned Jerusalem into ruins]" [Ps. 79:113].[24]

The place from which Naḥmanides imagined himself standing opposite the Great and Sacred House was likely the Mount of Olives. The actual sight that stood before his eyes was certainly not the ruined Jewish Temple but the extant Islamic shrines. While the outer walls of the Ḥaram al-Sharīf contain ancient layers of masonry, some of which date back to Second Temple times, Naḥmanides expressed no antiquarian interest. In fact, he seems to have ignored all the actual facts on the ground; he evoked the picture of a desecrated sanctuary that was no longer visible.

Though medieval Jerusalem might have contained numerous ruins, the frequent references in Jewish travel literature to its "desolate" state should not be taken at face value; nor is it to be confused with the nineteenth-century stereotype of the Orient as a region in decay. Rooted in collective memory and reinforced by ritual, Jewish travel writers continued to define the extant city—whether under Christian or Muslim domain—as "destroyed," and it was only to be rebuilt in messianic times. This generic convention appears to have shaped both the Jewish pilgrims' experience and their representation of the Holy City. As a result, the real and the envisioned Jerusalem were not only intertwined; the reality was hardly visible beneath the layers of religious imagination.

R. Isaac ben Meir Latif, who visited Mamluk Jerusalem in the mid-fifteenth century, seems to have been one of the few Jewish pilgrims who were not oblivious to the actual city they encountered. Latif opens his account with a phrase that echoes traditional pilgrimage literature: "On the mountains of Israel, there we sat and wept over the destruction of Zion."[25] Still, his point of reference immediately shifts from the Jewish past to a recognizable depiction of the contemporaneous city that he estimates to be "about twice [the size of] Ancona." To Latif, as implied by this comparison, Jerusalem was no timeless place but coterminous with his own Italian hometown. In addition to its religious significance, the Holy City boasted bustling markets and tumultuous streets: "Within [the city,] there is a daily market on five streets that are protected against heat and sun, since they are covered with domes . . . ; and on each side is a continuous [line of] shops that are graced by God's blessing, [as] nothing is missing in them. A person has difficulty passing through any of these streets due to the congestion."[26]

Arguably, Latif's more realistic attitude toward Jerusalem reflects the growing importance attributed to empirical observations during his time. Simultaneously, his account seems to exchange one literary topos for another—"desolation" and "ruin" for "a land flowing with milk and honey."[27] Contradictory as it might be, Latif's compatriot Meshullam even juxtaposes these two age-old conceptions of Palestine in the same sentence: "The Land [of Israel] is a land flowing with milk, although it is hilly and ruined and desolate."[28]

A Jewish Crusader City

Unlike other premodern Jewish travelers, Benjamin of Tudela does not open his chapter on Jerusalem with a traditional lamentation over its destruction but describes it as a walled—rather than ruined—city whose population is almost exclusively Christian: "Jerusalem is a small city and fortified by three walls. It is full of people whom the Ishmaelites call Jacobites, Arameans [Syrian Christians or Nestorians], Greeks, Georgians, and Franks, and of all nations [lit., tongues] of non-Jews [*goyim*]."[29] This ethno-religious survey reflects the official crusader policy of prohibiting non-Christians from settling in Jerusalem (though there were exceptions to the rule, as will become clear). Specifically, the "Franks," who lacked the numbers to repopulate the conquered city on their own—after its Muslim and Jewish population had been massacred in 1099—encouraged Near Eastern Christians to take up residence therein.[30] Only at this point does Benjamin mention the small Jewish presence: "There is a dyeing house that the Jews rent annually from the king [of Jerusalem], so that no one else may dye in Jerusalem besides the Jews. There are about [four] Jews who live under the Tower of David in a corner of the city."[31]Since the crusaders did not admit the establishment of a permanent Jewish community within the Holy City,[32] it was only thanks to these Jewish dyers—a profession that was very much at the low end of the social scale—that the occasional Jewish pilgrimage group could find lodging inside the walls (as stated). The Jewish tannery was situated on the western corner of town, near the medieval Citadel. From the Frankish period onward, the Citadel has been known as the Tower of David. (It goes back to the Hasmoneans.) Benjamin credulously adopts this name, for it points to the city's Jewish origins. In the same vein, he informs his readers that the Citadel's lower layers were built "by our forefathers," while the upper parts are said to have been added by the "Ishmaelites."[33]

Having completed his account of the Citadel, Benjamin unexpectedly proceeds to Christian landmarks, rather than the preeminent Jewish venue—the site of the former Temple. To begin with, he describes the Hospital, an institution near the Citadel, that was founded especially for Christian pilgrims: "There they lodge all the sick who come there, and they supply them with all their needs in life and in death."[34] It also served as the seat of the Knights Hospitalers (the same order that would later be headquartered at Rhodes, as stated in the previous chapter), one of the military-monastic orders that were established in Frankish Jerusalem (four hundred of which, as per Benjamin's count, were stationed in the city). The second major crusader institution was the headquarters of the Templar Knights, housed in the transformed al-Aqṣā Mosque. Notwithstanding the Jewish framework of his narrative, Benjamin echoes that generation's Christian perception of the site and its history. While he is apparently unaware of the building's Islamic past, he adopts the popular crusader account whereby it had once served as King Solomon's palace and even uses the period's Latin appellation for the edifice: Templum Salomonis (Solomon's Temple).[35]

Given its proximity to al-Aqṣā Mosque, one would have expected Benjamin to finally tend to the adjacent Dome of the Rock on the site of the ancient Temple. Instead, he leaps across town to, of all places, the Holy Sepulchre: "There is the large high place [*bamah*, church] that is called *Sepulchre*. There *that man* [Jesus] is buried to whom all the *errant ones* [*to'im*, Christian pilgrims] come."[36] Adhering to the era's Jewish literary norms, Benjamin avoids uttering the name of Jesus by replacing it with "that man." Nevertheless, it is odd that his account of the Holy City seems to follow the lead of a Christian guide. In contrast, most other Jewish travel narratives barely acknowledge the existence of Latin Jerusalem's religious center.[37] Therefore, the reader is left wondering whether the Tudelan's account incorporates any Christian sources. It is hard to avoid the impression that *Massa'ot*'s description of Jerusalem is conversant with the period's Christian itineraries, at least as an oral tradition (the Jewish traveler probably had no access to any Latin or vernacular *peregrinatio*).[38]

The polemical locution that Benjamin employs in his reference to the Holy Sepulchre leaves no room for doubt about his feelings: the center of the Christian universe is an idolatrous "high place," and the Christian pilgrims headed there are "misguided." *Massa'ot* bears witness to the fact that the new opportunities that the Latin Kingdom provided for both Christians and Jews interested in visiting Jerusalem inadvertently enabled the expression of marginalized voices that were normally silenced in the dominant (Christian) discourse.

Dome of the Rock: An Islamic Shrine Brimming with Jewish Memories

After the Holy Sepulchre, Benjamin takes his readers to each of the city's four gates before finally returning to the Temple Mount. Unlike other Jewish travelers, he sheds no tears for the sanctuary's destruction. Instead, *Massa'ot* offers a quasi-historical account of the site: "The Jehoshaphat Gate is in front of the Temple [*bet ha-miqdash*] that stood [there] in ancient times. There is [now] the Templum Domini [on what] was [once] the site of the Temple upon which 'Umar Ibn al-Khaṭṭāb erected a large and most beautiful dome. And the *goyim* [Christians] bring no image or icon into it but [only] come there to pray."[39] While the Tudelan previously equated al-Aqṣā Mosque with Templum Salomonis, he clearly distinguishes between the Dome of the Rock and the ancient Temple. The Dome of the Rock (Qubbat al-Ṣakhra) was built in the late seventh century during the reign of the Umayyad caliph 'Abd al-Malik (685–705), but Benjamin, like many Christian writers, erroneously credits the edifice to the second caliph, 'Umar Ibn al-Khaṭṭāb (r. 634–44), who ruled two generations earlier.[40] During the Frankish period, the shrine was transformed into a church that was christened Templum Domini (The Temple of the Lord), in commemoration of the Jewish Temple's role in the life of Jesus (the "Lord").[41] While Benjamin makes use of the Latin term, he clearly objects to the implied Christian claim to the building, as will be seen shortly. To him, its crusader-period name affirms the site as the focal point in any Jewish configuration of the Land of Israel.

Benjamin contends that Christians refrained from introducing into the Qubbat al-Ṣakhra what Jews deemed to be blasphemous images, such as crosses or representations of human beings. His account is contradicted by contemporaneous Christian and Muslim descriptions of the building, such as the report of the German cleric John of Würzburg, who visited Jerusalem in the 1160s, about the same time as Benjamin. According to John's detailed account of the Dome, several renderings of scenes from the Hebrew Bible and the New Testament as well as Latin inscriptions were mounted inside and outside the Templum Domini. He notes that "the sign of the holy cross has been fixed to the top by Christians, which is annoying to the Saracens."[42] Despite being a "Saracen," 'Alī bin Abī Bakr al-Harawī, a native of Aleppo and the author of a Muslim pilgrimage guide (*Kitāb al-ziyārāt*), was allowed into the shrine in 1173 and recalls seeing therein an icon of Christ (*sūrat al-masīḥ*) "in gold and incrusted with precious jewels."[43] Against this backdrop, Benjamin's assertion that the crusaders did not adorn the Dome with Christian images may be interpreted as a rhetorical strategy to deny the Latins' takeover of Judaism's most venerated site. By implication, this denial also included the Church's self-declaration as the New Israel after the Jewish people had been "forsaken" by God.[44] The Tudelan probably never went into the building because of halakhic restrictions prohibiting Jews from visiting the site of the former Temple or because the Latins prevented Jews from entering what was then a church. Thus he had to make do with reports, hearsay, and pious traditions about a place that he was obviously expected to describe. Whether he was unaware of historical reality or simply felt unconstricted by it, Benjamin reclaimed a lost

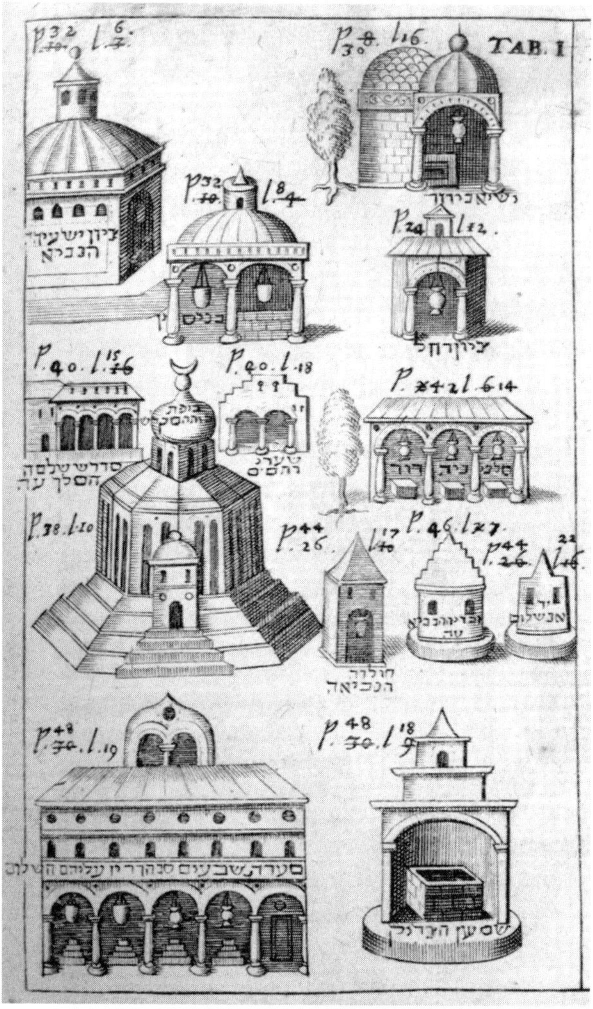

Figure 3. Johann Heinrich Hottinger, *Cippi Hebraici* (Heidelberg: Samuel Broun, 1662). *Cippi Hebraici* offers a bilingual Hebrew-Latin edition of *Yiḥus Avot* that was produced by the Christian Hebraist Hottinger (see Chapter 1). This copperplate image depicts the Dome of the Rock—here called "Dome of the Temple" (Hebrew: *kipat ha-miqdash*)—and (to its upper left) the al-Aqṣā Mosque—the "Study House [(*bet*) *midrash*] of King Solomon"—as well as a number of revered Jewish tombs in the vicinity of Jerusalem. Courtesy of the Library at the Herbert D. Katz Center for Advanced Judaic Studies, University of Pennsylvania.

sacred space for his Jewish audience, for whom this particular place was inextricably intertwined with their own constructions of community and identity.

In his roughly contemporaneous account, Petaḥyah adopts a slightly different strategy for coping with the Christian transformation of the Temple Mount: "There is a beautiful sanctuary [*hekhal*] that the Ishmaelites built in ancient times when Jerusalem was in the hands of the Ishmaelites. Then came insolent people who made the following slanderous report to the king of the Ishmaelites: 'There is an old man among us who knows the location of the sanctuary [*hekhal*] and [its] courtyard [*'azarah*].' And the king urged him to show it to him. Since the king was a friend of the Jews, he said: 'I want to build a sanctuary there, and no one else shall pray there save the Jews.' He built a sanctuary of marble stones, a fine structure, of red, green, and variegated marble."[45] This account constitutes an abridged version of the well-known legend of 'Umar Ibn al-Khaṭṭāb's discovery of the Temple's foundations, which turns up in both Christian and Islamic sources. In its Hebrew adaptation, Petaḥyah transforms the narrative into an edifying tale whereby the caliph, a "friend of the Jews," built a Jewish place of worship on the site of the Temple.[46] This idyllic picture becomes disturbed by a polemical note against those *Jewish* "slanderers" who passed on the information to the conqueror (which may hint at the source from which this tradition was drawn).[47] From the perspective of the Frankish era, the author views the construction of the Dome of the Rock not as a usurpation of a Jewish site, but the caliph comes close to restoring the Jewish institution! As such, Petaḥyah recasts an Islamic shrine as a semi-manifestation of the Temple, or as the presence of what is actually absent.

In marked contrast to Benjamin, Petaḥyah accuses the Christians of having introduced idols into the Dome of the Rock, thus violating the religious status quo. He then describes how the building's own prodigious powers repelled its Christianization: "Then came *goyim* [Christians] and put images [*ṣelamim*] in it, but they fell down. They then fixed the image within the thick wall, but it could not stand in the Holy of Holies."[48] The end result is the same as in Benjamin's story: both essentially deny that the Latins had converted the Dome of the Rock into a church. Their descriptions of the former Temple's site ignore historical reality in favor of a fiction that allows them to claim the "abiding presence of a lost center."[49]

Pilgrim literature's tendency to describe holy places according to pious conventions, as opposed to empirical observations, is most conspicuous in *Toṣ'ot Ereṣ Yisra'el*, which was penned during the early Mamluk era when the

Temple Mount was once again in Muslim hands. Did this change in sovereignty affect *Toṣ'ot*'s representation of the site?

From the vantage point of a ruined building overlooking the Ḥaram al-Sharīf, the anonymous author "*sees* the Temple Mount and the wall of the courtyard [*'azarah*]—the courtyard of the women, the courtyard of the [priests], and the courtyard of the Israelites—the site of the altar, the site of the Temple, the Sanctuary [*hekhal*], and the Holy of Holies."[50] Far from describing the actual mosques and shrines that stood before his eyes, this description echoes the idealized picture of the Second Temple in the Mishnah tractate Middot (Measures), which was composed after the destruction.[51] Based on collective Jewish memory, which had been shaped by this formative literature, the traveler reconstitutes in his religious imagination a vanished Temple in every detail.

Still, *Toṣ'ot* does not completely ignore the extant topography of the Ḥaram al-Sharīf, as observation and imagination do not necessarily cancel each other out. In fact, the author employs the Ḥaram's architecture as a foil on which to project elements of the destroyed Temple: "Above the Foundation Stone [*even shetiyah*, the Rock] the kings of Ishmael [Muslim rulers] built a very magnificent building. They made it a prayer house [*bet tefillah*] and erected above the building a very beautiful dome. This building [the Dome of the Rock] stands on [the site of] the Holy of Holies and above the Sanctuary [*hekhal*]."[52] Thereafter, the text identifies additional structures of the Ḥaram al-Sharīf with other parts of the Temple. For instance, Qubbat al-Silsila (the Dome of the Chain, to the east of the Dome of the Rock) is associated with the "outer altar that was in the courtyard of the Israelites."

Just as the Ḥaram's architectural landscape allows the onlooker to envision elements of the vanished sanctuary, an Islamic rite visualizes a bygone Jewish ritual: "We saw the Ishmaelites gather there on the day of their feast [Arabic: *'īd*], about three thousand, who were ambulating around this place [the Dome of the Chain] as in a procession, like the people of Israel used to ambulate around the altar on the seventh day of the Feast [of Sukkot]—[but one has] to distinguish between impurity and purity."[53] In their circumambulation of the Dome of the Chain, Muslims seemed to retain a central feature of the Hoshana Rabbah (the seventh day of Sukkot) processions as they were held before the Temple's destruction. Although this analogy makes Islam appear understandable by casting it in recognizable terms, the text also draws an unmistakable distinction between the "pure" Jewish practice and the "impure" Islamic one.[54] It bears noting that none of the works analyzed within this study draws similar parallels with Christian rites that are simply deemed to be idol worship.

In his own description of the Ḥaram (1481), Meshullam of Volterra also compares present Islamic ritual with past Jewish rites. However, in stark contrast to *Toṣ'ot,* Meshullam claims that ordinary Muslims observe certain rules of purity that applied solely to the Temple's high priest: "The Ishmaelites do not enter [the Dome of the Rock] without having performed an immersion [*ṭevilah*] five times."[55] Meshullam appears to be referring to the Islamic ablution that is performed before each of the five daily prayers. At the same time, his account evokes the image of the high priest who immersed himself five times before entering the Holy of Holies on Yom Kippur, the only occasion when any mere mortal was permitted into that hallowed space.[56] He also states that Muslims "do not touch a woman [for] three days before" visiting Qubbat al-Ṣakhra, thereby heeding to scriptural notions of ritual purity.[57] By projecting bygone rites onto Islamic praxis, Meshullam and the author of *Toṣ'ot* place Muslims in a time other than their own. These accounts underscore the Jewish pilgrim's limited interest in providing ethnographic accounts of Muslim customs, as current Islamic ritual merely serves to evoke a defunct Temple service that still plays a central role in the collective Jewish memory.

On another occasion, Meshullam has Muslims observing the Ninth of Av, a Jewish fast day marking the destruction of the First and Second Temples: "Let it be known to you, gentlemen, as there is no doubt about it: each year when the Jews go to the synagogue on the eve of the Ninth of Av, all the lights that are in the [Temple] courtyard [*'azarah*] go out by themselves. And they cannot rekindle them until that day has completely gone by; many times, the Ishmaelites tried to light them and were unable to do so. [Hence] the Ishmaelites know when the Ninth of Av is, which they thus observe almost like the Jews. This is clear and well known to everyone, without any doubt."[58] The Volterrean essentially contends that, despite the Muslims' dominion over the sacred space, they have to submit to a numinous power inherent in the Temple's former location. Like the tales about the Holy of Holies repelling Christian images, this miracle story—which Meshullam may have heard from local Jews—functions to attest to the irrevocably Jewish character of a lost place.

Beyond describing the Ḥaram al-Sharīf in terms of the Temple, some quattrocento Jewish pilgrims espoused a decidedly polemical attitude toward the Muslim presence on Jerusalem's sacred esplanade. R. Isaac ben Meir Latif's grievances are couched in midrashic metaphors that are seemingly timeless: he compares the Temple Mount to an empty throne, upon which "the feet of the

King [God] are not resting" and a "decorated table from which the sons [the Jews] have been driven away."[59] Latif bemoans the hallowed precinct's present status: "How much did our heart ache when we saw that our inheritance has become [the property] of foreigners, our house that of Gentiles [*nokhrim*]!" In a different historical context, these words would have referred to the Christian occupants of the Temple Mount. However, the rabbi then hints at the object of his polemic: "How can my soul be comforted when I saw the sanctuary of the King inhabited by the sons of the sorceress?"—where "sorceress" apparently stands for Hagar, the supposed ancestress of all Ishmaelites.[60]

In the sixteenth century, several Jewish letter writers mentioned portents of the imminent redemption that were connected to the Dome of the Rock. According to Moses Basola, the crescent on top of the shrine's cupola that hitherto faced south had turned to the east on Sukkot (1519), the traditional feast of the Temple's inauguration. The Jews interpreted the event as a sign that the Ḥaram would soon revert to its previous function as a Jewish sanctuary. Even the Muslims, Basola contends, "interpreted this as an evil omen for their faith and tried to turn it back to the south, which faces Mecca, but were unable to do so."[61] During Basola's time, these millenarian expectations were stoked by recent historical developments—chiefly, the migration of Sephardic refugees to the Ottoman Empire (in the wake of their expulsion from Spain in 1492). Some observers deemed the Ottoman conquest of Palestine (1516) to pave the way for the return of all Jews to their ancestral homeland.[62] Since this "ingathering of the dispersed" (*qibbuṣ galuyyot*) was a quintessential element of Jewish beliefs about the messianic age, it was also expected to lead to the restoration of the Temple and its sacrificial service.

The same motif resurfaces in Re'uveni's bizarre tale about his visit to the Ḥaram in March 1523. Not only does he claim to have been present when the Dome's crescent swung to the east, but he connects this "sign" with his own mission.[63] Wearing a green turban like a descendant of the Prophet Muhammad (*sharīf*), Re'uveni paid a visit to the Dome of the Rock, which he (like the other authors) identifies with the Holy of Holies. In what would have sounded rather shocking to a Jewish audience, the eccentric adventurer descended to the little grotto beneath the rock, where he spent five weeks fasting and praying—if his account is to be believed.[64] When the Muslim guardians treated Re'uveni as a descendant of Muhammad, kissing his feet and greeting him as "Blessed of the Lord, our lord son of our lord [Muhammad]," they appeared to be hailing a messianic figure. In Re'uveni's view, the crescent's shift was a sign from on high that he should embark on his fantastic mission to

Europe to rally the "liberation" of the Holy Land.[65] While a detailed discussion of this riveting story goes beyond the present framework, it evidently tries to address the incongruity between the Dome of the Rock as a real (Islamic) shrine and as an imagined (Jewish) shrine, declaring the building's present state deceptive and transitory in the face of imminent redemption.[66]

Mount Zion: Who Owns King David?

It may be of little surprise that the Ḥaram al-Sharīf emerges as a contested place in the travel accounts under review. However, Jewish visitors to Jerusalem faced similar dilemmas at other sites—among them the putative tomb of King David on "Mount Zion." Differing from the Temple Mount, the location of David's sepulchre had only recently been established. Benjamin offers a folkloristic tale about its accidental discovery and the miraculous prevention of its desecration by the Latin Christians. Before discussing this story and its function within *Massa'ot*, I will provide a historical sketch of the actual site.

According to the Hebrew Bible, David "was buried in the City of David" (1 Kings 2:10): on the southern slopes of the Ophel, southeast of the Temple Mount; this area was then equated with Zion (1 Kings 8:1). In contrast, the tradition locating David's grave on the southwestern promontory of Jerusalem, presently known as Mount Zion (and outside the Ottoman city walls), is apparently of Christian origin. Records of this later tradition only date back to the tenth century.[67] The institutionalization of David's chapel, including a large cenotaph (the "tomb"), may be an even later development, tied to the twelfth-century construction of the Latin Church of Saint Mary on the said hill.[68]

Notwithstanding the venue's dubious authenticity, crusader-period Jews claimed it as a biblical site, thereby illustrating how the competition with a rival faith may constitute sacred space in the Jewish collective memory. Benjamin seems to have had little doubt that "on Mount Zion are the tombs of the House of David and the tombs of the kings that rose after him."[69] However, he notes that the actual grave "is unknown" on account of the following chain of events: "Fifteen years ago, a [part] of the high place [*bamah*, i.e., the church] on Mount Zion collapsed. And the [Latin] patriarch [*patriarca*] told the one he had put in charge [with the rebuilding]: 'Take stones from the ancient walls and use them to rebuild the high place.'"[70] While two workers were "digging out stones from the base of the walls of Zion," they discovered the "mouth of a cave."[71] Hoping to find treasure, they entered the grotto, where they came upon "a large palace erected on marble columns overlaid with silver and gold. In front of it were a golden table, a scepter, and a crown. This was the tomb of King David. . . . These two men sought to enter the palace; but suddenly, a strong wind came out of the mouth of the cave and hit them, and they fell on the ground as though dead, and laid [there] until the evening. Suddenly, a wind came forth that shouted like a human voice: 'Get up and leave this place.'"[72] The folkloristic motif of laborers endangering their lives by entering a tomb is commonplace in stories about grave robbers. In this case, it also echoes ancient traditions concerning David's tomb, such as Josephus's account of King Herod's attempt to extract treasures from David's and Solomon's crypts.[73]

Returning to Benjamin's tale, the Latin patriarch was then informed of the discovery, whereupon he asked a local rabbi named Abraham of Constantinople (Arabic: al-Qūsṭanṭīnī) to confirm the site's authenticity. Benjamin attributes this entire narrative to the said rabbi, a "pious ascetic," who "told me these things"—a rare instance in which the Tudelan reveals his (oral) sources.[74] R. Abraham's appearance at this point in the story is apparently a narrative device that reflects a Jewish notion of ownership over the land's biblical localities, for the Christians required a Jewish seal of approval to affirm that this was David's sepulchre.[75] After verifying the site, R. Abraham suggested to the patriarch that they visit the tomb together the following day. However, the plan was aborted because the two bedridden workers refused to accompany them, "as God does not desire to show [the tomb] to any man. Therefore, the patriarch ordered that the place be sealed off and concealed from men to this day."[76]

The narrative's folkloristic style, its dialogues, dramatic turn, and attribution to a local eyewitness indicate that it originated as an oral tradition, but I am presently interested in its significance within the context of *Massa'ot*.[77] Elchanan Reiner, who first drew attention to the story's function as an anti-crusader polemic, contends that Benjamin "is proclaiming for all to hear that the site generally known as the 'tomb of David' is *not* the real tomb; the place usually shown as such is false—and the falsification is deliberate."[78] This seems to be an overstatement; Benjamin's caveat merely concerns the burial cave's precise location, given the fact that its entrance was sealed off.[79] The narrative does not challenge the popular belief that David and his successors were interred on Mount Zion.

Also, the images with which Benjamin (or his source) describes the burial chamber, such as the scepter and crown, evoke medieval Christian symbols of royalty. This Jewish adaptation of both the Christian pilgrimage site and the related imagery seems to be comparable to what postcolonial theorists describe as "ambivalent mimicry."[80] *Massa'ot* expresses a certain ambivalence toward Mount Zion, oscillating between a critique of a Christian "high place" and the attempt to appropriate it for a Jewish audience. The quoted narrative allows Benjamin to undercut the hegemonic discourse by a kind of counter-supersessionism: just as Christianity's claim to be the New Israel served to justify its exclusive control over both biblical past and sacred space, Benjamin reclaims the Davidic heritage for his own people by means of the pious figure of R. Abraham.

Following Saladin's victory (1187), the Ayyubids destroyed the crusader church; but Christian ownership of the venue was reestablished in the fourteenth century. On account of their trade interests with the West, the Mamluks granted the Franciscans the right to rebuild a monastery on Mount Zion and possession of the adjacent complex housing David's tomb. Yet another property included in this transfer was the Cenacle—a room above the Davidic sepulchre that was deemed to be the site of the Last Supper.[81] However, Catholic dominion over the compound was once again challenged during the early fifteenth century, when an Ashkenazi resident of Jerusalem sought to purchase the tomb. Taking advantage of the Jewish-Franciscan imbroglio, the Mamluk authorities converted the edifice into an Islamic house of worship, the shrine of Nabī Dā'ūd (Arabic: Prophet David). In 1488, Obadiah of Bertinoro summed up the developments at the contested site: "On [Mount] Zion, near the Tombs of the Kings, there is a large high place [*bamah*] of the priests of Francesco [Saint Francis]. In the past, the Tombs of the Kings were also under their control; but then a rich Ashkenazi came to Jerusalem and sought to purchase them from the king [the Mamluk sultan], and thus got himself embroiled in a conflict with the priests. At this time, [the Mamluks] took [the tombs] away from the priests, and they are now under the Ishmaelites' control."[82]

Whereas Obadiah's account suffices with single pejorative against the monastery ("high place of the priests"), the Franciscan guardian of Mount Zion, Francesco Suriano, exhibited considerably less restraint in his attacks against the Jews. In his Italian report from the turn of the fifteenth century, Suriano makes them responsible for the Cenacle's destruction by the Muslims: "And the reason for such ruin was the dogs of Jews, for they told the Saracens that under the chapel [the Cenacle] was the tomb of the prophet David.

When the lord sultan heard this, he ordered that the tomb and place be taken from the friars and dedicated to their cult [Islam], and so it was done. And the Saracens, considering it shameful that the friars should celebrate above themselves [in the Cenacle], . . . destroyed it."[83]

In 1481, Meshullam describes the church (Hebrew: *kenesiah*) of San Francesco and the tomb of King David as two distinct entities, one under Christian and the other under Muslim control. While the occasional Christian pilgrim—such as Felix Fabri (1483)[84]—still managed to slip in to the sepulchre, Meshullam fails to mention whether he was able to enter the holy place. In any event, he expresses no qualms about Muslim custody over the shrine.[85] Some forty years later, Basola, by contrast, openly laments that the Muslims only grant their coreligionists access. No less noteworthy is that Basola's account, which was composed shortly before the Franciscans were ousted from Mount Zion (by the Ottomans, in 1523), is free of antagonism toward the monks: "On Mount Zion, there is a place for priests similar in appearance to the monasteries [*conventi*] in Italy; adjoining it is a locked house with an iron door. They say that David and Solomon—may their memory be blessed—are buried there. Nearby is another house, also with a locked iron door; they likewise say that all the kings of the House of David are buried there. The Ishmaelites never allow anyone to enter these two places."[86]

To conclude, these various perspectives on David's tomb mirror a centuries-long conflict among Jews, Christians, and Muslims over a sacred shrine that—while of dubious authenticity—was equally claimed by all three religious communities as part of their Davidic legacy. At least between the twelfth and late fifteenth centuries, Christian control of the holy place aroused stronger feelings in Jewish travel narratives than the ensuing Muslim appropriation. It also bears noting that the terminology used for churches in the Hebrew accounts underwent a gradual change. Whereas Benjamin and Obadiah considered a church to be an idolatrous "high place," Meshullam and Basola referred to Christian institutions in a nonjudgmental fashion, using neutral Hebrew terms (*kenesiah* for church) or Italian loanwords (*conventi*). This is apparently indicative of a more relaxed attitude toward Christianity, once it had lost control over the sites in the Holy Land that were central to Jewish definitions of identity and community.[87] At the same time, Basola voices his frustration about the site's Ottoman custodians, who prevented non-Muslim pilgrims from visiting the shrine of Nabī Dā'ūd.

Subterranean Hebron: Religious Access Rights

Hebron's Tomb of the Patriarchs represents another site of discursive contest among the three Abrahamic religions. These tensions resound strongly in medieval Jewish travel literature, which raises questions concerning the impact of polemics on the representation of the real and vice versa.

The Hebrew Bible states that Abraham, Sarah, Isaac, Rebecca, Jacob, and Leah were buried in the Cave of Makhpelah "facing Mamre—now Hebron" (Gen. 23:19).[88] At the traditional site of their burial, a *temenos* (sacred precinct) was enclosed during the Hellenistic-Roman period (probably under Herod the Great, r. 37–4 BCE) with a finely crafted monumental wall, which by and large survives to this day to a height of about 60 feet (18 meters). (Petaḥyah marvels at the huge stones out of which "Abraham our father" constructed the "palace" or "sanctuary" [*hekhal*].)[89] The Byzantines then erected a basilica within the enclosure. After the Muslim conquest, the Christian structure was turned into a mosque known as Ḥaram al-Khalīl, the Sanctuary of Ibrahīm, the Friend (Arabic: *khalīl*) of God. When the crusaders conquered the area (in 1100), they converted the mosque back into a church, which Benjamin knows by its contemporaneous Romance name: "There is the large high place [*bamah*] that is called Saint Abram."[90] In his description of the site, Benjamin mediates various presents and pasts, much like the multilayered edifice itself.

The Tudelan contends that the shrine served as "a synagogue [*keneset*] of the Jews" during the early Islamic period ("in the days of the Ishmaelites"). This baffling claim is reminiscent of Petaḥyah's similarly outlandish statement about the Muslim conqueror of Jerusalem who built the Dome of the Rock as a sanctuary for Jewish worship. Tales aside, a letter from the year 1082 (shortly before the Latins' arrival) that was found in the Cairo Genizah sheds light on the site's pre-crusader status. When the letter was written, there was a Jewish society in Hebron that held a daily prayer service "in the Cave of Makhpelah."[91] It is unclear whether this Jewish ritual was conducted within the walls of the Ḥaram al-Khalīl, adjacent to it, or in a synagogue in the immediate vicinity. In any event, Benjamin and Petaḥyah, both of whose accounts date from the Frankish era, draw a sharp contrast between Christian and Muslim dominion over a place that is sacred to Judaism, as they idealize the Muslim past while bemoaning the Christian present.[92]

Benjamin accuses the current Christian overlords of fabricating a pilgrimage site (here Reiner's above cited statement does apply): "The *goyim*

[Christians] made there six tombs named after Abraham and Sarah, Isaac and Rebecca, Jacob and Leah. And they tell the *errant ones* [*to'im*, Christian pilgrims] that these are the tombs of the patriarchs. And [the pilgrims] give money there."[93]

Until this day the sanctuary contains six cenotaphs, each of which is enclosed in freestanding chapel-like structures. Benjamin knew that these monuments were not the real tombs. However, "misguided" Christian pilgrims were led to believe that they contain the patriarchs' remains, while only Jews were afforded the opportunity to visit the actual burial cave beneath the shrine's floor, as the Tudelan relates: "But if a Jew comes there, he shall give the guardian of the cave a fee and he will open an iron gate for him that was constructed by our ancestors; and one descends a staircase with a burning candle in his hand and gets down into a cave that is empty, as is the second [cave], until he reaches the third one.[94] Behold, there are six tombs: the tombs of Abraham, Isaac, Jacob, Sarah, Rebecca, and Leah, facing one another."[95]

Notwithstanding the different order in which the patriarchs and matriarchs are mentioned, their tombs' arrangement within the crypt appears to correspond to the chapels above (husband and wife face each other). Benjamin's account both mocks and mirrors the current Frankish Church of Saint Abram. Therefore, the case can be made that the Tudelan's descent to the real tombs was an imagined one. The most striking and paradoxical element of this story is its dual representation of a single place: the authentic burial site of the patriarchs below ground, which is reserved for Jews; and the spurious Christian shrines up in the church.

Petaḥyah's description of the expanse simultaneously ties into and diverges from that of his predecessor Benjamin. To begin with, *Sibbuv*'s protagonist gives the doorkeeper a gold coin in order to enter "the house of the patriarchs' tombs" (*bet qivre avot*)—the ground-level church; non-Christians were probably not admitted otherwise. Once inside, he notices three—rather than six—"alcoves" (*kokhin*),[96] which likely refer to the structures housing the cenotaphs. While this number may be the result of a scribe's slip (in premodern spelling, the Hebrew words for "six" and "three" differ by one letter only), some Christian pilgrimage accounts from the crusader period likewise speak of three chapels (one per couple).[97] Petaḥyah, like Benjamin, doubts whether they are the actual tombs. This critique of the Christian sanctuary seems to have been common among the Jewish residents of the crusader kingdom, as Petaḥyah received the following warning from the Jews of Acre before visiting Hebron: "Be aware that [the Christians] have placed three corpses at the entrance to the cave and they say that these are the patriarchs, which they are not."[98] Intent on seeing the genuine burial site, the Ashkenazi rabbi bribed the guard with an additional gold coin. Upon opening the door for the Jewish visitor, he allegedly confessed: "I have never let a *goy* [Christian] enter through this gate."[99]

As in *Massa'ot*, Petaḥyah then claims to have descended a flight of steps while brandishing a candle. His description of the subterranean passages is rather confusing, for the syntax seems to have been muddled during the transmission process of *Sibbuv*.[100] However, the picture that emerges is one of a "very spacious" outer cave. An opening on the stone floor is sealed off by sturdy iron bars, "the likes of which no man can make but only with the help of heaven"—time and again, the pilgrimage account employs the language of marvels—"and a raging wind blows out of the openings between the iron bars."[101] The gusts threaten not only to blow out the candles but to push the visitor backward. This same wind or draft turns up in several Jewish and Christian accounts of the site and is also redolent of the gusts emanating from David's tomb in Benjamin's aforementioned story. Petaḥyah interprets it as a miraculous sign that helped him realize "that the patriarchs are [down] there," and he prayed by the opening. However, unlike Benjamin, he does not purport to have entered the burial cave itself, as he got only as far as the bars.

Benjamin's and Petaḥyah's supposed descent into the crypt appears to offer a counternarrative against the Augustine monks' factual opening of the cave in 1119. This event is described in a twelfth-century Latin tractate about "the discovery of the holy patriarchs Abraham, Isaac, and Jacob" by one of the canons of Hebron: during prayer, one monk noticed "a light and sweet, yet cold wind" emanating from a crack in the pavement.[102] The clergy launched a protracted excavation that was carried out hesitantly by terrified workers (a motif that Benjamin also employs in his story about the discovery of David's tomb). They ultimately revealed the "most sacred corpse of Saint Abraham the Patriarch," the bones of Jacob and Isaac, and fifteen clay vessels containing more bones. After cleansing the relics in water and wine, they were displayed in a solemn procession.[103]

From a Jewish standpoint, the removal of their forefathers' remains was not only a desecration of Judaism's most venerated burial site but a blatant case of Christian supersessionism, as the Church had literally taken possession of the Jewish people's ancestors. Against this backdrop, one can readily understand Benjamin's and Petaḥyah's accounts of the Makhpelah as a form of narrativized polemic: while Christians exercise spatial control of the compound, it is the Jews—the legitimate heirs of the patriarchs—who are granted exclusive rights to the real graves, which are concealed from the general public. The Jewish authors' complete reversal of the actual balance of power vividly illustrates the potential of the travel narrative to reconfigure and subvert an existing hegemonic order.

Post-Crusader Era

In the wake of the battle of Ḥaṭṭīn (north of Tiberias, 1187), most of Palestine was back in Muslim hands after less than a century of Latin rule. From the standpoint of this study, the questions that beg asking are: How was the Muslims' renewed control over the Ḥaram al-Khalīl conveyed in the Hebrew travel narratives? Was it viewed in the same positive light as Muslim dominion before the crusaders, or did the Muslims now simply replace the Christians as the usurpers of "Jewish" sacred space?

Samuel ben Samson describes a pilgrimage to Hebron a generation after Saladin's victory over the crusaders. When his group of pilgrims, which comprised both French and Near Eastern Jews, tried to gain access to the Ḥaram al-Khalīl, only the most distinguished among them—an Iraqi exilarch (*rosh ha-golah*, or a scion of this Babylonian Jewish dynasty)—was allowed in.[104] The less privileged members of the company were denied entry into what was now an Islamic sanctuary. Nevertheless, they managed to gain the sympathy of a local dyer by telling him that "we came from a distant land to pray at this place and to prostrate ourselves at the place where our ancestors walked."[105] With the dyer's help, the pilgrims sneaked into the Ḥaram in the dead of night. Though the language is convoluted, it appears that Samuel also claims to have descended into the cave or some underground passage leading to it. Consequently, it stands to reason that he drew on some of the earlier Jewish traditions about the Makhpelah. Notwithstanding his surreptitious entry, the picture that emerges from this account is that Muslims granted Jews access to the mosque only under exceptional circumstances—as had been the case under the crusaders, according to Benjamin and Petaḥyah.

Under subsequent Mamluk and Ottoman rule, Jews were permitted only as far as the seventh step outside the Ḥaram al-Khalīl's southeastern entrance, where they prayed next to a hole that was believed to reach the cave. This state of affairs is supported by a list of pilgrimage places that was compiled in the fourteenth century by Yitgaddal, an Egyptian Jew.[106] Obadiah, who visited Hebron a few days before Passover 1488, offers a few more details: "There is a small window outside the wall [built] on top of the cave. They say that this window leads down to the tomb of our father Abraham. Jews are allowed to prostrate themselves and pray in front of this window. But they cannot enter the walled [compound] on top of the cave [the Ḥaram al-Khalīl]. I, too, prayed in front of this small window."[107]

This limited access of Jewish pilgrims to the site does not appear to trigger the same antagonism that informed the accounts of Hebron during the Frankish era. To wit: Muslims are not accused of idolatry, desecration, or supersessionism. On the contrary, Yitgaddal commends Muslims for "preserving the place's purity."[108] Perhaps drawing on the Egyptian Jew's account, *Yiḥus ha-Ṣaddiqim* (late fifteenth century) reports that "the Ishmaelites pray in purity and cleanliness" at the Cave of Makhpelah.[109] Similarly, Obadiah comments that Muslims "hold the place in much honor and awe."[110] The rabbi leaves no doubt that the burial cave is inaccessible to both Jews and Muslims. Instead, "the Ishmaelites stand above and lower lit lamps, which are always burning within the cave, by a chain through a shaft. And the Ishmaelites who come to prostrate themselves there throw coins into the cave through the shaft. . . . This is what I was told by some local Jews."[111] Though Muslims worship inside and Jews outside the sacred compound, Obadiah's and Meshullam's accounts demonstrate that the rituals of the two pilgrim groups closely resembled each other. According to Meshullam, the Jews also "throw money and various spices" through the mentioned hole in the outer wall[112]—a form of votive offerings that were thought to confer blessings upon the donor.

Not surprisingly, Re'uveni is the only other Jewish pilgrim who purports to have entered the Ḥaram al-Khalīl. In his account, which was penned shortly after the Ottoman conquest, the Jewish "prince" once more claims to have visited a Muslim site under the guise of a *sharīf*. On account of this assumed identity, he merited a grand tour from the mosque's attendants. Echoing the earlier Hebrew accounts, Re'uveni declares the cenotaphs to be a fraud and asks to see the real cave. He is thus led to the well-like shaft (also mentioned by Obadiah) from which lights are hung. After praying at this spot, the mysterious pilgrim badgers his hosts with additional questions about a possible entry into the cave, whereupon he is shown a sealed opening in the mosque's floor, which is usually covered with rugs.[113] Inquiring about the history of this entrance, Re'uveni is told how the cave was once blasphemously opened during the reign of the "second king after Muhammad" ('Umar Ibn al-Khaṭṭāb), after "the Ishmaelites had taken the Temple [Mount] from the Christians."[114] The caliph sent four men into the cave: three died shortly afterward, and the fourth was dumbstruck. As one can easily see, Re'uveni freely adopts several elements of Benjamin's earlier tale about the discovery of David's tomb. More pertinently, he is the only author who turns his predecessors' anti-Christian polemics against the Makhpelah's current Muslim custodians.

A number of Jewish travel narratives point to a flourishing Muslim *ziyāra* to Hebron in the post-crusader era. In particular, they elaborate on a custom peculiar to Muslim Hebron and known in Arabic sources as "Abraham's hospitality" (*ḍiyāfat al-khalīl*), or "Abraham's lentils" (*'adas al-khalīl*).[115] According to Yitgaddal, "four thousand pieces of bread and cooked lentils" are publicly distributed during the time of the Islamic afternoon prayer and "whoever wishes may partake."[116] Meshullam even claims that the Muslims "distribute at least 13,000 loaves of bread a day in honor of Abraham, Isaac, and Jacob"—a typical exaggeration by the Italian. Thereafter, Meshullam expounds upon the lavish menu: "In honor of Abraham, they distribute bread, tongues in mustard, and tender and delicious veal, such as Abraham gave to the angels; and in honor of Isaac, venison and delicacies such as he loved; and in honor of Jacob, bread and lentil stew, such as he gave to Esau; and this is [held] constantly, every day, and without fail."[117] Meshullam's detailed description of the menu is obviously a product of his imagination, which builds on midrashic associations. The meal of veal and "tongues in mustard" was, according to a Talmudic tradition, the meal that Abraham offered the "three angels" at the Terebinths of Mamre (Gen. 18);[118] and the "bread and lentil stew" (Gen. 25:34) is the same dish that Jacob fed Esau in exchange for his birthright.

Aside from the scriptural allusions, it bears noting that Meshullam paints a picture of extravagant Muslim hospitality in honor of the Jewish patriarchs. In fact, all Mamluk-era Jewish travelers display an unequivocally positive attitude toward this Muslim charity, which suggests that Jews were also beneficiaries of the largess. Obadiah's more realistic account leaves no room for doubt that the custom of "Abraham's lentils" was an interfaith experience: "Every day, they distribute bread, a stew of lentils, or some other dish of legumes to the poor—be they Ishmaelite, or Jewish, or uncircumcised [Christian]."[119] As reflected in *Yiḥus ha-Ṣaddiqim*, the food distribution went along with public jollity: "Every day at evening time, they blow [trumpets and strike] cymbals and sing songs at the entrance to the cave. And a number of people gather there, play music, and dance in honor of Abraham our father—may peace be upon him."[120]

All the above-mentioned accounts note that Jews were denied access to the shrine at Hebron once it was converted back into a mosque. In this sense, not much had changed since the crusader period. With the exception of Re'uveni, Muslim control of the sacred compound nevertheless did not elicit the same negative reaction from Jewish authors as its earlier Christian usurpation. This may be because Muslims tolerated a restricted Jewish presence outside the sanctuary's walls and allowed Jewish pilgrims to partake in the charity that was given in Abraham's honor. No similar accommodation of Jewish pilgrims—as limited as it may have been—is known from the Frankish period.

Chapter 5

Medieval Mingling at Holy Tombs

In addition to Jerusalem and Hebron, the age-old foci of Jewish journeys to the Levant, the accounts mention numerous burial sites of biblical figures and rabbinic sages in the Palestinian countryside that are collectively known as "tombs of [the] ancestors" (*qivre avot*) or "tombs of [the] righteous" (*qivre ṣaddiqim*) in Hebrew. The quintessential markers of the Land of Israel—as echoed in the cultural memory of premodern Jewry—seem to have been holy places and tombs rather than geographical features or political frontiers. The Hebrew itineraries tend to map these *qivre avot* by references to topographical elements, such as hills, caves, trees, or springs. Nonetheless, the texts reflect a conception of space from the perspective of an heir of religious traditions in lieu of an explorer.

In continuing the discussion of venerated tombs, this chapter raises a set of additional questions: Do medieval Jewish travelers evince any notion of sharing sacred space with a religious other—if not Christians, then perhaps Muslims?[1] Are they aware of pilgrimage sites as "liminal" spaces in which the boundaries of religion and social status potentially relax?[2] Alternatively, do they describe the interreligious convergence as an equal or an unequal encounter among followers of different traditions? Is there any perception in Hebrew travel writing of holy places as "contact zones," which Mary Louise Pratt describes as "social spaces where disparate cultures meet, clash and grapple with each other, often in highly asymmetrical relations of domination and subordination"?[3] Do the authors acknowledge an Islamic devotional landscape that is parallel to, and partly overlaps with, the Jewish one? Finally, how do their portraits of shared—or contested—religious sites in Palestine compare with their depictions of similar places in other parts of the Islamicate world? I begin my discussion in the Holy Land, and the second part of this chapter explores the sacred shrines of Iraq and Iran and their echo in the sources under review.

Sacred Shrines in Palestine

Nabī Ṣamwīl

One of the most frequently described *qivre avot* that attracted Jewish, Christian, and Muslim devotees is the aforementioned tomb of the prophet Samuel (Arabic: Nabī Ṣamwīl), near Jerusalem.[4] Like David's tomb, Samuel's reputed burial place was apparently established by the crusaders and subsequently claimed by both Judaism and Islam. Before analyzing its description in the travel accounts, it will be useful to look at the history and significance of this site.

According to the Hebrew Bible, Samuel was born in Ramatayim Ṣofim, in the hill country of Ephraim (1 Sam. 1:1), and was buried in his ancestral town, then called Ramah (1 Sam. 25:1, 28:3)—which scholars now believe to be the modern village of al-Rām (northeast of Jerusalem).[5] In contrast, the identification of current Nabī Ṣamwīl (northwest of Jerusalem) with Ramah probably dates back to the twelfth century.[6] Perched on a hilltop, this Frankish settlement was originally established purely for strategic reasons, as its occupants controlled the roads leading to the Holy City from the coastal plain. As noted, it was from this spot that the advancing crusaders first laid eyes on Jerusalem, in commemoration of which they christened the place "Montjoye." Shortly afterward, the church and monastery of Saint Samuel must have been established there.

Against this historical background, Benjamin's account of Samuel's tomb has a strong anti-Christian bent. However, differing from, say, his depiction of David's sepulchre on Mount Zion, the Tudelan is aware of the site's inauthentic character. In fact, *Massa'ot* accuses the crusaders of raiding Samuel's original burial site in (al)-Ramla and transferring the prophet's remains to Montjoye.[7] This claim is based on the erroneous identification of the city of Ramla (see Map 3)—which was established on the western plains at the turn of the eighth century—with the biblical hillside town of Ramah: "When the Edomites [Christians] took Ramla, namely Ramah, from the Ishmaelites, they found the tomb of Samuel of Ramah next to the synagogue of the Jews. And the Edomites exhumed him and transferred him to Shiloh and built above his [tomb] a large high place [*bamah*, i.e., church] that they call *Saint Samuel de Silo* unto this day."[8]

Benjamin clearly accuses the crusaders of violating Samuel's tomb and moving his remains to the Church of Saint Samuel (present-day Nabī Ṣamwīl), which he—here in accordance with medieval Christian tradition—also identifies with the biblical Shiloh.[9] He, moreover, claims that the prophet's "original" grave in Ramla (for which there is no evidence) had been marked by a synagogue; the Iberian traveler seems to imply that the Jews of Ramla owned the prophet's sepulchre and were then (literally) dispossessed by the crusaders. While Jews and Christians did revere the same prophet, the newfangled Church of Saint Samuel did not become a "liminal" space in which followers of both religions easily intermingled. Jews were probably barred from entering the sanctuary; and from a Jewish perspective, the Christian site was the ill-gotten fruit of the crusaders' usurpation of sacred tradition and relics. Hence the unwelcome Jews turned away in disgust from this idolatrous "high place," according to Benjamin.

Destroyed after Saladin's conquest of Jerusalem (1187), the ruins of the said church were later integrated into a newly constructed Islamic shrine marking the tomb of Nabī Ṣamwīl.[10] *Toṣ'ot Ereṣ Yisra'el* (dating to the thirteenth century) reflects this new state of affairs: "In Ramah, there is the tomb of Samuel of Ramah; there is also [the tomb of] his mother, Hannah, in a very beautiful building; and in front of the building is a prayer house [*bet tefillah*] of the Ishmaelites. Nearby is a well about which [the Jews] say that it is the *mikveh* [ritual bath] of Hannah."[11] The fact that *Toṣ'ot* lists other, adjacent stops on the Jewish circuit, such as the tomb of Hannah and her alleged *mikveh*, indicates that Nabī Ṣamwīl had by then become an accepted Jewish pilgrimage place.[12] At the same time, the Hebrew text uses a neutral term (prayer house) for the mosque that—in contrast to Benjamin's earlier invective against the idolatrous "high place" (church)—harbors no criticism of current Muslim dominion over the sacred venue.

In later accounts, the tone seems to shift: *Yiḥus Avot* (from the early sixteenth century) raises the question of whether the shrine of Nabī Ṣamwīl contained the biblical prophet's remains. Similar to the crusader-era portrayals of other holy tombs (David's tomb and the Cave of Makhpelah come to mind), *Yiḥus Avot* contends that Muslims worship at a mere cenotaph, while Samuel's actual burial place is in an inaccessible cave: "They made there the form of a tomb [a cenotaph] though [Samuel] is not buried there; and they did so for the sake of the Ishmaelites."[13] Its criticism of the site notwithstanding, the Hebrew source describes an annual Jewish pilgrimage to Nabī Ṣamwīl during the feast of Shavu'ot, on which occasion Torah scrolls were brought to the shrine from Jerusalem (Shavu'ot marks the revelation of the Torah).[14] In *Yiḥus Avot*, in other words, the contested holy place emerges as both fake and real at the same time.[15]

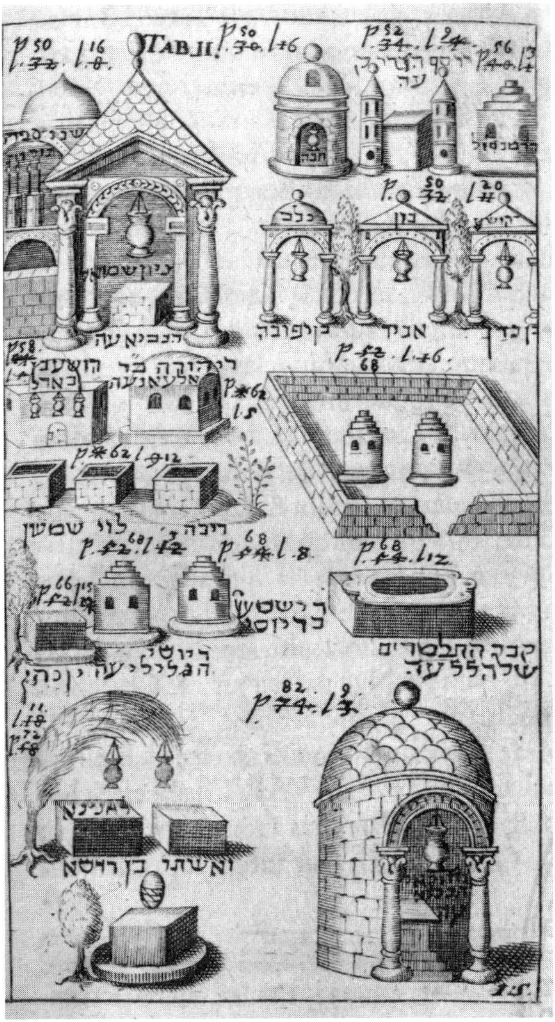

Figure 4. Johann Heinrich Hottinger, *Cippi Hebraici* (Heidelberg: Samuel Broun, 1662), a bilingual Hebrew-Latin edition of *Yiḥus Avot*; see Chapter 1. The reproduced page offers copperplate images of the traditional burial sites in Palestine of biblical prophets and Mishnaic sages. In the upper left corner is the tomb of Samuel, a pilgrimage place near Jerusalem that is commonly known by its Arabic name as Nabī Ṣamwīl. The shrine is here labeled *ṣiyyun shmu'el ha-navi*, "[funerary] monument of the prophet Samuel," in Hebrew. Courtesy of the Library at the Herbert D. Katz Center for Advanced Judaic Studies, University of Pennsylvania.

By the mid-fifteenth century, Nabī Ṣamwīl had become a religious "contact zone" between Jews and Muslims who were vying for control of the site, rather than sharing it. This is what is suggested by a tale told by the Italian pilgrim R. Isaac ben Meir Latif, whose anti-Islamic bias has been previously noted: "On one occasion, the Arabs prevented the Jews from entering the anteroom of the prophet Samuel's tomb for the purpose of prayer. But the righteous [prophet] . . . rose against them and choked [a Muslim's] throat for having prevented the Jews from coming to pray, and ordered him: 'Return the key to the Jews. They shall guard my doors, since they are my children, not you.' And he returned [the key] immediately."[16] In this story, which the author attributes to an old man from the vicinity (a frequently quoted source of pilgrims' tales), Samuel assumes the characteristics of a popular saint whose demise does not spell the end of his miraculous feats. Additionally, this uplifting story employs a frequent motif of hagiography whereby one who dares offend the saint (or desecrate his tomb) is immediately chastised through a punitive miracle.[17] However, the crux of the narrative seems to be the question of the sepulchre's legitimate custodians. To invoke Pratt's language again, R. Isaac bemoans the "asymmetrical relations" prevailing at the sacred venue. The return of the key to the Jewish community reverses their "subordination" by confirming the Jews' inalienable rights to their prophet's grave site.[18]

Regarding Samuel's tomb, Meshullam of Volterra (1481) bears witness to both Jewish-Muslim fraternity at and interreligious competition over jointly revered sites. He points out that the identification of numerous *qivre avot* was based on regional devotional culture.[19] Local Muslims not only endorsed Jewish traditions but proved to be indispensable sources for the identification of "Jewish" graves with which the pilgrims were previously unfamiliar: "The Ishmaelites honor all these places; and they have an oral tradition like ours; and they say to the Jews: Why don't you go to the tomb of such a righteous man [*ṣaddiq*] or to the tomb of the prophet whose name is such?"[20] Thereafter, Meshullam broaches the topic of Islamic worship at these same venues: "A number of times, the Ishmaelites wanted to close some of these tombs and transform them into sanctuaries under their [exclusive] control, but the Lord rendered their plans futile and would not listen to them, for 'the guardian of Israel neither slumbers nor sleeps' [Ps. 121:4]."[21] Though Meshullam believes that Islamic veneration affirms the sanctity of "Jewish" sites, he correspondingly portrays Jews in a precarious situation under Muslim dominion. Jewish access rights are a potential source of tension and, in this particular instance, are only upheld thanks to divine intervention. It thus stands to reason that the author had also heard a miraculous tale about Samuel's tomb.

A different picture of Jewish-Muslim relations at Nabī Ṣamwīl emerges from Obadiah of Bertinoro's account (which frequently diverges from Meshullam's). Obadiah strongly denies any rumors about the Jews' exclusion—quite possibly to encourage future pilgrims to flock to the hillside sanctuary: "The tomb of our lord Samuel of Ramah is still in the hands of the Jews. Every year, they come there from all the nearby areas to prostrate themselves on 28 Iyar [May to early June],[22] the day of his death; and they kindle above it large torches, in addition to the eternal lamp that burns there."[23] The esteemed rabbi stresses that Muslims would not tamper with pious donations to the saint; "The Ishmaelites hold this place in honor and are afraid to touch anything that has been dedicated in his name." In Obadiah's view, Jewish presence at the tomb was not subordinated to Muslim domination. In contrast, he accuses the Jewish community's own leadership of having stripped the shrine of its precious religious articles and votive offerings: "Once this place contained many silver utensils and gold-embroidered cloths that were very beautiful, but the wicked elders [of the Jewish community] of Jerusalem already sold all the donated property and estates, leaving nothing."[24] As a spiritual leader, Obadiah seems to downplay Jewish-Muslim competition over the devotional venue in comparison to intra-Jewish struggles.[25]

A generation later, Moses Basola reports that the Jews had their own prayer room "at one end of the building," which suggests that much of the compound was by then under Muslim custody.[26] Nabī Ṣamwīl was a crusader-era holy place, similar to David's tomb, which, after the Franks' defeat, became the focus of both Jewish and Islamic *ziyārāt* (plural of *ziyāra*). While several accounts testify that Jews and Muslims rubbed shoulders at the shared site, the majority religion, not surprisingly, asserted its dominance in the long run.

Beyond Jerusalem and Its Vicinity

Among Jewish pilgrims to the Holy Land, the purported burial sites of rabbinic sages and other *ṣaddiqim*, most of which were located in Galilee, were even more popular than the biblical tombs. This may have stemmed from Acre's transformation into the major port and center of the late crusader kingdom, as stated. When Jewish visitors disembarked in Acre, it was rather convenient for them to set out on their pilgrimages from the north. Whatever the reason, medieval Jewish travelers increasingly portrayed Galilee as a landscape with a special sanctity, even before the kabbalah of Safed (sixteenth century) would immortalize that image.[27] Time and again, the texts discussed throughout this book mention that the tombs of Jewish sages also attracted Muslim devotees who revered these local saints for their powers of healing and intercession.[28] (Christians, by contrast, do not seem to have venerated Jewish figures of postbiblical times.)

What is more, Hebrew itineraries from both the Frankish and early Mamluk period acknowledge Galilee's Islamic religious landscape, including Islamic shrines that mark a Jewish tomb. Surprising as it may be, many relevant passages in these works are free of polemical undertones and reflect that Jewish and Muslim pilgrims frequently intermingled at shared sites, where they similarly made supplications. Possibly, interfaith relations were more relaxed at these local shrines, since they were less significant to each community's self-definition than the highly contested sanctuaries of Jerusalem and Hebron.

A case in point is the reputed burial site of Jethro at Kefar Ḥiṭṭim (Arabic: Kafr Ḥiṭṭīn), a village nestled in the hills above the Sea of Galilee.[29] Islamic tradition identifies Jethro with Nabī Shuʿayb, a prophet mentioned in the Qur'an.[30] For this reason, the place is also discussed in the twelfth-century Muslim pilgrimage guide by al-Harawī.[31] While the anonymous author of *Toṣ'ot* (from the late crusader/ early Mamluk period) admits that the shrine was an Islamic sanctuary, he does not consider this a case of religious supersession. Instead, the Muslims' reverence for this "Jewish" holy place appears to confirm its sanctity, for "it is the custom of the Ishmaelites to build their prayer houses next to the tombs of the righteous."[32]

Another religious venue that features in Jewish (*Toṣ'ot*) as well as Islamic (al-Harawī's) pilgrimage guides is the tomb of Jonah ben Amittai, or Nabī Yūnis, in Kefar Kana (Arabic: Kafr Kanna), north of Nazareth. The Jewish source speaks glowingly of the Islamic shrine built over the tomb: "Over [Jonah's tomb] is a beautiful building, a house of prayer [*bet tefillah*] for the Ishmaelites."[33] In the early sixteenth century, Basola likewise points out that the tomb, which was marked by a "large distinguished building," was "in Ishmaelite hands." At the same time, he mentions that Jews were charged a five-dirham (a silver coin) admission fee that apparently was not levied on Muslim visitors; but in all likelihood, every pilgrim had to pay the additional dirham to light an oil lamp (after all, pilgrimage places are a source of revenue for their custodians).[34] In Basola's experience, the convergence of Muslim and Jew at this religious contact zone did not occur on an equal footing.[35]

At other sites, Jews and Muslims rubbed shoulders but disagreed over the identity of the person interred at a mutually revered shrine. For example, thirteenth-century Jews believed that a certain tomb in Yavneh (Yibnā, south of Jaffa) belonged to Rabban Gamliel "of Yavneh" (late first century), a founding figure of rabbinic Judaism; the Muslims held that it was the final resting place of Abū Hurayra (seventh century), a companion of the Prophet Muhammad. Though Jews and Muslims experienced their *ziyāra* to the same tomb as an affirmation of their particular identity, *Elleh ha-Massaʿot* does not mention a conflict over the sacred space and uses the now-familiar neutral phrase, a "prayer house [*bet tefillah*] of the Ishmaelites," in speaking about the shrine.[36]

Changing Rhetoric

While Muslims often began venerating established Jewish sites, the opposite also occurred. A clear example of a Jewish appropriation of a Muslim saint is the shrine (Arabic: *mashhad*) of Sitt Sukayna bint al-Ḥusayn, a granddaughter of Ali. Although she died in Medina in 736, her reputed grave at Tiberias has been revered since at least the twelfth century (it is mentioned by al-Harawī), and the extant structure was built a century later.[37] Jews not only participated in the saint's veneration but eventually Judaized her. After distorting the name Sukayna into the Hebrew *ha-zeqenah* (the Old Lady), her tomb was identified as that of R. ʿAqiva's wife, the daughter of Kalba Savuʿa.[38] The primary reason for this development was that the putative graves of R. ʿAqiva and his students are located in its vicinity. One of the earliest sources (1523) for this identification (of Sukayna with R. ʿAqiva's wife) is Basola's description of the mausoleum, which is tinged with polemical language: "The Ishmaelites have [there] a vexing [*meragez* or *margiz*, structure] with a large white tower [minaret]. [The Jews] say that R. ʿAqiva's wife, the daughter of Kalba Savuʿa, is buried there, and they call her the Old Lady."[39] Basola, who may be echoing local Jewish guides, essentially claims that it was the Muslims who usurped a Jewish holy place. In its choice of derogatory terminology for the Islamic shrine, his account clearly represents a discursive shift from earlier Jewish portrayals of sacred space that was shared by Jews and Muslims.

As shown above, the first instances of anti-Islamic content surface in Isaac ben Meir Latif's mid-fifteenth-century accounts of the Ḥaram al-Sharīf and Nabī Ṣamwīl.[40] Obadiah's anonymous student (1495) expresses similar sentiments by means of yet another folktale about a punitive miracle wrought by a deceased saint. In the student's telling, a Muslim woman had cursed R. Judah bar Ilaʿi (a second-century sage), whose tomb was shown at the

Upper Galilean village of 'Ain Zaitūn (Arabic for "spring of olives").[41] Having climbed an almond tree (she seems to have picked its fruit) that grew next to the pilgrimage site, the offender took a steep fall and broke her arms. When the rabbi later appeared to her in a dream, the woman understood the error of her disrespect. She proceeded to light candles at the tomb and was healed (shrines of saints were widely held to possess both curative and punitive properties). Less than three decades later, Basola repeats the same story (it may have been circulating among Italian Jewish pilgrims or their guides) but adds that the repentant blasphemer pledged her gold bracelets to the *ṣaddiq*. From the proceeds of their sale, she purchased olive trees that were used, along with contributions from other pilgrims, to cultivate a sacred grove in R. Judah's honor.[42] In both accounts, the Muslim perpetrator's initial punishment and subsequent "conversion" are obviously meant to bolster Judaism's self-perceived superiority over the younger religion—as well as its claim to the mutually revered holy tomb.

Basola recounts another folkloristic story with a similar message. About forty years before his visit in 1522, a legal dispute erupted between two other Upper Galilean villages, Farādiyya and Kafr 'Inan (Kufr 'Anan), over the water of a spring that flowed from the former to the latter. The residents of Farādiyya planned to dam up the brook; their downstream neighbors sought to prevent this by evoking ancient water rights. Though both parties involved in the dispute seem to have consisted mainly of Muslims, R. Ḥalafta—a venerated Mishnaic sage (*tanna*) who was interred in the area—intervened on behalf of the injured party. The rabbi appeared in a dream to a Jewish resident of Kafr 'Inan and instructed him to "search in my grave. There you will find a copper box. Inside, there is a deed recording how I purchased the spring from Naḥum of Gimzo [another Mishnaic sage], [and the agreement] that no man can dam up the water or irrigate his field until I first irrigate mine."[43] Following the dream, the Jew opened the grave (which is usually deemed to be a sacrilegious act) and found the writ. The residents of Kafr 'Inan presented the document to the Mamluk authority, who consequently upheld their rights. While R. Ḥalafta intervened on behalf of a village that by now had a Muslim majority, Basola's story ultimately confirms that the Jews were the historical owners of the tomb, the spring, and the village.

As evidenced by the above-cited examples, some Italian Jewish pilgrims from the mid-fifteenth century onward offer narrativized polemics against Muslim control of local tombs of saints. In earlier traditions, these holy places were perceived as a kind of common property that was shared by Muslim and Jewish devotees. Possibly, these later travelers echo a change in Muslim outlook and behavior. Following the ouster of the Franks from Palestine, Muslims were less inclined to welcome competition and may have asserted their ownership rights. If this was indeed the case, these folktales express the local Jewish population's anxieties over losing access to jointly revered sites. That these polemical stories are transmitted in the travel accounts of early modern Italian Jews seems significant, too. I suggest that the authors' representation of sacred space reflects their changing self-perception: as Italian Jews increasingly identified with their Gentile compatriots, they adopted certain Christian attitudes toward the Muslims' "occupation" of the Holy Land. In any event, it is remarkable how closely a few of Latif's and Basola's barbs against Islamic control of sacred space resemble the erstwhile Jewish polemic against the crusaders.

Sacred Shrines in Iraq and Iran

In the pages that follow, I reopen questions that were broached earlier concerning popular holy tombs that were revered by Jews and non-Jews alike. This time, the focus is on the pilgrimage sites and attendant customs in Jewish "Babylonia" (*bavel*) instead of the Land of Israel.[44] As opposed to medieval Palestine, Iraq never fell to the crusaders.[45] Another marked difference between the two areas was that the holy sites in Mesopotamia had not repeatedly changed hands among Jews, Christians, and Muslims. Against this backdrop, these questions beg to be asked: How are these historical and cultural distinctions reflected by Jewish travelers coming to Iraq from Europe? Were interfaith relations at the region's shrines viewed differently from those in Palestine, given that a competition with Latin Christianity had never been part of the local religious discourse?

Since few of the later travelers ventured as far as Mesopotamia, my discussion focuses on Benjamin of Tudela and Petaḥyah of Regensburg, who reported on the most famous Jewish shrines to the south of Baghdad. Some of these sites supposedly contain the tombs of biblical figures associated with the Babylonian captivity (sixth century BCE), such as Ezekiel and the exiled Judean kings Jeconiah and Zedekiah; others (which I do not discuss here) house the graves of eminent Talmudic sages (Babylonian *amora'im*) and later academy leaders (*ge'onim*). In all likelihood, the establishment of these sanctuaries indicates the local Jewish community's interest in confirming its own diasporic identity, as opposed to the legacy of their Palestinian brethren and that region's sacred space.

Correspondingly, Jewish pilgrimage in Iraq appears to have been part of a devotional culture that was unique to the area. For example, a brief perusal of the pilgrims' guide by al-Harawī—a near-contemporary of Benjamin—reveals a parallel ritual geography, since southern Iraq abounded with Muslim holy tombs, many of which were of particular importance to Shiites.[46] As opposed to the canonical pilgrimage to Mecca (*ḥajj*), the area's most significant Shiite *ziyāra* sites were (and still are) in the towns of Karbalā' (where Muhammad's grandson, al-Ḥusayn, was killed and buried) and Najaf, the next station on this literary tour.[47] If at all, how do Jewish travelers relate to this Islamic devotional culture?

The Shrine of Ali

Najaf (see Map 2) boasts the final resting place of Ali ('Alī Ibn Abī Ṭālib), the Prophet's cousin and son-in-law. Benjamin mentions the Islamic shrine, even though it was not venerated by Jews, but erroneously locates it in nearby Kūfa. This lack of geographical preciseness is not unique to the Jewish traveler, as Najaf is also overshadowed in Ibn Jubayr's account. Specifically, the Iberian Muslim chose to visit the mosque of Kūfa (in 1184), where Ali was assassinated.[48] When he later mentions Ali's burial shrine, Ibn Jubayr does so only in passing and without mention of the town (Najaf) that had sprung up around it: "A parasang to the west of the city [Kūfa] is the famous shrine named after Ali Ibn Abī Ṭalib—may God hold him in his favor—which is said to . . . hold his tomb. God knows the truth of this [matter] best. The construction of this shrine is most magnificent, according to what we were told, for on account of the shortness of our stay in Kūfa . . . , we did not see it."[49] Ibn Jubayr's skepticism about the authenticity of this site might betray his Sunni background (or, more accurately, his Almohad sympathies)—a topic beyond the framework of this book.[50]

In any event, Benjamin shares his fellow Iberian's bias against the sanctuary at Najaf, though he does not question whether Ali is buried there. He labels the funerary mosque a *bamah* (idolatrous "high place")—the same epithet that he employs for Christian churches.[51] Unless a copyist is responsible for this usage, the derogatory language is glaring because *Massa'ot* ordinarily refers to mosques by neutral terms, such as "prayer house" (*bet tefillah*).[52] In a similar polemical vein, the Tudelan calls Ali "the son-in-law of the madman," where "madman" serves as an invective against Muhammad. Much as Jesus is called "that man," premodern Hebrew literature commonly uses a substitute for the name Muhammad, which is derived from Hos. 9:7: "The prophet is foolish, the inspired man driven mad [*meshuga*'].”[53] Obviously, the rhetorical function of this invective is to deny any true prophethood after the last of the Hebrew prophets. To Benjamin, the status of Ali's shrine is on par with Jerusalem's Holy Sepulchre. It is the burial site of a saint that is not recognized by Judaism; and for this reason, he considers the shrine idolatrous.[54]

Massa'ot's description of Kūfa also stands out for its claim that the town housed the tomb of Jeconiah (Jehoiachin), the king of Judea who was exiled by Nebuchadnezzar in 597 BCE. The grave is said to have been covered by a “large building,” in front of which stood a synagogue.[55] In their juxtaposition, the shrines of Caliph Ali and King Jeconiah seem to epitomize how an important pilgrimage site belonging to the dominant religion led to the establishment of a similar structure by a minority community that sought to reinforce its own identity. That said, the Tudelan's book is the only source that locates Jeconiah's burial site in Kūfa.[56] Therefore, this royal tomb may be a mere fruit of the imagination of Benjamin, who felt a need to place it on the map, given the role played by the exiled king in the Jewish memory of Babylonia.

The Tomb of Ezekiel

In contrast to Kūfa, where Muslims and Jews, at least according to *Massa'ot*, venerated two different sites, a number of medieval Hebrew and Arabic accounts note that the prophet Ezekiel's burial place drew worshipers from both communities.[57] There is greater Muslim interest in Ḥizqīl (as Ezekiel is known in Arabic) than in other biblical figures that have been adopted in Islamic tradition, for he is identified with Dhū l-Kifl—a rather enigmatic Qur'anic prophet known as the “protector” or “guarantor.”[58] This identification surfaces in the guide for Muslim pilgrims by al-Harawī and Yāqūt's thirteenth-century *Geographical Dictionary*, both of which allude to the shrine's Jewish significance.[59] From a geographical standpoint, the sepulchral compound is situated between Karbalā' and Najaf, on the Euphrates, in a place that was called Bar Malāḥa in Benjamin's time but is presently known as (al-)Kifl, south of Baghdad (see Map 2).[60] Its mere location on the traditional route of *ḥajj* caravans from Iraq and Iran guaranteed the shrine a place on the Muslim pilgrimage circuit, a fact that Petaḥyah was well aware of: “Every Ishmaelite who goes to that place where Muhammad [is buried; i.e., Medina] goes via the tomb of Ezekiel and gives an offering and donation for Ezekiel and takes a vow and prays: Our lord Ezekiel, if I return, I will give you such and such.”[61] Petaḥyah states that pilgrims to the site believed that bringing votive deposits was likely to help them conceive children or render barren animals prolific. Whether under the name Ezekiel or Dhū l-Kifl, the saint was revered for his role as a protector or intercessor by Jewish and Muslim devotees alike.[62]

At the same time, Benjamin seems to be highlighting the site's Jewish character when calling it *keneset yeḥezqel*, Ezekiel's synagogue.[63] Petaḥyah similarly contends that the Jews possessed keys to its only entrance.[64] According to *Massaʿot*, the compound was maintained by an endowment, among whose assets were "estates, lands, and villages" that once belonged to the aforementioned King Jeconiah and later were confirmed by none other than Muhammad (the "madman").[65] In stating that the Prophet of Islam himself had reendorsed the pious foundation, Benjamin clearly attempts to showcase how Jewish institutions and rights were fully respected by the caliphal government. This stands in stark contrast to his account of Frankish Palestine, wherein he repeatedly inveighs against Christian usurpation of places sacred to Judaism.[66]

Neither Benjamin nor Petaḥyah takes issue with the Muslim presence at Ezekiel's shrine. In fact, both offer colorful canvases of an interreligious festival at the site, which the Tudelan likens to an annual fair (Castilian: *feria*). Generally, this sort of mass pilgrimage to a holy tomb took place on a fixed day or period on the religious calendar that was considered a particularly efficacious time for supplications. In the Islamic context, it would be called a *ziyāra* day, or *mawlid* (marking the saint's birthday); the corresponding Jewish term is *hillula*, which appears to be a relatively recent locution.[67] "Besides the Ishmaelites," as Petaḥyah relates, 60,000 to 80,000 Jews converged on Ezekiel's tomb during the week of Sukkot;[68] Benjamin speaks of an annual assemblage between Rosh Hashanah and Yom Kippur (perhaps the event covered the entire autumn holiday season). In his estimation, the crowd filled an entire campsite that was "about two miles" long.[69]

As was the case with many *mawlids* and *hillulas*, the festival of Ezekiel seems to have supported a market: Benjamin mentions "Arab merchants," who must have been selling provisions and souvenirs on the grounds. Not only did piety and commerce comingle at this site; the liminal space appears to have relaxed social and religious boundaries. The Tudelan reports that Muslim as well as Jewish dignitaries (including the exilarch and academy heads) attended the event.[70] Interreligious convergence, an annual fair, relaxation of social boundaries, and other elements of the quoted accounts conjure up an image of Ezekiel's tomb as a holy place that was shared by Jews and Muslims.

The Tomb of Ezra

Presently known as ʿUzayr (the Arabic name for Ezra), the tomb of Ezra is situated on the west bank of the Tigris, about 30 miles (48 kilometers) north of the Shaṭṭ al-ʿArab (the river's confluence with the Euphrates; see Map 2). Alternatively, Benjamin notes that it is "about two days" north from Basra.[71] Given that Ezra was one of the leaders of the returnees to Palestine from the Babylonian exile, it seems surprising that Jewish tradition would locate his grave in Iraq.[72] The explanation for this, according to *Massaʿot*, is that Ezra "went to King Artaxerxes and died there."[73] However, there is no evidence to support this claim. As in the case of Ezekiel, the tradition of Ezra's burial in Mesopotamia most likely stems from the Babylonian Jewish community's desire to assert its diasporic identity by establishing memorial sites for its most renowned historical figures. In addition, this tradition should be understood in the previously described regional context of Islamic shrines.[74]

As with Ezekiel's tomb, Benjamin depicts Ezra's burial site as a magnet for Jewish and Muslim pilgrims alike.[75] Yet the communities did not share the expanse; in an arrangement that may be described as a sort of cohabitation, they had separate places of worship adjacent to the burial chamber: "In front of the tomb, [the Jews] built a large synagogue [*keneset*]. And on the other side, the Ishmaelites built a prayer house [*bet tefillah*, i.e., mosque], on account of their great devotion [to Ezra]."[76] According to the Tudelan, the two communities rubbed shoulders at this sacred venue without ownership conflicts. As if to affirm this peaceful coexistence, Benjamin avoids any polemical reference to the mosque at Ezra's tomb, calling it a "prayer house" instead.

Daniel's Tomb

Following his account of southern Iraq, Benjamin turns to the Persian province of Khūzistān (the littoral lowlands of Iran). In the province's ancient city of Susa (Hebrew: Shushan; Arabic: al-Sūs), the Tudelan points to the reputed grave of the prophet Daniel—a shrine in the present-day Iranian town of Shūsh (see Map 2).[77] However, according to *Massaʿot* and a number of Islamic sources, the mausoleum no longer contained the prophet's remains:

> On the side [of the river] where the Jews live is the tomb of Daniel. Here the markets and abundant merchandise were located, and [the Jews] became rich. [The people living] on the other side of the bridge were poor because there were no markets and no merchants among

> them—only gardens and orchards. So they became jealous and said: "The only reason the others enjoy all this wealth is on account of the prophet Daniel, who is buried on their [side]." And they requested [permission] to [re]bury Daniel on their [side], but [the Jews] would not comply. As a result, [the two parties] fought against each other for a long time. And no one went forth or visited them because of the intense fighting . . . , until they grew tired, wised up, and reached a compromise among themselves to place the coffin of Daniel on this side one year and on the other side the next. Upon doing this, both sides grew wealthy.[78]

As per this narrative, which Benjamin seems to have taken from an oral source, both the Jewish and non-Jewish residents were convinced that good fortune emanated from the remains of Susa's patron saint, a supernatural power in which the heretofore neglected part of the town eventually demanded an equal share.[79]

Massa'ot omits the religious affiliation of the people living on the poor side of the river. In my opinion, they are not Muslims because Benjamin would have referred to them as "Ishmaelites." Since this tale subsequently speaks of "Arameans" (see below)—a term that the author otherwise uses to describe Syrian or Nestorian Christians—it is possible that he thinks of a Christian community.[80] Another version of this story turns up in the *Kitāb al-masālik wa'l-mamālik* (loosely translated as the Book of Roads and Realms) by the tenth-century Muslim geographer Abū Iṣḥāq al-Iṣṭakhrī. His version is set during the time of the Muslim conqueror Abū Mūsā al-Ash'arī, a companion of the Prophet Muhammad, who took Khūzistān between 638 and 642. Unlike Benjamin, al-Iṣṭakhrī expresses doubts as to the credibility of this tradition: "I have been told—but only God knows [the truth]—that a coffin was found in the days of Abū Mūsā al-Ash'arī. People said that the bones of the prophet Daniel—peace be upon him—were inside. And the People of the Book [*ahl al-kitāb*] circulated [the coffin] among their congregations in order to be blessed by it and to ask for rain in times of drought."[81]

As in *Massa'ot*'s version of the story, the remains of the prophet are passed around so that all can partake in the benefits, but the reward here consists of rain, not wealth. Of greater significance is the fact that the beneficiaries are the People of the Book (*ahl al-kitāb*), an Islamic category that includes both Jews and Christians. Hence it seems that the coffin of Daniel is passed back and forth between the town's Jewish and Christian "congregations."[82] Regardless of the Tudelan's actual source, it stands to reason that Benjamin's non-Jewish protagonists are indeed Christians.

In al-Iṣṭakhrī's tale, the above-mentioned Abū Mūsā al-Ash'arī settles the protracted conflict between the two sides by temporarily draining the riverbed and burying the prophet's remains in the middle of the waterway. Benjamin's version also features a Muslim leader in the role of mediator.[83] However, unlike the geographer's early Islamic backdrop, the Tudelan's story is set in the recent past, during the reign of the Seljuk sultan Sanjar bin Malik Shāh (d. 1157), arguably the most powerful Muslim leader of his time.[84] According to *Massa'ot*, when the sultan saw that "the coffin of Daniel was brought from one side to the other" through heavy traffic, he decided to put an end to the disgraceful treatment of the saint's relics. Specifically, Sanjar had the wooden coffin placed in a glass container (a kind of reliquary) and suspended by iron chains from the middle of a bridge spanning the river. He then issued the following order to the people of Susa: "At this place, you shall build an assembly house [or synagogue, *bet ha-keneset*] for all comers of the world. Whoever wishes may enter and pray, be they Jewish or Aramean [Nestorian Christian]."[85]

According to Benjamin's account, Daniel's coffin literally bridges the gap between the two sects. The Jews and Gentiles are able to share equally in the prophet's blessings, thanks to a Solomonesque sultan who finds a way to ensure the equitable distribution of the relics' powers. The Muslim ruler reportedly orders the construction of an interfaith venue reminiscent of *Massa'ot*'s description of Ezekiel's tomb. By calling Daniel's shrine a *bet ha-keneset*, the text appears to play with the dual meaning of the Hebrew term that may be translated as both "synagogue" or "assembly house," in a nonexclusive sense. If my interpretation of this story is correct, Benjamin is crediting a Muslim ruler with reconciling Jews and Christians vying over biblical relics. In this respect, Daniel's shrine at Susa emerges as the antithesis of Saint Samuel's church near Jerusalem (discussed above).

Massa'ot portrays Iraq and western Iran as a utopia of religious harmony: Islamic veneration of biblical tombs poses no threat to the access rights of Jewish worshipers; the two religions do not feud over the ownership of sacred space; and nothing suggests that Muslims are plotting to seize shared pilgrimage sites. Some rulers even strive to reestablish peace between Jews and Christians fighting over holy places and relics. This display of interreligious amity confirms, in Benjamin's view, the dignified status that his coreligionists enjoy in Muslim-ruled lands.

Why does the Tudelan offer such an idyllic picture of twelfth-century

Mesopotamia? As I argue in the following chapter, he deliberately employs Abbasid Iraq as a foil of crusader Palestine—as its desirable counterpart. This not only holds true for pilgrimage sites but for *Massa'ot*'s general picture of the Jewish communities in each of the two realms: whereas the Jewish population in the Land of Israel is small and humble, the Babylonian Jewish community is large and prosperous. It is tempting to speculate that Benjamin's portrait of harmonious Jewish-Muslim relations in the Middle East reflects a certain nostalgia for the conditions that had once prevailed in Muslim Spain, before the *reconquista* reached Tudela and other parts of central Iberia—a point to which I will return in the ensuing pages.

Chapter 6

Marvels of Muslim Metropolises

More than natural landscapes, cities feature prominently in premodern descriptions of foreign lands. Whether depicting a specific location in its own right or providing a backdrop for a historical narrative, urban environments play a crucial role in medieval Jewish travel writing about the Middle East. Against this backdrop, the present chapter addresses the following questions: What ideas about the Islamicate world are conveyed through representations of cityscapes? How are specific architectural features—such as palaces, mosques, and other monuments—depicted, and how do their images change across time? How and why do particular Near Eastern cities lend themselves to reflections about Muslim society, as well as the place of the Jews within that society, through their representation in travel writings?

Baghdad as a Caliphal Capital

Benjamin's account of Baghdad is one of the principal units of *Massa'ot*, as no other city—Jerusalem included—merits such a long description.[1] However, as in most of his book, the author is absent. Whether he actually visited the seat of the Abbasid caliphate (from 762 to 1258) or simply culled information about the city from other sources, Benjamin's chapter on Baghdad focuses on the caliph and his court in their capacity as a symbol of political, social, and religious order. The emphasis on royalty is evident from the outset of the Tudelan's disquisition on the Muslim metropolis: "Baghdad . . . is the great city and capital of the kingdom of the caliph [Arabic: *khalīfa*], commander of the faithful [Arabic: *amīr al-muʾminīn*], [a member of] the Abbasid [dynasty], from the family of the madman [Hebrew: *ha-meshuga'*, i.e., Muhammad]."[2]

The most striking feature of this citation is that the same sentence uses the caliph's official titles (*khalīfa, amīr al-mu'minīn*) along with the (by now familiar) epithet against the Prophet Muhammad: the "madman." To begin with, the Arabic terms that Benjamin intersperses within *Massa'ot*'s text (in Hebrew transliteration) should be considered a rhetorical device meant to support the illusion of authenticity of his account.[3] In the same sense, he refers to the Abbasids' (reputed) descent from the line of Muhammad (through 'Abbās, son of the Prophet's paternal uncle)—a genealogy that underpinned the family's bona fides to the caliphate. While "madman," in medieval Hebrew literature, is a commonplace substitute for the name Muhammad, this invective here clashes sharply with the dignified Arabic titles that precede it. This ambiguity testifies to the dilemma faced by a medieval Jewish author who sought to pen a credible account but was unable to acknowledge the religious authority implied by the titles he cited.

Benjamin's contention that the Abbasid caliph "is appointed over the religion of the Ishmaelites and that all the kings of Ishmael acknowledge him, and he is like the pope over the Christians" is anachronistic when related to the twelfth century.[4] Since its establishment in the mid-eighth century CE, the Abbasid caliphate had appreciably declined, as its succeeding representatives paled in comparison to such legendary figures as al-Mansūr (r. 754–775) or Hārūn al-Rashīd (r. 786–809).[5] Not only had the empire, which had once stretched from the Strait of Gibraltar to the Indus River, gradually fragmented, but the Abbasid caliph's supremacy over the entire Muslim community (Arabic: *umma*) was called into question by rival caliphates (most important, in Egypt, where the Fatimids had proclaimed themselves as Shiite counter-caliphs). Even as the nominal rulers of Baghdad, the Abbasids had long ceased to exercise their authority in person. What is more, they had basically lost control over the administrators—the Būyid *amīrs* in the tenth century and the Seljuk sultans from the mid-eleventh century onward—to whom they had formally delegated their power.[6] Thanks to Seljuk infighting, Caliph al-Muqtafī (r. 1136–60) and his son al-Mustanjid (r. 1160–70), whose tenures may have coincided with Benjamin's peregrinations, regained some of the caliphate's political and military independence, if only within the Abbasid heartland of Iraq. In any event, the Abbasids were still in the ascendancy as far as the Tudelan was concerned, and it is from this perspective that he depicts Baghdad as *the* capital of the Islamic world.

It is worth comparing Benjamin's account of Baghdad with the roughly contemporaneous one by Ibn Jubayr—another Iberian (albeit Muslim) traveler who visited the city in 1184: "Baghdad is an ancient city; and although it has never ceased to be the capital of the Abbasid caliphate . . . most of its traces have gone, leaving only a famous name. In comparison with its former state, before misfortune struck it and the eyes of adversity turned toward it, [Baghdad] is like an effaced ruin, a remain washed out, or the statue of a ghost."[7] Though Ibn Jubayr subsequently qualifies this statement to Baghdad's older areas on the west bank of the Tigris (where al-Mansūr had originally established the Round City in 762),[8] Benjamin's and Ibn Jubayr's respective city portraits nevertheless diverge: the latter describes the Abbasid capital as being in a state of decay, while the former still views it to be the undisputed center of the Muslim world.[9]

As opposed to his bare-bones descriptions of other places and rulers, Benjamin offers an in-depth account of the caliphal court and its trappings. A case in point is his depiction of the imperial palace that included a kind of botanical garden and hunting grounds: "[The caliph] has a palace in Baghdad that extends over three miles. Within the palace is a large forest with trees from all over the world, some of them fruit-bearing and others non-fruit-bearing; and there are all kinds of animals. The entire [expanse] is surrounded by a wall; and within the forest is a pool whose waters come from the River Hiddekel [the biblical name for the Tigris]. Whenever the king [the caliph] wishes to take an outing, feast and drink, [his servants] hunt birds, game, and fish for him."[10]

Over the centuries, almost every Abbasid ruler expanded and adorned the dynasty's legendary palaces on the east bank of the Tigris, to the point where the area had grown into a virtual city within a city.[11] Of all the royal residences, the most famous was the Crown Palace (Qaṣr al-Tāj). But the original edifice had burned down in 1154 and was never completely rebuilt,[12] so that it was probably under construction at the time of Benjamin's purported visit. The Second Crown Palace, which was built by al-Mustaḍī (r. 1170–80) farther upstream, was no less impressive, but there are doubts as to whether the residence was finished by the time the Tudelan may have passed through the city. Even so, there were still more than enough palatial complexes and royal gardens in Baghdad during the late Abbasid period.

However, it is unclear how a Jewish visitor to Baghdad, who seems to have traveled on no official mission, could possibly have secured information about the imperial residences, with the exception of hearsay. Also, Benjamin's account is rather dull compared with other portraits of caliphal plenitude—for example, the eleventh-century *History of Baghdad*, by al-Khaṭīb al-Baghdādī. A case in point is al-Baghdādī's description of a Byzantine delegation to the court of al-Muqtadir (r. 908–32). Among the many sights that were included in the ambassadors' tour of the caliphal estates was a sort of zoological garden with herds of wild animals, including elephants. Likewise, the chronicler mentions that a hundred lions were kept in one of the courtyards, "fifty to the right and fifty to the left, each handled by a keeper and collared and muzzled with chains of iron."[13] He also notes that the imperial compound contained all kinds of dazzling imitations of nature, such as an "artificial pond of white lead surrounded by a stream of white lead more lustrous than polished silver." There is no need to expand upon the reliability of al-Baghdādī's description: by the time of its writing, its motifs were already emblematic of the literary fame of Baghdad in the eyes of generations of readers.

In Benjamin's less elaborate account, the royal gardens similarly serve as representations of caliphal power and status.[14] Their exotic fauna and flora, in particular, are meant to underscore the opulence and cultural sophistication of Baghdad as an imperial capital and cosmopolitan center.[15] The same can be said with regard to *Massa'ot*'s depiction of the palace interiors: in pointing to costly material used all over the caliphal residence, the Tudelan clearly meant to evoke an aesthetic illusion of its opulence and ostentation; at the same time, his generic images and limited vocabulary undermine the desired verisimilitude: "Within the palace of the great king are large buildings of marble and columns of silver and gold, and ornaments of precious stones are fixed to the walls. In his palace are great riches and towers full of gold, silk robes, and every kind of precious stone."[16]

Also related to the royal household, both Benjamin and Ibn Jubayr depict the caliph as leading a life of splendid seclusion. The former reports that "he only leaves his palace once a year."[17] In Ibn Jubayr's words, the caliph "appears little before the public, being busy with his affairs concerning the palaces."[18] Despite similarities, there is a nuanced distinction between the two accounts. Ibn Jubayr interprets the caliph as being confined to his residence, while others wield the political power in his stead. Conversely, the Tudelan assumes that this state of affairs befits the monarch's elevated standing as the supreme ruler of the Islamic world. It is from this vantage point that the Jewish author paints a tableau of official court ceremonial.

A case in point is *Massa'ot*'s description of the caliph seeing off a caravan of Muslim pilgrims heading for Mecca (which Benjamin locates in Yemen!). Appearing at a palace window to greet the pilgrims, the caliph neither leaves the building nor addresses the people himself: "[The pilgrims] shout in front of the palace: Our lord, light of the Ishmaelites and splendor of our law [lit., Torah], show us the radiance of your countenance. But he pays no regard to their words. Then the tending ministers come and say: Our lord, spread forth your peace unto the people coming from distant lands who desire to take refuge in the shadow of your grace."[19] At this point, the caliph lowers the hem of his robe out of the window, so that his subjects can kiss the imperial garment. Although Benjamin clearly intends to give his readers a sense of the caliph's regal comportment, his message is impaired by the ambiguous language. Much like Christian Holy Land travelers, the Muslim pilgrims are "misguided" (*to'im*) in their aim.[20] In the eyes of his people, the monarch is "on par with the madman" (the Prophet Muhammad). Once again, the medieval Jewish author is unable to speak about a rival faith's prophet or pilgrimage destination in neutral terms. On the other hand, he deems Islamic law to be comparable with the "Torah"—a point I return to below.

To further illustrate the caliph's lofty status, the Tudelan elaborates on his attire during a public procession marking the end of Ramadan (the festival of 'Īd al-Fiṭr): "He rides on a mule dressed in the royal robes, which are made of silver, gold, and linen; on his head is a turban with precious stones of priceless value; but over the turban is a black shawl as a sign of modesty, as if to say 'Look! Darkness will cover all of this glory on the day of [the sovereign's] death.'"[21] As is often the case, there is a smattering of truth in Benjamin's narration: in commemoration of their mourning over the murder of Ḥasan and Ḥusayn (the Prophet's grandsons), black was the official color of the Abbasids.[22] The robes that were worn by the caliph at state events were usually black, and the same could be said for the garb of court bureaucrats and theologians. Benjamin, however, interprets this color scheme—like the caliph's ride on a mule—as a sign of modesty that evinces the transient nature of all human authority.

Thereafter, Benjamin paints a detailed picture of the caliphal entourage that includes "all the leaders of Ishmael dressed in fine robes and riding on horses," among them the princes of Arabia, Turkey, Persia, Media, and beyond.[23] The procession advances from the royal palace to the Congregational Mosque of al-Mansūr: "Along the road that [the caliph] takes to the prayer house [*bet ha-tefillah*], all the walls are adorned with garments of silk and purple, and men and women sitting in the street sing all kinds of songs and dance before the great king who is called *al-khalīfa* [the caliph], and they greet him in a loud voice saying: 'Peace unto you, our lord the king and light of the Ishmaelites.' He kisses his robe and gives them a sign of greeting—touching his robe with his hand. He then [goes] to the courtyard of the prayer house and ascends a wooden tower [a *minbar*, or pulpit] and expounds on their Torah [the Qur'an] to them."[24]

Given the unusually vivid description of this scene, should the reader assume that the Jewish traveler slipped into the mosque and witnessed the caliph delivering a *khuṭba* (Islamic sermon)? In the absence of any textual hint, it stands to reason that this passage draws on some unidentified source. It is worth noting that Benjamin employs here disinterested or positive terminology in all that concerns the Islamic religion. He calls the mosque a "prayer house" and the Qur'an "their Torah." He subsequently describes the caliph's slaughter of a camel on occasion of ʿĪd al-Fiṭr as "their paschal sacrifice [*sheḥiṭat pisḥam*]." The comparison that the Tudelan draws between the Islamic and Jewish rituals does not imply that they are interchangeable; rather, his objective is merely to decode an alterity into terms that are culturally acceptable to his readership. Benjamin is incapable of recognizing Muhammad's prophethood, but Islam frequently evokes positive associations—which stand in sharp contradistinction to his unequivocally negative outlook toward Christianity, as evidenced in previous chapters.

As firm evidence of the Muslim ruler's righteousness and philanthropy, Benjamin also elaborates on Baghdad's "great hospital," for which he once more uses the appropriate Arabic term: *dār al-māristān*. In fact, ever since the Būyid prince ʿAḍud al-Dawlah founded his famous clinic in the tenth century,[25] Baghdad's public hospitals became a staple of medieval travel writing about the Middle East. According to Ibn Jubayr, the medical center was situated in the aptly named western suburb of Sūq al-Māristān (Market of the Hospital).[26] While *Massaʿot* locates the hospital on the Euphrates, instead of the Tigris, and thus at quite a distance from the caliphal capital (this may have been a scribe's error), both Iberian voyagers note that the institution took up a colossal building and consider it an exceptionally advanced facility by any standard. In the Tudelan's words, "There are about sixty physicians' stores, and they all receive their drugs and all their needs from the king's house. Every patient who comes there is maintained by the treasure of the king, and is cured."[27] While some of the described cures sound rather backward (the mentally ill are shackled) to the modern reader, Benjamin is trying to prove that the caliph was exceedingly benevolent: "All this the king does out of charity to all who come to the city of Baghdad, whether they are sick or insane; for the king is a pious man and his intention is good in this respect."

Regarding topics and motifs, Benjamin's chapter on Baghdad clearly echoes medieval Arabic descriptions of the Abbasid capital. However, his rather limited Hebrew produces a far less informative and mellifluous account than, say, Ibn Jubayr's highly accomplished *Riḥla*. Given the doubts as to whether he was capable of consulting written Arabic, Latin, or vernacular texts, it stands to reason that the Jewish author drew on oral sources. But why did a Jew from Christian Navarre take the trouble to fashion such a detailed account of a distant Muslim metropolis? Aside from the fact that it was almost compulsory for medieval travel writers to spice their works with marvels of distant cities, Benjamin's portrait of caliphal splendor and piety appears to serve as a backdrop for his description of Baghdad's Jewish community, which "lives in peace, tranquillity, and honor under the great king."[28] As the Tudelan contends, the Jews' privileged situation was rooted in the fact that the caliph was "very fond" of them. Not only did the caliph employ many Jewish servants; he was well versed in the Torah and even knew how to read and write in the Hebrew language.[29]

Baghdad as a Jewish Capital

Beyond its function as the Abbasid capital, Baghdad emerges from Benjamin's account as the medieval Jewish world's principal metropolis. According to *Massa'ot* (MS London), there were "about forty thousand Jews" in twelfth-century Baghdad.[30] This exceptionally high estimate (Asher's text mentions only a thousand) is impossible to verify, and the author does not discuss how he obtained this information.[31] Regardless of its true size, it is obvious that Benjamin sought to portray Baghdad Jewry as the most prosperous Jewish community of his era. In the same sense, he mentions "twenty-eight synagogues of the Jews, some in Baghdad [itself] and [others in] al-Karkh, which is on the other side of the Hiddekel [Tigris] River, for the river divides the city."[32] The community's most prestigious house of worship was the Great Synagogue of the exilarch, or *rosh ha-golah* (the figurehead of Babylonian Jewry; see below), an impressive structure with "marble columns of all kinds of color overlaid with silver and gold."[33] (As in the case of the caliphal palace, Benjamin highlights expensive materials used in the building's construction.)

In addition, the Tudelan enumerates ten Jewish academies and identifies each of their leaders (*ge'onim*; singular, *ga'on*), most notable among them R. Samuel ben 'Eli (or 'Ali, d. 1194). According to *Massa'ot*, Samuel had a pedigree that went back to the biblical Moses.[34] Due to the rarity of this sort of genealogy, it stands to reason that Benjamin simply fabricates a lineage to rival the Abbasids' claim of descending from the Prophet Muhammad's family. Petaḥyah, by contrast, states that Samuel was a scion of (and hence named after) Samuel of Ramah;[35] the Tudelan traces the lineage of another Baghdad scholar, R. El'azar ben Ṣemaḥ, back to the same prophet. (This indicates that the traditions regarding the sages' pedigrees were mixed up at some stage.) Both texts highlight the putative biblical bona fides of the Iraqi Jewish leadership, as *Sibbuv* informs its readers that "all of them have a genealogy going back to the [biblical] tribes."

In many other ways, Benjamin embellishes his portrait of Baghdad's Jewish community with numerous biblical references and thereby creates a picture of the Abbasid capital that sharply contrasts with his account of Jerusalem. For example, he claims that the aforesaid R. El'azar ben Ṣemaḥ and his brothers "know how to cantillate the hymns like the singers at the time the Temple was standing."[36] The Tudelan perceives twelfth-century Iraqi Jewry to be a link in an unbroken chain that goes all the way back to the (First or Second) Temple. Far from being peripheral to Zion, diasporic Baghdad hosts the most vibrant of all Jewish centers, in Benjamin's worldview. Conversely, he and other contemporaneous Jewish travelers found only a handful of lowly Jewish tanners in crusader Jerusalem, as will be recalled.[37]

Baghdad Jewry's highest official was the Babylonian exilarch—the "head of the diaspora" (Hebrew: *rosh ha-golah*; Aramaic: *resh galuta*). With roots in pre-Islamic times,[38] this office reached the height of its prestige and power in the early Abbasid era, when the *rosh ha-golah* emerged as the Jewish community's representative before the caliph—who, at the time, was the unrivaled leader of the entire Islamic world.[39] By the twelfth century, however, both the Abbasid caliphate and Babylonian exilarchate—reduced to largely ceremonial status—were mere shadows of their glorious past. Against this backdrop, it may seem surprising that *Massa'ot* paints such an idealized portrait of Baghdad, its Muslim rulers, and Jewish elite. Whether he was unaware of the historical realities or chose to ignore them, Benjamin depicts Baghdad as a dual capital: the metropolis of the Abbasid caliphate, on the one hand; and the seat of Jewish royalty, on the other.

As reflected by *Massa'ot*, much of the *rosh ha-golah*'s mystique—even during a period of decline—was rooted in the fact that the holders of this hereditary position came from a family that supposedly descended from the House of David—through the exiled King Jeconiah, whose tomb Benjamin locates in Kūfa.[40] This fine pedigree is showcased by the Jewish traveler:

> At the head of all [the Jews] is Daniel ben Ḥisdai, who is called our lord the head of the diaspora of all of Israel; he has a written pedigree going

> back to David King of Israel; and the Jews call him our lord the exilarch, and the Ishmaelites call him our lord son of David [Arabic: *sayyidnā ibn dāwūd*]. He possesses great authority over all the communities of Israel at the hands of the commander of the faithful [Arabic: *amīr al-mu'minīn*, the caliph], the lord of the Ishmaelites, for thus the madman [Muhammad] commanded his descendants [the Abbasids, to do]. He gave [the exilarch] a seal of authority over all the holy congregations [of Israel] who are living under his jurisdiction [lit., Torah].[41]

Of course, the exilarch's position depended on the support of his constituents and the Muslim government, which could veto or confirm the Jewish community's candidate.[42] In tracing the caliphal appointment of the *rosh ha-golah* back to an order by Muhammad, the Tudelan aims to anchor this Jewish institution in the very roots of Islam. Although Islamic tradition does not attribute any saying (*ḥadīth*) concerning the exilarch to Muhammad, later Muslim writers accord a great deal of significance to the Davidic lineage of the *ra's al-jālūt* (the Arabic equivalent of the Aramaic *resh galuta*).[43] As with the Abbasids, genealogies were viewed to impart their medieval holders with authority.

According to *Massa'ot*, Muhammad even decreed "that everyone, be they Ishmaelite or Jew, or belonging to any other nation within his kingdom, should rise up before [the exilarch] and greet him. But whoever does not rise up before him should receive a hundred lashes."[44] This passage raises several questions concerning the status of non-Muslims in Islamic society, for it is hard to believe that the government would have required Muslims to publicly honor a representative of the *ahl al-dhimma* (the "protected" yet subjected non-Muslim minority), much less severely punish those who failed to do so. Benjamin's depiction of a court visit by the exilarch poses similar problems:

> Horsemen, non-Jewish and Jewish, escort [the *rosh ha-golah*] every Thursday when he goes to pay a visit to the great king [the caliph] and proclaim in advance: "Make way for our lord the son of David, as is his due." And they say in their [Arabic] language: "*I'amalū ṭarīq li-sayyidnā bin dāwūd* [Make way for our lord the son of David]." He rides on a horse and dons garments of silk and embroidery, along with a large turban on his head. On the turban is a large white shawl bearing a chain with the seal of Muhammad written on it.[45] He appears before the king and kisses his hand. Then the king rises before him and places him on the throne that Muhammad ordered to be made in his honor. And all

> the kings of the Ishmaelites who come to pay a visit to the king rise in front of [the exilarch]. The *rosh ha-golah* is seated on his throne opposite [the caliph], for in this fashion Muhammad commanded to uphold what is written "The scepter shall not depart from Judah; nor the ruler's staff from between his feet; until Shiloh comes and the homage of peoples be his" [Gen. 49:10].[46]

It bears emphasizing that, according to this passage, the Jewish representative had regular access to power, as he was received by the caliph "every Thursday." Moreover, the exilarch's procession through the streets of the capital was a spectacle in its own right. While the pomp that Benjamin describes was commensurate with that of the Abbasid court ceremonial, his account seems to be a secondhand report, at best. In fact, quoting the ushers' call in Arabic, the Tudelan employs yet another literary device for conveying authenticity and obtaining credit from his audience.

The above-cited passage elicits further questions concerning the position of *dhimmīs* (members of a "protected" non-Muslim minority) in Islamic society. At least according to the letter of the law (as laid down in the so-called Pact of 'Umar), all Jews (and Christians) were prohibited from wearing ostentatious garb or riding on horseback.[47] Since every Muslim regime's interpretation and enforcement of these rules varied appreciably, can Benjamin's account of the *rosh ha-golah*'s ride through the streets of Baghdad be considered evidence that these restrictions were neglected in twelfth-century Iraq—at least with respect to this Jewish leader of noble lineage? The rhetorical nature of this section precludes any such conclusion, for the author's gushing portrait of the exilarch appears to be a mirror image of his representation of the caliph. Put differently, depicting the Abbasids as if they were still the undisputed rulers of the Islamic world enables Benjamin to present the *rosh ha-golah* as the quasi-royal head of the Jews.

At the very least, the part about the caliph rising before the Jewish representative to seat him on a "throne that Muhammad ordered to be made in his honor" must be hyperbole. This gesture implies that the caliph recognizes the exilarch's status as a descendant of the royal House of David. What is more, the arrangement of both leaders' thrones opposite each other suggests that the *rosh ha-golah* is the caliph's equal, if not superior. This amounts to a role reversal of the *dhimmī*'s standing vis-à-vis the Muslim ruler. In a similar vein, Benjamin has Muhammad applying Gen. 49:10 (Judah's blessing from his father, Jacob) to the *rosh ha-golah*, thereby echoing the well-known rabbinic tradition: "'The scepter shall not depart from Judah'—these are the exilarchs in Babylonia who are *ruling* the people of Israel with a staff."[48] By putting this interpretation into the mouth of Muhammad, the traveler conveys the impression that even Muslims consider the exilarch to be the ruler of the Jews.

Benjamin clearly inflated the Jewish representative's status in his relationship to the Muslim government, as further illustrated by his narration of the *rosh ha-golah*'s installation. As indicated, any such appointee must be confirmed by the caliph. Although there is no extant writ of an exilarchal appointment, several documents pertaining to the inauguration of the Nestorian *katholikos,* the official head of the Nestorian Christians, have survived.[49] In fact, *Massa'ot* is the only source that even alludes to such an investiture of the Jewish dignitary. According to Benjamin, it was incumbent upon the exilarchal candidate to pave his way to office by means of large gifts of money "to the king, the princes, and the ministers."[50] This testimony is backed by a letter that was written (about two decades after Benjamin's journey) by the aforementioned *ga'on* Samuel ben 'Eli.[51] Therein the academy head questions the scholarly credentials of a recently installed exilarch and attributes his appointment solely to bribery and political connections.[52]

Massa'ot also touches on the *rosh ha-golah*'s inauguration ceremony: "On the day that the king [caliph] invests [the exilarch] with authority, they have him ride in the viceroyal carriage [Hebrew: *mirkevet ha-mishneh*]. And they accompany him from the palace of the great king to his [own] residence with drums and dances."[53] From a historical perspective, a procession accompanied by drums is well recorded in accounts of similar events for other (non-Jewish) Abbasid officials.[54] That said, the exilarch's carriage ride through the streets of Baghdad seems to be a figment of the Iberian Jew's imagination, for this means of transportation had been virtually gone from the Middle East since late antiquity.[55] (After Roman roads had fallen into disrepair, carriages—as differentiated from ox carts—were also a rare sight in medieval Europe.) As a result, it appears that Benjamin sought to draw a correlation between the *rosh ha-golah* and the biblical Joseph, who, in Gen. 41:43, is chauffeured in a "viceroyal carriage," as the pharaoh's second in command.[56]

There is another account by an Iberian Jew that has Jewish dignitaries riding carriages on occasion of their visit to the caliph. Glancing at Abraham Ibn Da'ud's chronicle of rabbinic history, *Sefer ha-Qabbalah* (Book of Tradition, 1160/61), will prove helpful in understanding Benjamin's representation of Abbasid Baghdad. For his part, Ibn Da'ud narrates that "seven hundred Jews" traveled "in seven hundred carriages" from Cordoba to Madīnat al-Zahrā' to meet the Andalusian caliph al-Ḥakam II (r. 961–76) at his country residence.[57] In another parallel to Benjamin's portrait of the exilarch, Ibn Da'ud relates that during their court visit, the Cordovan Jews were "attired in royal garb and wearing the headdress of Muslim officials." Because Ibn Da'ud composed his chronicle two centuries after the depicted events (around the time of Benjamin's travels), his account—written in Castilian Toledo—seems to be no more reliable than the Tudelan's. The argument can be made that Ibn Da'ud and Benjamin, in their descriptions of Jewish dignitaries at an Islamic court, voice a shared nostalgia for the bygone times of the Andalusian caliphate, as viewed by later generations of Jews living in Christian Spain.[58]

To return to Benjamin's representation of Baghdad as a Jewish metropolis: beyond exaggerating the *rosh ha-golah*'s standing at the caliphal court, the Tudelan also overestimates his position vis-à-vis other Jewish institutions. According to *Massa'ot*, the twelfth-century exilarchate was still at the height of its power, for the office's authority purportedly extended over all the Jewish communities in Mesopotamia, Persia, Khurāsān, Yemen, the "land of the Turks," Samarkand, and India.[59] "The exilarch authorizes them to appoint a rabbi or cantor [*ḥazzan*] in each community, as they come to him to receive ordination [*semikhah*] and authority [*reshut*], and they bring him presents and offerings from the ends of the earth."[60] In short, Benjamin contends that the *rosh ha-golah*'s powers and prerogatives were recognized by Jewish communities throughout the Abbasid Empire and beyond and thereby mirrored the caliph's authority as head of the universal Muslim community. However, the Tudelan's claims are contradicted by his contemporary Petaḥyah, who notes that it was the *ga'on* Samuel ben 'Eli, not Daniel ben Ḥisdai, who presided over the appointment of Jewish community officials "in all of Assyria [northern Mesopotamia], Damascus, in the cities of Persia and Media, and in Babylonia [central and southern Iraq]."[61]

While the present context is ill-suited for a disquisition on the exilarch's or the *ge'onim*'s purview, recent scholarship assumes that both the *rosh ha-golah* and the heads of the rabbinic academies claimed jurisdiction over the Jewish denizens of certain regions, which came to expression in matters of taxation, fund-raising, and the appointment of community officials.[62] At the same time, it appears as though there were overlapping areas of authority and that the officeholders frequently challenged one another's rights. In all likelihood, affiliations shifted and constituencies had a certain choice as to whom they paid religious dues—the yeshiva leaders or the *rosh ha-golah*. By the time of Benjamin and Petaḥyah, the once-famous academies of Sura and Pumbedita, much like the exilarchate, no longer commanded universal Jewish allegiance, as new distinguished centers of learning had sprung up in North Africa and Europe.[63]

Baghdad's decline as a Jewish metropolis is echoed by Judah Alḥarizi, roughly half a century after Benjamin and Petaḥyah. Assuming his usual satirical tone—he still jokingly calls Baghdad "the ornament of all cities"—the poet reports that the Jewish community's distinguished centers of learning had seen better days: "From [Mosul] I journeyed to 'Adinah [Baghdad].[64] It is the ornament of all cities. Since the days of old, there were world-renowned geniuses [*ge'onim*] and scholars there. But today, its sages have perished, and only callow youth remain. The fine flour has been removed, and the chaff is left behind. The lions are dead, and foxes have come in their stead."[65]

Despite these longtime developments, however, the symbol character of the *rosh ha-golah* as a descendant of King David continued to reverberate in the Jewish world well after the institution had lost its luster, much as Baghdad continued to serve as a pervasive cultural reference point long after its own fall from grace. Evoking the fantasy of a Jewish ruler of Davidic lineage, the Tudelan's account almost defies the fact that until the time of redemption, all Jewish communities—including those in the Land of Israel—were deemed to be a form of diaspora (*galut*). Baghdad emerges in Benjamin's account as the antithesis of crusader Jerusalem (as already stated). More specifically, the Muslim metropolis serves him as an "elsewhere" that offers much of what Zion lacked under Frankish rule: a viable Jewish community, respected Jewish dignitaries, and, above all, a certain degree of interreligious sociability. In providing a European Jewish readership with a means for reflection on the diaspora's potential of empowerment, such a counter-reality obviously offered a consoling message.

In contrast to nineteenth-century travel writers, the authors discussed in this study had yet to perceive the East as an aesthetic construct. Therefore, they eschewed painting picturesque city portraits in the Romantic sense. On the other hand, medieval travel literature is inclined to marvel at the wonders and curious sights of foreign places. In the ensuing pages, I track what the corresponding Arabic literature refers to as the "marvels of metropolises" (*'ajā'ib al-amṣār*) through descriptions of such evocative places as Damascus and Alexandria.[66] Benjamin's *Massa'ot* shares much of the lore about both cities that can be found in Muslim-authored travel accounts in more elaborate form. While he clearly engages in a conversation with these *'ajā'ib* traditions, it is doubtful that he read any of the *riḥla* literature (as stated above), wherefore they must have reached him through other—most likely, oral—sources. In telling his own versions of these Arabic tales, the Jewish traveler may offer a glimpse into his own personal encounters on the road, about which he is otherwise totally silent.

Damascus

Though written only about a decade apart, Benjamin's and Petaḥyah's respective accounts of Damascus mirror a slightly different historical background. The former experienced the city under the reign of Nūr al-Dīn Zangī, a member of the Turkish Zengid dynasty, who unified Syria under his rule (and hence posed a considerable threat to the crusaders).[67] In contrast, Petaḥyah already reflects a change in the political map after Nūr al-Dīn's death (1174), when Damascus fell into the hands of Saladin (the "king of Egypt"), who would later expel the Latins from much of the Levant.[68] Following passing references to the political situation, both travelers dwell on the Syrian metropolis's natural environment.

Only surpassed by his description of Baghdad, Benjamin's portrait of Damascus surely stands out within *Massaʿot* in its degree of detail: "Damascus . . . is a large and beautiful city that is surrounded by walls. It is [situated in] a country of gardens and orchards with an extent of fifteen miles in every direction. There is no land [full] of fruit like this in all the world. From Mount Hermon descend toward [the city the rivers] Amana and Pharpar, for it sits at the foot of Mount Hermon. The Amana flows through the city, and the waters are channeled through aqueducts [lit., bridges] to all the houses of the wealthy [lit., great ones] and to the streets and marketplaces. And the Pharpar flows between their gardens and orchards."[69] The city's unique location within a vast agricultural belt (the Ghūṭa Oasis) also attracted comment from Petaḥyah, who picked up the following saying that the "Ishmaelites" had about the place: "If paradise is on earth, then Damascus is paradise. If it is in heaven, then Damascus lies opposite it on earth."[70] He is obviously alluding to the same dictum as Ibn Jubayr, his Muslim contemporary: "Wherever you look on its four sides, its ripe fruits hold the gaze. By God, they spoke truth who said: 'If paradise is on earth, then Damascus without a doubt is in it. If it is in heaven, then it vies with it and shares its glory.'"[71]

Though he clearly takes interest in the city's natural environment, the focal point of Benjamin's attention is Damascus's major man-made monument: the renowned Umayyad, or Congregational Mosque, which was built during the reign of Caliph al-Walīd (r. 705–15). While it is noteworthy that an Islamic house of prayer catches the fancy of a medieval Jewish traveler, even more conspicuous is the religiously neutral terminology that he employs: "There is a [house of] assembly [*keneset*] of the Ishmaelites that is called the Congregational Mosque of Damascus [Arabic: *jāmiʿ dimashq*]; there is no building like this throughout the world."[72] Whereas the Tudelan usually dubs churches idolatrous "high places," the Umayyad Mosque is referred to as a *keneset.* In this context, the Hebrew word may be a mere translation for the Arabic *jāmiʿ*—as it similarly means an "assembly"; at the same time, it evokes the common term for synagogue: *bet keneset.*

Notwithstanding his positive characterization of the mosque, Benjamin tells that at its site, once stood the pagan "palaces of Ben Hadad" (Jer. 49:27), an ancient Aramean king. Until the first century BCE, Damascus's center was occupied by the Temple of the West Semitic storm god Hadad, which subsequently gave place to the Roman Temple of Jupiter, a Byzantine church, and finally, the said Umayyad Mosque. Though he mentions the name Hadad (the king rather than the god), it is doubtful that Benjamin was aware of the historical details; in all probability, he referred to the palace of a mythic king to explain the mosque's awe-inspiring architecture: "There is a wall of glass made by the work of magicians [*ḥarṭumim*], and within it numerous openings have been made, as many as the days of the year. [Over the course of the year,] the sun[light] enters each of them on its day and descends in [the specific opening] in twelve gradations, according to the hours of the day."[73]

In spite of its fairy-tale language, this fanciful picture seems to distantly echo certain elements that were described by Ibn Jubayr in a more reliable manner. Benjamin's "wall of glass," for instance, may refer to the magnificent mosaics that cover the mosque's courtyard and its inner walls. However, the famous water clock outside its eastern gate (Bāb Jayrūn) has apparently evolved into a sundial, in the Tudelan's account—which raises questions as to whether Benjamin actually saw the timepiece with his own eyes, or re-created it from the unreliable testimony of others.[74] Though the technical nature of this device would have stumped any writer lacking a background in horology, Ibn Jubayr explains that each passing hour was marked by a weight dropping from the beak of a sculpted bird into a vessel. He characterizes this chronometer as an "engineering contrivance" (Arabic: *tadbīr handasī*) that "imagination *might* conceive . . . to be a piece of sorcery [*siḥr*]";[75] the Tudelan considers it to be "the work of magicians."

As evidenced by other parts of this account, Benjamin let his imagination roam freely: "Within the palace [mosque] are chambers built of gold and glass. And if people are walking around the wall, each one sees the other whether he is inside or outside, even though the wall is between them. And there are columns overlaid with gold and silver, and [there are] marble columns of all kinds of colors."[76] What sounds like a romance description of a magical mirror palace might actually be a far-fetched rendering of the Umayyad Mosque's above-mentioned mosaics, its marble paneling, and other ornamental splendors (which continue to dazzle visitors to this day).[77] However, on account of the dreamlike character of this portrait, there are doubts as to whether the Jewish traveler was even allowed to enter the Islamic sanctuary. Also, the marble columns "overlaid with gold and silver" occur in a number of his references to architectural marvels, such as the caliphal palace and the exilarch's synagogue (discussed earlier).

The Tudelan's description seems to encapsulate some of the lore that had accumulated on the mosque's grandeur by the twelfth century. This assumption is bolstered by Benjamin's account of a fountain within the mosque's courtyard that he likens to "a head of a giant that is coated with gold and silver, and they fashioned it in the form of a bowl with rims of gold and silver. It is as big as a tub and about three people can enter it to bathe [at the same time]."[78] Once again, the Tudelan's penchant for fantastic descriptions is all the more glaring when compared with the report of Ibn Jubayr, though he also had a certain tendency to marvel at objects. In this case, the Muslim traveler simply speaks of large reservoirs (Arabic: *siqāyyāt*) and tanks of water for ritual ablution.[79] Benjamin's interpretation of the fountain basin as a giant's head is possibly a skewed allusion to one of the mosque's famous relics: the head of John the Baptist (known to Muslims as Yaḥyā bin Zakarīyyā').[80] On another occasion, at least, the Jewish author openly describes a relic from a mythological past: "Within the palace [mosque] hangs the rib of a certain giant [*'anaq*]; its length is nine spans, and its width is two spans.[81] And they say that he was a giant king of the giants of old and his name was King Abramaz; for they found [his name] engraved in a stone over his tomb where it was written that he ruled over the whole world."[82]

Both of Benjamin's motifs—the mosque's mythological past and its marvelous architecture—also surface in Moses Basola's travel diary, which was composed some 350 years later. Unlike the Tudelan, Basola readily admits that he caught only a fleeting glimpse of the Congregational Mosque because non-Muslims were not admitted: "In the middle of the city, in the commercial center, there is the Temple of Rimmon, a wondrous building. The dimensions of its courtyard are twice [the size of] San Marco Square. The floor is made entirely of shining marble; it is surrounded by colonnades with large columns, some [of which are] gilded. None but the Ishmaelites may enter. And it has four entrances through which it may be glimpsed."[83]

Instead of the palaces of Ben Hadad, Basola identifies the mosque with the ancient Temple of Rimmon, apparently in deference to another biblical verse that locates this particular building in Damascus (2 Kings 5:18). In the Bible's description of the temple at hand, the Arameans bow down to the god Rimmon—much as Muslims do in their own services: after Elisha had healed Naaman, the army commander acknowledges the God of Israel but nevertheless requests permission to "bow down" in the Temple of Rimmon. Against this backdrop, Basola's identification of the mosque with the ancient temple may be a playful hint at both the similarities and differences between Judaism and Islam. From the Italian rabbi's viewpoint, then, Islam appears to include elements of both his own religion and paganism.[84] Hence he does not consider the mosque to be a *keneset*, as Benjamin does. This seems to be another sign for a discursive shift in quattrocento Jewish travelers' attitudes toward Islam.

With respect to Basola's morphological descriptions, his estimation that the mosque's courtyard is twice the size of Venice's San Marco Square is a prevalent technique in travel writing—comparing foreign monuments with major landmarks back home. At the same time, he distorts the familiar through hyperbole (when claiming that the courtyard's measures are twice the size of Venice's main square)—an equally prevalent characteristic of the travel genre.

Alexandria

Alexandria merited even more attention than Damascus from European medieval travel writers.[85] There are a number of reasons for the Egyptian port town's popularity. To begin with, Alexandria was often the first stop of Jewish and Christian pilgrimages to the Holy Land. Because of the much-traveled sea lanes between Alexandria and other Mediterranean ports, the commercial hub was a convenient staging ground for a full circuit of the biblical sites (including those that were associated with the Exodus).[86] Also, for many Western travelers, their arrival in Alexandria was the first time that they had set foot on Islamic soil. As a result, they closely observed—and then described—everything that they encountered during their stay in an effort to fathom what awaited them on their trek through foreign lands. Last but not least, the ruins of the famous Hellenistic metropolis, founded by Alexander the Great in 332 BCE, served as highly evocative reminders of an ancient civilization that had a lasting impact on Judaism, Christianity, and Islam.[87]

Benjamin attributes many of the medieval city's structures to its ancient founder: "When Alexander the Macedonian built [the city], he . . . built it in an exceedingly strong and beautiful manner [*binyan*]; the construction [*binyan*] of the houses, palaces, and walls is exceedingly beautiful."[88] Above all, Benjamin marvels over Alexandria's water supply and distribution system. Largely dependent on the annual flooding of the Nile, the city boasted an elaborate network of conduits through which water was diverted into subterranean reservoirs and cisterns. The traveler notes that the city is "built over caverns by means of arches," which attest to the fact that "Alexander" constructed the settlement with "much wisdom." Furthermore, he admires its straight streets, going back to Hellenistic-Roman times, on which one might gain an unobstructed view for "a mile" ahead, from one city gate to the other.[89]

Alexandria's grid was unusual for medieval cities, and its subterranean waterworks also caught the eye of Benjamin's near-contemporary Ibn Jubayr.[90] While the Tudelan monotonously repeats certain Hebrew terms (such as *binyan*, and other derivatives of the verb *banah*, "build"), Ibn Jubayr displays a highly versatile Arabic vocabulary: "We have never seen a town with broader streets, or higher structures, or one more ancient and beautiful. Its markets are magnificent. A remarkable thing about the construction of the city is that the buildings below the ground are like those above it and are even finer and stronger, because the waters of the Nile wind underground beneath the houses and alleyways."[91]

Some three centuries after Benjamin and Ibn Jubayr, Meshullam of Volterra offers his own impressions of Alexandria. The Tuscan merchant equates its size with that of Florence. However, separating ancient from Muslim Alexandria, he reports that the city is now largely in ruins—as many other European travelers from the fifteenth century onward report.[92] More specifically, Alexandria's medieval walls encompassed only a portion of the ancient metropolis, whose architectural fragments were still visible in many places both within and beyond the city limits. From this standpoint, these accounts can be said to be relatively factual. Still, Meshullam's reference to urban decay seems to express his disillusionment with the reality that he encountered shortly after reaching the place that many Europeans considered the gateway to the East and its legendary riches (as discussed in Chapter 2).[93] The merchant's portrait of Alexandria appears to reflect this very confusion, as he describes the city as simultaneously grand and desolate: "Alexandria is as big as Florence and built comfortably. The city walls are high and beautiful, but the city is all dilapidated, as there are more ruins than standing structures. [Nevertheless,] the houses are beautiful; and in each house, you will find a courtyard [Italian: *cortile*] paved with white stones [*lastere*] and a tree in the middle of the courtyard."[94]

Obadiah of Bertinoro also conjures up contradictory images of Alexandria. To begin with, he notes that two-thirds of its space is "barren and desolate and large buildings are uninhabited."[95] He then offers a strikingly similar description of those residential compounds that were in use: "The inhabited courtyards are all paved with stones like a *mosaico*, with quince trees and date palms in the middle. And all the houses are large and beautiful."[96] As noted, the numerous similarities between the two accounts suggest that Obadiah had read Meshullam's travel diary. Alternatively, one might speculate that both were hosted in the same house owned by a local Jewish dignitary.

Among the city's ancient ruins, most medieval visitors were apparently taken to what was believed to be the academy of Aristotle, so that it is only natural for Benjamin to describe this mythical remnant of a refined civilization: "Outside the city is the academy [(*bet*) *midrash*] of Aristotle, the teacher [*rabbo*; lit., his rabbi] of Alexander. There is a large building [with] marble column[s] between each study hall [(*bet*) *midrash*]; and there are about twenty study halls where people came from all over the world to study the wisdom of the philosopher Aristotle."[97] While Aristotle did serve as Alexander's tutor, their sessions were never held in Alexandria. In fact, the ancient city's major academic institutions, the Mouseion and the Library, were founded by the Ptolemies long after Alexander's death (in the third century BCE). Still, locating Aristotle's academy in Alexandria, Benjamin faintly echoes the city's fame as one of the Hellenistic-Roman world's leading centers of philosophy and science. Similarly, Jacob ben Nathanel (a contemporary of Benjamin) may have assumed that the structure once served as an astronomical device: "In Alexandria of Egypt, I saw the academy [*bet ha-midrash*] of King Alexander [with] 365 columns corresponding to the days of the solar [year]."[98] At least, Ibn Jubayr explicitly argues that the ruins commonly thought to belong to Aristotle's academy were built "for the purpose of astronomical observations."[99]

One may infer from the early thirteenth-century description of Egypt by the Muslim polymath 'Abd al-Laṭīf al-Baghdādī that the ruins in question are what have since been identified as the ancient Serapeum (temple of Serapis).

Situated on a low hill to the southwest of the medieval city walls (Benjamin locates the ruins "outside the city"), the site still boasts a towering landmark: a 98-foot-high (30 meters) monolithic column, which today is widely referred to as Pompey's Pillar (an obvious misnomer).[100] 'Abd al-Laṭīf's account, the most reliable medieval source of its kind on Alexandria, helps check the Jewish travelers' descriptions against reality:

> I saw in Alexandria the Column of the Pillars [*'amūd al-sawārī*]. It is of that red spotted granite which is extremely hard. This column is of surprising dimensions and height. I can readily give credit to its being 70 cubits high: it is 5 cubits in diameter and stands on a base very large and proportioned to its height.[101] . . . Round the Column of the Pillars I likewise saw some considerable remains of [other] columns, part of them entire, and others broken. . . . I presume this was the portico in which Aristotle taught, and after him, his followers, and that this also was the academy erected by Alexander when he built his city.[102]

'Abd al-Laṭīf's rather precise description of the site (his measurements are close to the column's true height) show, by contrast, how fanciful the other writers' accounts are. Jacob ben Nathanel, depicts the Serapeum as a mysterious place that hovers between myth and reality. Next to the 365 columns, he also mentions some sculptural fragments that he relates to the four creatures in Ezek. 1:10: "There are two sarcophagi [*aronim*], one above and one below, with an image of the creatures on [each of] four [sides?], a face of a man, an eagle, a lion, and an ox."[103] While the Jewish travelers depict "Alexander's academy" in the language of marvels, their great interest in this ancient institution reflects the esteem with which Aristotle's teachings were held by medieval scholars, Jewish, Christian, and Muslim alike.

Practically all the accounts of Alexandria refer to one of the seven wonders of the ancient world—the Pharos.[104] The great lighthouse was built by the Ptolemies in the third century BCE at the entrance to the city's eastern harbor. Despite steady deterioration, including the partial collapse of its upper sections, the tower continued to serve the Mediterranean metropolis during the Middle Ages, until finally being toppled over by earthquakes in the early fourteenth century.

Crusader-era Jewish travelers such as Jacob ben Nathanel tend to wildly exaggerate the distance at which the Pharos's beacon could be seen: "There is a tower on the seashore that in Arabic is called *manāra* [lighthouse] where they put a light above at night, so that the ships will not deviate [from their course]. One can see the light in Africa, Provence, and in Acre. [The edifice] is constructed in such a marvelous way that two horsemen can ride up on their horses next to each other."[105] Ibn Jubayr, who limits the signal's visibility to seventy miles (which, because of the curvature of the earth, appears to be far-fetched as well), was also mesmerized by the ancient tower. He notes that "its interior is an awe-inspiring sight in its amplitude, with stairways and entrances and numerous apartments, so that he who penetrates and wanders through its passages may be lost."[106] However, modern readers are left with doubts as to whether Ibn Jubayr—as well as Jacob ben Nathanel—speaks from personal experience, for he admits that "words fail to give a conception of it."

Benjamin, who assumes that the Pharos was constructed by Alexander, offers his own version of a sort of medieval science-fiction thriller in which a Christian infiltrator causes irreparable damage to the "glass mirror" mounted atop the lighthouse. This device appears to function as a sophisticated telescope by the help of which "all the ships coming from Greece or the land[s] of the west from a distance of twenty days" could be detected.[107] "One day, long after the death of Alexander [Arabic: Iskandar], a ship arrived from Greece—the name of the sailor was Surudos, a Greek man of great guile."[108] He gained the lighthouse guardian's friendship and "made him drink much wine, him and all his servants, until they all fell asleep. Then the sailor and his servants got up, broke the mirror, and took off that same night." This narrative—which must have come to the Tudelan by way of an oral source—is clearly meant to explain why the lighthouse fell into disrepair. Correspondingly, it has a polemical bent against Christianity, for it is a Byzantine spy who smashed the mirror for the purpose of ending Muslim domination over the Mediterranean shipping lanes.

The major elements of Benjamin's narrative also turn up in al-Ḥimyarī's geographic dictionary (compiled in 1461), which abounds with legendary content.[109] This version of the story takes place in the caliphate of al-Walīd Ibn ʿAbd al-Malik (the early eighth century): the "King of Rūm [Byzantium] devised a cunning plot to get rid of the mirror in the lighthouse." At first, a Byzantine agent gained the caliph's trust by expressing his desire to embrace Islam. He then sought to lure the caliph into razing the Pharos by telling him that Alexander's treasures were buried beneath the structure. With the greedy caliph's approval, the spy proceeded to destroy the mirror and half the lighthouse. "When the news spread, the Rūmī [Byzantine agent] became afraid and fled during the night on a ship that was prepared for this purpose at the proper time."[110] The Tudelan, who apparently heard some version of this tale, appears to identify with Muslim anxieties over potential Byzantine expansion. Whatever his source, within the context of *Massa'ot*, the story allows him to depict Christianity as a barbaric force that destroyed one of the great wonders of antiquity. Similar to his chapter on Baghdad, Benjamin's account of Alexandria bolsters his hypothesis that the Islamicate world is culturally superior to Christendom.

Meshullam of Volterra, who visited Alexandria four centuries after Benjamin (in 1481), does not mention the Pharos any more, as his travelogue was penned well after the ancient tower had been destroyed. Instead, he offers a detailed picture of the fort that was erected on the ruins of the lighthouse (1477–79), as part of Mamluk sultan Qā'it Bāy's efforts to fortify the Egyptian harbor against the possibility of an Ottoman attack: "When you enter the port of Alexandria, you will find a beautiful citadel close to the city with thirty-two towers and a wall ten cubits thick, which stretches from tower to tower. . . . And with the exception of one side, it is surrounded by the sea. . . . I never saw such a fine fortress; it is new and [was constructed] about three years ago. As per the [standing] order[s], eight hundred *mamelucchi* [Mamluks] spend each night there. . . . Near the said citadel are twenty *moschee* [mosques]."[111]

Similar to Benjamin and other Jewish travel writers, Meshullam freely sprinkles his Hebrew account with Arabic terms, though he clearly could not speak the language. As indicated, the objective of this rhetorical device is usually to enhance the report's authenticity. In this instance, Meshullam utilizes Italianized loanwords—such as *soldano*, *mamelucchi*, and *moschee*—that in the fifteenth century had entered common usage. Here these evocative terms seem to underscore Alexandria's standing as the Muslim world's major port of arrival for European travelers who, upon disembarkation, first encountered a long-awaited exotic realm. Between the crusader period and Meshullam's time, the image of Alexandria in Jewish-authored travel accounts appears to have evolved from a site of ancient marvels to the symbolic gateway to the "Orient." From this standpoint, the Tuscan Jew once again embraces the larger trends of quattrocento travel writing.

PART III

Encountering the Other

Chapter 7

Ishmaelites and Edomites: Muslims and Christians

Opening Part III of this study, which is dedicated to the representation of people in the accounts, the present chapter investigates the various ways in which Jewish travelers from Europe reflected on their encounters with Muslims and Christians, the two ruling sects in the countries they visited or originated from. This investigation includes the cultural preconceptions that shaped their portrayals of the religious other.

Muslims: Benevolent Rulers or Uncivilized "Orientals"?

The images of Muslims conjured up by medieval Jewish travel literature are many and manifold. They oscillate between the idealization of Christendom's foes—a tendency that informs the crusader-era sources—and what may be considered early "Orientalist" stereotyping of Islamicate mores, the first traces of which surface in fifteenth-century accounts. The former tendency is evident throughout Benjamin of Tudela's portrait of Abbasid Iraq, as amply documented in previous chapters. Benjamin generally conveys a positive attitude toward Islam, which is reflected in his largely neutral choice of language when speaking about mosques ("house of prayer"; "assembly"). This sort of uncensorious attitude toward Islamic places of worship recurs throughout his *Massa'ot* and other itineraries from the same period, suggesting that it was Islam's unequivocal emphasis on the unity of God that enabled these Jewish authors to adopt a similar language for synagogues and mosques.

There are notable exceptions to these semantic tendencies. As discussed in Chapter 5, Benjamin refers to Ali's shrine at Najaf as a *bamah*—the same term that he applies to Jerusalem's Holy Sepulchre and other churches.[1] Among quattrocento authors, there seems to be a spike in polemical terms for Islamic sanctuaries, especially sites that were contested between Jews and Muslims. These crosscurrents make for a complex corpus in which only loose trends, rather than unbending ideological positions, can be traced. Also, the extant usage in the corpus at hand does not always reflect the original views of the authors but rather those of subsequent editors and copyists.

This sort of terminological survey is only one of several ways to assess the image of Islam in these texts. No less significant is the portrayal of Muslim leaders. As in medieval historical writing, the figure of the Muslim ruler in Jewish (as well as Christian) travel literature often represents the entire Islamic realm.[2] Over the next few pages, I discuss a couple of passages that shed light on the manner in which European Jewish travelers grasped the relationship between Levantine Jews and their Muslim rulers. While I have already expounded on Benjamin's anachronistic portrait of the Abbasid caliph, I offer a few more idealized portraits of certain sultans before turning to several polemical references to Muslim monarchs.

Saladin and the Ayyubids

Because of Saladin's leading role in the ouster of the Franks from much of the Levant, it is only natural that the authors in question are inclined to heap praise on him. Even a generation after the decisive Battle of Ḥaṭṭīn (1187), Judah Alḥarizi (in his *maqāma* on Jerusalem) composed an encomium of the Muslim ruler that is awash with messianic connotations. For with the end of Latin rule, the ban on Jewish residence in Jerusalem had also been rescinded—a ban that was based on the Christian claim that God had forsaken the Jews.[3] Against this backdrop, Alḥarizi likens Saladin to the ancient Persian king Cyrus (sixth century BCE),[4] as both rulers permitted the reestablishment of a Jewish community within the Holy City:

> The Lord, zealous for His Name's sake, had pity on His namesake [Israel], saying, "It is not right that Esau [Christians] seize Mount Zion's tents and Jacob be driven thence, lest the envious nations scoff, saying God has driven His firstborn off. . . ."
>
> So, 4,950 years[5] since the first day's light God roused the Ishmaelite ruler [Saladin] to fight . . . , so that he marched up from Egypt with his minions liege and against Jerusalem laid siege. God gave it to him

> to have and hold, and he told the city's dwellers young and old, "Speak unto Jerusalem's heart: let all the sons of Ephraim who dwell apart, yea, all Egypt's and Assyria's remnants speed like the hart! From every corner, come; build you your home!"[6]

Of course, the fact that the renewed Jewish presence in Ayyubid-ruled Jerusalem was too meager to justify associations of a messianic "ingathering of the dispersed" (*qibbuṣ galuyyot*) failed to inhibit Alḥarizi's vivid imagination.[7]

Another panegyric on the Ayyubids surfaces in Alḥarizi's *Kitāb al-Durar* (Book of Pearls). In a paean to Cairene Jewry, the poet alludes to the Fifth Crusade. Specifically, he refers to Sultan al-Malik al-Kāmil's victory over the Christians at Damietta (Arabic: Dimyāt; see Map 3), at the eastern mouth of the Nile. This event not only put an end to the Franks' short-lived occupation (1219–21) of the strategically important port city but paved the way to their ouster from all of Egypt. Among the gambits that the Ayyubids deployed at Damietta was to open the irrigation canals during the seasonal rise of the Nile waters, a tactic that left the crusader troops floundering through pools of mud with the sultan's cavalry at their heels. Since Egyptian Jewry could only expect to suffer from a crusader takeover of Cairo, Alḥarizi aptly compares the Christian defeat to the drowning of Pharaoh's chariots at the parting of the sea (Exodus 14).[8]

Written in Judeo-Arabic, Alḥarizi's work closely resembles Islamic terminology in its choice of words. For instance, the Jewish poet declares the Muslim victory a godsend, for "Allah moved the hearts of the kings of Islam," to whom He "granted great and everlasting victory."[9] With the rout of the crusaders, God gave victory to the entire "community of worshipers" (*jamī' al-'ibād*).[10] Similarly, Alḥarizi claims that the Muslims' triumph not only saved lives but also served the interest of true religion, from which he obviously excludes Christianity: through the Ayyubids, "Allah gave victory to [both] religion and worldly power [*al-dīn wa-'l-dunyā*]. May God prolong their days under the shade of felicity and let their banners be victorious."[11]

Is Alḥarizi implying that Jews and Muslims combined to form a greater "community of worshipers"? While the argument can be made that the Jewish poet's religiously suffused phrasing merely reflects the vocabulary of Arabic panegyrics, the enthusiasm with which he celebrates the "kings of Islam"—rather than the "Ishmaelite kings"—seems noteworthy. That said, it is the crusader threat that leads him to identify Jewish interests with those of the

Muslims. It also bears noting that the belief whereby God utilizes non-Jewish forces to carry out his plans for the people of Israel is a common theological paradigm with long-standing biblical precedents.[12]

Aside from descriptions of Muslim rulers guaranteeing the safety, autonomy, and prosperity of Jews, medieval Hebrew travel writings include popular tales that imply a reversal of the relationship between sovereign and subject. For instance, Petaḥyah of Regensburg tells of an unspecified sultan who commandeered a valuable stone from the steps leading to the purported tomb of R. Meir (the Mishnah's most frequently quoted sage) at Ḥillah, south of Baghdad.[13] However, after removing the stone, the sultan had a dream in which R. Meir seized him by the throat and nearly choked him to death. Like other medieval pilgrimage literature, *Sibbuv* includes a number of stories in which tomb desecrators are punished—or scared to death—by the very saint whose grave they had damaged.[14] In this case, the culprit begged the holy man for forgiveness, and the latter implored him to publicly repent: "The next morning, [the sultan] carried the stone on his shoulder, before the eyes of all, and returned it to its place, saying: 'I was wicked in robbing my righteous lord.'"[15] The story echoes the widespread practice of plundering shrines and other ancient structures for building material. However, in this instance, a mighty sultan is humbled by a deceased rabbi. In turning the true balance of power between the government and its *dhimmī* subjects on its head, Petaḥyah's miracle story is obviously expressing a fantasy of inversion. (For this reason, it may have originated in the local Jewish community.)

In yet another attempt to demonstrate Judaism's superiority over other religions, Petaḥyah tells of the near-conversion of a Muslim ruler on account of a discovery at the tomb of Baruch ben Neriah, a minor Jewish prophet, in southern Iraq. A rarity in Jewish travel literature from the crusader period, this narrative contains a polemical sideswipe at the Prophet Muhammad. While on the traditional pilgrimage route to Medina and Mecca, the Muslim "king" passes the said tomb. Upon opening the Jewish grave, the noble traveler finds a prayer shawl (*ṭalit*) sticking out between two marble slabs, and a miraculous brightness is emitted from the burial site.[16] As noted, Petaḥyah's *Sibbuv* was severely skewed over the course of the transmission process, so there is reason to believe that the extant account of brightness originally read as a "pleasant odor." Like the incorruptibility of a saint's remains, the "odor of sanctity" is a recurring theme in medieval narratives (of various religious provenance) about the identification of relics and holy tombs.[17]

In stark contrast to Baruch's remains, Muhammad's tomb (at Medina) was found to contain a decayed and unbearably malodorous corpse. Impressed by this striking dissemblance, the king "told all his people that there is no substance in either [Muhammad] or his religion."[18] However, owing to his premature death, the ruler "had no time to convert [to Judaism]," and his decision "to convert all his people was suspended." This motif is highly reminiscent of the traditions in classical rabbinic literature about Antoninus, a fictional Roman emperor, who either nearly converted or did embrace the Jewish religion.[19] Like other vulnerable minorities, the Jews hoped to gain the support of powerful leaders. These folkloristic tales give voice to this age-old desire. However, Petaḥyah's narrative stands out for its transformation of the burial site of a minor Jewish prophet into a derisive foil of Muhammad's tomb. Also noteworthy is that this anti-Islamic polemic occurs in the travel account of an Ashkenazi Jew. Possibly, Petaḥyah (or his editors) drew on Christian polemical traditions about Muhammad's death and burial.[20] That said, the contrast drawn here between a local Jewish shrine (the tomb of Baruch ben Neriah) and Muhammad's tomb seems to hint at the vituperative story's origin in the Iraqi Jewish community, which thereby vented its feelings about the ruling religion.

The "Turkish Menace"

With the exception of Alḥarizi's praise of the Ayyubids, the above-cited descriptions of Muslim rulers are purely imaginary. It is only in the late fifteenth century that Jewish travelers exhibit a greater awareness of and interest in political events in the Muslim world, though they are filtered through an Italian lens. For example, the accounts of Meshullam of Volterra and Obadiah of Bertinoro echo the Western notion of the "Turkish menace," which had gained currency following the Ottoman conquest of Constantinople (1453). Rife with bloody depictions of Turkish violence and cruelty, news accounts—that were rapidly disseminated by the recently invented printing press—reported on the latest Ottoman encroachments into Christian-held territories.[21] These same sentiments are discernible in Meshullam's description of the extensive damage to the city of Rhodes during the Ottoman siege of 1480, the year before his own arrival on the island.[22] As he reports, the Ottoman cannons had succeeded in destroying part of the city's fortifications at the site of the Jewish quarter. However, soon after entering the breach, the invasion force beat a hasty retreat.[23]

In all likelihood, Meshullam's account is partially based on testimony that he heard from members of the local Jewish community: "I have seen how the Turks totally destroyed [the city], especially in the Giudecca [Italian for "Jewish quarter"], on the left side, for the fighting was there. They tore down all the houses belonging to Messer Leon da Rhodi and R. 'Azaryah the Physician, as well as other houses; and the [town] wall came down near the synagogue."[24] However, the Tuscan's report also integrates the perspective of the island's rulers, the Knights Hospitalers, who took foreigners on tours of the battle site: "One day, as they say, the Turks, more than 10,000 men, climbed the walls and threw the *Gran Maestro* [Grand Master of the Knights] off the wall. But the Lord confounded [the Ottomans] so that 'one hit his brother or his relative,' and their hearts became weak, for the Lord helped [the people of Rhodes]."[25]

According to the religious worldview of the time, it was God who "confounded" the besieging Ottomans, much as he had "confounded the speech" of mankind at the Tower of Babel (Gen. 11:9). By preventing the Ottomans from capturing the Mediterranean island, heaven not only saved the Knights of Saint John but also the local Jews.

Seven years after Meshullam's journey, Obadiah offers a similar version of the Ottoman siege. It stands to reason that the Bertinorean drew upon comparable sources of information (that possibly included Meshullam's travel diary) in formulating his own account of this battle: "In the year of his death, the Turkish king [Meḥmed II, r. 1451–81] sent his army to besiege [Rhodes]. . . . They brought down the wall that surrounds the street of the Jews and destroyed all the Jews' homes. And the Jews told me that the Turks entered the city . . . and reached the entrance of the synagogue. But there God *confounded* them. And [the Turks] considered this a great miracle so they pushed one another and fled. And they slew one another and stumbled and nobody pursued [them]."[26]

Compared with Meshullam's account, Obadiah's version of the events makes even clearer that, in his estimation, the safety of the city's Jewish community was the major reason for the divine intervention (by "confounding" the Ottoman troops), for the "miracle" occurred on the synagogue's doorsteps. It was also the Jewish aspect of this episode that caused each of them to devote space in their accounts to the Ottoman siege of Rhodes. At the same time, both Italian Jews articulated the contemporaneous European perception of the Ottomans as a menacing juggernaut.[27]

Muslim Government

Other time-specific clichés can be found in Meshullam's and Obadiah's descriptions of their journeys east. For example, Meshullam appears to voice Western preconceptions as to the cruelty of "Oriental" rulers. A case in point is his account of a Mamluk sultan sentencing a Bedouin robber chief to death by flaying. The Volterrean indeed etches in toe-curling detail how "they began to strip off his skin, beginning from the ankles."[28] In yet another grueling image from Meshullam's diary, the skin was filled with straw, and the stuffed dummy was paraded through town on the back of a camel.[29] In revenge, the thief's brother mobilized a cavalry of some five hundred archers to wreak havoc on caravans in the eastern Egyptian desert, which Meshullam planned to traverse.[30] From the Tuscan's standpoint, the bloodthirsty despot's depravity seems to be matched by his subjects' unruliness.

For his part, Obadiah speaks of a "lack of political leadership and order" in Muslim lands, an observation for which the implicit point of comparison is apparently fifteenth-century Italy—a land that was well known for its own political strife. In Obadiah's estimation, the fact that a newcomer like himself might dare settle in the Levant was only possible thanks to the pious character of the Muslim populace: "If it were not for their fear of God, it would be impossible to live among them, due to their lack of political leadership and order and their nonexistent fear of the government."[31] Obadiah paints an extremely negative picture of the Mamluk judicial system: "They have unfair laws and twist the words as they like. . . . In Jerusalem, there are false witnesses from all over [lit., all places of the Gentiles]; at the courts, they do not investigate and do not question the witnesses. It goes without saying that they do not [have to testify under] oath but instantly reach a verdict according to their [the false witnesses'] words. If there were such courts in the lands of the uncircumcised [the Christians], people would swallow one another alive."[32]

In Obadiah's eyes, the European administration of justice is superior to the arbitrary system in Mamluk Jerusalem. These cultural sympathies for the "old country" and its courts notwithstanding, Obadiah immediately qualifies his statement. To paraphrase his words, if the Christians were not restrained by the rule of law, they would pose a far greater threat to Jews than Muslims; conversely the latter have no respect for their ineffective government, but at least they are a God-fearing people.

Once again, Meshullam and Obadiah do not see eye to eye. According to the former, "The Ishmaelites are wicked and sin against the Lord and their words are not to be trusted; they would be even worse if it were not for [their] fear of the government."[33] Put differently, it is only the truculent and fear-inspiring regime that somewhat restrains the inveterately wicked and iniquitous Muslims.[34] While Obadiah, who wrote his account five months after taking up residence in Jerusalem, may be considered better informed than Meshullam, who was just passing through the region, their contrasting descriptions of the relationship between the regime and its subjects should be considered equally stereotypical.

In sum, the idealized image of the benevolent Muslim ruler that was characteristic of earlier sources seems to give way to that of a malevolent and unreliable government in the accounts of the quattrocento Jewish travelers.

Islamic Ritual

The Ishmaelites' "sinful" character, as Meshullam lectures his readers, is further evidenced by their "false" religion. It is in this vein that the Volterrean offers a brief yet highly polemical account of Islamic ritual. While drawing certain parallels between Jewish and Islamic ceremonial life (both perform ablutions and have fixed prayer times, religious holidays, and fast days), the Muslims' distortion of true religion, according to Meshullam, seems to consist primarily of numerical errors: instead of Judaism's three daily prayers (on weekdays), Islam has five; in contrast to the Jewish Shabbat, Muslims observe their weekly rest day (Friday) for all of two hours ("as long as they perform their prayers"); their religious calendar has but two religious feasts ('Īd al-Aḍḥā and 'Īd al-Fiṭr); and whereas Judaism features a single major fast day (Yom Kippur) and a few lesser ones that are spread out over the entire year, Muslims fast "for *thirty* consecutive days" during the month of Ramadan.[35]

Similar comparisons were made by earlier Jewish polemicists who accused Muhammad of having arbitrarily altered divine commandments.[36] However, Meshullam's diatribe stands out for its emphasis on the numbers two, five, and thirty, which in Hebrew are represented by the letters *bet*, *heh*, and *lamed*, respectively. He claims that *'Alenu le-shabbeaḥ* (It is Our Duty to Praise), a controversial Jewish prayer that is often considered a veiled invective against Christians, is actually directed against Muslims: "It is with reference to them that the composer" of the *'Alenu* (named after its incipit) "composed [the phrase] 'who bow to something vain.'"[37] Meshullam is referring to the fact that "vain" [*hevel*] is spelled *heh-bet-lamed* in Hebrew. The letter *heh*, with a numerical value of five, "stands for the five ablutions that [Muslims] perform every day [before prayer]; the *bet* stands for the two feasts that they have during the year; and the *lamed* stands for the thirty days of fasting."[38]

Since the Middle Ages, the *'Alenu* has been the concluding declaration of all statutory Jewish prayer services and, for this reason, seems to be endowed with much significance.[39] As part of this prayer, Jewish worshipers thank God for not having created "us" like those "who *bow* to something vain." In a European environment, this passage was often understood as a cryptic anti-Christian reference (an interpretation found in both Christian and Jewish sources).[40] Against this backdrop, it is striking that Meshullam offers an anti-Muslim exegesis of this phrase, which might have been triggered by the conspicuous Islamic prayer ritual of prostration ("bowing"). This interpretation of the *'Alenu* may very well have originated in the Egyptian Jewish community, which the Italian Jew visited; alternatively, it could have been his own cultural transfer of an anti-Christian interpretation to an Islamic context.[41] In Meshullam's diary, this polemical reading of the *'Alenu* is another example of the attitudinal shift in fifteenth-century Jewish travel writing from an anti-Christian to an anti-Muslim bias.

Near Eastern Ways of Life

Yet another expression of Meshullam's blatantly judgmental attitude toward Levantine culture is his persistent mocking of the custom of sitting cross-legged on the ground.[42] For example, he uses bestial imagery in relationship to Muslims: "The Ishmaelites are to be likened to camels and are similar to beasts: as the camel goes without being shod, so they have no shoes; as the camel crouches and eats on the ground, so they crouch and eat on the ground without a [table]cloth but only a red leather [mat]. As the camel sleeps with its saddle [on], so they sleep and crouch on their legs and in their clothes and never take off their clothes at night."[43] Observing Levantine mores from an upper-class Tuscan perspective, Meshullam similarly declares that the fact that Ishmaelites "have neither bed nor table nor chair nor lamp" in their homes is uncivilized.[44] Though he admits that Muslims adhere to high standards of hygiene, he regards their eating habits as exceedingly vulgar, even likening them to those of swine—a rather harsh metaphor for a Jewish observer: "They are very clean in their person. . . . However, in their ways of eating they are pigs, for they [sit] on rugs [Italian: *tappeti*] on the ground and eat from . . . a copper dish of Damascene work [*ottone alla damaschina*] without a cover. They put neither cover, nor knife, nor salt on the table; they all eat out of one vessel—the slave with his master—and they always eat with their fingers, most of them sitting cross-legged [*coccolado*]."[45]

In Meshullam's account, Near Eastern table manners are an object of ridicule and amusement. As much as these tropes resemble later Orientalist works, it is worth remembering that his travel journal was written at a time when table manners, much like dress and speech, were barometers of class distinction. His remark about a slave and a master eating off the same plate attests to the fact that he believed Levantine table manners to be not only unrefined but a violation of social boundaries. Against this backdrop, Meshullam's deprecating portrait of Near Eastern customs appears to function, at least in part, as a satire of less sophisticated elements of Italian culture that, while still in existence, were increasingly identified with the lower strata of society. His outlook reflects the standards of the fifteenth-century Italian elite, which had only recently embraced an etiquette including the use of individual plates, utensils, and napkins.[46] As the Jewish merchant-banker carved out his own niche in the Tuscan upper class, he evidently mimicked its social and cultural discourse, including a condescending view of Islam and Near Eastern mores.

Christians: Idolaters or Countrymen?

In Jewish travel literature from the crusader period, as the cumulative evidence of previous chapters has shown, it is the Christian rather than the Muslim who draws almost uniformly unflattering comments. A semiotic survey of these texts points to a pronounced bias against Christianity, which is particularly manifest in Benjamin of Tudela's writing. Churches are commonly branded with the epithet *bamot* (high places), thereby reinforcing an age-old Jewish understanding of Christianity as idol worship. Even four centuries after Benjamin, Obadiah of Bertinoro shares this point of view. For example, he labels the Holy Sepulchre a *bet tarput* (house of idolatry)[47] and refers to a particular Christian as an "uncircumcised [one] who worships idols."[48]

To some degree, though, fifteenth- and sixteenth-century Italian Jewish pilgrims appear to have toned down the adversarial approach to Christianity—while some of them voiced increasingly negative opinions about Islam. Reflecting the extent of his own acculturation, Meshullam of Volterra, for instance, uses the Italian loanword *chiese* for churches on the island of Rhodes.[49] His description of the Holy Sepulchre is even more revealing. Far from employing polemical terminology, he echoes that of the Christians. To begin with, he speaks of the "*Sepolcro* . . . in Jerusalem . . . that the Gentiles [*lo'azim*] call *Golgotha*."[50] Most important, he refers to non-Jews with the religiously neutral term *lo'azim*, which originally meant speakers of other languages than Hebrew (and thus could also include Jews). Alternatively, Moses Basola can be said to occupy a middle ground on the topic of Christians. In contrast to many other premodern Jewish authors, Basola neither shuns the word Jesus nor does he replace it with a phrase like "that man." For him and his readers back home, Nazareth is known as the "the place of Jesus the Christian" (Hebrew: *ha-noṣri*).[51] However, in the case of the Holy Sepulchre, the rabbi seems to express conflicted feelings, for he calls it a *bamah* and the "burial place of Jesus" (*qevurat yeshu*) in the same breath.[52]

In Jerusalem and its vicinity, Jews adopted holy places that had been established by the Church, such as the tombs of David and Samuel (as discussed earlier).[53] Even so, Bethlehem rarely comes up in Jewish itineraries despite its being David's birthplace, probably due to its strong association with that of Jesus. To Obadiah, for example, the Church of the Nativity was another "high place of the Edomite [Christian] priests [*kemarim*]," and it was only worth mentioning on account of its proximity to a Jewish shrine, the much smaller tomb of Rachel.[54] Conversely, Basola had no qualms about entering the Church of the Nativity: "In Bethlehem, I saw the priests' convent [Italian: *convento*]; there is none to match it in Italy, with its sparkling marble floor and its twelve tall and exceedingly thick columns on each side."[55] Revealing his familiarity with churches back home, Basola took a touristic rather than a religious approach to this must-see site.

The dispute over holy places notwithstanding, what was the Jewish travelers' attitude toward the Christians they encountered along the way? And to what extent were they able to distinguish between the Christians of the Levant and their Latin counterparts, with whom they were already familiar from back home?

The answer to the last question is straightforward, for even Benjamin, one of the earliest authors under review, draws a clear distinction between the Latin and Greek Orthodox Churches. In his description of twelfth-century Constantinople, for instance, he speaks of the Hagia Sophia (another *bamah*) as the seat of the "pope of the Greeks" who "do not follow the religion of the pope of Rome."[56] Benjamin also enumerates the various Christian populations that resided in crusader-era Jerusalem: "Jacobites, Arameans [Syrians or Nestorians], Greeks, Georgians, and Franks."[57]

Three centuries later, Obadiah offers a similar list of the Christian denominations in the Mamluk-ruled city: "In Jerusalem, there live today [the followers of] five competing Christian confessions [*emunot*]: the Romans [Catholics], Greeks, Jacobites, Amalekites [Armenians?], and the Ethiopians [*ḥabisi*]. . . . Each one declares the belief [*emunah*] of the other to be false, like the Samaritans and Karaites do with the Rabbanites. And each sect [*kat*] has its own room within the *Sepolcro*, as it is a large high place."[58]

Since the days of Saladin, the Muslim authorities had parceled out the Holy Sepulchre, effectively auctioning off control over specific sections to competing Christian denominations. While these divisions were a major concern of Christian pilgrims, such as the Dominican friar Felix Fabri (from the German city of Ulm), who was a contemporary of Obadiah, it bears noting that the latter also comments on the compound's partitioning.[59] The rabbi must have learned about it from others, as it seems unlikely that he would have entered this "house of idolatry" (because of religious reasons or because of the substantial admission fee).[60] Though he might have been pleased with the fractured state of Christianity (the "external other"), the Bertinorean compares it to the rabbinic Jews' disputes with Samaritans and Karaites (the "internal other"), a topic discussed in the following chapter. Given the numerous accounts of discord among coreligionists in the travel literature on Jerusalem, it stands to reason that the Holy City turned out to be a disappointment for quite a few pilgrims.

The lack of gloating in Obadiah's reference to the Christians' disunity may be explained by his scholarly style of writing. Even more noteworthy are his apparent fellow-feelings for European Christian travelers (whom he here calls *noṣrim*, "Nazarenes," instead of "uncircumcised ones") that are hinted at in his account of Alexandria. Obadiah seems to empathize with Christian merchants who were locked in their *funduq* (hostelry) at nighttime, when the gates of most urban quarters were closed in medieval Egypt: "Every night, the Christians [*noṣrim*] staying there [at the *funduq*] have to shut themselves in their houses; the Ishmaelites close [the gates] from the outside and open them in the morning."[61] Also, reflecting certain restrictions imposed on local non-Muslims (*dhimmīs*), foreign Christians had to avoid the public sphere on Friday, the Muslim holiday, as Obadiah likewise notes: "It is the same on Friday, from midday until the evening, when the Ishmaelites congregate in their house of prayer: the Christians have to stay in their houses and shut [the doors]. But if a Christian is to be found outside at this time he will pay for it with his blood."[62] Since Italian Jews had to suffer similar restrictions during

Christian holidays as well as ghettos that were shut at nighttime, Obadiah might have been surprised to learn that comparable rules applied to Christians in a Muslim-majority country.

Beyond mere references to Jerusalem's diverse population, Basola, the latest of the travelers discussed in this book, is the only one who devotes some lines to the indigenous Christian population of the Levant: "In Bethlehem . . . they constitute more than half of the city. . . . There are many of them in Jerusalem as well. In Nazareth, they constitute the majority; and near Safed, there is a village named Yarun, where they are half of the population. There are large numbers of them in Damascus and Beirut as well. They are Christians [lit., uncircumcised] who settled there in ancient times, and their religion differs somewhat from that of the *goyim* in Italy."[63] Much like the yellow turban donned by Near Eastern Jews (see the following chapter), the traditional garb of the Levant's Christians complied with a dress code that was meant to ensure that *dhimmīs* stood out from Muslims (and one another). In addition to their blue turban, Basola notes the distinctive waist belt (Arabic: *zunnār*) of local Christians, who were hence dubbed *cristiani della cintura* (Christians of the girdle) in Italian.[64]

Basola appears to have had little qualms about socializing with Christians, be they Near Eastern or European. During his stay in Jerusalem, he even rented a room in what was known as the Casa di Pilato (House of Pilate). Located on the Via Dolorosa (a street name that only entered the lexicon at around the time of the rabbi's visit), this building was thought to have been the residence of Pontius Pilate, the Roman procurator who ordered the execution of Jesus. Venerated as the first Station of the Cross, the site was part of a devotional walk through the Holy City that was organized by Franciscans, wherefore it is frequently mentioned in Christian pilgrimage accounts.[65] By staying at this particular place, Basola apparently refrained from taking advantage of local Jewish hospitality. A possible reason for this choice of accommodations is what the wealthy rabbi deemed to be a lack of suitable alternatives. To be sure, Basola did not choose the Casa di Pilato for its connection with the martyrdom of Jesus but because it offered a rare scenic view over much of the Ḥaram al-Sharīf, which Jews were forbidden to enter by rabbinic law but still craved to see: "From the upper chamber where I lived, I could see the entire Temple, including the courtyard. No other house in Jerusalem boasts as good a view as this one. . . . Each morning at daybreak, I faced the Temple [Dome of the Rock] and recited the prescribed prayers before going to the synagogue. Blessed be God for granting me this privilege."[66] The fact that Basola was less perturbed by Christian sites than were other Jewish travelers seems to be only natural for a cinquecento rabbi and kabbalist who even socialized at home with Christian Hebraists, such as Guillaume Postel (their acquaintance was rooted in a shared interest in the kabbalah—the latter translated the Zohar into Latin).[67]

The ambiguity between fondness and ill will that European Jewish and Christian visitors to the Levant must have felt toward each other is best illustrated by Meshullam's account of his return trip. On the one hand, he seems to empathize with Christian pilgrims, who, according to Mamluk regulations, had to travel in a guarded convoy from Jerusalem to the coast.[68] Ostensibly, this arrangement was a security measure against highway bandits but also served the pilgrims' supervision on their way through Muslim territory.

On the other hand, Meshullam's account reflects how an encounter between Jewish and Christian pilgrims could be testy. At Jaffa, he and his companions boarded a galley owned by Agostino Contarini, one of a small number of Venetian shipowners who held a license to convey pilgrims to and from Palestine.[69] Anticipating possible troubles, Contarini concealed the new passengers' identity from the Christian travelers: "Hence they all believed," Meshullam writes, "that we were Gentile merchants—God forbid!"[70] As will be recalled, Meshullam had put on a white turban in order to pass for a Muslim while traveling across overland roads in the Levant.[71] Heading home in the company of Christian pilgrims, he was once again advised to hide his Jewishness lest his fellow Europeans receive him with animosity. Such fears were not without basis, as other passengers could very well have been smitten with religious fervor following their Jerusalem pilgrimage. The ability of Meshullam and his company to pass for "Gentile merchants" demonstrates that neither their dress nor language betrayed their religious affiliation. That said, Meshullam's actions on board express insecurity: "Since they were all wicked Germans and Frenchmen, all of them warriors, noblemen, and lords, I bestowed many favors upon them, so that they would refrain from doing me any harm should they later discover that I am a Jew. And as I foresaw it happened, for they were shaken upon hearing that I am Jewish, yet they could not change their attitude due to their initial great sympathy for me."[72]

While Meshullam saw himself as an Italian in relation to both Muslim and Jewish "Orientals," he still represented a confessional other to European Christians. The merchant may also be expressing an awareness of his belonging to an inferior class vis-à-vis the German and French "noblemen and lords." The encounter between European expatriates, then, did not seem to erode differences of class and religion.

Chapter 8

Near Eastern Jews: Brothers or Strangers?

Otherness and the unfamiliar are major themes of the travel genre. However, in describing their experiences with other cultures, travel writers often compare the alien societies with their own. As a result, their representations of foreign places and people also contemplate notions of the self and home. This is especially so when the destination is depicted as contrasting sharply with the author's native land or, conversely, when the subject is a "proximate other," such as a distant relative or coreligionist. To what degree, then, did European Jewish travelers identify with the Jews whom they met throughout the Islamicate world?[1] Did they view them as brothers or strangers?[2] Or did they recognize a familiarity that transcends and potentially debunks the alterity of the East? As the following roughly chronological discussions will show, the encounter between Western and Eastern medieval Jews engendered varied responses, giving rise to additional questions: To what extent are these different perspectives rooted in historical changes to the social and economic status of Near Eastern Jewry? And to what extent do they reflect changes in the European Jewish traveler's standing at home?

The Status of Jews Under Muslim Rule

In recognition of the revealed character of their scriptures, Islamic law placed both Jews and Christians under the category of *ahl al-dhimma* ("protected people"), a status that entitled them to the government's protection. At the same time, both groups had to categorically recognize Muslim suzerainty. The *dhimmī* standing entailed certain impositions, such as a special poll tax (*jizya*) and a dress code.[3] In light of the above, how did Jewish travelers from Christian lands grasp their Near Eastern coreligionists' place within society? How did they perceive the *jizya*, given its association with the subjected position of the non-Muslim?

As per the accounts of Benjamin of Tudela and Petaḥyah of Regensburg, the twelfth-century *jizya* was an annual head tax of one gold coin: a dinar. However, these reports as to a fixed contribution by every adult male *dhimmī*, regardless of his financial means, seem to contradict Muslim sources that refer to a graduated, income-related tax. Possibly one dinar was the amount levied from the lower societal strata; during the Fatimid period, the sum of two dinars was considered a monthly income of a lower-middle-class family.[4] Unclear also is the role of the Jewish community's own representatives in the tax collection. According to *Sibbuv*, the receipts from the poll tax in Mosul were equally divided between Muslim and Jewish authorities: "Of that coming from the Jews, half belongs to the king's [sultan or caliph] government," and "the other half of the tax" went to local members of the exilarchal family.[5] However, in Baghdad, "Each year, every Jew . . . gives a gold coin as a poll tax to the head of the academy [*rosh ha-yeshiva*], since the king does not receive any tax from them but the head of the academy."[6] Does Petaḥyah contend that the *jizya* in Baghdad had been entirely replaced by an internal Jewish tax?

Some of the apparent confusion may be attributed to the work's complex transmission process. As such, this passage should perhaps be emendated to read "the king *only* receives the tax from them *by way* of the head of the academy." It is often assumed that a Jewish representative (whether exilarch or academy leader) was charged with collecting the taxes from his constituents on the regime's behalf. There is little evidence in the twelfth century for this hypothesis, as suggestive as it may be.[7] (It was applied in later periods, though, as will be seen in a moment.) This system obviously would have strengthened the position of the religious minority's own officials. Probably for this reason, Petaḥyah views the Jewish leadership's involvement in the collection of the *jizya* as a sign of its wide-ranging autonomy. Far from depicting the head tax as a symbol of subjugation and discrimination, Petaḥyah's principal message seems to be encapsulated in the following remark: "In Babylon [Baghdad], the Jews are living in peace."[8]

Benjamin's treatment of the *jizya* sheds further light on his view of certain Near Eastern Jewish communities. The most striking feature of the Tudelan's reference to the poll tax is that it comes up only in the context of a peripheral community—what is presently referred to as Kurdistan Jewry—rather than in a Muslim metropolis like Damascus or Baghdad, which are discussed earlier in *Massa'ot*. In Benjamin's words, the Kurdish Jews were "under the rule of the king of Persia, and he collects a tax from them through his officer. And the annual tax that they pay is [one] *Āmirī* gold [dinar]."[9] The fact that this is the only place in *Massa'ot* that discusses the *jizya* may simply reflect the rather random organization of the book. In all likelihood, though, the decision to defer any mention of the poll tax until the section on northern Mesopotamia reflects a bias on the author's part. Like Petaḥyah, Benjamin considers Baghdad Jewry a largely self-governing community.[10] However, since the *jizya* is a symbol of Muslim hegemony, it does not conform with this picture of Jewish autonomy. For this reason, apparently, the tax only surfaces within the context of Jews in a remote land under Persian rule.[11] However, one of *Massa'ot*'s copyists seems to have felt the need to correct the somewhat misleading picture, according to which only the Persian king imposed a *jizya* on the Jews, by inserting the following sentence into Benjamin's account of Kurdistan: the head tax was paid "by every male [Jew] from the age of fifteen and onward *throughout* the kingdom of Ishmael [i.e., all Muslim-governed countries]."[12]

From the late fifteenth-century travel accounts on the Mamluk Empire, it seems that the *jizya* usually ranged from one and a half to two gold ducats, with certain local differences. (The frequent references to the ducat, instead of the dinar, in the more recent sources indicate that the Venetian coinage evolved into a kind of international currency in the eastern Mediterranean during early modern times).[13] The discrepancies among some of the accounts apparently reflect the varying economic conditions from region to region as well as the fluctuation of exchange rates. For example, according to Obadiah of Bertinoro's student, Jews had to pay a ducat and a quarter in Beirut, a bustling port city, and a mere ducat in the much poorer Galilean town of Safed. Additionally, once a *dhimmī* had paid the annual duties in one place, he could not be charged in other places, so long as he provided a receipt.[14] At least in this respect, the Muslim tax system was deemed to be well run.

Moses Basola, who visited the Near East in the 1520s, observes that the tax rate had not significantly changed in the aftermath of the Ottoman conquest (1517). In Tripoli (see Map 3), every adult male Jew had to pay an annual head tax of "around one gold ducat."[15] Perhaps the most surprising feature of Basola's account is that he evidently felt that the sultanate's taxation policy was reasonable and that local duties were predictable: "There are no other tax burdens, although each shopkeeper pays a monthly fee of six [silver] dirhams to the watchmen who light the street lamps and keep a close watch. This is the case across the Land of Israel."[16] Many of these Italian Jewish travelers perceived the *jizya* as a routine part of the Muslim system of government and were less inclined to consider it a discriminatory measure specifically targeted at Jews, since it also applied to local Christians.

The picture emerging from Obadiah's correspondence differs, to some extent, from the other travelers' testimonies. In one of his letters (1489), Obadiah notes that the Jews of Jerusalem had previously paid a fixed sum of four hundred gold ducats for the entire community. Under certain circumstances, such as towns with a large Jewish population, this arrangement could be convenient for both the taxpayer and the treasury; therefore, this method was, in some places, employed under later Ottoman rule.[17] However, if the actual number of taxpayers was shrinking, a fixed sum could become an unbearable burden on the non-Muslim populace. As spiritual leader of Jerusalem's "holy community," Obadiah faced this very problem but apparently managed to negotiate a return to the per-capita system: "Lately, the Lord had mercy and influenced the king [Mamluk sultan] [to decree] that everyone would pay a poll tax [on his own], which was a great reform such as has not been implemented in Jerusalem for fifty years."[18]

In contrast to Basola's statement that "there are no other tax burdens" besides the *jizya*, Obadiah's student mentions all kinds of arbitrary levies on commodities such as oil, sugar, and honey, which local governors occasionally imposed upon assuming office—probably to recover the bribes that they were forced to give to obtain the post. Those who refused to bear the expense, on the grounds that they lacked the economic wherewithal, would have their feet whipped until they either agreed to pay or died. The student also notes that, with respect to these particular duties, "there is one law for Jews, the uncircumcised [Christians], and Ishmaelites."[19] In other words, *dhimmīs* and Muslims all had to part with an identical amount or face the same consequences.

Far from complaining about taxes imposed on *dhimmīs*, the main source of Obadiah's ire was the Jewish community's own leadership (in the 1480s): "Claiming every week to have suffered losses and deficits," Jerusalem's "elders" demanded higher payments from the flock. If someone refused to pay, they hired Gentiles to beat him up.[20] Likewise, the officials who oversaw the community's religious endowments and held the so-called tax farm (*iltizām*) from the Mamluk government (sources of government revenue were frequently farmed out to the highest bidder) made a fortune, according to Obadiah, by abusing their authority at the expense of their constituents.[21] It is these venal acts, rather than the sultanic tax system, that Obadiah blames for the poverty and dwindling size of the city's Jewish community: "All the Jews once living in Jerusalem, who once numbered close to three hundred householders [families], disappeared one by one and emigrated due to the heavy taxes and burdens that were thrust upon them by the elders."[22] Upon arriving in Jerusalem, he observes that "only seventy heads of household, from the poorest of the people," had remained.[23]

Aside from the poll tax, *dhimmī* law stipulated certain dress codes that aimed to distinguish Muslims from the rest.[24] Minorities also had an interest in abiding by these conventions, as differences in raiment bolster in-group identities. As frequently mentioned in the travel accounts, Muslim men usually wore white turbans, while the prescribed color for Jews was yellow. Dark blue was often associated with Christians.[25] Differences in attire—whether based on religion, profession, social status, or gender—played an important role in European travelers' attempts to make sense of an otherwise undecipherable environment.[26]

Meshullam of Volterra refers to some of the rules of conduct that *dhimmīs* had to comply with in Mamluk Egypt. Given the fact that only Mamluk cavalry and high officials were permitted to ride horses, the Tuscan merchant and his company had to make the trip from Alexandria to Rosetta (see Map 3) on donkeys. Upon approaching the destination, "we alighted from our donkeys outside the city, since no Jew or Christian [*goy*] is permitted to ride in any city, even on donkeys."[27] Meshullam infers that a *dhimmī* who so much as slightly offends a Muslim might be compelled to embrace the ruling religion: "Jews or Christians [*goyim*] are prohibited from pointing [at Muslims] with their index fingers, lest they be forced to become Ishmaelites—God forbid—or they will kill him."[28] This case testifies to Meshullam's cultural ignorance, as finger-pointing was considered an insulting gesture in the Middle East (much like raising the middle finger in European society). For a *dhimmī*, then, pointing an index finger at a Muslim was equivalent to publicly shaming a member of the ruling faith and breaching the ingrained hierarchy of Muslim society.[29]

Islamic law placed height restrictions and other limitations on the construction of *dhimmī* residences and houses of worship.[30] The interpretation and enforcement of these rules seem to have varied widely. Some of those issues are broached in Obadiah's description of the Jewish neighborhood of Jerusalem at the end of the fifteenth century: "[The Jews] once had many houses that are now all but ruined and desolate and have become a permanent heap of rubble and will not be rebuilt. For according to the religion and law of the land, a Jew cannot build a house or courtyard without permission, even if it has fallen into ruin. And sometimes [attaining] permission costs more than the value of the house."[31] Inasmuch as *dhimmīs* had the right to own property in Muslim lands (a right they did not always enjoy in Christian Europe), it is surprising that the Jews of Jerusalem could not rebuild these structures in an unimpeded manner. In this case, the houses were probably part of the synagogue compound and thus subject to tighter rules governing the construction of non-Islamic places of worship. Indeed, Obadiah refers to a legal dispute over Mamluk Jerusalem's single synagogue.[32] As noted in his account, this entire affair was instigated by the synagogue's close proximity to a neighborhood mosque (commonly known as the 'Umarī Mosque). Obadiah explains the proximity between the two by an (otherwise unattested) story according to which the latter had once been a Jewish-owned house but was dedicated to Islamic worship when its owners embraced the ruling religion: "In the courtyard of the synagogue, close by, there is a *bamah* or mosque [*mosqeṭa*] of the Ishmaelites, for originally this house belonged to a Jew. But because of a quarrel and dispute he had with the [other] Jews he became an Ishmaelite. And when his mother saw that her son had converted on account of all the anger the Jews had caused him she donated her house, which was in the courtyard of the synagogue, as a house of idolatry [*bet tarput*] for Ishmaelites and [stipulated] that it be turned into a mosque, to spite the Jews."[33] Though the polemical barbs against this mosque betray Obadiah's indignation over the predicament—tellingly, he calls it a "house of idolatry" (much like churches)—he shifts the responsibility for the subsequent events, which I shall now survey, from the Muslims to the Jewish "apostate."

The chain of events that Obadiah maps out is corroborated by Muslim legal sources.[34] In 1473, one of the houses in the synagogue compound collapsed during a heavy storm, whereupon local Muslims sought to prevent the Jews from rebuilding the structure on the pretense that the land belonged to the adjacent mosque. However, an Islamic tribunal confirmed that the property was owned by Jews. Dissatisfied with the judges' ruling, some Muslim notables initiated a legal investigation into the status of the synagogue. They claimed that it was established after the Muslim conquest of the city (which was correct) and hence an illegal structure (according to the letter of the law, Christians and Jews were forbidden to construct new houses of worship once a place had come under Muslim dominion).[35] Over the next few years, the case was transferred back and forth among an array of courts in Jerusalem and Cairo, the Mamluk capital, and eventually became the object of a power struggle among various schools of Islamic law. Soon after a hearing that was favorable to the Jews, a riled-up Muslim mob took the law into its own hands and destroyed the synagogue overnight (1474). However, thanks to the personal intervention of Sultan Qā'it Bāy, the Jewish community was ultimately granted permission to reconstruct their synagogue.[36] While eschewing criticism of the Muslims, Obadiah praises the sultan's brave decision to rebuild the Jewish house of worship "more splendidly than before."[37]

The synagogue affair notwithstanding, Obadiah generally holds a negative view of the Mamluk judicial system, as already noted.[38] He specifically accuses Jerusalem's Islamic judges of turning *dhimmīs* into scapegoats. For instance, he tells how Jews and Christians were fined after a Muslim killed his mother under the influence of alcohol that he had purchased from minorities.[39] *Dhimmīs* were legally entitled to produce wine for their own consumption, given its ritual function in both Judaism and Christianity. "Since it is an abomination for the Ishmaelites to permit someone to produce wine," Obadiah notes, the Jewish community had to pay the governor of Jerusalem an annual fee of fifty ducats for this right.[40]

While consuming wine in public as well as selling it to Muslims was prohibited, according to Islamic law, it appears that the officials often turned a blind eye to such dealings. For this reason, cases involving the sale of wine frequently appeared in the local *sharī'a* courts.[41] In times of drought, in particular, the Muslim public was wont to demand stricter enforcement of the law, for the absence of rain was considered a sign of divine anger.[42] Moreover, during a dry spell, "the Ishmaelites may gather against us [the Jews]," Obadiah's student writes, "spill out the wine and break [the vessels], for they say that no rain has fallen on account of the Jews' sin of drinking wine."[43] Basola reports that the Jewish community of Jerusalem tried to avoid such conflicts by prohibiting the sale of alcohol to Muslims. However, some wealthy Jewish moneychangers seem to have obtained a special license to sell wine, despite the governor's official stance and the internal community-wide ban against such transactions. In addition, Basola mentions that a governor's threat to confiscate all the Jews' wine stocks could be averted by paying an exorbitant fine of two hundred ducats.[44]

The overall picture of the *dhimmī* experience that emerges from the accounts of these Italian Jewish travelers is ambiguous. For the most part, the Muslim government seems to have left the Jews alone so long as they paid their dues. In certain cases, though, governors might try to enrich themselves—or appease the majority and relieve tensions—by taking advantage of the awkward position that their non-Muslim subjects found themselves in.

Jewish-Muslim Encounters

Notwithstanding some remarks to the contrary, most travelers with an Italian background characterized daily Muslim-Jewish relations as basically peaceful. Despite his critique of the Mamluk judiciary, Obadiah holds that Levantine Jews did not feel oppressed: "From the side of the Ishmaelites, the Jews do not experience oppression [*galut*] in these parts. I have traveled the length and width of this land, and no one opened his mouth to utter a bad word. They are very kind to the foreigner, and particularly to someone who does not know the language. And even when they see many Jews gathered together, they are not hostile at all."[45] Similar sentiments were expressed in a letter by Samuel Ibn Picho (turn of the sixteenth century), wherein he attempts to persuade a relative to move to Palestine: "Thank God, here we do not experience such an onerous *galut*, though it is impossible for there not to be any [form of] *galut* [whatsoever]."[46] Though the phrasing sounds almost paradoxical, the author seems to play on the entire gamut of connotations for the Hebrew word *galut* (exile, diaspora, dispersion, oppression, etc.).[47] After the destruction of the Temple, Jewish existence was universally considered a form of exile, even in the Land of Israel. However, *galut* under Muslim rule was viewed differently by recent immigrants to Palestine, as they considered Jewish relations with their neighbors to be better than in the old country. Hence Ibn Picho adds: "In any case, it is not one-thousandth [as bad] as they say it to be there," meaning in Christian lands.

Numerous statements in the correspondence of quattrocento Jewish pilgrims describe a relatively friendly reception in the Levant. For example, Isaac ben Meir Latif writes that "the Arabs" are "peaceful toward us; they will never beat [a Jew]."[48] These feelings are shared by Joseph of Montagna: "On the road, we sometimes happened to be among many Ishmaelites . . . , and no one opened his mouth to utter a bad word."[49] Obadiah's student recounts how a crowd of poor Jewish pilgrims were generously welcomed upon disembarking at the port of Beirut: "The Ishmaelites had mercy with the poor and were very charitable and distributed money, wheat, bread, and fruit among them."[50] By contrast, the Christian pilgrims who arrived on the same two ships were the object of ridicule: "The Ishmaelites mocked the Christians [*goyim*], calling them 'son of a bitch' and frequently insulted and abused them with similar [words], while no dog barked at a Jew." He also notes: "They do not hate Jews to the point of reproaching and insulting us—as they do in your country [Italy]."[51]

The same can be said for the vocational integration of Levantine Jews, as it emerges from the travel accounts. In contrast to their experience in late medieval and early modern Christian Europe, several of the writers pointed out that Jews were not barred from certain occupations in Islamic lands. According to Elijah of La Massa (1438), "the Jews sit down to their work next to the Ishmaelites," from which it can be deduced that they all engaged in the same crafts. Moreover, the Muslims "are neither envious of [the Jews] nor do they harass them, as I have seen in other places."[52] Israel Ashkenazi (1522) was astounded by the Arabs' treatment of Jewish peddlers who passed through their villages and towns: "The Ishmaelites are very kind to them; they give them bread, honey, and fruit for free, as much as they need, and do not withhold their payment."[53] In Basola's estimation, Jews were better off in Ottoman Palestine than in Italy, from an economic standpoint. He attributes this state of affairs to amicable Jewish-Muslim relations: "for the Ishmaelites purchase more willingly from Jews than from others"[54] (perhaps he means other non-Muslims). In short, these travelers—most of whom hailed from Italy—viewed Jewish-Gentile relations in the Levant to be the antithesis of those back home.

Israel Ashkenazi—who had permanently relocated to Jerusalem—offers a rather complex picture of the Jewish experience in the Near East, which he articulated in response to a question that was sent to him from Italy as to whether it was preferable for a Jew to live under Muslim rule or under Christian rule. More specifically, R. Israel quotes his correspondent, R. Abraham of Perugia, as asking whether it is "better under Ishmael than under Edom"—a reference to an oft-quoted Talmudic saying.[55] The former answers that "in these parts [the Ottoman Empire], they say it is the opposite"—namely, it is "better under Edom than under Ishmael," as per the established Sephardic reading.[56] In discussing this aphorism, the two rabbis debated over the correct transmission of a Talmudic passage while simultaneously reflecting on the relative advantages and disadvantages of a Christian host society vis-à-vis a Muslim one.

With respect to the saying's correct version, R. Israel offers no conclusive answer ("there are arguments for both positions"). At the same time, he formulates an opinionated view of Jewish-Muslim relations, which seems to run counter to that of the authors cited above: "If [a Jew] accepts the yoke of oppression [*galut*] and submission [*hakhna'ah*], so that he raises neither his hand nor foot against the Ishmaelites—even if [a Muslim] deals dishonestly with you—and completely avoids speaking arrogantly, even to the lowest of the low, and behaves as if he were blind and does not hear, and like a mute does not open his mouth, except for placating words and to bribe [the Muslims] a bit—then [the Jew] will do well."[57] At first glance, R. Israel appears to endorse the view that, in real-life experience, it was "better under Edom than under Ishmael." Similar to Meshullam's remarks about the risks of finger-pointing, he seems to offer a rather cynical account of how Ottoman Jews had to humble themselves in their daily encounters with Muslims. However, the rabbi soon reveals that he is referring to another rabbinic source, Maimonides' *Epistle to Yemen* (from the late twelfth century), which includes a well-known harsh statement against Islam: "For I have seen letters sent by the Rambam [Maimonides] to Spain [it should read Yemen], where he writes that no nation in the world wishes to *humiliate* [*hakhni'ah*] and *debase* [*hashpil*] the Israelite nation as much as the Ishmaelites do."[58] However, this is a rather loose paraphrase of Maimonides' own words, which read: "no nation has ever done more *harm* to Israel; none has matched it in debasing and humiliating us."[59]

It is worth comparing R. Israel's paraphrase with the original, for the Italian rabbi conspicuously omits the matter of any "harm" being inflicted on the Jews. In so doing, R. Israel seems to imply that, so long as the Jews play by the rules and respect the existing social hierarchy in Muslim lands, they have nothing to fear: "For when the Ishmaelite sees the [Jew's] deference [*hakhna'ah*] and self-degradation [*hashpalah*], he becomes conciliatory; and even if he demands money, he will be content with a little."[60] The letter writer also notes that, despite having to keep his tongue in check, a Jew in the Levant "can go anywhere to do business and open a store in the market like an Ishmaelite, and no one says a bad word."[61] R. Israel denies that the rule whereby Jewish men under Muslim dominion must wear yellow turbans led to any restrictions on their movement or serious economic disadvantages comparable to those experienced by Italian Jews (who were required to wear a yellow badge).[62] Although his headgear sets him apart from others, a Levantine Jew is free to travel "wherever he wants," even on the overland roads, "and he is respected by everyone, except that he pays a higher toll."[63] While elaborating on the code of conduct that a *dhimmī* must abide by in Islamic lands, R. Israel conveys the message that the Ottoman Empire offered Jews certain advantages over contemporaneous Italy.

Levantine Jews: The Otherness of the Self

Having analyzed the status and living conditions of Near Eastern Jewry as perceived by their fellow Jews from Europe, the spotlight will now shift to a few questions that were posed earlier: To what extent did "Oriental" Jews serve as models of self-conceptualization for the writers under consideration? Were they perceived mainly as coreligionists and (distant) relatives, or as foreigners who were more representative of their Islamic environment than of a shared heritage? I will take stock of the various ways in which these authors constructed Jewish identity—both Western and Eastern—by means of a roughly chronological survey of relevant passages from the sources discussed in this study.

More than any other travelers, Petaḥyah of Regensburg extols the piety of his fellow Jews in the Middle East. A case in point is his glowing portrayal of twelfth-century Baghdad Jewry. To begin with, Jewish men walk the streets "wrapped in their woolen prayer shawls [*ṭalitot*]."[64] In addition, they maintain high standards of purity, as "everyone has a ritual bath [*mikveh*] in his courtyard" and no one prays without having immersed himself therein beforehand.[65] By projecting such ideals onto Baghdadi Jews, *Sibbuv* appears to echo values that were particular to the *Ḥaside Ashkenaz*.[66] This is evident in the following account of the Iraqi community's prayer services: although the custom of praying barefoot seemed exotic to the Ashkenazi rabbi, he depicts their services as a noteworthy example of orderly conduct: "No one talks to his friend in the synagogue. . . . While studying, if they should be mistaken in a tune, the head of academy gives them a sign with his finger and they understand how the tune should be."[67]

Petaḥyah once more appears to be contrasting Central European Jews with their Middle Eastern brethren when he claims that even ordinary Jewish men (*ʿam ha-areṣ*) in Iraq "know all twenty-four books" of the Hebrew Bible. Moreover, they are not impeded by the complexities of Hebrew grammar and punctuation or by instances of "defective spelling and superfluous" letters in the biblical text. As a result, there is no need for a cantor [*ḥazzan*] to recite the Torah on their behalf, for "whoever is called up to the Torah scroll" is capable of reading the portion aloud on his own.[68] Similarly, Petaḥyah claims that Near Eastern communities did not even employ a cantor, as each member was well versed in the liturgy.[69] His implicit criticism is perhaps that the growing importance of the *ḥazzan* in medieval Ashkenazi congregations reflected a decline in Hebrew knowledge among ordinary men (and was not the result of other factors, such as the increasing complexity of liturgical poetry). In hailing Mesopotamian Jewry as an example to be emulated, Petaḥyah is holding up a mirror to his home audience. The Middle East serves him as a critical foil of a Western Jewish world that, according to the heightened norms of the *Ḥaside Ashkenaz*, was in dire need of reinvigoration.

About a generation after Petaḥyah, Judah Alḥarizi (early thirteenth century) offers a sharply contrasting picture of Middle Eastern Jewry's religious erudition. Though it counted exilarchs among its illustrious members, insofar as Alḥarizi was concerned, the community of Mosul consisted entirely of ignoramuses. Still, he did see to it to put these words into the mouth of Ḥever the Kenite, the *Taḥkemoni*'s fictional narrator, who is an object of satire himself. In a particularly hilarious scene, Ḥever attends Friday evening services at which the *ḥazzan* makes "more than a hundred" errors. With respect to the following Shabbat morning prayers, Alḥarizi offers an eloquent parody of the cantor's performance. Riddled with mistakes and mispronunciations, this account must have seemed blasphemous to contemporaneous readers. For example, instead of "Blessed art Thou, O Lord . . . who created man *be-ḥokhmah* [with wisdom]," the boorish *ḥazzan* declaims with a booming voice, "Blessed art Thou, O Lord who created man a *behemah* [beast]."[70] And instead of "Let Israel be joyous *be-ʿosav* [in their Maker]" (Ps. 149:2), he reads "Let *Ishmael* be joyous *be-ʿesav* [in Esau]"[71]—an especially funny pun given that in rabbinic Hebrew, the biblical figures of Ishmael and Esau (or Edom) serve as the archetypes of Islam and Christianity, respectively. Over the course of the morning, the cantor tries to show off his skills by embellishing the statutory prayer with ostentatious renderings of liturgical poetry (*piyyuṭ*); however, because of their excessive length, the entire congregation walks out before the services are over.

From a biographical standpoint, this biting satire may be interpreted as Alḥarizi's sweet revenge for not having been hospitably received upon his own arrival in Mosul, "weary and sweating, on the eve of the Sabbath, as the sun was near setting."[72] The indignities suffered by an itinerant poet are a prevalent motif in the Arabic literary tradition, which Alḥarizi was steeped in. Thus it seems difficult to determine the extent to which the described scene reflects the poet's personal experience. In any event, Alḥarizi's caricature of an ignorant cantor should not be taken at face value—that is, as historical evidence of the Iraqi Jewish community's educational decline since the time of Petaḥyah's journey.[73] The amusing examples of the *ḥazzan*'s failed attempts at *piyyuṭ* betray Alḥarizi's unequivocal view that the Iberian tradition of synagogal poetry was far superior to that of the *mashriq* [East].[74]

The later travel accounts are informed by a wide range of opinions regarding the Jewish minority of Muslim countries, but the idealizing tendency seems to be once again in the ascendancy. For instance, three centuries after Petaḥyah, Obadiah of Bertinoro places a similar emphasis on the piety of Middle Eastern Jews, which he contrasts with that of his home audience: "I have noticed that by nature, all those who are living in the land of Ishmael [Islamic lands] . . . are more God-fearing than the people of these parts [Italy]"—an assessment in which he even includes Muslims: "Here you will find neither a Jew nor an Ishmaelite whose heart will turn away from the Lord to heresy [*minut*] or any evil belief."[75] (The rabbi may be alluding to secularizing trends in fifteenth-century Italy.)

Obadiah was especially impressed by the high level of religious observance among Levantine Jews. In his estimation, they "observe the Shabbat as it should be, namely much stricter than they do in these parts [Italy]; for no one leaves his house on Shabbat either for a walk or any [other] matter, except for a religious obligation or [to go] to the synagogue or the study hall [*bet ha-midrash*]."[76] Thereafter, he offers a barely veiled critique of Jewish observance in the old country: "It goes without saying that there is not even one [Jew] who on Shabbat would light a fire in his house or a lamp that went out by having a Gentile servant or maidservant [do so]." In a similar vein, he appears to subtly reprimand his readers for enjoying non-kosher wine:[77] "In all the parts I have passed through, except Italy, [the Jews] strictly abstain from the wine of Gentiles. . . . And there is no sinner or transgressor in these parts [the Levant] who would drink the wine that was touched by an Ishmaelite, much less by an uncircumcised idol worshiper [a Christian]."[78]

Writing from Jerusalem a generation later, R. Israel Ashkenazi reaches a similar conclusion: "In these parts, they hold the commandments very dear."[79] Like Obadiah, he contends that the local Jews consume neither wine nor cheese that was made by Gentiles and refrain from litigating internal disputes in non-Jewish frameworks.[80] Islamic law (much like premodern Christian law) granted Jewish communities juridical autonomy. This privilege was zealously guarded by rabbinic authorities, as communal leaders issued bans against Jews who dared to litigate in non-Jewish courts.[81] However, as sixteenth-century documents from Jerusalem's *sharīʿa* court amply demonstrate, Jews frequently brought disputes with their coreligionists before a *qaḍī* (Islamic judge), perhaps because the latter was better positioned to enforce rulings than his Jewish counterparts.[82] Even R. Israel seems to be aware of this, for he claims that when a Jew demands justice before an Islamic tribunal, "all Israel instantly unites against the destroyer."[83] They bribe the governor to have the culprit beaten and then pronounce a religious ban against him until he shows remorse and pays a fine to the community. In light of the above, R. Israel's initial statement according to which local Jews strictly observed the boundaries set by halakhah appears to have been yet another idealized depiction of Palestinian Jewry.

The picture that he renders of Jerusalem's Jews also serves R. Israel as a means to situate himself in cultural terms. The community, which during Obadiah's time was largely composed of Arabic-speaking (*musta'rab*) members, was now dominated by Sephardic Jews, on account of a recent (though relatively limited) surge in Jewish immigration to the Holy City following the Spanish expulsion (1492) and the Ottoman conquest of Palestine (1516).[84] As R. Israel observes, "Now that the *sefardim*—may their Rock save them and prolong their lives—have become numerous, they completely outnumber the other linguistic groups [lit., tongues] and do as they please."[85] This suggests that the writer, an Ashkenazi Italian, felt alienated by the Sephardic dominance, for sixteenth-century Jerusalem still had but one synagogue where each *ḥazzan* followed his own liturgical tradition. (His letter makes note of a single *musta'rab* and three Sephardic cantors, while failing to mention an Ashkenazi one.) However, R. Israel is flattered by the fact that "many [of his fellow congregants] tell me that I am one of the dear Italian [Jews] and not an Ashkenazi"—in spite of his epithet.[86] This indicates that, within an overwhelmingly Sephardic environment, he strongly identified with his Italian background. At the same time, he takes the trouble to deflate rumors as to intra-communal strife: "I assure you that there is great amity among all, between the *sefardim* and the *musta'rab* Jews."[87]

Aside from general praise of the community, R. Israel observes that the Talmudic erudition of Jerusalem's Jews lags well behind that of the Ashkenazi yeshivot in Italy: "What we studied in Perugia in one day exceeded what they learn here in a month, for there is no student who goes to the depths of the tradition, especially when it comes to the [work of] the Tosafists" (a school of medieval Ashkenazi commentators on the Talmud).[88] In brief, two tendencies can be ascertained from Israel Ashkenazi's letter: on the one hand, he pays tribute to the piety of the Jewish community in Palestine; on the other, he takes personal pride in his own Italian Ashkenazi heritage.

Among the later travelers, Meshullam stands out for his stereotyping and poor opinion of Levantine Jewry. As evidenced by the Volterrean's comments on his coreligionists' mores, his geographic dislocation was clearly matched by his sense of cultural and social dislocation. Reminiscent of his comparison of Muslims to camels on account of their frequent squatting on the ground, Meshullam claims that the habits of Alexandria's Jews "are like those of the Ishmaelites"—for instance, "they sit on the ground in the synagogue. They wear no shoes and do not enter the synagogue with shoes or stockings."[89] (The last custom also caught Petaḥyah's attention but did not diminish his overall impression that Near Eastern Jews conducted their prayers in an exemplary fashion.)[90] As will be recalled, a primary target of Meshullam's ridicule are the table manners that he observed during his peregrinations through Egypt and Palestine: like Muslims, "the local Jews are pigs at their eating, for they all eat from one vessel with their fingers."[91] These disparaging remarks confirm that from his point of view, the cultural difference largely overshadowed the common religious bonds that he shared with Near Eastern Jews. In Meshullam's opinion, the Muslims and Jews of the Levant formed a largely undifferentiated collective: "The Jews behave like the Ishmaelites in all the lands [and] provinces of the sultan [Italianized: *soldano*]."[92]

After rehashing the point that Levantines take their meals while sitting "on rugs [*tappeti*] on the ground," Meshullam describes how the guests toast one another before a festive meal: "When they want to honor someone, they bring raisin wine [Italian: *zibbibo*, from Arabic *zabīb*, "raisin"] which is a thousand times stronger than the *malvasia* [malmsey wine]. And you have to drink twice before they offer you anything to eat, save fruit. Finally, you have to drink to all the guests, for everyone who drinks says to the foreigner 'in your honor,' and then takes a fruit and says, 'to life and health,' and you will have to drink. Since each one does so, two hours pass before you can eat, and [then] you have already drunk twice, and they, too. If you were to refrain from drinking, you would greatly insult the host."[93] For this reason, Meshullam feigned medical problems to avoid having to partake in the wine. It bears noting that it is less than clear whether the host of this particular meal was Jewish or Muslim.[94] Probably, the Tuscan would have had more opportunities to dine and wine among his coreligionists; he mentions that he was hosted by several of the local Jewish notables—among them the highest representative of Egyptian Jewry, who was known as *nagid* (Hebrew for "lord" or "leader") or *ra'īs al-yahūd* (Arabic for "head of the Jews").[95]

As in other passages of this sort, Meshullam's underlying bias stands out all the more when compared with a similar one from Obadiah's account.[96] In the latter's description of a Shabbat dinner that he attended in Alexandria, he also notes that the Jews "in all of the land of Ishmael" have their meals "on a rug [*tappeto*, the same Italian loanword that Meshullam uses] without a table in front of them." Unlike the Volterrean, Obadiah offers no unflattering remarks about this custom. Thereafter, Obadiah provides a detailed account of the common Kiddush (blessing over the wine) ritual throughout the Near East: "The host takes a cup of wine, makes Kiddush, and drinks the entire cup. Then a wine pourer takes the cup from the host's hand and pours wine into it for each of the guests . . . , and each one drinks a full cup of wine. Then the host takes one, two, or three pieces of fruit, eats, and drinks a second cup; and all the guests say, 'to health and life.' Afterward, the one sitting next to him also takes from the fruit, and the wine pourer fills a cup of wine for him and says, 'to your joy.' And [the others] wish him 'health and life.' This is repeated for all the guests, one after the other. Then they take a second kind of fruit and pour a third cup of wine."[97]

Obadiah turns out to be not only a wine aficionado but a person with a sweet tooth. Before the meal, each guest would have "at least six or seven cups" of "strong" wine and some fruit, such as "yellow plums [*mirabolani*], candied fruit [*canditi*], fresh ginger, dates, raisins, almonds, and a confectionary [*confetti*] of coriander seeds; and with each item, a glass of wine" is consumed, "sometimes raisin wine, which is very good, and sometimes *malvasia di Candia* [a sweet Cretan malmsey wine], or local wine; and I drank with [the host] and was exhilarated." Only then, "a large bowl filled with cooked [vegetables] and meat is brought out. Each one stretches out his hand and takes whatever he desires from this bowl."[98]

Although Meshullam makes no mention of Kiddush, the resemblance between the two authors' scenes is striking. For instance, the raisin and the malmsey wines are included on both menus, and a number of the same Italian loanwords turn up in each of the accounts. If, as I assume, Obadiah had read Meshullam's earlier travelogue, it stands to reason that his account constitutes a dialogic response to that of his contemporary.[99] The rabbi not only expands upon the merchant's scene but transforms his critique of Levantine habits into a paean of Near Eastern Jewish hospitality. But regardless of whether Obadiah was aware of his countryman's letter, he puts a positive spin on a custom that was belittled by the other. Whereas Obadiah chooses a form of participant observation (he freely describes his personal joy), Meshullam emerges as a distanced, slightly disdainful spectator (he abstains from the wine). The Volterrean was once more dismayed at the presumed erosion of social boundaries: had he taken part in the merrymaking, it would have meant acknowledging the egalitarian aspect of drinking with people whom he apparently deemed to be of a lower status than himself. Not surprisingly, he notes that his servant was far from bashful in accepting his host's alcohol.

Chapter 9

Karaites, Samaritans, and Lost Tribes

Even more than their meeting with Near Eastern fellow Jews, the European Jewish travelers' encounter with Karaites and Samaritans in the Levant gave rise to questions of in-group and out-group identity. To some extent, the authors merely echoed earlier statements from rabbinic literature about Karaites and Samaritans. Others actively developed and modified those statements in ways that spoke to their readers' contemporary interests. Classical Jewish sources had already expressed a variety of opinions about these nonrabbinic communities. The travel writings similarly reflect that "Rabbanites" and Karaites—or Jews and Samaritans, for that matter—did not always find themselves on opposite ends of the spectrum but shared numerous traditions and practices. Otherness is not necessarily "there" or "beyond" but can also be here and within. In consequence, the "proximate other" could occasionally be acknowledged as a variation of the self, as some of the following examples show.

Above all, Obadiah of Bertinoro approaches the topic from a scholarly perspective when summarizing the commonalities and differences between Rabbanites (as rabbinic Jews are called when contrasted with Karaites) and Karaites for his readership back in Italy, where any information about the other branch of Judaism will have been largely limited to polemical literature. As he duly notes, the main divide between the two communities pertains to the Rabbanites' fundamental doctrine of the Oral Torah, according to which rabbinic interpretations (Oral Torah) of the Bible are considered nearly as authoritative as the Written Torah: "As you know, the Karaites do not believe in the words of our rabbis—may their memory be blessed."[1] At the same time, he concedes their erudition in the Hebrew Bible. Obadiah even admits to having read some classical Karaite Bible commentaries (or excerpts thereof), including those of Yefet ben 'Eli (second half of the tenth century) and Aaron ben Elijah of Nicomedia (fourteenth century). However, Obadiah questions the Karaite principle whereby each generation is entitled to reinterpret the so-called literal meaning of the biblical text (*peshaṭ*) and to determine the "essence of a commandment" (*'iqar ha-miṣvah*) on its own, thereby overturning the authority of earlier exegetes.[2]

While these ideological questions appear to have mainly concerned the learned elites, divergent forms of observance carried more weight in the daily encounters between Levantine Rabbanites and Karaites. (They also would have been of greater interest to Obadiah's readership.) As reflected by the traveler, calendrical adherence was the most important criterion of denominational allegiance to each of these communities, which often lived side by side in the eastern Mediterranean.[3] Both the rabbinic and Karaite calendars are based on the biblical one, so each consists of twelve lunar months (of twenty-nine to thirty days). However, the two groups periodically add a thirteenth month to balance the difference between the lunar and solar year (the former loses approximately eleven days annually vis-à-vis the solar year), for the purpose of ensuring that the Jewish festivals fall during their biblically prescribed seasons. While the rabbinic calendar was already pre-calculated by the high Middle Ages, the Karaite calendar was not.[4] As Obadiah explains, the determination of the latter necessitated frequent decisions that were predicated on two factors: an eyewitness testimony that the crescent moon had become visible was a prerequisite for declaring the first day of a new month; and annual reports from Palestine on the state of its barley crop. If the festivals and the agricultural seasons fell out of sync, a leap year had to be proclaimed.[5] Communication problems between the far-flung Karaite diasporas could result in local calendrical discrepancies: "Sometimes the Karaites in Cairo will determine Rosh Hashanah and Yom Kippur on a different day from the Karaites in Jerusalem . . . ; and they say that there is nothing wrong with this. . . . If the Karaites in Egypt intercalate, for example, the Karaites in Constantinople may not do so. There is no one to blame, as everyone does what seems right to him."[6] The resulting disunity in observance seems intolerable from Obadiah's rabbinic vantage point. Though his critique is largely implicit, he apparently views Karaism as a case of exaggerated individualism that triggers intra-community friction.

At the same time, Obadiah commends Karaites for having adopted certain rabbinic laws and practices, such as the rules of slaughtering, even though its details are "not written in the Torah."[7] Sometime before his visit there, the Karaites in Cairo embraced the rabbinic custom of reading the Torah during Monday and Thursday prayer services.[8] He also praises the Karaites for not consuming wine that was produced by non-Jews. In this respect, they even served as a positive example for Italian Jews who, to the Bertinorean's dismay, saw no harm in drinking "Gentile wine" (as discussed in the previous chapter).

Travelers' reports that depicted the Samaritans as a kind of biblical Judaism frozen in time were sure to arouse even greater curiosity among readerships than largely academic discussions of Karaite/Rabbanite discrepancies. In the Hebrew travel accounts analyzed here, Samaritans are usually called *kutim* (or *kutiim*) but only rarely *shomronim* (Samaritans). Hewing to the nomenclature of classical rabbinic literature, the prevalence of the term *kutim* (derived from 2 Kings 17:24 and 30) indicates that, insofar as rabbinic Jews were concerned, the Samaritans belonged to the people that the Assyrians exiled to Samaria in the eighth century BCE; they were deemed to be of foreign, non-Israelite descent.

Nonetheless, Jewish and Samaritan communities often lived side by side in the medieval Levant, as can be gleaned from Benjamin of Tudela's *Massa'ot*.[9] In Damascus, say, Benjamin counts three thousand Jews alongside "about one hundred Karaites and about four hundred *kutiim*."[10] While "there is peace between them," communal boundaries are being upheld, as "they do not intermarry." With regard to crusader-ruled Ashkelon, which was then a bustling port city involved in trade with Egypt, Benjamin even speaks of a Samaritan majority: "There are about two hundred Rabbanite Jews . . . , about forty Karaites, and about three hundred *kutim*."[11]

Of particular interest to the discussion at hand is the following line from *Massa'ot*'s account of Caesarea (see Map 3), where both communities were equally strong, in Benjamin's estimation: "There are about two hundred Jews and two hundred *kutiim*, who are the Samaritan Jews [*ha-yehudim ha-shomronim*] who are called *Samaritanos* [in Romance language]."[12] Based on this passage, does the Tudelan recognize the Samaritans as Jews—as a kind of variation of the self? Probably not, for Benjamin draws a clear line between other and self in his account of Nablus (see Map 3): "There are *no* Jews" in this town, but it does have "about a thousand *kutiim* . . . and they are called *Samaritanos*."[13] Here the text lacks any parenthetical explanation about *kutiim* being Samaritan Jews, which probably indicates that the remark concerning the Caesarean Samaritans originated as a marginal commentary and was later inserted into the text by a medieval scribe.

Benjamin lists some major points of tension between the two ethnoreligious communities. For instance, the Samaritans only follow the "Torah" (the Pentateuch) but do not recognize the other two parts of the Hebrew canon (Prophets and Writings), not to mention the rabbinic Oral Torah. The main difference between Jews and Samaritans was the question of which mountain was divinely chosen as the center of worship: Jerusalem's Temple Mount, or Mount Gerizim (Arabic: Jabal al-Ṭūr), near Nablus. With respect to Gerizim, the Tudelan elaborates: Samaritans "say that this is the [true site] of the house of God—praised be He. On Passover and the [other] holidays, they bring a burnt offering onto the altar, which they built on Mount Gerizim, as it is written in *their* Torah."[14] The claim that the Samaritans offer sacrifices on the biblical festivals is a common imprecision of travelers' reports (both Jewish and Christian, medieval and modern). While their Passover celebration does involve the slaughtering, roasting, and eating of lambs—an element conspicuously absent from the rabbinic seder, even though it is prescribed in Exodus 12—the Samaritan ritual is not considered a sacrifice as such, and no similar rite is performed on other festivals.[15] Benjamin's account of the Samaritans proves to be an early example for how quasi-ethnographic observations are tinged by the visitor's own preconceptions.

Another object of curiosity that numerous Jewish (and Christian) travelers to Palestine felt compelled to remark on is the Samaritan Pentateuch. In this case, Benjamin seems to draw on some polemical source, for he proves to be relatively well informed about the major differences between the Masoretic (rabbinic) text of the Torah and the Samaritan Pentateuch, which he refers to as "*their* Torah." In the latter, the view according to which Mount Gerizim is the site that God chose for His sanctuary is buttressed by a reading of Deut. 27:4 ("Upon crossing the Jordan, you shall set up these stones, about which I charge you this day, on Mount Ebal"), which has Gerizim instead of Ebal.[16]

In addition to this objective disagreement over the biblical text, the Tudelan clearly questions the Samaritans' Israelite lineage. Rather than offer historical reasons (such as the Assyrian population transfer), he (somewhat surprisingly) grounds his argument on the Samaritans' use of a different alphabet from that of the Jews: "They lack three letters: [*heh*],[17] *ḥet*, and *'ayin:* the *heh* of Abraham our forefather's [name], for they lack *hod* [magnificence]; the *ḥet* of *Yiṣḥaq* [Isaac] our forefather, for they lack *ḥesed* [mercy]; and the *'ayin* of *Ya'aqov* [Jacob] our forefather, for they lack *'anavah* [modesty]. Instead of these letters, they use an *alef.* Hence, it is evident that they do not descend from Israel; though with the exception of these three letters, they do know the Torah of Moses."[18]

Given the fact that the Samaritan alphabet does include all three letters, it is obvious that Benjamin did not have any firsthand knowledge of the

Samaritan Torah. Indeed, their Pentateuch would have been illegible to him because, unlike in rabbinic Judaism, which adopted the square Aramaic ("Assyrian") characters, the Samaritans preserve a form of the paleo-Hebrew script. Another possibility is that Benjamin is referring to the common pronunciation of the said consonants, as these so-called gutturals tend to be neutralized in the Samaritan articulation of Hebrew.[19] Meshullam of Volterra, who seems to draw on similar polemical traditions, explicitly ties the Samaritans' lack of certain characters to their pronunciation of the holy tongue.[20] By associating each of the three characters with one of the patriarchs, Benjamin argues that the Samaritans are not of Jewish origin. Since he considers the absence of certain letters to be a sign that they are bereft of the central virtues of Abraham, Isaac, and Jacob, the *kutiim* cannot be their progeny—a conclusion that is probably based on the widespread rabbinic belief that the merits of the forefathers (*zekhut avot*) are passed down to their descendants.[21] The fact that Jews and Samaritans use different scripts is not seen as resulting from a historical schism but as a sign of their different origins.

As if to dismiss all theories about the Samaritans lacking certain letters (and virtues), Obadiah draws on Maimonides to clarify that they continue to write "the Hebrew script that was originally used by the Israelites before they were exiled to Assyria."[22] Arguably, it was a humanist impetus that caused some Italian Jewish travelers to take an antiquarian interest in the Samaritan script, as opposed to a merely polemical one. In the early sixteenth century, Moses Basola even offered his readers a table of the Samaritan alphabet, which he identified with the paleo-Hebrew characters known from ancient shekel coins.[23] That he responded to the interests of an early modern Jewish audience is illustrated by the fact that this specific passage from Basola's travelogue caught the eye of 'Azaryah de' Rossi, who cited it in his *Me'or 'enayim* (Light of the Eyes, first printed in Mantua, 1573–75), in the context of his own discourse on the history of the Hebrew alphabet and Jewish numismatics.[24]

To return to Obadiah: while he mostly emphasizes the commonalities between Jews and Samaritans, the following statement of his—which repeats allegations already made by Abraham Ibn Ezra (twelfth century)—seems to harbor a faint yet derisive undertone: "Wherever the tetragrammaton occurs in the Torah, it is written *ashima*" in the Samaritan Pentateuch.[25] Evidently, Obadiah had never seen a copy of the Samaritan Bible, for the difference is limited to Jewish and Samaritan reading practices rather than the text itself. Whereas rabbinic Jews avoid pronouncing the tetragrammaton by uttering *adonai* (Lord) or *ha-shem* (the Name) in its place, Samaritans enunciate *shema* ("the Name" in Aramaic). In claiming that the Samaritan Pentateuch substitutes the divine name by the similar-sounding word *ashima*, Obadiah appears to echo an ancient polemical tradition whereby the Samaritans worshiped a goddess who went by the name Ashima and whose cult was imported by some of those people whom the Assyrians settled in Samaria.[26] Between the lines, then, Obadiah may also be casting doubt on the Samaritans' Israelite origin.

Though hardly an impartial reporter, Obadiah, the scholar, avoids outright polemics and appears to consciously disassociate himself from such bias when stating that the Samaritans "are extremely hated by the Jews because they sacrifice and burn frankincense on Mount Gerizim."[27] While Obadiah stops short of outwardly accusing the Samaritans of idolatry (instead, he pins them with violating the Sabbath), his contemporary Meshullam of Volterra exhibits no such restraint. The latter claims that they put a "golden dove" on their altar at Mount Gerizim, a contention that—though lacking any historical evidence—comes with a Talmudic antecedent.[28]

Regardless of his claims about the Samaritan Pentateuch, Obadiah reveals a rather inclusive attitude toward Samaritans and Karaites when counting them among Cairene Jews: "In Cairo, there are today about seven hundred Jewish households: fifty of them are *shomronim* [Samaritans] who are called *kutim*, and 150 Karaites, and the rest are Rabbanites."[29] Here he evidently draws on information gained during his personal stay in Cairo, as opposed to mere book knowledge. Giving a rundown of Egyptian Jewry's social pyramid, Obadiah once more embraces Karaites and Samaritans as part of the self: "The Samaritans are richer than the *rest of the Jews* in Cairo; they serve in high [governmental] offices in Cairo, and among them are treasurers and administrators. One of them has 200,000 and another one 100,000 gold coins. And the Karaites are richer than the Rabbanites."[30]

Nevertheless, Obadiah does not fail to mention that "among the Rabbanites are rich people, too. However, the practice of the Jews in the land of Ishmael [Muslim-ruled countries] is to present themselves as poor. And they always carry themselves as weak, despised, and bent down in front of the Ishmaelites."[31] While this behavior may have been rooted in the desire of the Jewish minority to avoid undue attention and envy (as reflected in the previous chapter), Obadiah also bemoans the lack of internal solidarity among rabbinic Jews: "They are neither charitable nor generous at all and do not love one another. Everyone is seeking only his own good. In this respect, the sect [*kat*] of the Karaites is more commendable than the sect of the Rabbanites; [the former] are generous toward one another. They also mix with the Rabbanites and befriend them."[32]

Of course, this is an idealized picture that could easily be challenged by accounts in other sources that reflect the tensions and strife between Mamluk Cairo's rabbinic Jews and Karaites.[33] In depicting the other as more charitable, Obadiah once again holds up a mirror to his own sector. What is to be made of his inclusive attitude toward Samaritans and Karaites? In part, it may stem from his personal encounter with members of the other groups during his sojourn in the Egyptian capital. His caravan from Cairo to Gaza included some Samaritans who were making the pilgrimage to Mount Gerizim.[34] The long desert trek may have afforded him an opportunity to learn more about his fellow travelers' actual practices and opinions. Perhaps this is why he does not repeat the age-old misinformation that the Samaritans worship a dove. Obadiah's ostensibly objective account of nonrabbinic communities is also part of his self-representation. By positioning himself as a philosophically detached observer rather than a polemicist, the renowned Mishnah commentator enhances his own scholarly reputation and authority in all matters of Jewish law and ritual.

While shedding positive light on the competing Jewish identities, the demographic numbers that Obadiah provides show to whom the future belongs: "There are only a few [Samaritans] left out of [what was once] a large number; for according to what they told [me], there are fewer than five hundred households left throughout the entire world."[35] Obadiah reckons that Samaritans and Karaites may be perched atop the social ladder; however, rabbinic Jews not only follow the correct tradition but constitute the future of Judaism. Declining numbers made these rival identities appear less threatening to the rabbinic one.

Legends of Independent Jewish Tribes

Besides being the home to Rabbanite, Karaite, and Samaritan communities that were more-or-less known to a European audience, the medieval travel writers imagined the Muslim world as a place inhabited by autonomous warrior Jews, some of whom they identified with the Lost Tribes of Israel. While such tales are central to the more imaginary works (the *Book of Eldad* and Re'uveni's travel narrative) discussed here, they also come up in the letters of relatively reliable authors who, in this case, often admit to depending on hearsay. The popularity of this topic among both Jews and Christians heightened during the fifteenth and sixteenth centuries against the backdrop of widespread millenarian expectations. The reunion of the Lost Tribes with their known brethren was considered a harbinger of the redemption.[36] In this context, early modern readers were particularly eager to receive any news that a traveler had to report in this respect, as evidenced by the fact that R. Israel Ashkenazi in his letter explicitly responds to such questions by his addressee, R. Abraham of Perugia.[37]

The entire spectrum and history of these legends, as well as their attraction to both Jewish and Christian audiences, lie beyond the scope of this book.[38] I will focus on selected passages from the travel accounts that situate these tribes in or near Islamic territory. Within this context, I will attempt to answer several questions: What role do these legends play in the Jewish writers' mental map of the Middle East?[39] To what extent do they shed light on medieval Jewish notions of home and abroad, diaspora and the Land of Israel? And what sort of Jewish self-conceptualizations do these legends imply?

Among the earliest travel narratives to include the motif of independent Jewish tribes is the so-called *Book of Eldad*. Here the idea can already be found that some of these Jewish warriors are living on the Arabian Peninsula, not far from the holy cities of Islam. According to the author of the book (commonly attributed to Eldad ha-Dani), the tribe of Ephraim and half the tribe of Manasseh are dwelling in the mountains "overlooking the city of Mecca," which he tellingly calls "the error of the Ishmaelites."[40] The book describes them as mounted highway bandits who "do not spare their enemies and live on booty only." Indeed, they are such "valiant warriors that one of them goes out [to fight] a thousand [men]." The other half of Manasseh and the tribe of Simeon are living in the "land of the Chaldeans [*kasdim*]," according to the same narrative. Since the patriarch Abraham originated from Ur of the Chaldeans (Gen. 11:31), a logical place of residence for these tribes would be southern Iraq. However, the *Book of Eldad* imagines them in a proverbial faraway land, at a distance of a six-month journey (from Mecca?). Not only are Simeon and Manasseh free from the yoke of foreign rule, but they "take tribute from twenty-five kingdoms," including "some of the Ishmaelites."[41] The apparent objective behind this sort of wishful thinking is to symbolically subvert the established political order, for it suggests the potential reversal of Jewry's subjection to either Muslims or Christians in the near or distant future. In this respect, the Arabian Desert is a utopia where elements of the messianic age are already a reality.

Benjamin places yet another, otherwise unknown, tribe called "Khaybar, the people of Tema," in the Arabian Peninsula.[42] Later he identifies them with the "lost" tribes of Reuben, Gad, and half of Manasseh. Khaybar (see Map 1) and Taymā' were two ancient oases towns, the former in the region of Medina and the latter in the peninsula's northwest.[43] Both settlements had Jewish communities during the early days of Islam. After initially resisting Muhammad's troops, the Jews in these towns surrendered and were allowed to retain their lands in return for an annual tribute (the precursor of the *jizya*). Like the rest of the Hijāzī Jews, they were expelled by the caliph ʻUmar in the seventh century.[44] While *Massaʻot* triggers distant memories of Khaybar's Jewish past, it offers no credible evidence that "50,000 Jews" were still living there five centuries later.[45]

From a biblical standpoint, the assumption of Reuben, Gad, and half the tribe of Manasseh living in Khaybar is problematic. As per the Book of Kings, following Assyria's conquest of Samaria in 723 BCE, its population was uprooted to northern Mesopotamia—not the Arabian Peninsula. Among the locations in which they were resettled was a place (or river) called Ḥabor (2 Kings 17:6).[46] The phonetical proximity between Ḥabor and Khaybar is apparently what led Benjamin (or his unknown source) to identify this Arabian oasis as the northern tribes' place of exile.[47]

In yet another wild fantasy of geography and demographics, the Tudelan claims that the land inhabited by the Arabian Jews is surrounded by the "mountains of the north" and takes sixteen days to traverse. Within the region's provinces, Jews inhabit "large and fortified cities" and number about 300,000 people.[48] (According to these figures, the Arabian Peninsula was home to the largest Jewish community in the world!) "The yoke of Gentiles" is not upon these Jews; in fact, they regularly "go forth to pillage and capture booty from distant lands along with the Arabs who are their allies."[49] For this reason, "all the neighbors of [these] Jews fear them."[50] Despite their violent exploits, the Arabian Jews are portrayed as leading a pious and ascetic life. For instance, they fast forty days a year so that God may liberate their Jewish brethren around the world from their onerous state of "exile" and "oppression" (two connotations of the term *galut*). One may thus deduce that Benjamin considered these sovereign Jewish tribes to be free of the plight of *galut*, even though they resided outside the Land of Israel. In other words, the Tudelan believes that a part of the Middle East other than Palestine has the potential for a Jewish existence that is not in thrall to Edom (Christianity) or Ishmael (Islam).[51]

Three centuries after Benjamin, the myth of the tribes had not lost its allure. David Re'uveni's purported origins call to mind several elements in *Massa'ot*'s portrait of the Khaybar Jews: Gad, Reuben, and the half-tribe of Manasseh live in the "wilderness of Ḥabor," here situated a ten-day journey from the Red Sea port of Jeddah; the Jewish population in this region is 300,000 strong;[52] and Re'uveni constantly boasts of having fasted for extended periods of time—a form of asceticism that also surfaces in the Tudelan's corresponding account of the tribes. Although these similarities are not enough to conclusively state that Re'uveni drew on *Massa'ot* (these traditions may have reached him through other channels), he appears to have styled himself as a Jewish prince in the image of these Arabian Jews.[53]

Even Obadiah of Bertinoro, who usually displays a healthy skepticism toward fanciful tales, conveys stories about Jewish warriors in the Arabian Peninsula. For example, he has heard that these "giants" attack *ḥajj* caravans heading to Mecca. Moreover, "the Ishmaelites assert that one of them is able to carry a camel-load on one shoulder while the other hand holds the weapon to fight. It is known that their religion is that of the Jews, and it is said that they are the Rechabites."[54] In one of the more far-fetched items in his account, Obadiah reports that, owing to their trademark battle cry, the divine name of *shadday,* the Rechabites are known as "Arabs [who are] sons of *el* [the god] *shadday*."[55]

While he characterizes as hearsay the kind of lore that situates the Lost Tribes behind the mythical River Sambatyon (which rests each Shabbat; hence its name),[56] Obadiah gives greater credence to contemporaneous news about a distant Christian empire, where some of the tribes are said to be living: "What is clear to me without any doubt is that in one of the regions of the kingdom of Prester John [*Preste Ioanni*]—a land of mountains and hills, and the mountain ranges are very high and [the region is] said to be a ten-day journey—there undoubtedly dwell Israelites, and they have five princes [*nesi'im*] or kings."[57]

In the medieval imagination, the realm of the legendary Prester John was commonly located in India or Ethiopia. Both regions were thought to be overlapping spheres because at the time, it was still uncertain how Asia was separated from Africa. From the fourteenth century on, news about a Christian kingdom in Ethiopia found its way to Europe, and a number of travelers even claimed to have reached this fabled land.[58] Any information about Ethiopia and its supposed priest-king were highly valued, for Prester John was considered a potential ally in the Portuguese effort to break the Muslim grip—be it Mamluk or Ottoman—over the Red Sea route to India.

According to rumors transmitted by Obadiah, these warrior Jews are pitted against Prester John. In other words, unlike their brethren on the Arabian Peninsula, they are locked in combat against *Christian* forces.[59] Far from being invincible, these tribes share the fate of *galut* with the rest of the Jewish people. In fact, since Prester John "dealt them a crushing defeat" they pay tax to the ruler of India-Ethiopia—a claim redolent of a Christian version of these same legends that was meant to deny the possibility of Jewish independence.[60] (The lack of Jewish statehood since late antiquity was interpreted by the Church as divine punishment for the Jews' alleged responsibility for the death of Jesus.)

In another possible reference to Ethiopian Jews, R. Israel Ashkenazi disseminates tantalizing rumors about "several thousand, [even] myriads" of black Jews (*kushim*) living somewhere along the Nile; and their king similarly "wages daily war against the Christians."[61] R. Israel relates a story about a Portuguese Jew (perhaps a converso) who had visited the courageous Jews. This report echoes several Portuguese expeditions to Ethiopia that were initiated in the hopes of making contact with its Christian ruler (supposedly Prester John) but yielded little, if any, success.[62] In contrast to Obadiah's largely subdued warrior Jews, R. Israel's tribes are clearly of the utopian kind: they asked their visitor about the fate of the "people of the diaspora" (*anshe ha-golah*) and the state of Jerusalem and the Temple. In response, the visitor told them "that we [the known Jews] are in great distress and wander from one nation to another in captivity and distress, and the Temple is destroyed and Jerusalem ruined and in the hands of foreigners."[63] Isolated from the rest of the world, these newly discovered black Jews not only stand in stark contradistinction to the known Jews but are unaware of the plight of their brethren. Upon receiving this terrible news, "they instantly tore their clothes [in grief] and wept bitterly for many days."

The raft of stories in Hebrew travel writings about the Lost Tribes demonstrates how, from a Jewish perspective, distant lands could be conceptualized as both domicile and exile.[64] On the one hand, the Middle East was portrayed as the home of Jewish warrior tribes who defied all the well-known attributes of *galut*. On the other, these tribes could also be viewed as part of a universal diaspora, which would come to an end only through the messianic "ingathering of the dispersed" (*qibbuṣ galuyyot*). While the first type of traditions locates these tribes largely in an Islamic setting, the second—which is characteristic of sources from the late fifteenth century onward—imagines them living under Christian rule. This shift of the Lost Tribes from Arabia to Ethiopia in Jewish travel writings occurred in response to the Portuguese exploration and related Christian news about the "discovery" of Prester John's kingdom.

Chapter 10

Assassins, Blacks, and Veiled Women

During the Middle Ages, most Muslim, Christian, and Jewish writers of travel were fascinated by the strange and exotic. When describing alien societies on the fringes of their cultural and geographic universe, they could take advantage of a literary license that was unavailable to them when writing about places with which their readership was somewhat familiar. At the same time, classical authors, such as Pliny, had established a certain set of images with respect to this world beyond. Consequently, medieval Jewish travelers, in representing "outlandish" people, drew on motifs shared by premodern travel writing, regardless of linguistic and cultural boundaries.

Besides entertaining their readers, what interest did Jewish authors have in people outside mainstream Sunni society, such as Ismailis and Druze? How did they perceive these others in relation to their own Jewish identity? What notions of race and human diversity were expressed in their portrayals of black Africans? What rhetorical strategies did they adopt to explore fantasies of unknown human societies? With these questions in mind, I will analyze a number of textual examples that depict geographically, culturally, or socially peripheral societies in the Muslim world from the perspective of medieval Jewish travelers.

"Assassins"

Following the establishment of the crusader states in the Levant, rumors began to spread in the Latin world about the so-called Assassins. Benjamin of Tudela is one of the first non-Muslim authors to refer to this Shiite sect, "a people who are called *al-ḥashīshīn*" ("hemp smokers" in Arabic): "They do not believe in the religion of the Ishmaelites [Islam] but in one [person] of their own whom they consider to be a kind of prophet. Whatever he tells them they will do, whether for death or for life. They call him *shaykh al-ḥashīshīn* ["sheik of the hemp smokers" in Arabic]. He is their Elder, and on his word, all the people from the mountains come and go. And their [major] settlement is the city of Qadmūs."[1]

The Arabic term *ḥashīshīn* (or *ḥashīshiyyīn*)—the errant source for the Western word "assassin"—is obviously pejorative in nature. Benjamin must have picked it up from Sunnis polemicizing against the Nizaris (*nizāriyya*), the more appropriate term for this Shiite subgroup. A branch of the so-called Ismailis, the Nizaris materialized out of an intra-Muslim dispute over the legitimate claim to the supreme leadership (imamate) of the Islamic community, following the death of the Fatimid caliph al-Mustanṣir in the late eleventh century. (The faction that backed his eldest son, Nizār, who was subsequently murdered, was known as the *nizāriyya*.)[2] After the emergence of the first independent Nizari principalities in northern Iran, similar strongholds were established in the Syrian mountains (Jibāl Anṣāriyya), within a largely hostile Sunni environment that was controlled by Seljuk Turks. By Benjamin's time, the Nizaris were also waging war against some of the regional crusader lords: "They are fighting against the Edomites [Christians] who are called Franks [*franqos*] and with the ruler of Tripoli."[3]

The Nizaris left few written records. On the other hand, most contemporaneous Sunni authors were prejudiced against them, and Christian accounts were similarly informed by clichés.[4] As a result, it is difficult to get a true feel for this group. More than anything, outsiders were intrigued by exaggerated reports about *fidā'īs*, Nizari warriors who carried out death missions. As related by Benjamin, "They faithfully follow the order of their Elder and are feared everywhere because they murder the kings while sacrificing [their own lives]."[5] Pervasive myths describe the Assassins' addiction to drugs (hence the "hemp smoker" epithet), their indoctrination, and their unwavering devotion to a figure that Marco Polo dubbed "the Old Man of the Mountain," a century after the Tudelan globetrotter.[6]

The most interesting facet of the above-quoted account is that Benjamin deems the Nizaris to be non-Muslims, a claim that is also raised by Ibn Jubayr, the Sunni Iberian traveler who was a near-contemporary of the former. While all Benjamin knew was that the sect was headed by a certain *shaykh*, his Muslim counterpart was familiar with its current leader, Rāshid al-Dīn Sinān (died 1192/93), who ruled the Nizaris for about three decades and occasionally resided at the Syrian fortress of Qadmūs (which also comes up in the cited passage from *Massa'ot*).[7] Ibn Jubayr's account features some well-known motifs of anti-Ismaili legends, such as the claim that Sinān's devotees were willing to leap to their death at his command. Although the Nizaris, like other Shiite communities, believed in divinely instituted religious authority and had certain esoteric traditions, it is unclear what role their leader claimed for himself. In any event, Ibn Jubayr accuses them of apostasy from Islam because of their "vesting divinity in a man."[8] As he had no stake in the Sunni-Shiite controversy, Benjamin merely presents them as one of many non-Jewish communities that believe in a false prophet.

Druze

Among the various ethnicities and sects inhabiting the mountains of Lebanon (to this day) are the Druze. In Benjamin's words, "They live in the high mountains and the clefts of the rocks. There is no king or ruler who governs them, as they live independently between the mountains and rocks. Their territory extends till Mount Hermon, a distance of three days."[9] As in the case of the Nizaris, the Iberian Jew was one of the first European authors to put the Druze on the regional map—a fact that once again situates his book within the historical context of the crusaders' penetration into the Levant. Not coincidentally, he tells of an armed conflict between the Druze and the city of Sidon, which then belonged to the Latin kingdom of Jerusalem. Though their religion is related to that of the Ismailis from a historical standpoint, the Druze—who see themselves as true "unitarians" (*muwaḥḥidūn*)—are usually not considered Muslims.[10] Possibly influenced by this Muslim perspective on the Druze, Benjamin deems them *paganos* (a Romance loanword for "pagans") who "have no religion at all."[11]

As a close-knit society that keeps its doctrines secret, the Druze have long lived under a shroud of mystery. Attributing all kinds of licentious activities to the Druze, *Massa'ot* reflects commonplace medieval Christian and Sunni prejudices against this sect.[12] Especially repugnant, albeit riveting, stories appeared of their alleged sexual deviances, such as incest and wife swapping—a well-known topos of travel literature that has been associated with many "exotic" peoples.[13] According to Benjamin, "They are steeped in incestuous vice; they take their sisters, and a father takes his daughter [to bed]." And they engage in ritual libertinism: "Once a year, they have a feast where everyone, men and women, comes to eat and drink together, and [then] they exchange their wives, each one with his friend."[14] Many medieval readers were doubtless intrigued by these raunchy stories.

Infidel Turks

Like the mountains of Lebanon, central and eastern Iran (Khurāsān) are regions that were largely beyond the ken of premodern European audiences. Benjamin believes this area to be home to other Jewish warrior tribes (different from those discussed in the previous chapter), which are allied with a fearsome people called Kuffār al-Turk, or infidel Turks—an Arabic term that may hint at the oral source of this tradition. Beyond the colorful character of the related tales (see below), this purported Jewish link of the Kuffār al-Turk explains the Tudelan's interest in them. He considers them one of a handful of Turkic tribes that are known as Ghuzz in Arabic (a name that Benjamin is also acquainted with), or Oghuz in Turkish.[15] "Fifteen years ago," he writes, they "came to Persia with a large army and took the city of Rayy, smote it with the sword, took all of its spoils, and left by way of the wilderness."[16] Thereafter, the "king of Persia" launched a campaign against the Kuffār al-Turk, but was forced to retreat after losing most of his troops on the battlefield.[17]

Given this description's matter-of-fact tone, a historical verification seems warranted. The city of Rayy (a southeastern part of greater modern-day Tehran; see Map 1) was laid waste by an Oghuz invasion in 1035, almost a century and a half before the Tudelan penned his account. A few years later, Rayy fell into the hands of the Seljuks, another Turkish clan.[18] In contrast to *Massa'ot*'s description, both the Oghuz and Seljuks were Muslims ("Ishmaelites"), not "infidels." However, during the first half of the twelfth century—much closer to Benjamin's own time—Transoxania was invaded by the Qarā Khiṭāi, a nomadic people originating from northern China; and unlike other nomads who conquered Islamic lands, the Qarā Khiṭāi never embraced Islam. Their advances roughly coincided with an Oghuz rebellion against the Seljuk sultan, Sanjar bin Malik Shāh, whom they defeated in 1153—a date that approximates Benjamin's suggested time frame ("fifteen years ago").[19] It stands to reason that *Massa'ot* essentially combines both nomadic waves of migration, that of the Oghuz and the Qarā Khiṭāi, into one.

Regardless of the historical events that Benjamin is echoing, they have been richly embellished by legend and fantasy, as illustrated by his colorful portrait of the Kuffār al-Turk: "They worship the wind and inhabit the wilderness and neither eat bread nor drink wine, but [live] exclusively [on] raw meat that is not cooked. They have no noses, and instead of the nose they have two small holes through which the breath emits. They eat all kinds of animals, be they [ritually] unclean or clean [according to Jewish law]. But they love Israel very much."[20]

The lack of noses places this particular account within the tradition of Eastern marvels, such as "monstrous" races that live beyond the borders of the known world.[21] Together with other fantastic aliens, such as the mouthless (*astomi*) and headless (*acephali*), these noseless people can be traced back to Pliny's *Natural History* (first century) and the many appropriations from his work on the part of medieval authors of encyclopedias, anthologies, and travel accounts.[22] Most prominent among the last genre is *The Book of Mandeville*, which features an entire chapter on remote islands populated by marvelous aliens, including a "people who have a completely flat and completely level face, noseless and eyeless, except for two small round holes instead of eyes and a mouth as flat as a lipless slit."[23]

The raw-meat diet of Benjamin's "infidel Turks" is another well-known motif of travel literature; Petaḥyah of Regensburg offers a similar description of a nomadic people: "In the Land of Kedar, they eat no bread but only rice and millet boiled in milk as well as milk and cheese. [When they are] on horse[back], they put slices of meat . . . under the saddle, and they tire out the horse so that it sweats; [in this fashion] the meat gets warm and [then] they eat it."[24] The Land of Kedar seems to be Petaḥyah's toponym for the southern Ukraine of today or Crimea (see Map 1). This citation is perhaps one of the earliest references to the Crimean Tatars.

Benjamin's reference to a diet of unclean meat echoes a prominent theme from the *Alexander Romance*. A compilation of legends about Alexander the Great and his Eastern exploits, this book came out in numerous versions and languages, including Greek, Latin, Arabic, Hebrew, and most medieval European vernaculars. While other versions refer only to an exotic people subsisting on raw meat, the medieval Hebrew rendering relates that Alexander came to "a land in the East" where he "found a despised and lowly people" who consumed "reptiles, horses, swine, and all kinds of birds, beasts and unclean swarming and creeping creatures."[25] In addition, the *Alexander Romance* accuses these savages of eating their dead, a claim that is absent from Benjamin's account.

Despite their unkosher diet, the Tudelan contends that the Kuffār al-Turk "love Israel very much."[26] Conjuring up the image of a most exotic people that challenge the mighty "king of Persia" is thus part of Benjamin's larger vision of Khurāsān as a utopian home of valiant warrior Jews in league with the "infidel Turks."

Black Africans

Aside from legends about the mythical Lost Tribes (discussed in the previous chapter), the *Book of Eldad* offers a first-person account of Eldad ha-Dani's purported adventures "beyond the rivers of Cush." A rather elastic geographical reference (derived from Isa. 18:1), Cush in this context may allude to the Upper Nile region and Ethiopia. Before arriving in Africa, Eldad and his travel companion (another member of a Lost Tribe) had been on an unspecified maritime journey. Their ship was tossed about in a violent storm "until the sea cast us among a people called Romranos," who were "black Cushites."[27] The biblical name Cush, a descendant of Noah and a son of Ham (Gen. 10:6), is the root of a common Hebrew term, *kushi* (hence Cushite), for black people as well as their place of origin.[28] Adopting a prevalent and enduring stereotype, Eldad describes the Romranos as beastlike subhumans who walk about stark naked and practice anthropophagy (the eating of human flesh). Accordingly, the protagonist's travel companion was eaten by the Cushites. Eldad was spared this fate because he had fallen ill on the high seas and the savages wished to fatten him up. In the meantime, the Cushites were "miraculously" attacked by a foreign army, which took Eldad captive, thus saving his life and enabling him to face more adventures.[29]

Some of these topoi are expanded in David Re'uveni's highly fanciful narrative of his own forays into northeastern Africa, a region where he probably never set foot. From Jeddah, the self-styled Jewish prince claims to have taken a sea passage to the port city of Suakin (Sawākin, in northeastern Sudan of modern times). As opposed to Eldad, Re'uveni was not shipwrecked, but he, too, became grievously ill on the high seas and sought succor through bloodletting, the application of hot nails, and protracted fasts. Upon reaching Suakin, he joined a caravan of more than three thousand camels that was headed for the legendary kingdom of Sheba (which otherwise is often located in Yemen). After a two-month journey "through vast deserts and forests . . . and over rivers and mountains,"[30] he reached the capital of Cush on the banks of the Nile. The king of this exotic polity was called 'Amarah, a black man who ruled over black and white subjects alike.[31] Some of the places and names that come up in this context seem to fit Ethiopia or modern-day Sudan. For example, the said monarch could be ʿAmāra Dūnqas, the early sixteenth-century ruler of the Funj, a nomadic cattle-herding people on the Blue Nile.[32] For the most part, though, Re'uveni's route seems to go through imagined geography with only a tenuous relation to actual terrain. Therefore, the few identifiable details therein should be considered authenticating devices that were used to lend verisimilitude to an otherwise imaginary voyage of a hero who overcomes the most perilous of circumstances.

In his representation of ʿAmarah's court, Re'uveni employs some prevalent stereotypes of exoticism: nudity and colorful jewelry. "The king, whom I accompanied, had female and male servants, most of whom were naked."[33] The queen, concubines, princesses, and maidservants all sport golden armlets, bracelets, and anklets. In addition, they wear a sort of golden chastity belt: "And they cover their nakedness with a hand-wrought chain of gold, a cubit wide, which goes round the loins and is locked in front and behind; the rest of the body is naked. And all the women wear gold nose rings."[34] Re'uveni himself was given four female and four male slaves, whom he insisted on clothing, in an apparent effort to civilize the savages. The story's erotic character is intensified when the protagonist tells how he almost succumbed to the temptation (the "evil inclination," or *yeṣer ha-ra*ʿ in Hebrew) of having sex with a slave girl. Having already conducted her to his bed, it was only the Jewish adventurer's "good inclination" that helped him resist the exotic-erotic pull (though he could not fall asleep the rest of the night). The state of utter barbarity in which these African people ostensibly live is underscored by a diet consisting of exotic, unkosher animals (elephants, wolves, tigers, dogs, camels, mice, frogs, and snakes) and even human flesh.[35] All told, Re'uveni's story of his African travels and travails seems to reflect the early modern era's ambivalence to the so-called Dark Continent, both a repugnance and fascination with, say, "savage" nudity and (alleged) cannibalism.[36]

While Benjamin does not narrate any personal adventures in Africa (as will be recalled, he is not the protagonist of his book), *Massaʿot* does include various references to black Africans. As far as the twelfth-century author can tell, they live beyond Aswan (see Map 1), the historic border town between Egypt and Nubia. In this particular context, it serves as a boundary marker between the known and unknown world. The fact that Benjamin calls the Cushite king *sulṭān al-ḥabasha*, the traditional Arabic title for the ruler of Ethiopia, seems to be another indication that his information draws on Arabic (oral) sources.[37] The Jewish traveler merely repeats ancient stereotypes and commonplace value judgments regarding African ethnicity and color in general.[38] Specifically, he believes that blacks have "bestial" habits as well as a lower mental capacity than other humans: "There is a people among [the Cushites] who are like beasts eating the weeds on the bank of the Pishon [in this context, the Nile River] and in the fields. They walk about naked and don't have the [same] intelligence [Hebrew: *da'at*] as humans. They have intercourse with their sisters and with whomever they find."[39] As noted, Benjamin similarly accuses the Druze of incest and promiscuity. Against this backdrop, this claim may be less a product of racial prejudice than stereotypes associated with all sorts of "barbaric" people.

His paternalistic portrait of black Africans is rooted in the reality of black (and white) slavery in the Islamicate world. Cairo's Jewish merchant class, which the Tudelan would have encountered on the Egyptian leg of his peregrinations, is known to have maintained domestic slaves, some of whom originated from Sudan.[40] Whatever his personal encounter with slaves may have been, Benjamin presents blacks as beastlike and gullible, to the point where they are easily taken captive by Aswan's slave traders: "When the people of Aswan set out on raids of [the blacks'] land, they take bread, wheat, raisins, and figs with them and throw it to them; and when they come after the food, they take many of them captives. They sell them in Egypt and in all the kingdoms around them. These are the black slaves, the children of Ham."[41] Despite the fact that it was another son of Ham, Canaan (the eponymous ancestor of the Canaanites), who was cursed to "be the lowest of slaves to his brothers" (Gen. 9:25), Cush's descent from Ham often served to legitimize (as it were) the enslavement of black Africans in Christian and Jewish sources. By referring to the biblical forefather of all blacks, both human diversity and inequality seemed tenable from a religious standpoint.

Aside from these biblical "rationalizations," Benjamin's unquestioned assumption that the enslavement of black people is the natural course of things derives from a tradition of prejudice with roots in Greek and Roman antiquity. According to a prevalent explanatory model (that hearkens back to Aristotle and Pliny), differences in skin color were a product of disparate climate zones—a hypothesis that seems to undergird Benjamin's description of human diversity, for he highlights that the black slaves' country of origin "is very hot."[42] As illustrated by the Tudelan's portrayal of Africans, balmy environments were often associated not only with dark skin but with moral laxity and cowardice.

With regard to India, *Massa'ot* offers an image of blacks that is at variance with the prevailing stereotypes: there are also "children of Cush" who "are all black" on the west coast of India.[43] While these Cushites worship the sun, they are honest merchants, in the Tudelan's reckoning. Among them are even black adherents of his own religion who are "good Jews observing the commandments."[44] As Benjamin may have realized, the dispersion of Jews throughout the then-known world challenged theories whereby human dispositions were conditioned by climate.[45] In this sense, Benjamin's discourse on blackness even includes potential variations of the self.

The Male Gaze: Women and Gender

The following pages discus the portrayal of another marginalized group: women. Among the various issues to be addressed in this context is the function of a representational mode: How are Levantine women exoticized by male Jewish travelers from Europe, and for what purposes? Why is female veiling considered a form of either modesty or subversion? And what is the role of these "strange" women in the writers' larger conceptualization of the Middle East?

It has been noted that none of the texts under review was authored by a woman. There are several reasons for this: the era's defined gender roles and most women's comparative lack of independent financial means limited their possibilities to set out on the road.[46] Specifically, questions of physical security imposed constraints on a woman's wanderlust. Even so, there are numerous references in the literature to Jewish women going on pilgrimage, which was one of the socially more acceptable forms of female long-distance travel.[47] However, the exceedingly low literacy rate among premodern women (Jewish and non-Jewish alike) prevented them from recording their experiences abroad.[48] As a result, all the sources discussed in this book represent the privileged position of a literate male elite.

Against this background, I here draw on the theoretical model of the "male gaze," by which I mean the representational power that was wielded by a travel writer against the depicted female object.[49] While most of the Jewish travelers discussed in this study hailed from Christian lands, such a perspective about foreign women appears to characterize male-authored travel literature in general, irrespective of the author's cultural background. In an illustrative example for the male gaze, the Iberian poet Judah Halevi evokes the following scene of bejeweled girls standing along the Nile:

> On the Nile's bank are girls, and not just one; gazelles yet not as fleet—
> Their arms weighed down by bangles and anklets halt their steps.[50]

Had these lines been composed by a traveler from northern Europe, one would be inclined to classify these expressions of male visual appreciation as an early "Orientalist" trope. However, in Halevi's work, they are classical elements of Andalusian poetry, in both its Hebrew and Arabic forms. Tellingly, the poet hints that these are the erotic fantasies of a man—namely, himself—in his sixties ("the heart enticed forgets its age").

After these theoretical reflections, I now turn to what have become prominent cultural markers of the "exotic" East in the eyes of Western audiences: gender separation and female veiling. As early as the twelfth century, Petaḥyah of Regensburg depicts the veil as a fabricator of invisibility; "he repeatedly told [his audience] that he saw no woman all the time he was in Babylon [Baghdad] because they are veiled and modest."[51] In this context, it may seem surprising that Petaḥyah applauds the strict gender codes that were observed by Iraqi Jews: "In the city of Baghdad . . . no [Jewish] man looks at a woman; and no man goes to the house of his friend, lest he see the wife of his friend who would immediately say to him: 'Insolent man, why have you come?' But he knocks with a tin [knocker], and [the friend] comes out and speaks with him."[52] As a manifestation of the moral values held by the *Ḥaside Ashkenaz*, this portrait of Babylonian Jewry serves Petaḥyah as a foil for the perceived shortcomings of mainstream Ashkenazi culture.[53]

Yet another surprising anecdote in *Sibbuv* tells of the precocious daughter of a famous Baghdad scholar, the aforementioned *ga'on* Samuel ben 'Eli.[54] This young woman, whose name is glaringly absent in the story, was an "expert in Scripture and Talmud."[55] While literacy was largely limited to the elite in medieval Jewish society, boys were ideally taught some basic reading skills, with the principal objective of enabling them to participate in synagogue services. As a rule, girls were denied such an education, for they lacked an active role in the liturgy. That said, early rabbinic sources discuss whether a father may privately teach his daughter Torah.[56] In light of other such cases that turned up in the Cairo Genizah, there is reason to believe that the *ga'on*—who had no sons, according to *Sibbuv*—gave his daughter an education that was ordinarily the prerogative of boys.[57] It is also known that learned women were excluded from the male domain, and female instructors could only teach pupils of minor age.[58]

Against this backdrop, it is even more startling that Samuel's daughter taught young men the Hebrew Bible, according to Petaḥyah.[59] Even so, this anecdote ultimately affirms that the community's public and private spaces were gendered and that literacy was reserved for males; Petaḥyah notes that she instructs her male students "through a window, while she remains within the building and the students are outside below and do not see her."[60] It is also worth noting that Petaḥyah was evidently drawn to this case not because of the gender issue but because it supported his idealized vision of Iraqi Jewry as a learned and pious community par excellence.

A prime indicator of both gender and social status, the peculiarities of Levantine women's garb are a well-worn theme in Occidental representations of the Middle East, even before illustrations of Oriental custom and costume would become a staple of early modern travel accounts and printed fashion books.[61] As transitions from one ethno-religious space to another are often marked by descriptions of women's attire, Meshullam of Volterra discusses the female dress mode shortly after setting foot in the "strange" new world of Alexandria: "I have explored Alexandria and their customs and found that they have very strange customs. The women see without being seen, for over their faces they wear a black cloth [Hebrew: *miṣnefet*] with small holes. On their head they wear a miter [Italian: *mitra*] of paper that is folded many times, glued [Italian: *incollata*], and decorated. Over it [they wear] a white cloth that reaches their ankles and covers them up to the nose."[62]

This passage's convoluted mix of Hebrew and Italian words reflects the writer's attempt to offer a precise image along with his feelings of cultural dislocation. However, the major elements of Mamluk ladies' street apparel (Figure 5)—a black facial veil, a paper-padded bonnet (Arabic: *ṭarṭūr*), and a large white wrap (known as an *izār*)—clearly emerge from his description.[63] To put Meshullam's observations into perspective, honorable women in the streets of Medici Florence might have similarly concealed themselves from "common" eyes under capacious cloaks (*mantelli*) that came with a hood or could simply be pulled over the head.[64] Above all, it was the quasi-netted veil—worn by wealthy ladies as an indicator of status more than religion—that the Volterrean considered one of the "strange" ways of Mamluk society, as it allowed women to "see without being seen."[65] This phrasing seems to express the uneasiness felt by Meshullam when he became the object of a *female* gaze that he was unable to return. One may infer from his description that he considered the facial veil a mask-like disguise.

This interpretation is supported by Meshullam's reference to some Jewish women in Hebron whose full covering granted them entry into the Ḥaram

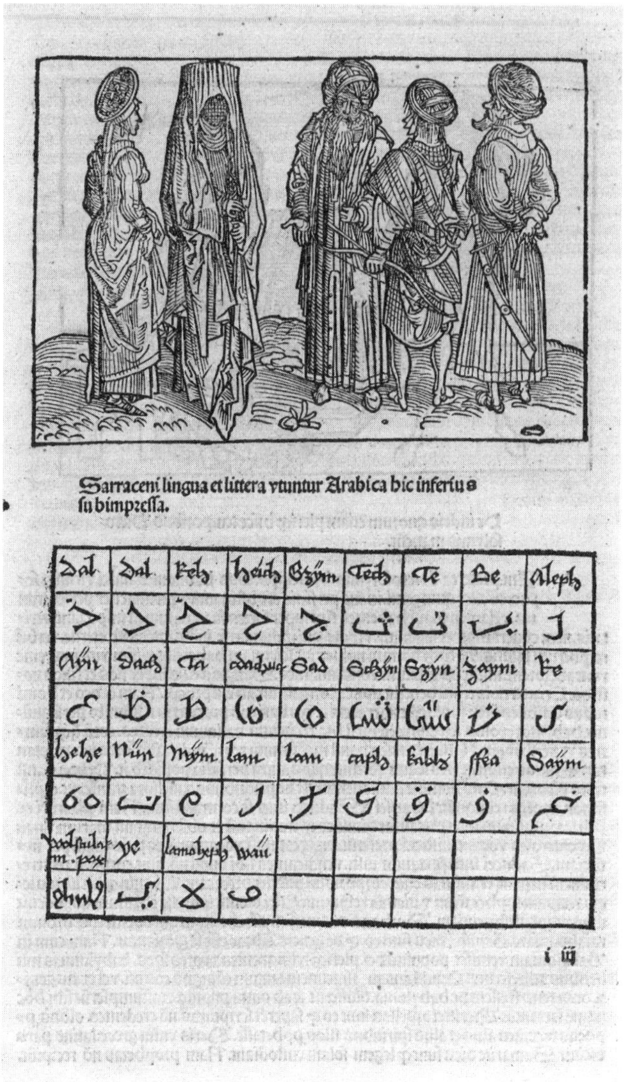

Figure 5. "Saracen" costumes, showing varieties of male and female dress from the late Mamluk Empire. The first figure on the left dons a paper-padded bonnet (Arabic: *ṭarṭūr*); the second wears a facial veil and a large white wrap (*izār*) that is thrown over the said bonnet. This image stems from Bernhard von Breydenbach's *Peregrinatio ad Terram Sanctam*, which describes the German canon's travels to Jerusalem in 1483–84. Lavishly illustrated by Erhard Reuwich of Utrecht, the first Latin and German print editions of this pilgrimage account appeared in Mainz in 1486. The image reproduced here is from the Speyer edition of 1490 (by Peter Drach), in which the original woodcuts were reused. Courtesy of Van Pelt–Dietrich Library, University of Pennsylvania.

al-Khalīl (Tomb of the Patriarchs), a site that Jews were otherwise barred from during the Mamluk period.[66] In a similar vein, Obadiah's anonymous student writes about an Italian Jewish lady who gained access to Jerusalem's al-Aqṣā Mosque: "Lady Stella . . . , the wife of the Honorable Rabbi Moses of Loborgo . . . , saw its inside with the help of an Ishmaelite townswoman, a prominent lady who resides next to the [*bet*] *midrash* [of Solomon, i.e., the Mosque]. And I heard from Lady Stella that it is built of very handsome stones as bright as the pure sky, and on top it is covered with pure gold that was fashioned by craftsmen."[67] Though unstated in the letter, it can be assumed that both women were fully veiled while touring the Islamic sanctuary.[68]

The above-cited authors broach this topic to offer their readers a glance at "veiled" spheres, sacred places that were off-limits to Jews and other non-Muslim visitors. By securing women freedom of movement and thus social liberties that were denied the male traveler, veils assume a subversive quality in these passages.[69] Like other aspects of Islamicate culture, the positive image of female coverings appears to take a turn for the worse in Jewish travel accounts between the twelfth and early sixteenth centuries.

An exception to this rule among the period's Italian pilgrims was R. Israel Ashkenazi, who echoes Petaḥyah's earlier sentiments about the garb of Middle Eastern women. Perhaps it was his own Ashkenazi cultural background that caused him to praise the modest dress worn by Jerusalemite women, Muslim and Jewish alike. Having settled in Ottoman Palestine during the early sixteenth century, he not only advised his eldest daughter to adopt the local dress code but seemed to prefer it to the latest fashion in Italy:

> The women [of Palestine] conduct themselves with great modesty; their garments [reach] up to the neck and do not reveal so much as a finger of flesh. When they go out, they are totally wrapped in a white garment [the aforementioned *izār*], a black veil entirely of silk covers the face, [allowing] her to see without being seen. Consequently, even a husband does not recognize his wife. They cover the entire body; and if they were to show only a small finger, this would be a great disgrace to them. They scorn the way our women are dressed, and they are right. And shortly after arriving here, I adapted my eldest daughter's clothes to the customs of the land.[70]

Returning to Meshullam, the veil was but one of Levantine society's many "strange" ways. To him, the Islamic realm was a topsy-turvy world in which gender roles were partially reversed. For example, men "go without shoes or stockings" in Alexandria "but [wear] linen robe[s] that reach down to the knee, while the women wear trousers."[71] In Cairo, too, "women wear trousers, instead of the men."[72] Unlike the fashionable men in quattrocento Florence who sported tight-fitting hose (Italian: *calze*), Egyptian males in gowns and robes appeared to be donning women's clothes.[73] Conversely, a trend in Mamluk Egypt was for women to wear long drawers (*sarāwīl*).[74] From Meshullam's standpoint, Near Eastern people were engaged in cross-dressing (an act explicitly prohibited in Deut. 22:5).

Similar statements can be found in contemporaneous Christian pilgrimage accounts, thereby reconfirming the degree to which Meshullam had embraced his fellow countrymen's cultural values. For instance, Santo Brasca, a chancellor at the Sforza court in Milan who journeyed to the Holy Land in 1480 (a year before Meshullam), is also astounded by the fact that Muslim women "wear breeches, but not the men." However, the Milanese administrator strikes a much harsher polemical tone than his Jewish counterpart: women's faces, according to Brasca, were "completely covered by a black veil so that neither their eyes nor the slightest inch of flesh is visible." As a result, they looked "like the devil from hell."[75]

Meshullam offers an intimate description of female jewelry as well. Given that in Mamluk Cairo, wealthy women fully shrouded themselves in public, how was he able to observe that, say, the bands of their drawers were embroidered with jewels and pearls or that their ears were pierced with "ten or eight holes into which they thread precious stones"?[76] It is unlikely that Meshullam was exposed to these details inside the homes of local Jewish dignitaries, for the hostess would probably have covered her hair in the reception room (though not her face), and no male travelers ever laid eyes on the more informal private quarters of a Near Eastern house. Is the Volterrean's observation merely another example of male fantasies about otherwise "invisible" women? This may indeed be the case; but one must also remember that Meshullam traded in pearls and gemstones and thus took a professional interest in such matters. For instance, he knew that "Moorish" (*mori*) gentlemen "do not wear gold rings but silver rings in which they set precious stones and pearls."[77] Therefore, it is conceivable that he learned about women's domestic clothing and jewelry from his business partners in Cairo, where he purchased some pearls and precious stones.[78]

In another prominent facet of Meshullam's cultural commentary, he depicts Islamic law as repressive toward women. In his opinion, Muslim women do not enjoy the same rights as their Jewish counterparts. Whereas rabbinic law obligates a husband to provide his wife with clothing throughout the course of the marriage, the Volterrean contends that the Muslim husband is soon freed from that duty (a claim whose erroneous nature does not need to be discussed here):[79] "When they take a wife, the groom gives them a dowry and from that day on, the man is only obliged to provide her with provisions, food and drink alone; but [with respect to] her clothing, she needs to dress herself out of her own [money]; what is more, upon giving birth to sons, she must supply their provisions."[80] Given the presumed requirement of paying for their own cloths and their children's food, Meshullam holds that Muslim women "are all well known to be prostitutes."[81] He may have been under the impression that the veil enabled them to venture off on sexual escapades much like Florentine carnival masks provided a temporary respite from quotidian norms and stricture. Moreover, he avers that Muslim women can easily secure a divorce (somewhat contradicting his previous argument that they are being taken advantage of): "If they do not want to stay with their husband, they go to the governor of the city and state that the husband does not provide them with food, and their words are believed; and the husband soon has to grant them a writ of divorce [*geṭ*]; for the Ishmaelites give a writ of divorce like the Jews."[82]

Owing to Western men's fascination with the Islamic allowance of polygyny, Meshullam repeatedly makes the absurd claim that Muslim men take "twenty to thirty" wives.[83] In so doing, he gives voice to male fantasies of boundless sexuality and domination. He fails, though, to reflect on the perpetuation of multi-wife families in Judaism. While Ashkenazi ordinances prohibited a man from taking more than a single spouse and Near Eastern Jews often signed prenuptial agreements to that effect, polygyny was not unheard of in the Jewish Levant.[84] According to Meshullam, the Muslim practice offered a solution for certain sexual restrictions that were imposed on the husband by Islamic law: "When she is pregnant, the husband is not permitted to touch her any more because to them it is a transgression to spill semen in vain, even with their own wives. For this reason, they take twenty or thirty wives, and there are Ishmaelite men who have twenty sons and daughters in a single year."[85]

It seems that fantasies about the hidden attractions of the harem were encouraged by the very limited contact between European travelers like Meshullam and Near Eastern women. As a result, he depicts "Oriental" women as sexualized and promiscuous, on the one hand, and subjugated and oppressed, on the other. Either way, his exoticized portrait of Near Eastern women adds to the general picture that he draws of the Islamicate world as a place that is both desirable (commercially and sexually) and disorienting.

Conclusion

Throughout this study, I have attempted to describe the Muslim world as it was encountered, envisioned, and elaborated by Jewish travelers and writers during a period that, from a European perspective, is broadly considered the late Middle Ages but extends into the early modern era. Far from clearly distinguishing between East and West, medieval Jewish travel literature does not know any hegemonic discourse of the Orient. Just as the European Jewish traveler to the Levant represented multiple categories, the analyzed texts do not speak with one voice but offer a kaleidoscope of perspectives, including contradictory ones. In so doing, they confute any notion of (Muslim or Jewish) culture and identity as fixed and reducible to an immutable essence. On the contrary, the Middle East that emerges from the discussed sources is a region with diverse attributes and shifting dynamics.

As the writers' cultural backgrounds, individual preferences, travel routes, and destinations varied and changed, so did their points of interest and perceptions. In addition to describing places, the texts convey their authors' proclivities, intended audiences, and time periods. Between the twelfth and early sixteenth centuries, Hebrew travel writing underwent fundamental changes in all that concerns perception and representation. The authors of crusader-era itineraries largely shunned explicitly self-revealing content. In the case of Benjamin of Tudela, for instance, there is almost no trace of the traveler in his impersonal accounts of foreign cities and marvels. From his vantage point, the precise description of a specific place or event was of little value when the same passage could be recruited (and often transformed) in the service of a greater religious truth. Conversely, fifteenth- and sixteenth-century travelers reveal a clear consciousness of themselves as both observers and authors. Circulated among Italian Jewish communities, their diaries and letters attest to a growing interest in providing accounts of the Middle East that were more contemporary and more engaged with the specific historical circumstances of the day than, say, Benjamin's—by then, thoroughly outdated—*Massa'ot*, which nonetheless was still copied, printed, and read by early modern Jewry.

Adopting a variety of genres and forms, medieval Jewish travel writers provided their audiences with diverse portraits of the East as an actual, imaginary, and conceptual realm. Judah Halevi, for instance, used the pilgrimage to Zion as a metaphor for a mystical quest. In his poems, he conjured up a spiritual East that was inherently superior to the West, which he identified with Andalusian court culture and its worldly riches rather than Christian Europe. Judah Alḥarizi, by contrast, viewed both the Arabic and Jewish culture of the *mashriq* (the Islamicate East) to be vastly inferior to that of the more refined *maghrib* (West), despite ultimately settling down in Aleppo following his lengthy peregrinations. As these examples demonstrate, the travel writers often employed the journey as a vehicle for reflecting on their place of departure.

Another case in point is Petaḥyah of Regensburg's pilgrimage account. By envisioning an exceptionally pious and erudite Jewish community in Iraq, *Sibbuv*'s narrator (or his editors) used the travel genre to criticize what he probably saw as the laxity of contemporaneous Ashkenazi Jewry. By extension, Petaḥyah challenged the centrality and normative character of Europe and its (Jewish) moral codes. In repudiating their country of origin and declaring it a place of exile vis-à-vis Zion, a number of this study's protagonists attempted no less than a cultural reorientation. At the same time, they reoriented a European vision of the East, for they overtly distanced themselves from any conceptualization of the Land of Israel as a Christian *terra sancta*. But where, exactly—if at all—did the travelers draw a border between East and West?

In fact, the transition was gradual for those who took one of the long and complicated land routes from Europe to the Levant. If a transformation in these cases was discernible, it was due to the change in the religious affiliation of the people encountered along the way. As Petaḥyah puts it, "the people believe in the law of Muhammad" from the "land of the Turks" onward.[1] For Meshullam of Volterra, by contrast, the cultural boundary between Orient and Occident was clearly traversed upon debarking at Alexandria.[2] Other seaborne travelers (for example, Obadiah of Bertinoro and Moses Basola) describe the Mediterranean as a site of mass transit, commercial exchange, and religious interaction—instead of separation—and, in this sense, offer support to a Braudelian conceptualization of this historic sea as a contact zone between East and West.[3]

This transnational cultural awareness among a number of the authors seems to reflect that, traveling between Iberia and Iraq, Venice and Cairo, Jewish pilgrims and merchants passed through numerous Jewish diasporas. In so doing, they relied on kinship networks that extended beyond cultural, political, and linguistic boundaries. While Obadiah marveled at the different customs and traditions of local Jewish communities, he also expressed a sense of belonging that undermines the foreign-versus-familiar dichotomy. Though some authors rendered Near Eastern Jews, Karaites, and Samaritans as aliens, others explored potential conceptualizations of the self in their portraits of a distant relative. The Middle East that takes shape in these descriptions turns out to be far from uniformly (Sunni) Muslim; it is home to numerous other minorities besides Jews, such as Ismailis, Druze, and "Christians of the girdle" (Levantine Christians).[4]

Given the relative prominence of business information in the sources, I shall revisit here a question that was raised in the Introduction: Did these Jewish travelers' descriptions of the Middle East betray fledgling attitudes of what would later epitomize the age of European expansion and commercial hegemony? As a product of the twelfth century, Benjamin was still far removed from notions of Western economic predominance. Describing an interconnected world of commerce stretching from Iberia to India, *Massaʿot* reflects a transnational trade network that, according to Janet Abu-Lughod, "finally attached" Europe "more firmly to the ongoing world system."[5] In particular, the Tudelan mirrors two of the important trade routes that linked the medieval Christian world to the Middle East (even if the author himself did not reach the end of either line): "the central route connecting the Mediterranean with the Indian Ocean via Baghdad, Basra, and the Persian Gulf" and "the southerly route connecting the Alexandria-Cairo-Red Sea complex with the Arabian Sea and then the Indian Ocean."[6]

What Abu-Lughod terms the "interdependent world system" of the later Middle Ages seems to have fallen apart in the mid-fourteenth century (the spread of the bubonic plague along some of the same routes was just one factor in this breakdown in communications). At the turn of the sixteenth century, the Portuguese fleet threatened the Mamluks' and later the Ottomans' naval hegemony over the spice trade. Nonetheless, Meshullam, Obadiah, and Basola highlighted cities such as Cairo and Alexandria as trade hubs on the commercial networks spanning the Mediterranean Sea and the Indian Ocean.

Over the course of this book, I have largely tracked Jewish perspectives on the Middle East during two historical ages: the crusader era; and the Ayyubid to the early Ottoman period. A quintessential example of the first category, Benjamin's *Massa'ot*, appears to be the product of a complex and intense encounter with Christianity. Although European Jewish pilgrimage to the Levant took advantage of the improved transportation services between outremer and Latin Europe, twelfth-century Hebrew itineraries assailed Christian claims to exclusive ownership over sacred places that were deeply ingrained in the Jewish cultural memory. Reclaiming King David's tomb and the Cave of Makhpelah for his Jewish readership, the Tudelan (more than any of the other writers) subverted Christian supersessionism. Christian as well as Jewish pilgrimage accounts from the Middle Ages were doubtless Jerusalem-oriented. However, the Jewish authors of the crusader era shifted the spotlight from the Holy Sepulchre (a place of "idolatry") to the Temple Mount, which, despite its appropriation by the Latin Church, continued to be the symbolic center of the Jewish universe. Echoing medieval Judaism's generally negative attitude toward Christianity, the binary opposite and antagonist of these travel accounts was "Edom," not "Ishmael."

None of the authors preferred Muhammad over Jesus, both of whom they commonly referred to with derogatory epithets (the "madman" and "that man," respectively). Still, these Jewish travelers' engagement with Christianity determined their construction of the Islamic world. In *Massa'ot*, for instance, Abbasid Iraq serves as a canvas on which to project ideal images of Jewish dignity, authority, and self-rule.[7] Against the backdrop of twelfth-century Iberian history, Benjamin's glowing portrait of Jewish-Muslim relations in Baghdad may be expressing a certain nostalgia for the conditions prevailing in al-Andalus, before the Christian *reconquista* inexorably altered the political and religious landscape of medieval Iberia.[8]

In another difference from their representation of Christian-Jewish relations, travelers from both the crusader and early Mamluk periods attest that Jews and Muslims frequently rubbed shoulders at Near Eastern shrines. Similar reports of amicable interfaith relations are to be found in several works by fifteenth-century Jewish authors who depicted the Levant as a place that stands in stark contradistinction to Europe in all that concerns the majority's treatment of the Jewish populace. As opposed to the restrictions against Jews in early modern Italy (not least their exclusion from numerous professions by Christian guilds), they faced no economic discrimination of this sort in Islamic lands. By their account, residents of the Levant expressed little animosity toward Jewish pilgrims and immigrants.

In contrast, other quattro- and cinquecento Jewish travelers struck a more polemical tone in their descriptions of Muslim-Jewish relations at what they considered to be contested holy places. Following the expulsion of the crusaders from Palestine, Muslims apparently asserted their hegemony over sacred space and were less inclined to welcome other worshipers than at earlier stages of Islamic rule. On the other hand, the fact that these accounts were penned by Italian Jews might attest to the impact of the contemporaneous Christian discourse regarding the "infidel's occupation" of the Holy Land. Together with the lifestyle and mores of their Christian peers, these Jewish travelers apparently absorbed some negative rhetoric about Muslims and Islam. There is a strong resemblance between the earlier Jewish polemic against the crusaders and, say, Isaac ben Meir Latif's or Basola's jibes against Muslim control over "Jewish" sites. Whatever his origins, David Re'uveni, the most oscillating figure among the discussed travelers, doubtlessly echoed sixteenth-century calls for renewed crusading with his fantastic plans for a Christian-Jewish military campaign against the Ottomans.

I began this study by asking whether European Jewish travelers shared certain "Western" perceptions of the Middle East with their Christian counterparts. The analyzed sources clearly have brought considerable nuance to what might otherwise be an overstated and static dichotomy between Jewish and Christian perspectives on the "Orient." In fact, the travel corpus reveals shifting views of the Islamicate world on the part of European Jews. There is no clear cutoff year (say, 1450) between pro-Islamic and anti-Islamic sentiments. Likewise, there is no evidence in support of the claim that Orientalism ultimately reared its head at the dawn of the early modern era (whenever exactly that may have been), or that from then on, the opinions expressed by Europe's Christian and Jewish travelers concerning the Levant were uniformly negative. Despite their shared Italian background and travel routes, even contemporaries such as Meshullam of Volterra and Obadiah of Bertinoro voiced sharply contrasting views on the Near East and its people, thereby attesting to a broad spectrum of cultural attitudes in Italian Jewish society (and the same holds arguably true for the Christian travel writers of that period).

Meshullam's accounts of Muslims and Near Eastern Jews are undoubtedly permeated with a bias that does and does not conform to the prejudices, fantasies, and assumptions of later Orientalism, as described by Said. Within the context of his descriptions of everyday life, the upper-class merchant explicitly assumes the superiority of Italians over the people of the Mamluk Empire—and thereby, his, the writer's positional superiority vis-à-vis his subjects. Much of what the Volterrean states about local customs is based on presuppositions, as he cannot be said to have made a genuine attempt to understand a foreign culture. In construing the Islamicate world, the norms and values of the home—the Tuscan Jewish elite, in his case—serve the merchant as a "universal" point of comparison. His portrait of Near Eastern people features confident generalizations, ethnic stereotyping, and cultural condescension. Like other male travelers, Meshullam was especially curious about the sexual practices of the Levant, such as polygyny and harems. However, due to his limited access to the gendered sphere of the home, he leaves his readers with contradictory clichés about "Oriental" women, such as their invisibility in public or, alternatively, promiscuity in private.

Unlike his status-driven contemporary and compatriot, Obadiah displays remarkably little religious or cultural bias toward the Near East. In his letters, the late Mamluk Empire comes across as a multiethnic society in which the Muslim majority cohabitates with a plethora of religious and ethnic minorities. Relatively impartial to other people, local customs, and religious differences, the Mishnah scholar's account reflects an educated man's values and sensibilities; it offers genuine examples of cross-cultural understanding. If Obadiah, as I have suggested, had read Meshullam's travel diary, he may well have made a conscious decision to portray the Levant in a different light.

Meshullam's and Obadiah's divergent accounts of what must have been a very similar journey from Italy to Palestine, via Egypt, are indicative of the various ways a foreign country can be experienced. This incongruity sheds light on the difference between the objectivity of travel (actually being there) and the subjective memory or reconstruction of a trip in hindsight (having been there). Bear in mind that Obadiah had permanently left his place of origin and then assumed a resident's perspective of his adopted home. Meshullam, by contrast, had planned to return to Italy from the outset, and his contact with Near Eastern cultures was exceedingly superficial and fleeting. The merchant subsequently used the travel journal to reaffirm his standing in the home culture, where knowledge of distant places conferred status. In this respect, Meshullam's Near Eastern journey invites comparison with modern tourism. For "tourism involves a temporary change of the *status quo.* However, it ends up as protection and reproduction of the *status quo*."[9]

By casting himself as a dispassionate, rational, and thus reliable observer, Obadiah, too, may have been cultivating a desired image: the man of learning had to take into account his own reputation upon penning letters that were likely to be circulated beyond their immediate addressees. Since travel writers were susceptible to charges of exaggeration and mendacity, Obadiah had to safeguard his own rabbinic authority, intellectual respectability, and, not least, his newfound position as leader of the Jewish community in Jerusalem. Therefore, his travel account may no less reflect the self-image he wished to communicate to his readers than Meshullam's diary of his Levantine voyage. Though each adopted a vastly different strategy, both Italian Jews construed their social personae by means of a journey and availed themselves of the travel account to enhance their prestige.

With respect to Meshullam, it behooves us to judge his writing in the context of its own time to avoid reducing the quattrocento Jew to the stereotype of a nineteenth-century Orientalist. If Orientalism is taken to mean an attitude by which the other is defined from the vantage point of the author's own perceived cultural superiority, then his travel journal is perhaps an example of an incipient or "proto-Orientalism" (Barbour).[10] Meshullam's conventionalized distinctions between Italian and Levantine mores are certainly value-laden; they are consonant with opinions about the Islamicate world that were about to take root in European thought. However, if Orientalism is viewed as a discursive tool for controlling, subjugating, and exploiting the other, then the merchant's travelogue fails to qualify. It bears noting that even the most disparaging elements of his rhetoric about the Near East can hardly be considered a discourse from a position of genuine hegemony. Bound to schedules and traveling over routes that he had little input over, the displaced Tuscan was forced to respond to unpredictable encounters with unfamiliar norms and people. Time and again, he was thrust into situations where he felt vulnerable, rather than in control. For example, Meshullam tells how he was tricked by unreliable guards and guides turned robbers. For the sake of blending in and traveling inconspicuously, he even temporarily adopted the same Oriental clothes and mores that he otherwise ridiculed.[11] Inadvertently, the status-conscious merchant had to admit that cultural encounter involves crossing and mixing.

Meshullam's upper-class airs did not spare him from the indignities of anti-Jewish prejudice. To Christian sailors and pilgrims, he was a loathsome Jew, not a cultivated Tuscan.[12] Performing various roles in different circumstances—an Italian among Christians, a Turk among Muslims, an Italian Jew among his Levantine coreligionists—Meshullam had to repeatedly position himself anew with regard to conventions of rank. By emphasizing traits that the European elite had only recently cultivated, he staked his own claim in "respectable" (Italian) society. In so doing, the Volterrean may have unconsciously hinted at the incertitude and ambivalence of his position as a Jew. As such, his scornful depiction of Near Eastern customs and costumes should be interpreted as expressions of social aspiration and achievement by a Jew of fine lineage. One should not presume that, by dint of their own status as the non-Christian other, European Jewish travelers were naturally inclined to display a greater openness to and sympathy for foreign cultures.

Medieval Jewish travel writings echo the tremendous transformation of the Near Eastern political map between the twelfth and sixteenth centuries—a change that went along with an altered religious topography. At the same time, these texts reflect and refract the evolution of Jewish self-perceptions. Growing commerce and accelerated mobility appear to have been among the factors that compelled Europe's Jews to reorient themselves in an ever-expanding world. In addition, the social aspirations of early modern Italian Jews had a profound effect on their perceptions of the Muslim world; as their self-image underwent change, their views toward the other were modified as well. Despite their apparent essentialist character, such definitions as "self" and "other"—or exile and domicile—turn out to be historically situated; they take on different meanings, depending on time, location, and political conditions. Far from simply pitting East against West, the travel narratives analyzed in this book demonstrate the manifold ways in which premodern Jews negotiated their mingled identities: European and Jewish, Western and Eastern.

Chronology of Travelers and Works

Date of Travels	*Traveler/Author*	*Works Discussed*	*Date of Composition*
late ninth century?	Eldad ha-Dani	*Sefer Eldad* (Book of Eldad)	before the mid-twelfth century
1140–41	Judah Halevi	several poems	1141 and earlier
before 1173	Benjamin of Tudela	*Sefer ha-Massaʿot* (Book of Travels)	after 1173
before 1187	Jacob ben Nathanel ha-Kohen	*Sippur Massaʿot* (Story of Travels)	late twelfth century
before 1187	Petaḥyah of Regensburg	*Sibbuv* (Circuit)	late twelfth century
1210	Samuel ben Samson	itinerary	in or after 1210
ca. 1215 and subsequent years	Judah Alḥarizi	*Kitāb al-Durar* (Book of Pearls), *Taḥkemoni*	ca. 1215–25
1265–67	Naḥmanides (Ramban)	letter	1267
	Anonymous	*Elleh ha-Massaʿot* (These Are the Travel Routes)	before 1291
	Anonymous	*Toṣʾot Ereṣ Yisraʾel* (Extremities of the Land of Israel)	late thirteenth century
	Yitgaddal the Scribe	list of holy places	fourteenth century
1437	Elijah of La Massa	letter	1438

Date of Travels	*Traveler/Author*	*Works Discussed*	*Date of Composition*
ca. 1455	R. Isaac ben Meir Latif	letter	ca. 1455
1480	R. Joseph of Montagna	letter	1480
1481	Meshullam of Volterra	letter	in or after 1481
1486–87	R. Obadiah of Bertinoro	three letters	1488, 1489, and 1492
1495	Student of R. Obadiah of Bertinoro	letter	1495
late fifteenth century	Samuel ben Joseph Ibn Picho	letter	late fifteenth century
	Anonymous	*Yiḥus ha-Ṣaddiqim* (Lineage of the Righteous)	late fifteenth century
1520	R. Israel ben Yeḥiel Ashkenazi	letter	ca. 1522
1521–23	R. Moses Basola	*Elleh Masʿay* (These Are My Travels)	in or after 1523
ca. 1523–27	David ha-Re'uveni	*Sippur David ha-Re'uveni* (Story of David ha-Re'uveni)	ca. 1528(?)
	Uri ben Simeon of Biella (copyist)	*Yiḥus Avot* (Lineage of the Ancestors)	1564

Glossary

Abbasids—caliphal dynasty ruling (mostly) from Baghdad (750–1258)

ahl al-dhimma (Arabic)—"protected people"; collective term for religious communities, primarily Jews and Christians, to which Islamic law granted protection

Ashkenazi—Jew of French or Central or Eastern European cultural background

Ayyubids—dynasty of sultans founded by Saladin that ruled greater Syria and Egypt (1171–1250)

bamah (Hebrew)—"high place"; idolatrous shrine (see 2 Kings 23:8 and 15; and 2 Chron. 31:1); polemical reference to churches in medieval Hebrew literature

ben (Hebrew)—"son of"; forms part of a name

Cairo Genizah (Hebrew)—repository of discarded texts at the medieval Ben Ezra Synagogue of Cairo-Fusṭāṭ

dhimmī (Arabic)—"protected person"; member of the *ahl al-dhimma* (s.v.)

dirham—Islamic silver coin

Edom, Edomite—typological reference in medieval Hebrew to Christianity or a Christian

ereṣ yisra'el (Hebrew)—Land of Israel, Palestine

exilarch—see *rosh ha-golah*

Fatimids—dynasty of Shiite (s.v.) caliphs that ruled in Egypt (969–1171), North Africa, and other parts of the Near East

funduq (Arabic)—hostelry for foreign merchants in Muslim cities that also provided storage for merchandise

galut (Hebrew)—"exile," "diaspora," "oppression"

ga'on (Hebrew; plural: *ge'onim*)—"eminence"; head of a post-Talmudic rabbinic academy (yeshiva, s.v.), especially those of Abbasid Baghdad between the ninth and twelfth centuries

Genizah—see Cairo Genizah

ḥajj (Arabic)—Islamic pilgrimage to Mecca

halakhah (Hebrew)—rabbinic legal tradition, Jewish law

Ḥaram al-Khalīl (Arabic)—sanctuary of Abraham the "friend" of God; Islamic term for Hebron's Tomb of the Patriarchs, the Cave of Makhpelah

Ḥaram al-Sharīf (Arabic)—Noble Sanctuary; Islamic term for Jerusalem's Temple Mount

Ḥaside Ashkenaz (Hebrew)—medieval Jewish pietists whose centers were in the south German city of Regensburg (on the Danube) and the Rhineland

Ishmael, Ishmaelite—typological reference in medieval Hebrew to Islam, Muslims, or Arabs

Islamicate—referring to aspects of Muslim society and culture that were shared by non-Muslims

itinerarium (Latin)—list of places on a given route, late antique or medieval travel log

jizya (Arabic)—annual poll tax levied on *dhimmīs* (s.v.) in medieval Muslim societies

Judeo-Arabic—Arabic written in Hebrew characters

Kingdom of Jerusalem—crusader state in the Levant (1099–1291)

maghrib (Arabic)—west

Mamluks—a military caste recruited from the ranks of former slave soldiers; a few rose to become sultans of Egypt and greater Syria (1250–1517)

maqāma (Arabic; plural: *maqāmāt*)—prose poem

mashriq (Arabic)—east

Massaʿot (Hebrew)—"travels"; title of Benjamin of Tudela's book

midrash—rabbinic scriptural interpretation, specific interpretative tradition, or compilation thereof; in the Hebrew travel accounts, the term is sometimes used as a shortform for *bet midrash,* "study house"

Mishnah—earliest compilation of rabbinic laws and traditions, redacted in Palestine around 220

mustaʿrab (Arabic)—"Arabized"; an Arabic-speaking Jew, to be differentiated from a *sefardi* (s.v.)

Ottomans—dynasty of Turkish sultans (ca. 1300–1922), rulers of the Ottoman Empire, or their subjects

parasang—a measure of Persian origin (*farsang, farsakh*) that is about three and a half miles (5.6 kilometers) long

patrone (Italian; plural: *patroni*)—shipmaster

peregrinatio (Latin)—"pilgrimage"; late antique or medieval Christian pilgrimage account

Peṣaḥ (Hebrew)—Passover, a weeklong Jewish festival (eight days in the diaspora) commemorating the Exodus; celebrated in March or April

piyyuṭ (Hebrew)—liturgical poem or poetry

qibbuṣ galuyyot (Hebrew)—"ingathering of the dispersed"; the return of all Jews to the Land of Israel (s.v.) during the messianic age

qivre avot (Hebrew)—"tombs of the ancestors"; tombs of biblical figures

Qubbat al-Ṣakhra (Arabic)—Dome of the Rock

riḥla (Arabic)—"journey"; genre of Arabic travel literature

rosh ha-golah (Hebrew)—"head of the diaspora" or exilarch; Jewish representative to the Abbasid (s.v.) caliph, figurehead of Babylonian Jewry

Rosh Hashanah—Jewish New Year; falls in September or October

ṣaddiq (Hebrew; plural: *ṣaddiqim*)—"righteous"; a Jewish holy person

sefardi (Hebrew; plural: *sefardim*)—Sephardic Jew, Jew of Iberian heritage

Seljuks—Turkish dynasty that ruled in West and Central Asia in the eleventh and twelfth centuries *sharīʿa* (Arabic)—Islamic law

sharīf (Arabic)—"noble"; descendant of the Prophet Muhammad

Shavuʿot—the Jewish Festival of Weeks, which commemorates the revelation of the Torah; falls in May or June

Shiite—a member of the branch of Islam known as *shīʿa* (or *shīʿat ʿalī*, "faction of Ali) that regards Ali and his descendants as the only legitimate successors to Muhammad; cf. Sunni (s.v.)

Sibbuv (Hebrew)—"circuit," "circular voyage"; pilgrimage account of Petaḥyah of Regensburg

Sukkot—the weeklong Jewish Feast of Booths (eight days in the diaspora), which commemorates the wandering of the Israelites in the desert; falls in September or October

Sunni (Arabic)—member of the majority ("orthodox") branch of Islam (*ahl al-sunna*) that regards the four "righteous" caliphs (Abu Bakr, ʿUmar, Muʿawiya, and Ali) as Muhammad's legitimate successors; cf. Shiite (s.v.)

toʿeh (Hebrew; plural: *toʿim*)—"wanderer," "errant one"; polemical term in medieval Hebrew for Christian pilgrims and crusaders

Tosafists—school of medieval Ashkenazi commentators on the Babylonian Talmud

Umayyads—first dynasty of caliphs that ruled the early Muslim empire (661–750)

yeshiva (Hebrew; plural: yeshivot)—rabbinic academy

Yom Kippur—Day of Atonement, eight days after Rosh Hashanah (s.v.); falls in September or October

ziyāra (Arabic; plural: *ziyārāt*)—"visitation"; Muslim or Jewish pilgrimage to a local holy place, to be differentiated from the central or scriptural pilgrimage such as the *ḥajj* (s.v.)

Notes

Introduction

Epigraph: Alḥarizi, *The Book of Taḥkemoni: Jewish Tales from Medieval Spain*, trans. David S. Segal (London: Littman Library of Jewish Civilization, 2001), 231 (slightly modified). For more on Alḥarizi and his use of the travel motif, see Chapter 1 in this volume.

1. The most comprehensive study on this particular topic remains that of Mary B. Campbell, *The Witness and the Other World: Exotic European Travel Writing, 400–1600* (Ithaca, N.Y.: Cornell University Press, 1988). A more recent investigation of medieval Christian constructions of the East is Iain Macleod Higgins, *Writing East: The "Travels" of Sir John Mandeville* (Philadelphia: University of Pennsylvania Press, 1997), which offers a methodologically impressive, in-depth study of what was arguably the most influential travel book of its time (see the following note).

2. Until the nineteenth century, a fourteenth-century English knight named Sir John Mandeville was seen as the unquestioned author of this guidebook and supposed record of a journey from England to the Far East, via Constantinople and Jerusalem. Today, the *Book of Mandeville* is commonly considered a "forgery," as it is almost entirely based on previous travel accounts and other authoritative literature. The original Old French version is available in the critical edition by Christiane Deluze, *Le livre des merveilles du monde* (Paris: Centre Nationale de la Recherche Scientifique, 2000); this version has been recently translated into modern English by Iain Macleod Higgins, *The Book of John Mandeville with Related Texts* (Indianapolis: Hackett, 2011).

3. *The Itinerary of Benjamin of Tudela: Critical Text, Translation and Commentary*, ed. Marcus N. Adler (London: H. Frowde, 1907), vii. In speaking about a "struggle between Cross and Crescent," Adler, however, does not limit himself to the Crusades. He holds that the entire "history of the civilized world from the downfall of the Roman Empire to the *present day* may be summarized" as such a struggle (ibid., my emphasis).

4. This has already been pointed out by Michael Harbsmeier, "Reisen in der Diaspora: Eigenes in der Fremde in der jüdischen Reiseliteratur des Mittelalters," *Das Mittelalter: Perspektiven mediävistischer Forschung* 3, no. 2 (1998): 63–80. Medieval Christian travelers

throughout the Islamic world likewise found hospitality among local Christian communities. To them, however, their countries of origin would not appear to be a form of exile (Hebrew: *galut*) in the same sense as for Jews (see also the following note).

5. On the construction of exile and domicile in medieval Jewish literature, see Yosef H. Yerushalmi, "Exile and Expulsion in Jewish History," in *Crisis and Creativity in the Sephardic World, 1391–1648*, ed. Benjamin R. Gampel (New York: Columbia University Press, 1997), 3–22; and Esperanza Alfonso, *Islamic Culture Through Jewish Eyes: Al-Andalus from the Tenth to the Twelfth Century* (London: Routledge, 2008), 61–64, 70–71, 112, who focuses on these concepts as expressed in Hebrew poetry from Muslim Iberia.

6. My argument finds certain parallels in Simon Gaunt's most recent analysis of Marco Polo's *Description of the World*. According to Gaunt, "Marco Polo's view of the world turns out to be quite the opposite of what we now call Eurocentric: the *Devisement* portrays distant lands and cultures as significantly more sophisticated, powerful and opulent then Europe." Gaunt, *Marco Polo's Le Devisement du Monde: Narrative Voice, Language and Diversity* (Cambridge, U.K.: D. S. Brewer, 2013), 37.

7. From the crusader period, about a dozen so-called T-O maps survive (consisting of a circle divided by a T or a Y), which indicate three continents, with Jerusalem at the center; see Catherine Delano-Smith, "The Intelligent Pilgrim: Maps and Medieval Pilgrimage to the Holy Land," in *Eastward Bound: Travel and Travellers, 1050–1550*, ed. Rosamund Allen (Manchester: Manchester University Press, 2004), 107–29.

8. The term "Orientalism" was coined by Edward Said in his pathbreaking study *Orientalism* (New York: Pantheon, 1978; reprint, New York: Vintage, 2003) to describe the European construction of the Orient as "other." According to Said, this concept enabled the Occident to dominate and ultimately colonize the Orient. However, it is unclear whether Said believed the Orientalist discourse to have originated in the late eighteenth century (see ibid., 22), or to have much earlier roots in medieval Christian or even ancient civilization (see ibid., 59). This is not the place to discuss Said's profoundly influential thesis or to critique some of its well-known generalizations and shortcomings. For an accessible disquisition on Said's work as well as its impact and aftermath, see Zachary Lockman, *Contending Visions of the Middle East: The History and Politics of Orientalism* (Cambridge: Cambridge University Press, 2004), 182–214.

9. Syed Manzurul Islam, *The Ethics of Travel: From Marco Polo to Kafka* (Manchester: Manchester University Press, 1996), 123. By contrast, Gaunt argues that Polo "assumes neither the pre-eminence of European culture nor a stark, binary contrast between Europe and the rest of the world"; Gaunt, *Marco Polo's Le Devisement*, 146.

10. Campbell, *The Witness and the Other World*, 93; for a contrary viewpoint, see Gaunt, *Marco Polo's Le Devisement*, 149, who expresses doubts that "trade is the *Devisement*'s principal aim or main preoccupation."

11. Mary Louise Pratt, *Imperial Eyes: Travel Writing and Transculturation* (London: Routledge, 1992), 4.

12. Josephine W. Bennett, *The Rediscovery of Sir John Mandeville* (New York: Modern Language Association, 1954), 234. In contrast to Bennett, Stephen Greenblatt calls

into question interpretations that perceive Mandeville's book to be an agent of empire. Instead, he argues that it articulates a relatively tolerant attitude toward cultural diversity; see Greenblatt's *Marvelous Possessions: The Wonder of the New World* (Chicago: University of Chicago Press, 1991), 26–51. On the reception of Marco Polo during the age of exploration, see John Larner, *Marco Polo and the Discovery of the World* (New Haven, Conn.: Yale University Press, 1999), 151–60, who doubts that Polo's book had any significant impact on Columbus's expeditions.

13. Benjamin of Tudela's *Itinerary* gained a new Christian readership during the sixteenth century when it was first translated to Latin—which put the medieval Jewish travel account in the context of the European expansion; see, in this volume, Chapter 1 n. 45.

14. As Said has argued, not only scholars of Oriental studies "but also works of literature . . . and *travel books*" have sown the seeds for the imperial project, instead of furthering the understanding of the Islamic world (*Orientalism*, 23; my emphasis). For a fairly recent, constructive critique of Said's travel theory, see Steve Clark, ed., "Introduction," in *Travel Writing and Empire: Postcolonial Theory in Transit* (London: Zed, 1999), 10–13.

15. Medieval geography did not divide the world into just the Asian Orient and European Occident, but knew of three continents (Asia, Europe, and Africa). According to Suzanne Conklin Akbari, the dichotomy of Orient and Occident may be the by-product of the late medieval shift from maps with an eastern orientation to those oriented toward the north; see Akbari, "From Due East to True North: Orientalism and Orientation," in *The Postcolonial Middle Ages*, ed. Jeffrey J. Cohen (New York: St. Martin's, 2000), 19–34; and Akbari, *Idols in the East: European Representations of Islam and the Orient, 1100–1450* (Ithaca, N.Y.: Cornell University Press, 2009), 3, 20–23, 48.

16. With the exception of Benjamin of Tudela, premodern Jewish travel writing does not cover the Far East. His brief references to India and China reflect common medieval lore, as opposed to personal experiences; see Chapter 1 in this volume; and my detailed discussion in "Flying Camels and Other Exotic Species: Natural Marvels in Medieval Jewish Travel Writing" (forthcoming).

17. For this reason, it seems, Roxanne L. Euben asks: "What would it mean to invert the questions that reproduce the West as the epicenter of the world? Instead of only investigating how Western travel writing produces the 'colonized other,' what features of travel . . . might be brought into view by shifting the theoretical perspective?" Euben, *Journeys to the Other Shore: Muslim and Western Travelers in Search of Knowledge* (Princeton, N.J.: Princeton University Press, 2006), 2.

18. The first journal written by a westbound Jewish traveler dates to the late eighteenth century. It was written by Ḥayim Joseph David Azulai (known by his acronym as the Ḥida), who journeyed from Hebron to Europe as an emissary of the Palestinian Jewish community. His travel diary (*Ma'gal Ṭov*, Good Circuit) provides a rare example of an Ottoman Jew encountering Western Europe; the text was edited by Aharon Freiman, *Sefer ma'gal ṭov ha-shalem* (Jerusalem: Meqiṣe Nirdamim, 1934). A rather liberal English translation was published by Benjamin Cymerman, *The Diaries of Rabbi Ha'im Yosef David Azulai* (Jerusalem: Bnei Issakhar Institute, 1997). For a recent analysis, see Matthias B.

Lehmann, "Levantinos and Other Jews: Reading H. Y. D. Azulai's Travel Diary," *Journal of Jewish Studies* 13, no. 3 (2007): 1–34. Also, Nabil I. Matar offers intriguing descriptions of journeys by early modern Muslims to the West: *In the Lands of the Christians: Arab Travel Writing in the Seventeenth Century* (New York: Routledge, 2003); idem, "Arab Views of Europeans, 1578–1727: The Western Mediterranean," in *Re-Orienting the Renaissance: Cultural Exchanges with the East*, ed. Gerald MacLean (Houndsmills, U.K.: Palgrave Macmillan, 2005), 126–47.

19. See Joshua Prawer's classic study "The Hebrew Itineraries of the Crusader Period," in *The History of the Jews in the Latin Kingdom of Jerusalem* (Oxford: Clarendon, 1988), 169–250.

20. The term "Islamicate," which I occasionally use instead of Islamic or Muslim, was coined by Marshall G. S. Hodgson to describe aspects of society and culture that are found throughout the Muslim world, even among non-Muslims; Hodgson, *The Venture of Islam: Conscience and History in a World Civilization* (Chicago: University of Chicago Press, 1974), 1:49.

21. As David Nirenberg has forcefully argued with respect to medieval accounts of the persecution of minorities, any study of premodern times guided by the question of "When did Europe go wrong?" imposes a questionable, "teleological" model on history; see the introduction to his *Communities of Violence: Persecution of Minorities in the Middle Ages* (Princeton, N.J.: Princeton University Press, 1996), 3–7.

22. On (mainly) Christian authors, see the extensive bibliography collected by Stéphane Yérasimos, *Les voyageurs dans l'empire ottoman (XIVe–XVIe siècles): Bibliographie, itinéraires et inventaire des lieux habités* (Ankara: Türk Tarih Kurumu, 1991); and Suraiya Faroqhi, *Approaching Ottoman History: An Introduction to the Sources* (Cambridge: Cambridge University Press, 1999), 110–33.

23. Among sixteenth-century Jews, Abraham Farissol of Ferrara was one of the first to respond to the recent expansion of the European geographical horizon. In his *Iggeret orḥot 'olam* (Ways of the World), published in 1525, he included excerpts from non-Jewish travel accounts that he translated into Hebrew; see David B. Ruderman, *The World of a Renaissance Jew: The Life and Thought of Abraham ben Mordecai Farissol* (Cincinnati: Hebrew Union College Press, 1981), 131–43. At the same time, Farissol affirmed a traditional worldview and aimed to prove that authoritative texts such as the Hebrew Bible already announced or implied these recent discoveries (ibid., 137, 142). A similar approach was adopted by the physician and chronicler Joseph ha-Kohen of Genoa, whose historical works include Hebrew paraphrases of Spanish accounts of the Americas; see my "Joseph ha-Kohen, Paolo Giovio, and Sixteenth-Century Historiography," in *Cultural Intermediaries: Jewish Intellectuals in Early Modern Italy*, ed. David B. Ruderman and Giuseppe Veltri (Philadelphia: University of Pennsylvania Press, 2004), 75–76.

24. On Jewish migration in the early modern period, see David B. Ruderman, *Early Modern Jewry: A New Cultural History* (Princeton, N.J.: Princeton University Press, 2010), 23–41.

25. The Hebrew text was published by Avraham Ya'ari in his anthology *Iggerot ereṣ*

yisra'el (Ramat Gan: Masada, 1971), 183–87; an abridged translation, which I have slightly modified, can be found in Norman A. Stillman, *The Jews of Arab Lands: A History and Source Book* (Philadelphia: Jewish Publication Society, 1979), 290–92.

26. Eighteenth-century Hebrew literature devised novel forms of travel writing, such as Azulai's aforementioned travel diary; see n. 18 above. In addition, Samuel Romanelli's description of his sojourn in Morocco needs to be mentioned, as it constitutes a blend of traditional modes of Hebrew travel writing and Jewish Enlightenment (*haskalah*) thought. At the same time, Romanelli's account provides an example of how North African Muslims and Jews were being Orientalized from the perspective of a European Jew around the time of the French Revolution. First published in Berlin in 1792, *Massa' ba-'rav* (Vision of an Arab Land; an allusion to Isa. 21:13) was reissued by Ḥayyim Schirmann in his collection of Romanelli's writings: *Ketavim nivḥarim: Massa' ba-'rav, leqeṭ shirim, qeṭa'im mit-tokh maḥazot* (Jerusalem: Mosad Bialik, 1968), 17–149; trans. Yedida K. Stillman and Norman A. Stillman, *Travail in an Arab Land* (Tuscaloosa: University of Alabama Press, 1989). For recent studies, see Daniel Schroeter, "Orientalism and the Jews of the Mediterranean," *Journal of Mediterranean Studies* 4 (1994): 183–96; Andrea Schatz, "Detours in a 'Hidden Land': Samuel Romanelli's *Masa ba'rav*," in *Jewish Studies at the Crossroads of Anthropology and History: Tradition, Authority, Diaspora*, ed. Ra'anan S. Boustan, Oren Kosansky, and Marina Rustow (Philadelphia: University of Pennsylvania Press, 2011), 164–84; and Asher Salah, "The Otherness of the Self: On Romanelli's Travelogue," *European Journal of Jewish Studies* 5 (2011): 219–40.

27. Leopold Zunz, "An Essay on the Geographical Literature of the Jews, from the Remotest Times to the Year 1841," published in the appendix to Adolf Asher's edition and translation, *The Itinerary of Rabbi Benjamin of Tudela*, 2 vols. (New York: Hakesheth, 1840–41), 2:230–317. (Asher's text was later superseded by Adler's aforementioned critical edition; see also Chapter 1 in this volume.) Zunz originally composed the essay in German, but its English translation was published first; the German version, "Geographische Literatur der Juden von den ältesten Zeiten bis zum Jahre 1841," was only to appear in his *Gesammelte Schriften* (Berlin: Louis Gerschel, 1875; reprint, Hildesheim: Olms, 1976), 1:146–216.

28. Zunz, "Essay on the Geographical Literature," 231–32.

29. This approach characterizes, e.g., the work of Abraham David, this generation's most prolific researcher of Hebrew travel accounts; see his *To Come to the Land: Immigration and Settlement in Sixteenth-Century Eretz-Israel*, trans. Dena Ordan (Tuscaloosa: University of Alabama Press, 1999).

30. As described by Prawer, *History of the Jews*, 191.

31. Zunz, "Essay on the Geographical Literature," 252; my emphasis.

32. Elliott S. Horowitz, "Towards a Social History of Jewish Popular Religion: Obadiah of Bertinoro on the Jews of Palermo," *Journal of Religious History* 17 (1992): 148.

33. On the ethnographic dimension of late medieval pilgrimage accounts, see Joan-Pau Rubiés, "The Emergence of a Naturalistic and Ethnographic Paradigm in Late Medieval Travel Writing," in *Voyages and Visions: Towards a Cultural History of Travel*, ed. Jaś Elsner and Joan-Pau Rubiés (London: Reaktion, 1999), 31. On sixteenth- to eighteenth-century

travel literature, see Rubiés, "Travel Writing and Ethnography," in *The Cambridge Companion to Travel Writing*, ed. Peter Hulme and Tim Youngs (Cambridge: Cambridge University Press, 2002), 242–60; an expanded version of this essay was published as chapter 4 in Rubiés, *Travellers and Cosmographers: Studies in the History of Early Modern Travel and Ethnology* (Aldershot, U.K.: Ashgate, 2007).

34. Here I am borrowing a metaphor first used by Ezel Kural Shaw, "The Double Veil: Travelers' Views of the Ottoman Empire, Sixteenth Through Eighteenth Centuries," in *English and Continental Views of the Ottoman Empire, 1500–1800*, ed. idem and C. J. Heywood (Los Angeles: W. A. Clark Memorial Library, 1972), 13.

35. *From Italy to Jerusalem: The Letters of Rabbi Obadiah of Bertinoro from the Land of Israel* (Hebrew), ed. Menahem E. Artom and Abraham David (Ramat Gan: Bar-Ilan University, 1997), 79. For more on Obadiah's diaristic letters, see Chapter 1 in this volume. Obadiah's skepticism in this respect seems all the more remarkable, given the Talmud's discussion (b. Berakhot 54a) of the appropriate prayer when a person sees the pillar of salt that Lot's wife had become.

36. See Chapter 9 in this volume.

37. François Hartog, *The Mirror of Herodotus: The Representation of the Other in the Writing of History*, trans. Janet Lloyd (Berkeley: University of California Press, 1988), 3–4.

38. See ibid., 230–37.

39. In a hagiographic tradition reaching back to late antiquity, travels and miracles appear to go hand in hand; they were similarly considered instances of *thaumata* (wonders), as John (Jaś) Elsner has pointed out with reference to Apollonius of Tyana: "Hagiographic Geography: Travel and Allegory in the *Life of Apollonius of Tyana*," *Journal of Hellenic Studies* 117 (1997): 23.

40. In so doing, I am adopting an approach that was first used by Ivan G. Marcus in his study on Jewish historical narratives from the Middle Ages. In Marcus's estimation, "The goal is not 'facts' or 'literary creativity' but something I would call 'historiographical creativity.' At issue is not many literary genres of stories that represent the world but many types of pasts remembered in symbolic forms"; Marcus, "History, Story, and Collective Memory: Narrativity in Early Ashkenazic Culture," *Prooftexts* 10 (1990): 367.

41. With this subheading, I am obviously alluding to the aforementioned (see n. 15 above) study of the same title, edited by Jeffrey J. Cohen.

42. Clark, in his introduction to *Travel Writing and Empire*, 2.

43. Against the charges of anachronism, the use of postcolonial theory in medieval studies has been defended, inter alia, by Bruce W. Holsinger, "Medieval Studies, Postcolonial Studies, and the Genealogies of Critique," *Speculum* 77 (2002): 195–227; and Nadia R. Altschul, "Postcolonialism and the Study of the Middle Ages," *History Compass* 6 (2008): 588–606.

44. In an important review article, M. G. Aune similarly speaks of "skewed readings of early modern cross-cultural encounters that attempt to establish originary points for later colonial projects"; see Aune, "Early Modern European Travel Writing After Orientalism," *Journal for Early Modern Cultural Studies* 5, no. 2 (2005): 121.

45. Richmond Barbour, *Before Orientalism: London's Theatre of the East, 1576–1626* (Cambridge: Cambridge University Press, 2003), 16, 17, 22, 29, and passim. In his study, Barbour focuses on dramatic representations of the East as staged in English theaters of the Shakespeare era but draws on contemporaneous travel literature as well. As the author argues in this context, "pre-Enlightenment 'orientalisms' expressed material, political, and discursive relations profoundly different from those Said finds typical of modernity" (ibid., 3). Similar to Barbour's "proto-Orientalism," Akbari speaks of "medieval Orientalism," a notion that she traces back to Said and simultaneously differentiates from his original definition of Orientalism; see her *Idols in the East*, 3, 5, 6, 13, 18, 283.

46. Ram Ben-Shalom has recently raised similar questions with regard to the fourteenth-century Jewish philosopher and exegete Joseph ben Abba Mari Ibn Caspi, who, in his biblical commentaries, occasionally refers to his journey from southern France to Egypt; Ben-Shalom, "The Unwritten Travel Journal to the East of Joseph Ibn Caspi: Images and Orientalism" (Hebrew), *Pe'amim* 124 (2011): 7–51. However, since Ibn Caspi did not compose any "travel writing" per se, I have omitted these references from the corpus discussed here. (On my understanding of travel writing, see Chapter 1 in this volume.)

47. See Chapter 10 in this volume.

48. Henceforth, I will be using the terms "cultural" and "collective" memory interchangeably; on these concepts, see Jan Assmann and John Czaplicka, "Collective Memory and Cultural Memory," *New German Critique* 65 (1995): 125–33.

49. See Nicole Chareyron, *Pilgrims to Jerusalem in the Middle Ages*, trans. Donald W. Wilson (New York: Columbia University Press, 2005). The Christian pilgrims' accounts from the twelfth to the sixteenth centuries discussed by Chareyron include not a few similarities to Jewish-authored texts from the same period. Though Chareyron offers a lively synthesis culled from numerous sources, rather than a critical analysis of each text, I occasionally refer to her study as a matter of comparison.

50. Commonly regarded as one of the most notorious polemicists against Islam, even the Dominican friar Riccoldo da Montecroce (ca. 1243–1320) expressed a spectrum of views (including positive ones) about his encounters with Muslims, as Rita George-Tvrtković argues; see her most recent study of Riccoldo's account of his extended stay in Baghdad: *A Christian Pilgrim in Medieval Iraq: Riccoldo da Montecroce's Encounter with Islam* (Turnhout: Brepols, 2012).

51. With these methodological reflections, I have obviously taken inspiration from Joan-Pau Rubiés and his contextualized readings of early modern travel accounts; see Rubiés's preface to his *Travel and Ethnology in the Renaissance: South India Through European Eyes, 1250–1625* (Cambridge: Cambridge University Press, 2000), x–xix.

52. Here I am indebted to Barbara E. Mann, who, in the context of Jewish studies, first treated this concept in a sustained fashion. Her recent study *Space and Place in Jewish Studies* (New Brunswick, N.J.: Rutgers University Press, 2012) has helped me clarify my own thoughts in this respect.

53. On pilgrimage as a "liminal" or "liminoid" experience that transcends social boundaries, see the classic studies by Victor Turner, "The Center Out There: Pilgrim's

Goal," *History of Religions* 12 (1973): 191–230; and Victor Turner and Edith L. B. Turner, *Image and Pilgrimage in Christian Culture: Anthropological Perspectives* (New York: Columbia University Press, 1978; reprint, 1995), 1–20.

CHAPTER 1. MEDIEVAL JEWISH TRAVELERS AND THEIR WRITINGS

1. See *Dictionary of Literary Themes and Motifs*, ed. Jean-Charles Seigneuret, 2 vols. (Westport, Conn.: Greenwood, 1988), s.v. "Travel"; Jan Borm, "Defining Travel: On the Travel Book, Travel Writing and Terminology," in *Perspectives on Travel Writing*, ed. Glen Hooper and Tim Youngs (Aldershot, U.K.: Ashgate, 2004), 13–26; and *Historisches Wörterbuch der Rhetorik*, ed. Gert Ueding, 10 vols. (Tübingen: Max Niemeyer, 1992–2011), s.v. "Reiseliteratur."

2. Joan-Pau Rubiés, "Travel Writing as a Genre: Facts, Fictions and the Invention of a Scientific Discourse in Early Modern Europe," *Journeys* 1 (2000): 6 (my emphasis; reprint in Rubiés, *Travellers and Cosmographers*, chap. 1).

3. By including in my discussion poetic descriptions of travel, I follow Zweder von Martels, who considers both prose and poetic works as legitimate parts of the body of travel literature; see his "Introduction: The Eye and the Mind's Eye," in *Travel Fact and Travel Fiction: Studies on Fiction, Literary Tradition, Scholarly Discovery and Observation in Travel Writing*, ed. von Martels (Leiden: Brill, 1994), xi.

4. Cf. Bernard Cerquiglini's statement that medieval literature does not "produce variants; it *is* variance"; Cerquiglini, *In Praise of the Variant: A Critical History of Philology*, trans. Betsy Wing (Baltimore: Johns Hopkins University Press, 1999), 78. On the different recensions of Benjamin of Tudela's book, see below.

5. The most frequently quoted English translations of premodern Jewish travel writings are those edited by Elkan N. Adler (a half-brother of Marcus N. Adler, the modern editor of Benjamin's *Massa'ot*) in his *Jewish Travellers* (London: Routledge, 1930); this anthology was later reissued as *Jewish Travellers in the Middle Ages: Nineteen Firsthand Accounts* (New York: Dover, 1987). In his choice of texts, E. Adler largely followed Judah D. Eisenstein's Hebrew anthology, *Ozar Massaoth: A Collection of Itineraries by Jewish Travelers to Palestine, Syria, Egypt, and Other Countries* (Hebrew) (New York: Or Yom, 1926; reprint, Tel Aviv, 1969). However, many of the translations published by Adler are abridged and slightly adapted reprints of earlier English renderings by other scholars—a fact that Adler does not always make clear. Another problem with these translations is that most of them are based on uncritical editions of the Hebrew original.

6. Lacking a specific Hebrew word, Prawer first applied the Latin term to the genre's Jewish works; see his *History of the Jews*, 169.

7. For more on these lists, see Elchanan Reiner, "Traditions of Holy Places in Medieval Palestine—Oral Versus Written," in *Offerings from Jerusalem: Portrayals of Holy Places by Jewish Artists*, ed. Rachel Sarfati (Hebrew and English) (Jerusalem: Israel Museum, 2002), English part, 9–19; Reiner, "'Oral Versus Written': The Shaping of Traditions of Holy Places

in the Middle Ages" (Hebrew), in *Studies in the History of Eretz Israel: Presented to Yehuda Ben-Porat*, ed. Yehoshua Ben-Arieh and Elchanan Reiner (Hebrew) (Jerusalem: Ben-Zvi Institute, 2003), 308–45.

8. On Christian T-O maps, see, in this volume, Introduction, n. 7. In medieval Hebrew literature, the only maps known to me are the diagrammatic depictions of the Holy Land that accompany Rashi's commentary on the Pentateuch; see Benjamin Z. Kedar, "Rashi's Map of the Land of Canaan, ca. 1100, and Its Cartographical Background," in *Cartography in Antiquity and the Middle Ages: Fresh Perspectives, New Methods*, ed. Richard J. A. Talber and Richard W. Unger (Leiden: Brill, 2008), 155–68.

9. On medieval Christian pilgrimage guides and narratives, see Donald R. Howard, *Writers and Pilgrims: Medieval Pilgrimage Narratives and Their Posterity* (Berkeley: University of California Press, 1980), 11–54; reprint in *Pilgrimage: Jews, Christians, Moslems: Collected Essays* (Hebrew and English), ed. Ora Limor and Elchanan Reiner (Raanana: Open University of Israel, 2005), 95E–136E; Jean Richard, *Les récits de voyage et de pèlerinage* (Turnhout: Brepols, 1981); and M. Alison Stones, "Medieval Pilgrimage Writing and Its Manuscript Sources," in *Encyclopedia of Medieval Pilgrimage*, ed. Larissa J. Taylor et al. (Leiden: Brill, 2010), 395–413.

10. The intertextual character of travel literature (irrespective of the authors' religious background) has already been highlighted by Manfred Pfister, "Intertextuelles Reisen, oder: Der Reisebericht als Intertext," in *Tales and "Their Telling Difference": Zur Theorie und Geschichte der Narrativik, Festschrift für Franz K. Stanzel*, ed. Herbert Foltinek, Wolfgang Riehle, and Waldemar Zacharasiewicz (Heidelberg: Carl Winter, 1993), 109–32.

11. See my "The Sacred Text as a Mental Map: Biblical and Rabbinic 'Place' in Medieval Jewish Travel Writing," in *Envisioning Judaism: Studies in Honor of Peter Schäfer on the Occasion of His Seventieth Birthday*, ed. Ra'anan S. Boustan et al. (Tübingen: Mohr Siebeck, 2013), 1.395–417.

12. For an English translation of Egeria's Latin account, see *Egeria's Travels to the Holy Land*, trans. John Wilkinson (Jerusalem: Ariel, 1981). For discussions on her pilgrimage and the attendant scholarly debate, see Ora Limor, *Holy Land Travels: Christian Pilgrims in Late Antiquity* (Hebrew) (Jerusalem: Ben-Zvi Institute, 1998), 39–114; and Maribel Dietz, *Wandering Monks, Virgins, and Pilgrims: Ascetic Travel in the Mediterranean World, A.D. 300–800* (University Park: Pennsylvania State University Press, 2005), 44–54.

13. Campbell, *The Witness and the Other World*, 22.

14. On Muslim and Jewish constructions of sacred space, see Josef W. Meri, *The Cult of Saints Among Muslims and Jews in Medieval Syria* (Oxford: Oxford University Press, 2002), 12–29.

15. Carl Thompson, *Travel Writing* (London: Routledge, 2011), 10.

16. Thus Joshua Prawer, "Gefälschte hebräische Itinerarien des Heiligen Landes aus dem Mittelalter," in *Fälschungen im Mittelalter: Internationaler Kongreß der Monumenta Germaniae Historica, München, 16.–19. September 1986*, Monumenta Germaniae Historica 33, no. 5 (Hanover: Hahnsche, 1988), 505–18.

17. In fact, Carmoly only published a French "translation" of the undocumented

Hebrew "original," titled *Shevile d'Irushalayim* (Paths of Jerusalem): "Les Chemins de Jérusalem, par Ishak Chelo en 1344," in Eliakim Carmoly, trans., *Itinéraires de la Terre Sainte traduit de l'hébreu* (Brussels: A. Vandale, 1847), 217–320. Thereafter, Eisenstein included a Hebrew rendering of Carmoly's French text in his *Ozar Massaoth*, 72–79; and E. Adler provides an English translation in his *Jewish Travellers*, 130–50. Obviously, Carmoly compiled this fabrication on the basis of medieval Jewish and Christian itineraries. See the compelling arguments by Gershom Scholem, "Shevile d'irushalayim ha-meyuḥas le-r. yiṣḥaq ḥelo—mezuyaf," *Me'asef Ṣion* 6 (1934): 39–53; Michael Ish-Schalom, "'Al shevile d'irushalayim le-r. yiṣḥaq bar yosef ḥelo," *Tarbiz* 6 (1935): 197–209; and Prawer, "Gefälschte hebräische Itinerarien," 514–18. "Isaac Chelo's itinerary" has frequently been mistaken for a primary source; recent examples include Elka Weber, "Sharing the Sites: Medieval Jewish Travellers to the Land of Israel," in *Eastward Bound: Travel and Travellers, 1050–1550*, ed. Rosamund Allen (Manchester: Manchester University Press, 2004), 36 and passim; Weber, *Traveling Through Text: Message and Method in Late Medieval Pilgrimage Accounts* (New York: Routledge, 2005), 45 and passim; and B. Mann, *Space and Place*, 50.

18. Prawer, *History of the Jews*, 137, 143.

19. See Ross E. Dunn, *The Adventures of Ibn Battuta: A Muslim Traveler of the 14th Century*, 2nd ed. (Berkeley: University of California Press, 2005), 3–4. The standard Arabic edition of Ibn Jubayr's work was prepared by William Wright and Michael J. de Goeje, *The Travels of Ibn Jubayr* (Leiden: Brill, 1907). The translation quoted herein was rendered by Roland J. C. Broadhurst, *The Travels of Ibn Jubayr* (London: Jonathan Cape, 1952). In the case of Ibn Baṭṭūṭa, the Arabic text was established by C. Defrémery and B. R. Sanguinetti, eds., *Voyages d'Ibn Batoutah*, 4 vols. (Paris: Imprimerie Nationale, 1853–59; reprint, Paris: Vincent Monteil, 1979); this edition includes a French translation. Throughout, I am quoting from H. A. R. Gibb's English translation, *The Travels of Ibn Baṭṭūṭa (A.D. 1325–54)*, 4 vols. (Cambridge, U.K.: Hakluyt Society, 1958–94); index volume by A. D. H. Bivar (Aldershot, U.K.: Ashgate, 2001).

20. Prawer, *History of the Jews*, 169.

21. The manuscript (MS Cambridge Add. 539) was published by Lazar (El'azar) Grünhut under the heading *Sippur Massa'ot* (Story of Travels) as an appendix to his edition of Petaḥyah of Regensburg's account (see below): *Die Rundreise des R. Petachjah aus Regensburg*, 2 vols. (Hebrew) (Jerusalem: J. Kauffmann, 1905), 2:4–14. Adler's English rendering (*Jewish Travellers*, 92–99) is unreliable and leaves out some passages. On the itinerary's date, see Prawer, *History of the Jews*, 184–91.

22. Jacob ben Nathanel ha-Kohen, *Sippur Massa'ot*, 9, 12.

23. Ibid., 4.

24. The parasang (Persian: *farsang, farsakh*) is called *parsa* in Hebrew and measures about three and a half miles (5.6 kilometers), though its length varies historically.

25. This itinerary was first edited—on the basis of MS Parma (de Rossi 563)—by Abraham Berliner in *Oṣar Ṭov* (1876), 35–38; cf. Berliner's notes in *Magazin für die Wissenschaft des Judentums* 3 (1876): 157–60. I will be quoting the far superior edition (based on the same manuscript) by Fülöp Schulcz, *Mikhtav me-rabbi shmu'el b"r shimshon 'al pi*

k"y parma (Vác: Kohn, 1929). For an English translation (which I do not follow), see Adler, *Jewish Travellers*, 103–10.

26. On the exilarch as the figurehead of Babylonian Jewry, see Chapter 6 in this volume. Some members of the exilarchal dynasty resided in cities other than Baghdad, such as Mosul, and the person in question may not have held the office of *rosh ha-golah*.

27. Samuel ben Samson, *Mikhtav*, 5.

28. Prawer ("Gefälschte hebräische Itinerarien," 510–14; *History of the Jews*, 246–49) deems *Elleh ha-Massa'ot* to be a plagiary based on *Toṣ'ot Ereṣ Yisra'el*. Reiner—whose assessment I follow here—argues that the latter is an expanded version of the former; see Reiner, "Traditions of Holy Places," 13–14, and "Oral Versus Written," 328–42.

29. The title alludes to Num. 33:1: "These were the travel routes of the Israelites" (*Elleh mas'e vene yisra'el*). The edition that I cite is based on MS Rome (Biblioteca Casanatense, codex no. 3097), a composite manuscript that was copied by Isaac ben Menaḥem of Pisa in 1428 and also includes Benjamin of Tudela's itinerary and other travel-related texts. Lazar Grünhut published this version of *Elleh ha-Massa'ot* in the appendix to his edition of Benjamin's book: *Die Reisebeschreibungen des R. Benjamin von Tudela: Nach drei Handschriften, aus dem 13. und 14. Jahrhundert stammend und ältern Druckwerken ediert und übersetzt* (Frankfurt am Main: J. Kauffmann, 1903), 145–64. (For Benjamin's work, I am citing from Adler's superior edition, instead of Grünhut's; see below.)

30. See Chapter 2 in this volume. On the fact that contemporaneous Christian pilgrimage developed similar routes starting in Acre, see Denys Pringle, *Pilgrimage to Jerusalem and the Holy Land, 1187–1291* (Farnham, U.K.: Ashgate, 2012), 7. In its style and organization, *Elleh ha-Massa'ot* particularly resembles an anonymous French guidebook (ca. 1229–39) whose opening reads: "These are the holy pilgrimages that one must seek out . . . in the Holy Land"; see its description and translation by Pringle, ibid., 34–35, 165–72.

31. Prawer's translation, "Comings and Goings in the Land of Israel" (*History of the Jews*, 233), is unconvincing because the biblical term *toṣ'ot* is often used in the context of territorial boundaries. Therefore, it is best translated as "limits" or "extremities" (see Num. 34:4, 8, 9, 12; Josh. 15:4, 7, 11, 19:22; and Ezek. 48:30). An incomplete edition was provided by Simḥah Assaf, "Toṣ'ot ereṣ yisra'el," in *Yerushalayim: Qoveṣ ha-ḥevrah ha-'ivrit le-ḥaqirat ereṣ yisra'el ve-'atiqoteha, muqdash le-zekher r. avraham moshe lunṣ*, ed. A. L. Sukenik and Y. Peres (Jerusalem: Bet Misḥar and Derom, 1928), 51–66; reprint in Assaf, *Texts and Studies in Jewish History* (Hebrew) (Jerusalem: Mosad ha-Rav Kook, 1946), 74–90. Henceforth I will be quoting both the folio and the page number according to Assaf's original publication.

32. Here I follow Reiner's dating of the text; "Oral Versus Written," 337.

33. This attribution is based on the writer's ostensible reference to Naḥmanides as "my teacher," Hebrew: *RBY* (*Toṣ'ot*, fol. 1, 44), which turns up in the context of Naḥmanides' tomb (at the foot of Mount Carmel). However, this reading seems to be the result of a copyist's negligence that turned a Hebrew abbreviation for "our teacher" (*RBY'*, for *rabbenu*; a general honorific) into "my teacher"; see Reiner's detailed discussion, "Oral Versus Written," 339–42. On Naḥmanides and his own relocation to Acre, see Chapter 4 in this volume.

34. The manuscript, which is housed in the British Library's collection (Add. 27.125, fol. 145a), was published by Zvi Ilan, *Tombs of the Righteous in the Land of Israel* (Hebrew) (Jerusalem: Kanah, 1997), 131–44; for a facsimile, see Sarfati, *Offerings from Jerusalem*, Hebrew part, 33, fig. 10.

35. See Jacob Mann, *The Jews in Egypt and in Palestine Under the Fāṭimid Caliphs*, 2 vols. (London: Oxford University Press, 1920–22; reprint, 1969), 1:174, 2:207–8.

36. The version of *Yiḥus ha-Ṣaddiqim* that will be discussed here appears in Ilan, *Tombs of the Righteous*, 145–75, based on MS Günzburg (National Library of Moscow, Coll. 579/2), from ca. 1490; it is also known as *Elleh mas'e vene yisra'el* ("these are the travel routes of the Israelites"). *Yiḥus ha-Ṣaddiqim* was first printed at Constantinople in 1520, and subsequently at Mantua in 1561.

37. One of the most important manuscript versions of *Yiḥus Avot* was copied by Uri ben Simeon of Biella, a later resident of Safed, in 1564 (this version is said to have been printed in Venice in 1575, but no such copies are extant). The text was published by Moshe Luncz, "Yiḥus Avot," *Ha-Me'amer* 3 (1920): 209–23; a French translation was rendered by Carmoly, *Itinéraires de la Terre Sainte*, 433–60.

38. For a more detailed discussion that also refers to the possible influence of earlier Hebrew manuscripts, see Rachel Sarfati, "The Illustrations of *Yiḥus ha-Avot*," in Sarfati, ed., *Offerings from Jerusalem*, English part, 21–29; for reproductions of such illustrations, see ibid., Hebrew part, 35–46, figs. 11–19. In some cases, these illustrations depict tombs or places not mentioned in the text itself and hence seem to adapt it to an audience's expectations. On illustrations as a "paratext," see Gérard Genette, *Paratexts: Threshold of Interpretation*, trans. Jane E. Lewis (Cambridge: Cambridge University Press, 1997), 406.

39. Other such illustrations were rendered apparently by the travelers themselves, among them the anonymous Casale Pilgrim (1598). Having returned from Palestine to the northern Italian town of Casale Monferrato, he drew on *Yiḥus Avot* for his "own" pilgrimage account, making few significant alterations and additions to the text of his source; see the facsimile edition by Cecil Roth, *The Casale Pilgrim: A Sixteenth-Century Illustrated Guide to the Holy Places* (London: Soncino, 1929), which comes with an English translation.

40. Its longer title reads *Cippi Hebraici: Sive Hebraeorum, tam veterum, Prophetarum, Patriarcharum; quam recentiorum, Tannaeorum, Amoraeorum, Rabbinorum monumenta* (Heidelberg: Samuel Broun, 1659). The 1662 edition (housed at the rare-book room of the University of Pennsylvania's Herbert D. Katz Center for Advanced Judaic Studies) that was available to me includes two copperplates of various shrines, one between pp. 32 and 33, and the other between pp. 50 and 51. According to Reiner ("Traditions of Holy Places," 16–17), the Hebrew text published by Hottinger traces back to the version copied by Uri ben Simeon of Biella; see n. 37 above.

41. See Pamela Berger, "Jewish-Muslim Veneration at Pilgrimage Places in the Holy Land," *Religion and the Arts* 15 (2011): 1–60, including numerous reproductions.

42. Upon his return, Benjamin seems to have made his home in neighboring Castile rather than in Navarre; *Itinerary of Benjamin*, Hebrew part, 2 (anonymous prologue). The

distinction between the kingdoms was still somewhat evanescent during the period under consideration, and borders tended to shift.

43. For more on the concept of hybridity, see Ania Loomba, *Colonialism/Postcolonialism*, 2nd ed. (London: Routledge, 2005), 145–53.

44. Adler, *Itinerary of Benjamin*, English part, 1–2 n. 2 (on Marcus N. Adler, see the Introduction in this volume); and David Jacoby, "Benjamin of Tudela and His 'Book of Travels,'" in *Venezia incrocio di culture: Percezioni di viaggiatori europei e non europei a confronto: Atti del convegno Venezia, 26–27 gennaio 2006*, ed. Klaus Herbers and Felicitas Schmieder (Rome: Centro Tedesco di Studi Veneziani, 2008), 144–49.

45. The Latin translation of Benjamin's work (*Itinerarium Beniamini Tudelensis . . . ex Hebraico Latinum factum*) merits special notice, as it made a medieval Jew's travel account accessible to a learned Christian readership during the period of New World explorations. It was rendered by Benito Arias Montano, a renowned Spanish humanist and Bible scholar, and printed in Antwerp in 1575 at Christopher Plantin's, a leading publishing house of the time. As Zur Shalev has recently argued, Montano considered Benjamin a precursor of later Spanish explorers; Shalev, "Benjamin of Tudela, Spanish Explorer," *Mediterranean Historical Review* 25, no. 1 (2010): 17–33.

46. Both the Constantinople and Ferrara prints seem to hint at the displaced Sephardic communities' keen interest in *Massa'ot*. On early print editions of Benjamin's book, see the introduction to Asher's edition, *Itinerary of Rabbi Benjamin*, 1:1–9. On modern editions and translations, see the detailed bibliography by Abraham David, "Benjamin ben Jonah of Tudela," in *Encyclopedia of Jews in the Islamic World*, ed. Norman A. Stillman (Brill Online, 2013), http://referenceworks.brillonline.com/entries/encyclopedia-of-jews-in-the-islamic-world/benjamin-ben-jonah-of-tudela-COM_0003980 (accessed June 26, 2013).

47. See the Introduction to this volume, n. 27.

48. See Adler's introduction, *Itinerary of Benjamin*, xiv. MS London (Add. 27089) is a composite manuscript containing a range of writings of disparate character and origin, including Benjamin's book in sec. 19 (fols. 149a–161b). For more on this manuscript, see George Margoliouth, *Catalogue of the Hebrew and Samaritan Manuscripts in the British Museum* (London: British Museum, 1915; reprint, 1965), 3:466; and Jacoby, "Benjamin of Tudela," 136 n. 4.

49. The Casanatense manuscript (MS Hebr. 3097), which, in addition to Benjamin's *Massa'ot* (in sec. 1, fol. 1a–27b), includes fourteen other Hebrew treatises, dates from 1428; see n. 29 above. Adler's and Grünhut's editions both offer *variae lectiones* from MS Rome in the apparatuses of their respective editions, but it has never been published in full. The different recensions of *Massa'ot* demand new studies in their own right.

50. My translation is based on *Itinerary of Benjamin*, Hebrew part, 1, which provides a synopsis of the three major textual witnesses: MS London, MS Rome, and Asher's text. That the prologue calls the traveler *Rabbi* Benjamin may be a mere honorific and does not mean that he was a rabbi by training.

51. See the nonpaginated prologue (*haqdamah*) to *Itinerary of Rabbi Benjamin*, ed.

Asher, vol. 1, Hebrew part. A very similar text is represented by MS Vienna (or MS Epstein; now housed at the National Library of Israel, Heb. 80 2647, fol. 1a–39a), apparently from the late fifteenth or sixteenth century, which was used by Grünhut as the ground text of his above-mentioned *Reisebeschreibungen des R. Benjamin* (for the quoted passage, see ibid., 1). The Ferrara print may actually be based on this manuscript—a question that goes beyond the scope of this discussion.

52. Marco Polo's *Description of the World* has been transmitted in numerous manuscript versions so different from one another that it is impossible to reconstruct an ur-text. Throughout, I am quoting Ronald Latham's readable and easily accessible translation: Marco Polo, *The Travels* (Harmondsworth, U.K.: Penguin, 1958), 33. This rendition is based on the Franco-Italian version ("F"), which is considered the most reliable. It was first published by Luigi F. Benedetto, *Il Milione: Le Divisament dou monde* (Florence: Leo S. Olschki, 1928), and intermittently corrected in the revised edition by Gabriella Ronchi (Milan: Mondadori, 1982); the Franco-Italian words in parentheses are taken from ibid., 3. For a discussion on Rustichello and his role in the composition of *Divisament dou Monde*, see Leonardo Olschki, *Marco Polo's Asia: An Introduction to His "Description of the World" Called "Il Milione"* (Berkeley: University of California Press, 1960), 5, 7, 12, 48–51; Dietmar Rieger, "Marco Polo und Rustichello da Pisa: Der Reisende und sein Erzähler," in *Reisen und Reiseliteratur im Mittelalter und der Frühen Neuzeit*, ed. Xenja von Ertzdorff, Dieter Neukirch, and Rudolf Schulz (Amsterdam: Rodopi, 1992), 289–312; and Gaunt, *Marco Polo's Le Devisement*, 42–61.

53. *Itinerary of Rabbi Benjamin*, ed. Asher, vol. 1, Hebrew part, 2. In contrast, MS London reads here: "First, I set out from *my city* to the city of Saragossa" (*Itinerary of Benjamin*, ed. Adler, Hebrew part, 2), which seems to represent a copyist's addition meant to clarify that Benjamin set out from Tudela.

54. *Itinerary of Benjamin*, Hebrew part, 3.

55. Prawer, *History of the Jews*, 197–98. Distances are measured in parasangs (see n. 24 above), miles, or the rather sketchy spatio-temporal unit of a "day's journey," which may hint at different sources used by Benjamin or his editor.

56. There are two more instances of first-person narration in *Massa'ot*, but neither describes Benjamin's progress on the road or personal observations; in both cases, the author quotes an informant who "told *me* [all] these things"; *Itinerary of Benjamin*, Hebrew part, 26, 57.

57. This does not prevent me from asking questions concerning the book's portrayal of the Islamicate world, as collective works arguably reflect the cultural attitudes of their intended audiences.

58. This is not the place to list the myriad studies that touch on Benjamin's descriptions of specific places along this route, most of which tend to take the general reliability of his statements for granted. Still, I would like to draw attention to a recent article by Marie Thérèse Champagne and Ra'anan S. Boustan that reads *Massa'ot*'s account of Rome as a mirror of specific cultural memories related to that imperial city; Champagne and Boustan, "Walking in the Shadows of the Past: The Jewish Experience of Rome in the Twelfth Century," *Medieval Encounters* 17 (2011): 464–94.

59. *Itinerary of Benjamin*, introduction, ix; ibid., English part, 48–49 n. 1; 66 n. 1. Benjamin's book, which was composed a century before Marco Polo's, contains one of the first "European" references to China. On this topic, see also the Introduction to this volume, n. 16.

60. In the case of the *Book of Mandeville*, Higgins (*Writing East*, 17–19) has conclusively proved how medieval travel literature was continuously re-created in transmission.

61. See Michael Signer's introduction to the 1983 reprint of Adler's translation: "Aside from other motivations, the Itinerary of Benjamin of Tudela represents a contribution to the literature of consolation for the Jewish people"; *The Itinerary of Benjamin of Tudela: Travels in the Middle Ages*, introductions by Michael A. Signer, Marcus N. Adler, and A. Asher (Malibu, Calif.: Joseph Simon / Pangloss, 1983), 26.

62. See the detailed discussion of specific examples by Hans Peter Rüger, in the introduction to his partial German translation of Benjamin's book, *Syrien und Palaestina nach dem Reisebericht des Benjamin von Tudela* (Wiesbaden: Harrassowitz, 1990), 2–3.

63. See, in this volume, Chapter 6 n. 89.

64. Petaḥyah, *Sibbuv*, 1:1 and 36, which is based on the editio princeps (Prague, 1595). In contrast, MS Warsaw deviates significantly from the received text and contains neither the introduction nor the colophon. This manuscript was unknown to Grünhut and was subsequently published by Abraham David, "Sibbuv r. petaḥyah me-regensburg be-nusaḥ ḥadash," *Qoveṣ ʿal Yad* 13 (1996): 237–69. Although its date of origin (the late fifteenth century) predates the other known manuscripts, MS Warsaw is even less complete; I refer to it only when its readings are relevant to the topic under discussion. For an English translation of *Sibbuv*, see the uncritical, bilingual edition by Abraham Benisch, *Travels of Rabbi Petachia of Ratisbon* (London: Trubner, 1856). This outdated translation (which I will not be quoting) has been adopted, with minor alterations, by Adler, *Jewish Travellers*, 64–91.

65. Prawer establishes its *terminus a quo* and its *terminus ad quem* as 1174 and 1187, respectively, in *History of the Jews*, 209.

66. Petaḥyah, *Sibbuv*, 1:2.

67. Ibid., 1:3.

68. See Chapter 3 in this volume.

69. Petaḥyah, *Sibbuv*, 1:7.

70. In being based on the traveler's oral report, *Sibbuv* also resembles earlier Christian pilgrimage accounts, e.g., those of Arculf and Willibald (from the late seventh and early eighth century, respectively), both of which were put into writing by a different author from the traveler himself; see Thomas O'Loughlin, "Adomnan and Arculf: The Case of an Expert Witness," *Journal of Medieval Latin* 7 (1997): 127–46; and Ora Limor, "Pilgrims and Authors: Adomnán's *De locis sanctis* and Hugeburc's *Hodoeporicon Sancti Willibaldi*," *Revue Bénédictine* 114 (2004): 253–75.

71. Petaḥyah, *Sibbuv*, 1:2. The phrasing of this passage echoes the introduction to Asher's edition of Benjamin's *Massaʿot*.

72. In differentiating between a travel account's persona and author, I follow Rubiés, "Travel Writing as a Genre," 20.

73. Similar questions have been raised by Limor regarding Arculf's and Willibald's pilgrimage accounts; Limor, "Pilgrims and Authors," 257–58. In Galit Hasan-Rokem's estimation, *Sibbuv* constitutes an example of folk literature that "reveals clear traces of orality and interactivity with the audience"; Hasan-Rokem, "*Homo viator et narrans judaicus*—Medieval Jewish Voices in the European Narrative of the Wandering Jew," in *Europäische Ethnologie und Folklore im internationalen Kontext: Festschrift Leander Petzoldt*, ed. Ingo Schneider (Frankfurt am Main: Peter Lang, 1999), 93. Regarding Marco Polo's work, Gaunt (*Marco Polo's Devisement*, 41) similarly speaks of "ambiguous narrative voice(s)."

74. Petaḥyah, *Sibbuv*, 1:7. Interestingly, the Warsaw manuscript offers a much more detailed account of this exchange; David, "Sibbuv r. petaḥyah," 240–43. Nonetheless, it is unclear whether MS Warsaw contains the passage, which was censured by R. Judah, or a later interpolation, which was prompted by the remark about R. Judah's unwillingness to elaborate on this issue.

75. See Gershom Scholem, *Major Trends in Jewish Mysticism* (New York: Schocken, 1941), 88–91.

76. *Sibbuv*'s moralist tendencies do not necessarily conform to Judah he-Ḥasid's teachings. For a discussion on the socioreligious outlook of the Ashkenazi Pietists in general and Judah he-Ḥasid in particular, see Ivan G. Marcus, *Piety and Society: The Jewish Pietists of Medieval Germany* (Leiden: Brill, 1981), 21–36, 55–65; and Haym Soloveitchik, "Piety, Pietism and German Pietism: Sefer Ḥasidim and the Influence of Ḥasidei Ashkenaz," *JQR* 92 (2002): 455–93. On the relation between *Sibbuv* and the Ashkenazi Pietists, see also Hasan-Rokem, "Homo Viator," 96–97, 99.

77. On MS Warsaw, the earliest extant manuscript, see n. 64 above. A bilingual Hebrew-Latin edition of *Sibbuv*, trans. Christopher Wagenseil (Altdorf, 1687), was published almost a century after the editio princeps. For more on the history of this text, see David, "Sibbuv r. petaḥyah," 237–39.

78. On Naḥmanides' letter sent from Jerusalem in 1267, see Chapter 4 in this volume.

79. See Chapter 3 in this volume.

80. The letter by R. Elijah of La Massa has survived in a single Hebrew manuscript, which is housed at the Bibliothèque Nationale in Paris (no. 1049). Several errors were committed in its earlier publications, such as Eisenstein, *Ozar Massaoth*, 83–84; and Ya'ari, *Iggerot ereṣ yisra'el*, 86–89. E.g., these versions date the letter to 1435 and refer to its author as R. Elijah of Ferrara. Throughout, I will be quoting the superior edition by Joseph R. Hacker, "R. Elija of Massa Lombarda in Jerusalem" (Hebrew), *Zion* 50 (1985): 241–63. Hacker's text (*sans* his introduction) has been republished by Abraham David, *Reflections on Jewish Jerusalem: An Anthology of Hebrew Letters from the Mamluk Age* (Hebrew) (Tel Aviv: Hakibbutz Hameuchad, 2003), 67–73. For an (outdated) translation, see Adler, *Jewish Travellers*, 151–55. While Hacker identified the letter writer's place of origin with Massa Lombarda (a town between Bologna and Ravenna), David argues for Massa Fiscaglia because of its vicinity to Ferrara; David, *Reflections on Jewish Jerusalem*, 67 n. 2.

81. He may have been related to Isaac ben Abraham Ibn Latif (1210–80), a Neoplatonic philosopher, kabbalist, and biblical exegete from Toledo. In fact, the letter writer

has erroneously been identified with the thirteenth-century luminary—a confusion finally clarified by Shaul H. Kook, *ʿIyyunim u-meḥkarim*, 2 vols. (Jerusalem: Mosad ha-Rav Kook, 1959–63), 2:142–46. R. Isaac ben Meir Latif's letter has survived in MS Parma-Palatina 2445 (de Rossi 402), fol. 154. It was first published, on the basis of this manuscript, by Abraham Berliner and David Hoffmann, *Oṣar Ṭov* (1878): 33–35; reprint, Moshe A. Luncz, *Ha-Meʿamer* 3 (1920): 175–82; and Yaʿari, *Iggerot ereṣ yisraʾel*, 94–98. A different version of the letter (once a part of Eliakim Carmoly's collection) was published by Naftali Ben-Menaḥem, *Sinai* 53 (1963): 258–62. Abraham David's recent edition, *Reflections on Jewish Jerusalem*, 89–98, which I will be quoting here, is also based on the MS Parma-Palatina but offers some new readings and refers to variants in the other version as well.

82. See, in this volume, Chapter 10 n. 47.

83. The letter has been preserved in two almost identical copies from the sixteenth and eighteenth centuries (MS Warsaw, Institute for Jewish History, no. 253, fol. 120a–b; and MS Oxford, Bodleian Library, Opp. Add. 4° 178, fol. 92a–b). Moshe A. Luncz first published the epistle, on the basis of the second manuscript, in his yearbook *Yerushalayim* 6 (1903): 336–38, and then in *Ha-Meʿamer* 3 (1920): 89–92, followed by Yaʿari, *Iggerot ereṣ yisraʾel*, 89–93. I am quoting the new critical edition by David, *Reflections on Jewish Jerusalem*, 111–19.

84. The letter by Obadiah's anonymous student (the Günzburg Collection at the National Library of Moscow, no. 333), along with Adolf Neubauer's translation into German, was first published by Senior Sachs; "Ein anonymer Reisebrief vom Jahre 1495," *Jahrbuch für die Geschichte der Juden und des Judenthums* 3 (1863): 271–84 (edition), 285–300 (translation). Several other editions and reprints have appeared over the years: Eisenstein, *Ozar Massaoth*, 124–30; Luncz, *Ha-Meʿamer* 3 (1920): 151–70; and Yaʿari, *Iggerot ereṣ yisraʾel*, 144–60. Throughout this work, I am translating passages from the most recent edition by David, *Reflections on Jewish Jerusalem*, 142–70, which is the only version to offer the entire text. An abridged English translation can be found in Kurt Wilhelm, ed., *Roads to Zion: Four Centuries of Traveler's Reports* (New York: Schocken, 1948), 15–27. This rendition has been slightly adapted by Lawrence Fine, "Travel in the Land of Israel," in *Judaism in Practice*, ed. Fine (Princeton, N.J.: Princeton University Press, 2001), 237–47.

85. The most famous representatives of this illustrious family are Joseph Picho (or Pichon, d. 1379) and ʿAzaryah Figo (1579–1647). In his capacity as chief tax collector, Joseph was one of the highest-ranking officials at the court of Henry II of Castile. ʿAzaryah served as rabbi and preacher of Venice's Sephardic community.

86. The letter was published by Yaʿari, *Iggerot ereṣ yisraʾel*, 178–81. For more on the date of writing, see Yaʿari's introductory remarks.

87. The only surviving copy of this letter is from 1523; the exact date on which it was originally penned has been lost to history. The manuscript, housed in Florence's famous Biblioteca Medicea Laurenziana (Plut. 2.35), has been published several times. The first edition was produced by Adolf Neubauer, "ʿInyene ʿaseret ha-shevaṭim," *Qoveṣ ʿal Yad* 4 (1888): 25–37. David Castelli's edition, in *Ha-Meʿamer* 3 (1920): 183–96, was based on a new reading; see also Yaʿari, *Iggerot ereṣ yisraʾel*, 167–77, whose text draws heavily on Neubauer's.

I am using the most recent and reliable edition by Abraham David, "The Letter of R. Israel Ashkenazi of Jerusalem to R. Abraham of Perugia" (Hebrew), *Alei Sefer* 16 (1990): 95–122, which includes an introduction and notes.

88. See Alessandra Veronese, *Una famiglia di banchieri ebrei tra XIV e XVI secolo: I da Volterra* (Pisa: Edizione ETS, 1998). For a detailed look at the family's business interests, see ibid., 107–11, 129–42.

89. The letters were published by Umberto Cassuto, "La famille des Médicis et les Juifs," *Revue des Études Juives* 76 (1923): 132–45.

90. See Chapter 2 in this volume.

91. See Veronese, *Una famiglia di banchieri*, 211–23.

92. The manuscript (Plut. 44.11) is among the treasures of the Biblioteca Medicea Laurenziana of Florence. Its first thirty-three of originally fifty-four double-sided (and paginated) pages are missing; see Avraham Ya'ari's description of the manuscript in the introduction to his edition, *Massa' meshullam me-volṭera be-ereṣ yisra'el* (Jerusalem: Mosad Bialik, 1949), 30. Adler's outdated English translation (*Jewish Travellers*, 156–208) is based on the faulty edition by Eisenstein (*Ozar Massaoth*, 86–106), leaves out certain passages, and misinterprets others. Vastly superior is Daniel Jütte's recent German translation, which features an erudite introduction and helpful notes: Meshullam da Volterra, *Von der Toskana in den Orient: Ein Renaissance-Kaufmann auf Reisen*, trans. Daniel Jütte (Göttingen: Vandenhoek and Ruprecht, 2012).

93. For a brief disquisition on autobiographic writings by fifteenth- and sixteenth-century Jews, see Fabrizio Lelli, "The Origins of the Jewish-Autobiographic Genre: Yohanan Alemanno (1434 to 1504) and Abraham Yagel (1553 to After 1623)," *European Association of Jewish Studies Newsletter* 12 (March 2002): 4–11; and Lelli, "Biography and Autobiography in Yoḥanan Alemanno's Literary Perception," in *Cultural Intermediaries: Jewish Intellectuals in Early Modern Italy*, ed. David B. Ruderman and Giuseppe Veltri (Philadelphia: University of Pennsylvania Press, 2004), 25–38.

94. See Deborah Howard, "The Status of the Oriental Traveller in Renaissance Venice," in *Re-Orienting the Renaissance: Cultural Exchanges with the East*, ed. Gerald MacLean (Houndsmills, U.K.: Palgrave Macmillan, 2005), 29–49.

95. *Massa' meshullam*, 43.

96. The family name Yare seems to be an acrostic for Deut. 33:24, "May he be the favorite of his brothers." For an in-depth look at Obadiah's family and his life prior to his emigration to Palestine as reflected in both archival and Hebrew sources, see Ariel Toaff, "New Information on the Life of R. Obadia of Bertinoro in Italy" (Hebrew), *Pe'amim* 37 (1988): 24–30; and Toaff, "Ovadiah da Bertinoro nella realtà italiana del suo tempo," in *L'interculturalità dell'ebraismo: Atti del Convegno internazionale, Bertinoro-Ravenna, 26–28 maggio 2003*, ed. Mauro Perani (Ravenna: Longo, 2004), 257–68.

97. The town is often misspelled in traditional editions of R. Obadiah's works, as a result of which his Mishnah commentary is largely known as the Barṭenura.

98. See Toaff, "New Information," 27.

99. See Obadiah's first letter (henceforth, Letter A), *From Italy to Jerusalem*, 37. In line

12, the rabbi mentions that he departed from Città di Castello on "the first of the ninth month," while omitting the year. In dating the start of his journey to 1486, I follow Abraham David, who argues for 1 Kislev 5247 (October 29, 1486); other scholars believe that the voyage began a year earlier; see ibid., 9 and n. 14. Obadiah's letters were first published by Menaḥem Artom in Ya'ari's anthology, *Iggerot ereṣ yisra'el*, 98–144. This text is, by and large, identical to Artom's above-cited edition, to which Abraham David added a critical apparatus and an introduction. In fact, the Artom-David edition first appeared as a chapter in *Jews in Italy: Studies Dedicated to the Memory of U. Cassuto on the 100th Anniversary of His Birth* (Hebrew), ed. Haim Beinart (Jerusalem: Magnes, 1988), 24–108. Throughout this book, I am referring to the separate reprint titled *From Italy to Jerusalem*, cited above. The first English translation of Obadiah's letters, which was published by the Society of Hebrew Literature in London, is characterized by a heavy Victorian style, omissions, and misinterpretations: *Miscellany of Hebrew Literature* 1 (London: Trübner, 1872), 113–50. Nonetheless, this rendition is still widely quoted because it was adopted by Adler, *Jewish Travellers*, 209–50. Yaakov D. Shulman's more recent translation simplifies the original and was rendered in a nonacademic style: *Pathway to Jerusalem: The Travel Letters of Rabbi Ovadiah of Bartenurah, Written Between 1488–1490* (New York: CIS, 1992).

100. Obadiah, Letter A, *From Italy to Jerusalem*, 37. An especially intriguing example is his portrait of the Jewish community of Palermo; see Elliott S. Horowitz, "Religious Practices Among the Jews in the Late Fifteenth Century According to Letters of R. Obadiah of Bertinoro" (Hebrew), *Pe'amim* 37 (1988): 31–40; and Horowitz, "Towards a Social History," 138–51 (which is a revised version of the former article).

101. For examples, see Chapters 3 and 8 in this volume.

102. See Chapter 3 in this volume.

103. *From Italy to Jerusalem*, 83; henceforth Letter B.

104. Whereas the letter (Letter C) itself only provides the day and month (22 Ṭevet), the secondary heading states that the year was 5250 (1489/90). However, given the fact that Obadiah mentions the Ottoman-Mamluk peace agreement of 1491, the epistle could not have been written before Ṭevet 5252 (December 1491); see Artom and David, *From Italy to Jerusalem*, 88–89 n. 1.

105. In the letter to his brother, Obadiah mentions that the banker transferred a hundred Venetian gold ducats, along with a note promising to send him the same amount on an annual basis; see Letter B, ibid., 87.

106. See Isaac Ben-Zvi's introduction to his edition of the account: *A Pilgrimage to Palestine by Rabbi Moshe Basola of Ancona*, 2nd ed. (Hebrew) (Jerusalem: Jewish Palestine Exploration Society, 1939), 10–11. This edition is based on the only known manuscript, which is housed at the National Library of Israel (Heb. 8° 1783). Abraham David's recent edition provides a few corrections: *In Zion and Jerusalem: The Itinerary of Rabbi Moses Basola (1521–1523)* (Hebrew and English) (Jerusalem: Bar-Ilan University Press, 1999), English trans. Dena Ordan. For the most part, I am quoting from Ordan's translation, and any modifications that I make are duly noted. For more on Basola's biography, see David's introduction, ibid., 14–28; David, "From Italy to Jerusalem: R. Moses Basola

and His Travelogue in 1521–1523" (Hebrew), *Miscelánea de estudios árabes y hebraicos* 57 (2008): 109–24.

107. Basola's emigration is corroborated by his contemporary Gedalyah Ibn Yaḥia, author of a chronicle of rabbinic scholarship, *Shalshelet ha-Qabbalah* (Chain of Tradition): "Rabbi Moses Basolo [*sic*], head of the yeshiva in the Marches, went to the Land of Israel and died there in [5]320 [1560] at the age of eighty"; *Shalshelet ha-Qabbalah* (Venice, 1587), fol. 65v.

108. See 'Azaryah de' Rossi, *Sefer me'or 'enayim*, ed. David Cassel, 2nd ed. (Warsaw: Alapin, 1899), 394; here I quote the translation by Joanna Weinberg, *The Light of the Eyes* (New Haven, Conn.: Yale University Press, 2001), 666 (slightly modified). On this passage in *Me'or 'enayim*, see also Chapter 9 in this volume.

109. See David's introduction to *In Zion and Jerusalem*, 34–35.

110. See Chapter 9 in this volume.

111. Abraham Epstein and David Heinrich Müller published separate editions of this correspondence on the basis of both manuscripts and early print versions: Epstein, *Eldad ha-Dani: Seine Berichte über die X Stämme und deren Ritus in verschiedenen Versionen nach Handschriften und alten Drucken* (Pressburg/Bratislava: Adolf Alkalay, 1891), 3–8; and Müller, *Die Recensionen und Versionen des Eldad had-Dânî*, Denkschriften der Kaiserlichen Akademie der Wissenschaften in Wien, Philosophisch-Historische Classe 41 (Vienna: Tempsky, 1892), 16–20. For an English translation, see Adolf Neubauer, "Where Are the Ten Tribes?" *JQR* 1, no. 2 (1889): 104–8; or Adler, *Jewish Travellers*, 15–21.

112. For more on his identification as R. Ṣemaḥ ben Ḥayyim and on the widely accepted date of this correspondence, see Neubauer, "Where Are the Ten Tribes?" 104, 108–9; and Epstein, *Eldad ha-Dani*, 9 n. A. The problems with this identification have been discussed by David J. Wasserstein, "Eldad ha-Dani and Prester John," in *Prester John, the Mongols and the Ten Lost Tribes*, ed. Charles F. Beckingham and Bernard Hamilton (Aldershot, U.K.: Variorum, 1996), 223–24.

113. In the late nineteenth century, Neubauer had already deemed Eldad to be an impostor; Neubauer, "Where Are the Ten Tribes?" 98, 109. In contrast, Shlomo Morag has tried to prove that Eldad hailed from Najran (historically a part of Yemen but today in Saudi Arabia) by dint of a philological analysis of his Hebrew. I am skeptical as to the validity of Morag's theory; see Morag, "Eldad Haddani's Hebrew and the Problem of His Provenance" (Hebrew), *Tarbiz* 66 (1997): 223–46.

114. Epstein published the *Book of Eldad* (in Epstein, *Eldad ha-Dani*, 22–29) on the basis of the Constantinople print of 1519; see also the discussion of the different textual witnesses by Müller, *Recensionen*, 21–25. For a translation, based on the Epstein edition, see B. Halper, *Post-Biblical Hebrew Literature: An Anthology—English Translation* (Philadelphia: Jewish Publication Society, 1921), 49–54.

115. See the motifs and themes listed by Edward Ullendorff and Charles F. Beckingham, *The Hebrew Letters of Prester John* (Oxford: Oxford University Press, 1982), 161–72; and the recent discussion by Micha Perry, "The Imaginary War Between Prester John and Eldad the Danite and Its Real Implications," *Viator* 41 (2010): 1–23. On the history of the

Prester John legend, see Bernard Hamilton, "Continental Drift: Prester John's Progress Through the Indies," in *Prester John, the Mongols and the Ten Lost Tribes*, ed. Charles F. Beckingham and Bernard Hamilton (Aldershot, U.K.: Ashgate, 1996), 237–69 (reprint in Joan-Pau Rubiés, ed., *Medieval Ethnographies: European Perceptions of the World Beyond* [Farnham, U.K.: Ashgate, 2009], as chap. 4).

116. As evidenced by the fact that the Karaite Judah Hadassi mentions the book in *Eshkol ha-Kofer*, which he composed in Constantinople ca. 1148; see *Sefer eshkol ha-kofer* (Gozlow: Mordekhai, 1836), 29d, § 60. Another twelfth-century reference to the *Book of Eldad* turns up in Abraham Ibn Ezra's commentary on Exod. 2:22.

117. *The Story of David Hareuveni* (Hebrew), ed. Aaron Z. Aescoly, 2nd ed., with new introductions by Moshe Idel and Eliahu Lipiner (Jerusalem: Bialik Institute, 1993), 7. The abridged English translation of Re'uveni's account in Adler (*Jewish Travellers*, 251–328) is not based on Aescoly's edition and glosses over many of the text's problems.

118. At some point in his diary, Re'uveni claims to be of Davidic descent (*Story of David Hareuveni*, 76), which contradicts his alleged Reubenite origin and hints at the possibility that he laid stake to a messianic role.

119. See Chapter 9 in this volume.

120. Azriel Shoḥat believed that Re'uveni was from Yemen; Shoḥat, "Notes on the David Reubeni Affair" (Hebrew), *Zion* 35 (1940): 96–116. Alternatively, Ervin Birnbaum argued that he was from India; Birnbaum, "David Reubeni's Indian Origin," *Historia Judaica* 20 (1958): 1–10. Based on a linguistic analysis of his "diary," Aaron Z. Aescoly concluded that Re'uveni was an Ashkenazi Jew who had traveled to Africa; Aescoly, "David Reubeni in the Light of History," *JQR* 28 (1937–38): 1–45; and idem, "Leshono shel David ha-Re'uveni," *Leshonenu* 5 (1932–33): 39–48 (reprint in the appendix to the *Story of David Hareuveni*, 195–220). In contrast, A. S. Yehuda's linguistic analysis led him to believe that Re'uveni was a Sephardic Jew: "David ha-Reuveni, moṣa'o, leshono u-te'udato," *Ha-Tequfa* 34–35 (1950): 599–625. The disparate conclusions attest to the problems with this sort of analysis.

121. See Miriam Eliav-Feldon, "Invented Identities: Credulity in the Age of Prophecy and Exploration," *Journal of Early Modern History* 3 (1999): 203–32; and Martin Jacobs, "David ha-Re'uveni: Ein 'zionistisches Experiment' im Kontext der europäischen Expansion des 16. Jahrhunderts?" in *An der Schwelle zur Moderne: Juden in der Renaissance*, ed. Giuseppe Veltri and Annette Winkelmann (Leiden: Brill, 2002), 191–206.

122. See Robert Silverberg, *The Realm of Prester John* (Garden City, N.Y.: Doubleday, 1972), 212–19; and Avraham Gross, "The Ten Tribes and the Kingdom of Prester John: Rumors and Investigations Before and After the Expulsion from Spain" (Hebrew), *Pe'amim* 48 (1991): 5–41.

123. *Story of David Hareuveni*, 143.

124. The relationship of the political and messianic motifs in Re'uveni's bizarre mission will not be discussed here anew (Moshe Idel examines these motifs in his introductory chapter to the 2nd ed. of *Story of David Hareuveni*, xix–xliii), but it is likely that his objective was to precipitate the eschatological war between Gog and Magog (Christendom

and Islam). Moti Benmelech argues that Re'uveni was motivated by the predictions of the kabbalist Abraham ha-Levi; Benmelech, "History, Politics, and Messianism: David Ha-Reuveni's Origin and Mission," *AJS Review* 35 (2011): 35–60.

125. Most of the corroborative evidence has been reprinted in the appendix to *Story of David Hareuveni*, 151–91. Some additional documents from the National Archive in Lisbon can be found in Lipiner's new introduction, ibid., xlv–lxvi.

126. To date, *Dîwân des Abû-l-Hasan Jehuda Halevi*, ed. Heinrich Brody, 4 vols. (Berlin: Mekiṣe Nirdamim, 1894–1930) is considered the classical edition; selections of Brody's text were reissued in the following bilingual edition: *Selected Poems of Jehuda Halevi*, trans. Nina Salaman (Philadelphia: Jewish Publication Society, 1924; reprint, 1974). Since the opening of Russian archives, scholars have discovered other compilations in the Firkovich collection of Hebrew manuscripts at the Russian National Library of Saint Petersburg. Consequently, Joseph Yahalom is preparing a new critical edition of Halevi's poems, which will be based on the most complete collection, known as the Ḥiyya *dīwān*. According to Yahalom, some of the poems underwent what can only be referred to as censorship; see Yahalom, *Yehuda Halevi: Poetry and Pilgrimage*, trans. Gabriel Levin (Jerusalem: Magnes, 2009), 138–39, 145, 180–93.

127. For an in-depth look at Halevi's life as reflected in Genizah fragments, particularly his friendship with Ḥalfon, see Moshe Gil and Ezra Fleischer, eds., *Yehudah Ha-Levi and His Circle: Fifty-Five Genizah Documents* (Hebrew) (Jerusalem: World Union of Jewish Studies, 2001), 174–257.

128. The letter (ENA NS 1, f. 5), which was first published by Shlomo D. Goitein in "Autographs of Yehuda Hallevi" (Hebrew), *Tarbiz* 25 (1956): 408–12, is now available in Gil and Fleischer's aforesaid new edition; see document no. 19 in *Yehudah Halevi and His Circle*, 325, fol. a, lines 9–10. For a full translation of the letter, see Goitein, *A Mediterranean Society: The Jewish Communities of the Arab World as Portrayed in the Documents of the Cairo Geniza*, 6 vols. (Berkeley: University of California Press, 1967–93; reprint, 1999), 5:465.

129. See Chapter 2 in this volume.

130. In particular, Alḥarizi emulated the works of al-Ḥarīrī, one of the most famous authors of classical Arabic *maqāmāt*, some of which he translated into Hebrew. On the Arabic *maqāma*, see Devin Stewart, "The *Maqama*," in *The Cambridge History of Arabic Literature: Arabic Literature in the Post-Classical Period*, ed. Roger Allen and D. S. Richards (Cambridge: Cambridge University Press, 2006), 145–58. On Alḥarizi's adaptation of the *maqāma* and its conventions, see the introduction by Joseph Yahalom and Naoya Katsumata to their most recent edition of Alḥarizi's *Taḥkemoni: Or the Tales of Heman the Ezraḥite* (Hebrew) (Jerusalem: Ben-Zvi Institute, 2010), 16–19, 26–40; an English translation of this introduction has been added as an appendix, ibid., ix–xiv, xxii–xxxv.

131. For a survey of the most up-to-date research on this poet and his oeuvre, see Joshua Blau and Joseph Yahalom, "Kitab Aldurar: An Unpublished Work by Judah Alharizi" (Hebrew), *Pe'amim* 108 (2006): 19–51.

132. This collection was published in Alḥarizi, *The Wanderings of Judah Alharizi: Five Accounts of His Travels*, ed. Joseph Yahalom and Joshua Blau (Hebrew) (Jerusalem: Ben-Zvi Institute, 2002), 77–89 (chap. 3).

133. This title, which is the correct one, has only recently been established, thanks to the discovery of an additional manuscript fragment; see Alḥarizi, *Kitāb al-Durar: A Book in Praise of God and the Israelite Communities* (Hebrew and English), ed. Joshua Blau, Paul Fenton, and Joseph Yahalom (Jerusalem: Ben-Zvi Institute, 2009), which includes Hebrew and English translations. On the discovery of the book and its relation to Alḥarizi's other works, see ibid., 26–32 (Hebrew), and 33*–41* (English). Some of the poems relating to Alḥarizi's travels have been previously published by Yahalom and Blau under the title *al-Rawḍa al-Anīqa* (The Pleasant Garden), in *Wanderings of Judah Alharizi*, 91–167.

134. In its expanded version, this portrait of Jewish notables is largely identical with the received text of *Taḥkemoni*, ed. Yisra'el Toporovsky (Tel Aviv: Maḥbarot la-Sifrut and Mosad ha-Rav Kook, 1952), 344–66 (Gate 46). However, the new edition of *Taḥkemoni*, ed. Yahalom and Katsumata, 433–57, counts it as the 39th *maqāma*, of which it offers both the short (A) and the expanded version (B), thereby documenting the complex revisions of his work that Alḥarizi undertook toward the end of his life. Given that Alḥarizi's playfulness gets lost in literal translation, I frequently quote from Segal's English rendering (*Book of Taḥkemoni*), which endeavors to capture the rhetorical puissance of the original. However, wherever certain details that are important to my discussion have been omitted from Segal's rendering, I cite from the literal translation by Victor E. Reichert, *The Tahkemoni of Judah al-Ḥarizi*, 2 vols. (Jerusalem: R. H. Cohen's, 1965–73).

135. On the patronage relationship and its insecurities as reflected in Arabic panegyrics, see Jocelyn Sharlet, *Poetry and Patronage in the Islamic World: Social Mobility and Status in the Medieval Middle East and Central Asia* (London: Tauris, 2011).

136. See, in this volume, Introduction n. 2.

137. In referring to, say, his assistant Raphael, Meshullam uses the Hebrew *ḥaver* for *compagno*, which, in this case, means servant rather than friend; see Ya'ari's introduction to his edition of *Massa' meshullam*, 27–28. In general, my identification of Italian loanwords draws on Ya'ari's notes and Alessandra Veronese's Italian translation, *Mešullam da Volterra, Viaggio in Terra d'Israele* (Rimini: Luisè, 1989).

CHAPTER 2. TRAVEL MOTIVATIONS

1. On the conditions of medieval travel as reflected in a variety of (mainly Christian) sources, see Norbert Ohler, *The Medieval Traveller*, trans. Caroline Hillier (Woodbridge, Suffolk: Boydell, 1989), 3–140. Goitein, *Mediterranean Society*, 1:273–81, sheds light on medieval Jewish travel by land and sea based on Genizah documents. On Jewish migration during the early modern period, see David B. Ruderman, *Early Modern Jewry: A New Cultural History* (Princeton, N.J.: Princeton University Press, 2010), 23–41.

2. See Ohler, *Medieval Traveller*, 56–64; cf. Goitein, *Mediterranean Society*, 1:44–55.

3. That said, one of the fifteenth-century travel accounts included in the corpus was written by an anonymous Italian Jew who traveled to Palestine with the explicit purpose to study with the renowned R. Obadiah of Bertinoro; see Chapter 1 in this volume. On

the quest for knowledge (Arabic: *ṭalab al-ʿilm*) as a major motive for the travel of medieval Muslims, see Sam I. Gellens, "The Search for Knowledge in Medieval Muslim Societies: A Comparative Approach," in *Muslim Travelers: Pilgrimage, Migration and the Religious Imagination*, ed. Dale F. Eickelman and James Piscatori (Berkeley: University of California Press, 1990), 50–65.

4. See Chapter 1 in this volume.

5. This is not to say that medieval Jewish scholars studied at local academies exclusively; during the thirteenth and fourteenth centuries, the Cairo school of Maimonides attracted a number of Jewish scholars from as far away as Provence. Among them was the philosopher and exegete Joseph Ibn Caspi, who came to Egypt to study with a descendant of Maimonides. However, Ibn Caspi was deeply disappointed with the lack of philosophical erudition that he found there; see Ben-Shalom, "Unwritten Travel Journal," 16–19.

6. See the Introduction in this volume.

7. *Itinerary of Benjamin*, Hebrew part, 18, 20, 58–59.

8. See Lionel Casson, *Travel in the Ancient World* (London: George Allen and Unwin, 1974; reprint, Baltimore: Johns Hopkins University Press, 1994), 98.

9. Detailed information of this sort may be gleaned from the correspondence of Jewish merchants that was preserved in the Cairo Genizah; see Goitein, *Mediterranean Society*, 1:149–266; Moshe Gil, "The Jewish Merchants in the Light of Eleventh-Century Geniza Documents," *Journal of the Economic and Social History of the Orient* 46 (2003): 273–319; and the recent study by Jessica L. Goldberg, *Trade and Institutions in the Medieval Mediterranean: The Geniza Merchants and Their Business World* (Cambridge: Cambridge University Press, 2012). However, most of the relevant material dates earlier than the travel accounts that form the basis of this study. Also, the India trade as reflected in the Genizah goes beyond the book's geographical and time limits. On this topic, see Goitein's posthumously published *India Book*, which was completed by Mordechai A. Friedman: Goitein and Friedman, *India Traders of the Middle Ages: Documents from the Cairo Geniza: India Book* (Leiden: Brill, 2008); and Roxani E. Margariti, *Aden and the Indian Ocean Trade: 150 Years in the Life of a Medieval Arabian Port* (Chapel Hill: University of North Carolina Press, 2007), 109–214.

10. See Gil and Fleischer, *Yehudah Halevi and His Circle*, 427–29, doc. no. 41; a translation of the fragmentary letter can be found in Raymond P. Scheindlin, *The Song of the Distant Dove: Judah Halevi's Pilgrimage* (Oxford: Oxford University Press, 2008), 103–4.

11. *Massaʿ meshullam*, 54.

12. On Meshullam's caravan trip through the Sinai Peninsula, see Chapter 3 in this volume.

13. Campbell, *The Witness and the Other World*, 93.

14. *Itinerary of Benjamin*, Hebrew part, 69. As in medieval Arabic texts, "India" here refers to the whole region of the Indian Ocean.

15. Ibid., 58.

16. Ibid., 59.

17. See the seminal work by Olivia R. Constable, *Housing the Stranger in the*

Mediterranean World: Lodging, Trade, and Travel in Late Antiquity and the Middle Ages (Cambridge: Cambridge University Press, 2003), 68–79. On the *funduq* in the later Middle Ages, see ibid., 234–305.

18. *Massa' meshullam*, 56.

19. Ibid., 59. On the Egyptian spice trade and Venice's role in it, see Frederic C. Lane, *Venice: A Maritime Republic* (Baltimore: Johns Hopkins University Press, 1973), 285–94; Walter J. Fischel, "The Spice Trade in Mamluk Egypt," *Journal of the Economic and Social History of the Orient* 1 (1958): 157–74; and Eliyahu Ashtor, "The Volume of Levantine Trade in the Later Middle Ages (1370–1498), *Journal of European Economic History* 4 (1975): 573–612 (reprint in Ashtor, *Studies on the Levantine Trade in the Middle Ages* [London: Variorum, 1978], chap. 10).

20. Based on correspondence preserved in the Genizah, Goitein estimates that some two hundred different goods passed through eleventh-century Cairo; see idem, *Mediterranean Society*, 1:209–10; cf. Goldberg, *Trade and Institutions*, 230.

21. Hebrew text in David, *Reflections on Jewish Jerusalem*, 153.

22. Basola, *In Zion and Jerusalem*, Hebrew part, 13; I am quoting the translation in ibid., English part, 58.

23. *Massa' meshullam*, 80.

24. *Yiḥus ha-Ṣaddiqim*, in Ilan, *Tombs of the Righteous*, 158.

25. *Yiḥus Avot*, in *Ha-Me'amer* 3 (1920): 213.

26. Letter by Isaac ben Meir Latif in David, *Reflections on Jewish Jerusalem*, 94.

27. That said, the defeat of the crusaders elevated Jerusalem's religious standing in the Muslim world. Consequently, the Mamluks erected numerous religious structures and foundations therein, which boosted the meager local economy; see Joseph Drory, "Jerusalem During the Mamluk Period (1250–1517)," *Jerusalem Cathedra* 1 (1981): 190–213.

28. Obadiah, Letter A, *From Italy to Jerusalem*, 73. Obadiah's anonymous student offers a similar assessment of the economic situation in Jerusalem; see David, *Reflections on Jewish Jerusalem*, 163.

29. Basola, *In Zion and Jerusalem*, Hebrew part, 15; I have adopted the translation in ibid., English part, 64; cf. Israel Ashkenazi, letter, 112. On the occupations of Jerusalemite Jews in the sixteenth century, see Amnon Cohen's studies of Ottoman court documents (all of which are later than Israel Ashkenazi's time), *Jewish Life Under Islam: Jerusalem in the Sixteenth Century* (Cambridge, Mass.: Harvard University Press, 1984), 140–98, esp. 160–70.

30. Obadiah, Letter C, *From Italy to Jerusalem*, 90.

31. Hebrew text in David, *Reflections on Jewish Jerusalem*, 163.

32. Basola, *In Zion and Jerusalem*, Hebrew part, 23–24; I have modified the translation in ibid., English part, 86, and added the Italian loanwords in parentheses. On Jewish involvement in the Italian Levant trade, see Aryeh Shmuelevitz, *The Jews of the Ottoman Empire in the Fifteenth and Sixteenth Centuries: Administrative, Economic, Legal, and Social Relations as Reflected in the Responsa* (Leiden: Brill, 1984), 134–35.

33. Pratt, *Imperial Eyes*, 5.

34. Alison Games similarly draws a distinction between earlier British accommodation

to existing Mediterranean trade systems and later colonialism and imperialism; Games, *The Web of Empire: English Cosmopolitans in an Age of Expansion* (Oxford: Oxford University Press, 2008), 47–53.

35. Hacker, "R. Elija of Massa Lombarda," 259 (reprint in David, *Reflections on Jewish Jerusalem*, 70).

36. On early modern travelers to the Levant and their references to the local practice of medicine and science, see Sonja Brentjes, "Early Modern Western Travellers in the Middle East and Their Reports About the Sciences," in *Sciences, techniques et instruments dans le monde iranien (Xe–XIXe siècle)*, Actes du colloque tenu à l'Université de Téhéran, 7–9 June 1998, ed. N. Pourjavadi and Z. Vesel (Louvain: Peeters, 2004), 379–420 (reprint in Brentjes, *Travellers from Europe in the Ottoman and Safavid Empires, 16–17th Centuries* [Farnham, U.K.: Ashgate, 2010], chap. 5).

37. Hebrew text in David, *Reflections on Jewish Jerusalem*, 118.

38. The scriptural basis for this commandment is to be found in Exod. 23:14–17 and Deut. 16:16. On Jewish pilgrimage during Second Temple times, see the seminal study by Shmuel Safrai, *Pilgrimage at the Time of the Second Temple* (Hebrew) (Tel Aviv: 'Am ha-Sefer, 1965); and Martin Goodman, "The Pilgrimage Economy of Jerusalem in the Second Temple Period," in *Jerusalem: Its Sanctity and Centrality to Judaism, Christianity, and Islam*, ed. Lee I. Levine (New York: Continuum, 1999), 69–76 (reprint in Goodman, *Judaism in the Roman World: Collected Essays* [Leiden: Brill, 2007], 59–68). According to Goodman, there was no such mass pilgrimage to Jerusalem before the reign of King Herod (37–4 BCE). On this topic, see also Catherine Hezser, "Travel and Mobility," in *The Oxford Handbook of Jewish Daily Life in Roman Palestine*, ed. Hezser (Oxford: Oxford University Press, 2010), 220–21; and idem, *Jewish Travel in Antiquity* (Tübingen: Mohr Siebeck, 2011), 365–88.

39. Presumably, the Jewish practice of visiting the Tomb of the Patriarchs (and burial sites of other biblical figures) has roots in late antiquity; see John Wilkinson, "Jewish Holy Places and the Origins of Christian Pilgrimage," in *The Blessings of Pilgrimage*, ed. Robert Ousterhout (Urbana: University of Illinois Press, 1990), 41–53; and Allen Kerkeslager, "Jewish Pilgrimage and Jewish Identity in Hellenistic and Early Roman Egypt," in *Pilgrimage and Holy Space in Late Antique Egypt*, ed. David Frankfurter (Leiden: Brill, 1998), 99–225. However, the evidence for Jewish tomb veneration during this period is scarce, and very little is known about the associated customs; see Hezser, *Jewish Travel*, 385–88. On the veneration of holy tombs in Christian late antiquity, see the classic study by Peter Brown, *The Cult of the Saints: Its Rise and Function in Latin Christianity* (Chicago: University of Chicago Press, 1981), 1–22.

40. See Christopher S. Taylor, *In the Vicinity of the Righteous:* Ziyāra *and the Veneration of Muslim Saints in Late Medieval Egypt* (Leiden: Brill, 1999); Josef W. Meri, "The Etiquette of Devotion in the Islamic Cult of Saints," in *The Cult of Saints in Late Antiquity and the Middle Ages: Essays on the Contribution of Peter Brown*, ed. James Howard-Johnston and Paul A. Hayward (Oxford: Oxford University Press, 1999), 263–86; idem, *Cult of Saints*, 120–41; and *EI*, s.v. "*Ziyāra*." On the inner-Jewish debate about the suitability of pilgrimage to holy tombs, see Elliott Horowitz, "Speaking to the Dead: Cemetery Prayer in Medieval and Early Modern Jewry," *Journal of Jewish Thought and Philosophy* 8 (1999): 303–17.

41. Making physical contact with a revered tomb is only one of the common phenomena of a *ziyāra* that, besides the obvious supplications, may include some of the following customs: circumambulation, kindling of lights, votive offerings, and sprinkling of fragrances. For a detailed account on Muslim *ziyāra* practices, see Niels H. Olesen, *Culte des saints et pèlerinage chez Ibn Taymiyya (661/1263–728/1328)* (Paris: Paul Geuthner, 1991), 140–83. In the same context, the author discusses the polemics of Ibn Taymiyya against such customs.

42. On the two major Jewish pilgrimage circuits that developed in crusader Palestine, one having its origin in Acre, the other starting in the south from Egypt, see Reiner, "Traditions of Holy Places," 11–12. In medieval Europe, Jews, too, visited the tombs of their martyrs and venerated rabbis, yet most of the evidence seems to be later than the crusader period; see Lucia Raspe, "Sacred Space, Local History, and Diasporic Identity: The Graves of the Righteous in Medieval and Early Modern Ashkenaz," in *Jewish Studies at the Crossroads of Anthropology and History: Tradition, Authority, Diaspora*, ed. Ra'anan S. Boustan, Oren Kosansky, and Marina Rustow (Philadelphia: University of Pennsylvania Press, 2011), 147–63.

43. Alḥarizi, *Kitāb al-Durar*, 218 (Judeo-Arabic), 120* (English translation). On the tombs of Ezekiel and Ezra, see Chapter 5 of this volume.

44. See Moshe Gil, "Aliya and Pilgrimage in the Early Arab Period (634–1009)," *Jerusalem Cathedra* 3 (1983): 163–73; Gil, *A History of Palestine, 634–1099* (Cambridge: Cambridge University Press, 1992), 622–31; Miriam Frenkel, "'Yated ha-tequ'ah be-makom ne'eman': Poliṭiqah ve-koaḥ ba-'aliyah le-regel ha-yehudit l-irushalayim ba-tequfah ha-faṭimit," in *Ut Videant et Contigant: Essays on Pilgrimage and Sacred Space in Honor of Ora Limor*, ed. Yitzhak Hen and Iris Shagrir (Hebrew) (Raanana: Open University of Israel, 2011), 135–56.

45. See Elchanan Reiner, "A Jewish Response to the Crusades: The Dispute over Sacred Places in the Holy Land," in *Juden und Christen zur Zeit der Kreuzzüge*, ed. Alfred Haverkamp (Sigmaringen: J. Thorbecke, 1999), 211. Reiner goes as far as to characterize medieval Jewish pilgrimage to Palestine as "a mirror image of Latin-Christian pilgrimage, imitating the Latin itineraries, religious values, myths and folk culture." Joseph Shatzmiller similarly contextualizes medieval Jewish pilgrimage within contemporaneous Christian culture; see Shatzmiller, "Jews, Pilgrimage, and the Christian Cult of Saints: Benjamin of Tudela and His Contemporaries," in *After Rome's Fall: Narrators and Sources of Early Medieval History: Essays Presented to Walter Goffart*, ed. Alexander Callander Murray (Toronto: University of Toronto Press, 1998), 337–47.

46. See Reiner, "Oral Versus Written," 312–14.

47. The crusader ban on Jewish settlement in Jerusalem was linked to the Church's claim of having superseded Judaism; see Prawer, *History of the Jews*, 46–49, 94.

48. On the Hebrew sources reflecting this fact, see Chapter 4 of this volume. Jews seem to have monopolized the dyeing business in Syria-Palestine under both Muslim and Christian rule; see Rüger, *Syrien und Palaestina*, 6. For medieval Christian, Jewish, or Muslim travelers in foreign lands, "lodging with those of the same faith" was the preferred, if not only, option; see Ohler, *Medieval Traveller*, 81–89. There is particularly rich documentation

for Egyptian Jewish communities that provided travelers with lodging and other forms of support; see Goitein, *Mediterranean Society*, 2:135–36.

49. See Elchanan Reiner, "Pilgrims and Pilgrimage to Eretz Yisrael, 1099–1517" (Hebrew) (Ph.D. diss., Hebrew University of Jerusalem, 1988), 30.

50. See Ephraim Kanarfogel, "The *'Aliyah* of 'Three Hundred Rabbis' in 1211: Tosafist Attitudes Toward Settling in the Land of Israel," *JQR* 76 (1985): 191–215. On this topic, see also Alexandra Cuffel, "Call and Response: European Jewish Emigration to Egypt and Palestine in the Middle Ages," *JQR* 90 (1999): 61–102; as Cuffel points out, this immigration wave was not confined to famous rabbis but included minor scholars and nonrabbinic figures as well.

51. Petaḥyah, *Sibbuv*, 1:12. On Samuel ben 'Eli and his portrayal by Petaḥyah, see also Chapter 6 in this volume.

52. Halevi's travel poetry and its relation to his Near Eastern journey is the topic of several recent studies, foremost among them Scheindlin, *Song of the Distant Dove*, 97–152; and Yahalom, *Yehuda Halevi*, 107–60. Here is not the place to discuss these monographs in detail (that said, see nn. 59 and 62 below); see, however, David J. Malkiel's recent review essay "Three Perspectives on Judah Halevi's Voyage to Palestine," *Mediterranean Historical Review* 25, no. 1 (2010): 1–15.

53. Among Muslim travelers, Ibn Baṭṭūṭa (see Chapter 1 n. 19) similarly names penitence as a major motive for his travels—which, however, should take him far beyond a mere pilgrimage to Mecca.

54. For the date of Halevi's arrival, see the letter published by Gil and Fleischer, *Yehuda Halevi and His Circle*, 422, doc. no. 40, fol. a, lines 35–36; an abridged translation is offered by Scheindlin, *Song of the Distant Dove*, 97–98. For a vivid reconstruction of Halevi's encounters in Egypt with Jewish businessmen, scholars, and dignitaries, see ibid., 97–152.

55. Halevi's ship finally set sail on May 14, the first day of Shavu'ot; see Gil and Fleischer, *Yehuda Halevi and His Circle*, 482, doc. no. 52; translated in Scheindlin, *Song of the Distant Dove*, 149.

56. See Gil and Fleischer, *Yehuda Halevi and His Circle*, 484–94, doc. nos. 53 and 54; and Scheindlin, *Song of the Distant Dove*, 150–52. It is often assumed that Halevi was trodden to death by a Muslim with his horse shortly after having reached the gates of (crusader-ruled!) Jerusalem. However, this legend is unknown prior to the sixteenth-century chronicle of Gedalyah Ibn Yaḥia, who attributes it to hearsay ("an old man"); *Shalshelet ha-qabbalah* (Jerusalem: Ha-Dorot ha-rishonim ve-qorotam, 1962), 92.

57. According to manuscript versions (MS London) of *Massa'ot*, Judah Halevi is buried near Tiberias, next to the tomb of R. Yoḥanan ben Zakkai (*Itinerary of Benjamin*, Hebrew part, 29), leading Adler to conclude (ibid., English part, 29 n. 1): "Jehuda Halevi died about thirty years before Benjamin's visit, and the question of the burial-place of our great national poet is thus finally settled." However, since Yoḥanan ben Zakkai lived during the first century, the print version that reads "R. Jonathan ben Levi" (another Mishnaic sage) instead of Judah Halevi makes more sense. In any case, the manuscript mentioning the poet's tomb may already echo the medieval lore that had developed around his pilgrimage and mysterious death.

58. Judah Halevi, *Dîwân*, 2:184; idem, *Selected Poems*, 39; cf. Scheindlin, *Song of the Distant Dove*, 203–9. On the timing of the poem, see Gil and Fleischer, *Yehuda Halevi and His Circle*, 187.

59. Here, I disagree with Scheindlin (*Song of the Distant Dove*, 211–12), who appears to construct an artificial contrast between theoretical (Neoplatonic or mystical) vision and actual pilgrimage. When Neoplatonic language is interpreted through the lens of Sufism, the experiences do not exclude but potentially complement each other; see Diana Lobel, *Between Mysticism and Philosophy: Sufi Language of Religious Experience in Judah Ha-Levi's Kuzari* (Albany: State University of New York, 2000), 22–28.

60. Judah Halevi, *Dîwân*, 2:296; idem, *Selected Poems*, 115; cf. Scheindlin, *Song of the Distant Dove*, 85.

61. This terminology closely resembles the Neoplatonic language of Solomon Ibn Gabirol (ca. 1021–58), author of *The Fountain of Life* (*Mekor Ḥayim*), whose thought had a strong impact on Halevi; see Scheindlin, *Song of the Distant Dove*, 29. On Halevi's poems on the soul and their relationship to Neoplatonism, see Adena Tanenbaum, *The Contemplative Soul: Hebrew Poetry and Philosophical Theory in Medieval Spain* (Leiden: Brill, 2002), 174–94.

62. Hence Scheindlin (*Song of the Distant Dove*, 32–33) believes that Halevi later turned away from Neoplatonic thought and its desire for the soul's reunion with the divine (see also n. 59 above). Instead, Halevi then voiced his hope for a "national restoration" of the Jewish people, in Scheindlin's view. However, the notion of Jewish "nationalistic thought" (ibid., 33) constitutes an anachronism when related to premodern times.

63. Shlomo D. Goitein, "The Biography of Rabbi Juda ha-Levi in the Light of the Cairo Geniza Documents," *Proceedings of the American Academy of Jewish Research* 28 (1959): 55–56; cf. Gil and Fleischer, *Yehuda Halevi and His Circle*, 251–53.

64. "Vaults of the wind" alludes to Ps. 135:7.

65. Here, I quote only the first lines of the Hebrew source; Judah Halevi, *Dîwân*, 2:171; idem, *Selected Poems*, 24.

66. Cf. what is arguable Halevi's most famous line: "My heart is in the East, and I at the edge of the West." The Hebrew text of the poem, which Halevi composed well before his voyage to the Levant, is to be found in Halevi, *Dîwân*, 2:155; and Yahalom, *Yehuda Halevi*, 85, which comes with a translation by Gabriel Levin.

67. In Arabic literature, by contrast, it is the eastern wind that has nostalgic associations, as Scheindlin, *Song of the Distant Dove*, 228, points out.

68. In the former sense, it occurs in Ps. 84:4: "Even the sparrow has found a home, and the swallow [*dror*] a nest for herself . . . near Your altar, O Lord of hosts, my king and my God." If the poet has this psalm in mind, the swallow also stands for Halevi's longing to reach the site of the former Temple. This interpretation is supported by the ensuing reference to *mar-dror* ("pure myrrh"), an ingredient of the anointing oil at the Tabernacle (Exod. 30:23).

69. Cf. the more detailed interpretation of this poem by Marc Saperstein, "Halevi's West Wind," *Prooftexts* 1 (1981): 306–11.

CHAPTER 3. LEVANTINE JOURNEYS

1. On the conditions of medieval travel, see also, in this volume, Chapter 2 n. 1.

2. See Scheindlin, *Song of the Distant Dove*, 99 and 268 n. 3; and Malkiel, "Three Perspectives," 3–4.

3. On Venice as a facilitator of Latin pilgrimage to the Holy Land, see Deborah Howard, *Venice and the East: The Impact of the Islamic World on Venetian Architecture; 1100–1500* (New Haven, Conn.: Yale University Press, 2000), 189–216; and Chareyron, *Pilgrims to Jerusalem*, 16–18.

4. *Massa' meshullam*, 60–62.

5. Obadiah, Letter A, *From Italy to Jerusalem*, 41. As there is no evidence that Meshullam had undergone rabbinical training, Obadiah here seems to use the term "rabbi" as an honorific.

6. Ibid., 42.

7. Ibid., 51.

8. Ibid., 61.

9. See Chapter 1 in this volume.

10. Petaḥyah, *Sibbuv*, 1:7.

11. *Massa' meshullam*, 60.

12. On Mediterranean shipping lanes and the various effects of currents and winds on them, see Peregrine Horden and Nicholas Purcell, *The Corrupting Sea: A Study of Mediterranean History* (Oxford: Blackwell, 2000), 137–43. On the sea lanes connecting Italy with the Levant during the fifteenth and sixteenth centuries, see David, *To Come to the Land*, 8–13.

13. See Hilda F. M. Prescott, *Jerusalem Journey: Pilgrimage to the Holy Land in the Fifteenth Century* (London: Eyre and Spottiswoode, 1954), 46–56; Eliyahu Ashtor, "Venezia e il Pellegrinaggio in Terrasanta nel Basso Medioevo," *Archivio Storico Italiano* 143 (1985): 197–223; J. Kenneth Hyde, "Navigation of the Eastern Mediterranean in the Fourteenth and Fifteenth Centuries According to Pilgrims' Books," in *Literacy and Its Uses: Studies on Late Medieval Italy*, ed. Hyde and Daniel P. Waley (Manchester: Manchester University Press, 1993), 87–111; and Deborah Howard, *Venice and the East*, 190–200.

14. Nonetheless, Meshullam boarded such a pilgrim galley at Jaffa; see below and Chapter 7 in this volume.

15. See also Chapter 4 in this volume.

16. Obadiah's description of the conflict, which was penned about sixty years later, seems to partially corroborate the Franciscans' accusations; see Chapter 4 in this volume. The exact time period in which the prohibition was in force and the extent to which it was heeded by port authorities and shipowners remain the subject of debate; see Shlomo Simonsohn, "Divieto di transportare Ebrei in Palestina," *Italia Judaica* 2 (1984): 39–53; and David Jacoby, "The Franciscans, the Jews, and the Issue of Mount Zion in the Fifteenth Century" (Hebrew), *Cathedra* 39 (1986): 51–70.

17. See Shlomo Simonsohn, "Dalla Sicilia a Gerusalemme: *'Alyyah* di ebrei siciliani nel Quattrocento," *Materia Giudaica* 11, nos. 1–2 (2006): 43–50.

18. Obadiah, Letter A, *From Italy to Jerusalem*, 81–82.

19. Basola, *In Zion and Jerusalem*, Hebrew part, 36; English part, 115.

20. Ibid., Hebrew part, 36; I slightly modify the translation in ibid., English part, 115–16. Other Jewish travelers, too, would offer detailed advice on "How to Travel from Venice to the Land of Israel"—to quote the title of an anonymous travel guide from the fifteenth century (MS Cambridge Add. 10.46, fol. 6a). The manuscript was published by Adolf Neubauer, *Hebräische Bibliographie* 21 (1881–82): 136. For a few additional sources, see Abraham David, "New Sources Describing Travel by Sea from Venice to the Orient and Eretz Israel (Palestine) in the Fifteenth to the Seventeenth Centuries" (Hebrew), *Shalem* 6 (1992): 319–33.

21. Shlomo D. Goitein's translation of the Hebrew document from the Cairo Genizah; Goitein, *Letters of Medieval Jewish Traders* (Princeton, N.J.: Princeton University Press, 1974), 41 (no. 3), slightly edited. For further travelers' reports about dangers incurred on a Mediterranean passage, see idem, *Mediterranean Society*, 1:320–22. Other letters deposited in the Genizah tell about ships that were pursued by pirates; see Goitein, *Letters*, 42–45 (no. 4); and Goitein, *Mediterranean Society*, 1:327–32. On the hazards and risks experienced by India merchants, including shipwreck and piracy, see Goitein and Friedman, *India Traders*, 157–64.

22. *Massa' meshullam*, 82.

23. Ibid., 83.

24. Ibid., 65–66. "Horses that are swift as leopards" is an allusion to Hab. 1:8.

25. *Massa' meshullam*, 60. Not only when crossing the desert but also in populated areas, overland travel in the Middle East was largely done in caravans for safety as well as convenience; see Goitein, *Mediterranean Society*, 1:276–80.

26. *Massa' meshullam*, 67.

27. A different picture of the same trek emerges from the account by 'Ayyāshī, a seventeenth-century Muslim jurist from Morocco who, on his *ziyāra* to Jerusalem, also joined a caravan going from Egypt to Palestine. In his account (as summarized by Matar), the Bedouin of the Sinai Peninsula are not portrayed as "merciless brigands intent on pillage and murder." Having been informed that the caravan consisted of poor pilgrims, they let it move on without demanding any payment; see Nabil Matar, "Two Journeys to Seventeenth-Century Palestine," *Journal of Palestine Studies* 29, no. 4 (2000): 38; cf. ibid., 44.

28. Petaḥyah, *Sibbuv*, 1:6.

29. Hacker, "R. Elija of Massa Lombarda," 258 (David, *Reflections on Jewish Jerusalem*, 69).

30. On the plague of 1438 that struck Egypt and Syria particularly hard, see Eliyahu Ashtor (Strauss), *Toledot ha-yehudim be-miṣrayim ve-suriyah taḥat shilṭon ha-mamlukim*, 3 vols. (Jerusalem: Mosad ha-Rav Kook, 1944–70), 2:116 n. 7.

31. *Massa' meshullam*, 63.

32. Cf. Exod. 8:12–13.

33. *Massa' meshullam*, 63.

34. Ibid., 76.

35. Ibid., 77.

36. Obadiah, Letter A, *From Italy to Jerusalem*, 82.

37. See Goitein, *Mediterranean Society*, 1:347.

38. How much attention the Jem affair received among contemporaries is also illustrated by Meshullam of Volterra's report. He claims to have seen Jem and his men in Ramla (on August 26/27, 1481), when the latter was on his flight to Cairo; *Massa' meshullam*, 77–78.

39. Instead, the knights transferred Jem to Rome (in 1489) as per an agreement with the pope. The most detailed account of the affair is still to be found in Joseph von Hammer-Purgstall, *Geschichte des Osmanischen Reiches*, 2nd ed. (Pest: Hartleben, 1834), 1:602–22; for more recent scholarship, see *EI*, s.v. "Djem."

40. Obadiah, Letter A, *From Italy to Jerusalem*, 46.

41. Ibid., 46–48.

42. *Massa' meshullam*, 45–46. The thorough search that foreigners had to undergo after disembarking in Alexandria is also commented on by many Christian travelers; see Chareyron, *Pilgrims to Jerusalem*, 191. Similarly, Ibn Jubayr criticizes the fleecing of poor Muslim pilgrims upon their arrival at Alexandria; see his *Riḥla*, 39–40; *Travels of Ibn Jubayr*, 31–32. Social status and connections seem to have determined the individual treatment more than religious affiliation did.

43. See Wilhelm Heyd, *Histoire du Commerce du Levant au moyen-age*, 2 vols. (Leipzig: Harrassowitz, 1885–86), 2:449–52; and *EI*, s.v. "Ḍarība." Even so, Obadiah says that one had to pay only 2 percent on currencies imported into Egypt; Letter A, *From Italy to Jerusalem*, 51. But he was spared any such payment, having been accompanied by a well-connected dragoman (see below). On the workings of the customs administration, cf. Margariti's study of the Aden customhouse, *Aden and the Indian Ocean Trade*, 110–40.

44. On a twelfth-century Jewish customs officer at Alexandria, see Miriam Frenkel, *"The Compassionate and Benevolent": The Leading Elite in the Jewish Community of Alexandria in the Middle Ages* (Hebrew) (Jerusalem, Ben-Zvi Institute, 2006), 33. On Jewish customs officers in Ottoman Egypt, see Shimon Shtober, "On the Issue of Customs Collectors in Egypt: Jews as Tax Farmers in Ottoman Egypt" (Hebrew), *Pe'amim* 38 (1989): 68–94.

45. *Massa' meshullam*, 49.

46. Obadiah, Letter A, *From Italy to Jerusalem*, 48. Basola mentions a Jewish customs agent in Beirut, a certain Abraham Castro, who determined the tax "as he pleases"; Basola, *In Zion and Jerusalem*, Hebrew part, 13. I am quoting the translation in ibid., English part, 59.

47. Basola, *In Zion and Jerusalem*, Hebrew part, 12; English part, 57.

48. During the reign of Catarina Cornaro (r. 1474–89), a Venetian noblewoman by birth and widow of the Cypriot king James "the Bastard," Venice increasingly gained control over the Mediterranean island. At the same time, Cyprus was tributary to the Mamluks. According to Meshullam, Catarina was on a court visit to Cairo when he met her majordomo; *Massa' meshullam*, 50. Fears that she might conspire with the sultan against

her Venetian advisers were among the reasons that the Serenissima later forced Catarina to abdicate her crown to the republic (1489); see Irene Zanini-Cordi, "Cornaro, Catarina (1454–1510)," in *Encyclopedia of Women in the Renaissance: Italy, France, and England*, ed. Diana Maury Robin et al. (Santa Barbara, Calif.: ABC-CLIO, 2007), 98–99.

49. *Massa' meshullam*, 50.

50. The mu'ayyadī was named after the Mamluk sultan al-Mu'ayyad Sayf al-Dīn Shaykh (r. 1412–21). Meshullam uses an Italianized form of the term (*maiidi*).

51. *Massa' meshullam*, 52.

52. *Itinéraire d'Anselme Adorno en Terre Sainte (1470–1471)*, ed. and trans. Jacques Heers and Georgette de Groer (Paris: Éditions du Centre national de la recherche scientifique, 1978), 174–77 (Latin with French translation); cf. Chareyron, *Pilgrims to Jerusalem*, 189–90. Though attributed to Anselmo Adorno, the account of their shared journey seems to have been penned by his son Giovanni (Jean, 1444–1511).

53. *Massa' meshullam*, 69–71.

54. Similar attitudes are expressed in the pilgrimage account by one seventeenth-century Englishman, who is known only by his initials "T.B." This traveler repeatedly complains about Arab "savages" and "molesters" trying to extort money from him; see Matar, "Two Journeys," 47–48.

55. Adorno, *Itinéraire*, 238–39 (Latin with French translation).

56. Hebrew text in David, *Reflections on Jewish Jerusalem*, 158.

57. Ibid., 158–59.

58. See Chapters 4, 5, and 7 in this volume.

59. Basola, *In Zion and Jerusalem*, Hebrew part, 14. I slightly modify the translation, ibid., English part, 61.

60. Obadiah, Letter A, *From Italy to Jerusalem*, 57.

61. Hebrew text in David, *Reflections on Jewish Jerusalem*, 149, 167.

62. Basola, *In Zion and Jerusalem*, Hebrew part, 38; English part, 116. Christian pilgrims, too, often brought cookware on board, as one could not rely on the meal service that was supposedly included in the fare; see Prescott, *Jerusalem Journey*, 53.

63. *Story of David Hareuveni*, 31.

64. An anonymous *baraita* restricts the permission to set out on a sea journey to the first three days of the week (t. Shabbat 13:13; *The Tosefta: According to Codex Vienna with Variants from Codex Erfurt, Genizah MSS. and Editio Princeps* [Hebrew], ed. Shaul Lieberman, 4 vols. [New York: Jewish Theological Seminary, 1955–73], 2:16). However, the Talmudic discussion (b. Shabbat 19a) questions this limitation. On the potential conflicts of holiday observance and sea travel as reflected in classical rabbinic texts and later halakhic literature, see Jacob Katz, *The Sabbath Gentile: The Socio-Economic and Halakhic Background to the Employment of Gentiles on Jewish Sabbaths and Festivals* (Hebrew) (Jerusalem: Shazar Center, 1983), 33–42; Hezser, *Jewish Travel*, 305–6; and Hezser, "Travel and Mobility," 219.

65. The date of his departure is mentioned in Gil and Fleischer, *Yehuda Halevi and His Circle*, 482, doc. no. 52; for a translation, see Scheindlin, *Song of the Distant Dove*, 149.

66. Basola, *In Zion and Jerusalem*, Hebrew part, 9; English part, 48.

67. Ibid., Hebrew part, 10–11; English part, 50–52.

68. Ibid., Hebrew part, 11; English part, 55.

69. Hebrew text in David, *Reflections on Jewish Jerusalem*, 114.

70. *Massa' meshullam*, 60.

71. Obadiah, Letter A, *From Italy to Jerusalem*, 61.

72. Genizah documents reflect that some Jewish travelers paid escorts when staying behind a caravan in the open field to observe Shabbat; see Goitein, *Mediterranean Society*, 1:280–81. Because of danger, certain rabbinic authorities even argued that Jewish travelers were permitted to continue their desert trek on Shabbat once they were traveling under the protection of a non-Jewish caravan. See the respective responsum by the Aragonese R. Isaac bar Sheshet Perfet (Rivash, 1326–1408, who later migrated to Algeria), where Bar Sheshet draws an analogy between desert travel and a sea journey. At the same time, the rabbi argues that Jews should avoid setting out on a caravan trip during the second half of the week, when it was foreseeable that they would have to desecrate the Shabbat; *She'elot ve-teshuvot le-rabbenu yiṣḥaq bar sheshet*, ed. David Metzger (Jerusalem: Makhon Yerushalayim, 1993), 1:92–95, no. 101.

73. Lit., "close to 24 o'clock"; Meshullam uses the Italian counting of hours that starts at 6 PM.

74. *Massa' meshullam*, 62.

75. Basola, *In Zion and Jerusalem*, Hebrew part, 37. I am quoting the translation in ibid., English part, 116.

76. For vivid descriptions of life on board, see Prescott, *Jerusalem Journey*, 60–62; and Chareyron, *Pilgrims to Jerusalem*, 48, 50.

77. Obadiah, Letter A, *From Italy to Jerusalem*, 43.

78. *Massa' meshullam*, 42.

79. On Jewish captives taken in the eastern Mediterranean during the fifteenth to seventeenth centuries, see Eliezer Bashan, "Captivity and Ransom in Mediterranean Jewish Society During the Medieval Period and up to the New Times" (Hebrew) (Ph.D. diss., Bar-Ilan University, 1971), 151–64.

80. These pilgrim galleys have been described in much detail by Felix Fabri, a Dominican friar from Ulm, within the account of his (second) Jerusalem journey (1483); for the Latin text, see *Fratris Felicis Fabri Evagatorium in Terrae Sanctae, Arabiae et Aegypti peregrinatio*, ed. Conrad D. Hassler, 3 vols. (Stuttgart: Literarischer Verein, 1843–49), 1:117–22; trans. Aubrey Stewart, *The Wanderings of Felix Fabri*, 4 vols. (London: Palestine Pilgrims' Text Society, 1896–93), 1:125–31. On this topic, see Frederic C. Lane, *Venetian Ships and Shipbuilders of the Renaissance* (Baltimore: Johns Hopkins University Press, 1934; reprint, New York: Arno, 1979), 17–22; and Deborah Howard, *Venice and the East*, 26–28. On the Contarini brothers and their role in the Venetian pilgrim traffic, see *Canon Pietro Casola's Pilgrimage to Jerusalem in the Year 1494*, trans. M. Margaret Newett (Manchester: Manchester University Press, 1907), 98–100; and Prescott, *Jerusalem Journey*, 51–52.

81. See Chapter 7 in this volume.

82. *Massa' meshullam*, 61.

83. Ibid.

84. See Chapters 7 and 8 in this volume.

85. *Massa' meshullam*, 62.

86. Ibid., 66.

87. Ibid., 67. The Irish Franciscan Symon Semeonis (who undertook a Jerusalem pilgrimage in 1323–24) likewise draws attention to the fact that Middle Eastern men urinated squatting: "We could hardly dare urinate standing while in their [the Bedouin] presence, when my nature called, because they . . . never urinate except *as females*, and while doing so always look towards their rears, affirming that all who urinate standing offend the omnipotent God and incur without doubt his malediction"; Latin text in *Itinerarium Symonis Semeonis ab Hybernia ad Terram Sanctam*, ed. and trans. Mario Esposito (Dublin: Dublin Institute for Advanced Studies, 1960), 102. As Esposito omits the cited passage from his translation, I am quoting here the English rendering by Eugen Hoade, *Western Pilgrims* (Jerusalem: Franciscan, 1952), 41 (my addition and emphasis). It is noteworthy that Meshullam does not draw any such feminizing comparisons.

88. *Massa' meshullam*, 67.

89. At one point on their desert trek, Meshullam's interpreter was given away as a Jew, wherefore the locals demanded a much higher way toll (two ducats). The caravan master managed to resolve the conflict; ibid., 61.

90. See Obadiah, Letter A, *From Italy to Jerusalem*, 80.

CHAPTER 4. FACING A GENTILE LAND OF ISRAEL

1. For Damascus, see *Itinerary of Benjamin*, Hebrew part, 31; and Petaḥyah, *Sibbuv*, 1:28. For Aleppo, see *Itinerary of Benjamin*, Hebrew part, 32; Asher's edition reads here 1,500 (*Itinerary of Rabbi Benjamin*, vol. 1, Hebrew part, 50). It is unclear whether these figures refer to individuals, males, or households.

2. Petaḥyah, *Sibbuv*, 1:29.

3. Here I am borrowing the phrase "landscape of Jewish cultural memory" from Ra'anan S. Boustan, "The Spoils of the Jerusalem Temple at Rome and Constantinople: Jewish Counter-Geography in a Christianizing Empire," in *Antiquity in Antiquity: Jewish and Christian Pasts in the Greco-Roman World*, ed. Gregg Gardner and Kevin L. Osterloh (Tübingen: Mohr Siebeck, 2008), 341.

4. *Itinerary of Benjamin*, Hebrew part, 21.

5. Josh. 19:24–31; Judg. 1:31.

6. For the definition of Acre as lying outside the Land of Israel, see m. Giṭṭin 1:2; and t. Shevi'it 4:11.

7. *Itinerary of Benjamin*, Hebrew part, 21.

8. In an apparent act of censorship, the word *to'im* has been crossed out in MS London and erased in MS Vienna. Regarding this term, crusaders are likewise called *to'im* in the

Hebrew accounts of the persecution of the Rhineland Jews; e.g., see Solomon ben Simson's chronicle, in the edition by Eva Haverkamp, *Hebräische Berichte über die Judenverfolgungen während des Ersten Kreuzzugs* (Hanover: Hahnsche, 2005), 299, 609; for an English translation, see Shlomo Eidelberg, *The Jews and the Crusaders: The Hebrew Chronicles of the First and Second Crusades* (Madison: University of Wisconsin Press, 1977), 24. On the polemical language of these accounts, see Anna Sapir Abulafia, "Invectives Against Christianity in the Hebrew Chronicles of the First Crusade," in *Crusade and Settlement*, ed. Peter W. Edbury (Cardiff: University College Cardiff Press, 1985), 66–72.

9. In describing pilgrimage as a "contested" activity, I am following John Eade and Michael J. Sallnow; see the introduction to their edited volume *Contesting the Sacred: The Anthropology of Christian Pilgrimage* (London: Routledge, 1991), 1–29.

10. On this background, Benjamin refers to the Apulian city of Trani as an important port of embarkation for Holy Land pilgrims (*to'im*); see *Itinerary of Benjamin*, Hebrew part, 10–11.

11. Benjamin's *Massa'ot* is considered one of the earliest sources for the establishment of a crusader church on the Carmel; see Denys Pringle, *The Churches of the Crusader Kingdom of Jerusalem: A Corpus*, 2 vols. (Cambridge: Cambridge University Press, 1993), 2:227.

12. *Itinerary of Benjamin*, Hebrew part, 21. Elijah's restoration of the altar is mentioned in 1 Kings 18:30. The site is traditionally located on the southeastern peak of the Carmel range at al-Muḥraqa.

13. These "high places" were to be destroyed, following the example of 2 Kings 23:8 and 15; and 2 Chron. 31:1; cf. Deut. 12:2.

14. Mutatis mutandis, this tendency may find a parallel in Christian pilgrimage accounts describing the Holy Land as an "imaginary spot on the world's atlas, a Holy Land with no life of its own"; Campbell, *The Witness and the Other World*, 42.

15. *Massa' meshullam*, 71.

16. During the Fifth Crusade, when Damietta was taken by the crusaders (1219), the Ayyubids considered the necessity of ceding Jerusalem to Christendom and, in anticipation thereof, dismantled the Holy City's fortifications; see Steven Runciman, *A History of the Crusades*, 3 vols. (Cambridge: Cambridge University Press, 1951–54), 3:158. On the largely undefended character of Mamluk-ruled Jerusalem, see Drory, "Jerusalem During the Mamluk Period," 192–93.

17. Cf. Obadiah of Bertinoro's account, written seven years later: "Jerusalem is largely ruined and deserted, and it goes without saying that there is no wall surrounding it"; Letter A, *From Italy to Jerusalem*, 64.

18. A critical edition of the letter was rendered by Benjamin Z. Kedar, "The Jewish Community of Jerusalem in the Thirteenth Century" (Hebrew), *Tarbiz* 41 (1972): 82–94; reprinted as "The Jews of Jerusalem, 1187–1267, and the Role of Naḥmanides in the Re-Establishment of Their Community" (Hebrew), in *Jerusalem in the Middle Ages: Selected Papers* (Hebrew), ed. Kedar (Jerusalem: Ben-Zvi Institute, 1979), 122–36; this version of the letter was republished by David, *Reflections on Jewish Jerusalem*, 40–43.

19. *Massa' meshullam*, 71. According to the Talmud (b. Mo'ed Kaṭan 26a), Jews are

obliged to rend their garments twice at the sight of Jerusalem. Discussing the reason for these two rends, the Talmud declares the first to be a sign of mourning over the destruction of the Temple and the second to commemorate the destruction of the city itself. In the same context, another opinion is quoted that implies the opposite order.

20. *Toṣ'ot ereṣ yisra'el*, fol. 2, 55.

21. A place called Ṣofim is already mentioned in the Talmud (b. Mo'ed Kaṭan 26a), but its location is left unclear there. In medieval Hebrew itineraries, the place name Ṣofim seems to echo Christian traditions in yet another way. The crusaders had identified Montjoye with biblical Ramah, which is also called Ramataim Ṣofim (1 Sam. 1:1). On Nabī Ṣamwīl, see Chapter 5 in this volume. This hill is not to be confused with modern Mount Scopus (Hebrew: Har ha-Ṣofim), a Jerusalem neighborhood to the north of the Mount of Olives.

22. For the Latin text of Theoderic's account, see *Peregrinationes Tres: Saewulf, John of Würzburg, Theodericus*, CCCM 139, ed. R. B. C. Huygens (Turnhout: Brepols, 1994), 186; I am slightly altering the translation found in John Wilkinson, Joyce Hill, and W. F. Ryan, eds., *Jerusalem Pilgrimage 1099–1185* (London: Hakluyt Society, 1988), 310. On other Christian descriptions of the pilgrims' arrival at Montjoye, see Chareyron, *Pilgrims to Jerusalem*, 78–79.

23. *Toṣ'ot ereṣ yisra'el*, fol. 2, 55.

24. Hebrew text in *Kitve rabbenu moshe ben naḥman*, ed. Ḥayim (Charles) Chavel, 2 vols. (Jerusalem: Mosad ha-Rav Kook, 1963–64; reprint, 1982), 1:429; for an English translation of the entire prayer, see *Ramban (Nachmanides), Writings and Discourses*, trans. Charles B. Chavel, 2 vols. (New York: Shiloh, 1978), 2:702–25 (my translation differs from Chavel's). Historically, the biblical verses quoted in this prayer refer to the destruction of the First Temple (586 BCE); the classical rabbis applied them to the Second Temple (70 CE) as well. Accordingly, the "heathens" who had "entered" God's "inheritance" can allude to any of the city's subsequent conquerors. In this sense, the notion of a barren city and land had become a timeless motif.

25. The phrasing alludes to Ps. 137:1. The Hebrew text of the letter can be found in David, *Reflections on Jewish Jerusalem*, 92.

26. David, *Reflections on Jewish Jerusalem*, 92. For further descriptions by the authors of Jerusalem's covered market streets, see Chapter 2 in this volume.

27. This phrase occurs in Num. 13:27 and Jer. 11:5, inter alia.

28. *Massa' meshullam*, 75.

29. *Itinerary of Benjamin*, Hebrew part, 23.

30. On the killing of Jerusalem's inhabitants by the crusaders and the pertinent scholarly discussion, see Benjamin Z. Kedar, "The Jerusalem Massacre of July 1099 in the Western Historiography of the Crusades," *Crusades* 3 (2004): 15–75. The diverse Christian communities that made up the population of Frankish Jerusalem have been described in detail by an anonymous Christian pilgrim whose account (in translation) can be found in F. E. Peters, *Jerusalem: The Holy City in the Eyes of Chroniclers, Visitors, Pilgrims, and Prophets from the Days of Abraham to the Beginnings of Modern Times* (Princeton, N.J.: Princeton University Press, 1985), 307–8.

31. *Itinerary of Benjamin*, Hebrew part, 23. In reading "four" Jews, I am following MS Rome, while MS London, the base text of Adler's edition, has "two hundred." The different readings are easily explained, as the letters *dalet* (standing for "four") and *resh* (with a numerical value of 200) are often confused in Hebrew manuscripts. That the Jewish presence in Frankish Jerusalem was restricted to a tannery is confirmed by Petaḥyah (*Sibbuv*, 1:32), who mentions one dyer called R. Abraham. A century later, Naḥmanides similarly speaks of two dyers as the sole Jewish inhabitants of the by-then Mamluk-ruled city (see his above-cited letter from 1267, in Kedar, "Jewish Community of Jerusalem," 94). Though he explains the community's small size with the earlier Mongol invasion, Naḥmanides may be following here an older tradition going back to crusader times.

32. See Chapter 2 in this volume.

33. *Itinerary of Benjamin*, Hebrew part, 23.

34. Ibid.; the Hospital near the Holy Sepulchre was in the area of the Old City that still is known as Muristan (a Persian loanword, meaning hospital). For contemporaneous descriptions of the Hospital by Christian pilgrims, see Peters, *Jerusalem*, 324–27.

35. *Itinerary of Benjamin*, Hebrew part, 23–24. Manuscripts and printed texts offer corrupted versions of the Latin term, but the original is still recognizable; MS Rome reflects an Italian pronunciation (*templo*). For Christian accounts of the Templars' headquarters, see Peters, *Jerusalem*, 320–24.

36. *Itinerary of Benjamin*, Hebrew part, 24. Asher's edition (*Itinerary of Rabbi Benjamin*, vol. 1, Hebrew part, 36) suggests a Romance-pronunciation of Sepulchre, whereas other textual versions offer a corrupted rendering of the loanword.

37. For a few more Jewish references to the Holy Sepulchre, most of which are polemical in tone, see Chapter 7 in this volume.

38. Another reason for his mention of the Holy Sepulchre may consist in relatively current events. The rebuilding of the church, which had been largely destroyed in 1009 (during the reign of the Fatimid caliph al-Ḥākim), was completed in 1149, the fiftieth anniversary of the crusaders' conquest of Jerusalem. Since this event took place not long before Benjamin's ostensible visit, it may partly explain why Christianity's most revered site receives his attention.

39. *Itinerary of Benjamin*, Hebrew part, 24.

40. On the Dome of the Rock's construction, see Gil, *A History of Palestine*, 90–96.

41. The Byzantines had left the Temple Mount in ruins to visibly document the fulfillment of the prophecy by Jesus that "there shall not be left here one stone upon another" (Matt. 24:2). By contrast, the Templum Domini (Dome of the Rock) played a central role in the crusader reconfiguration of Islamic Jerusalem and, next to the Holy Sepulchre, became a focal point in Latin processions in the city; see Sylvia Schein, *Gateway to the Heavenly City: Crusader Jerusalem and the Catholic West (1099–1187)* (Aldershot, U.K.: Ashgate, 2005), 97–106.

42. For the Latin text of John of Würzburg's account, see *Peregrinationes Tres*, 90–95; for a translation, see Wilkinson, *Jerusalem Pilgrimage*, 246–50 (based on an older edition). On the Dome of the Rock in its crusader transformation, see also Heribert Busse, "Vom

Felsendom zum Templum Domini," in *Das Heilige Land im Mittelalter: Begegnungsraum zwischen Orient und Okzident*, ed. Wolfdietrich Fischer and Jürgen Schneider (Neustadt an der Aisch: Degener, 1982), 19–32.

43. Abū l'Ḥasan 'Alī bin Abī Bakr al-Harawī, *Kitāb al-ishārāt ilā ma'rifat al-ziyārāt*, ed. Janine Sourdel-Thomine (Damascus: al-Ma'had al-Faransiyy li-'l-Dirāsāt al-'Arabiyya, 1953), 25. I am quoting the translation by Josef W. Meri, *A Lonely Wayfarer's Guide to Pilgrimage: 'Alī ibn Abī Bakr al-Harawī's Kitāb al-Ishārāt ilā Ma'rifat al-Ziyārāt* (Princeton, N.J.: Darwin, 2004), 70.

44. As Andrew S. Jacobs argues, already Egeria (late fourth century) takes part in Christian supersessionism and a related imperial discourse; see *Remains of the Jews: Holy Land and Christian Empire in Late Antiquity* (Stanford, Calif.: Stanford University Press, 2004), 119–21.

45. Petaḥyah, *Sibbuv*, 1:32–33.

46. On the topos of the Muslim ruler as a friend of the Jews, see Chapter 7 in this volume.

47. On the legend's various versions, from Christian and Muslim sources, see Johann Gildemeister, "Die arabischen Nachrichten zur Geschichte der Harambauten," *ZDPV* 13 (1890): 1–24; Keppel A. C. Creswell, *Early Muslim Architecture*, 2nd ed. (Oxford: Clarendon, 1969), 1:32–33; and Gil, *History of Palestine*, 65–68. At times, the person leading 'Umar to the site of the Temple is said to have been the Christian patriarch. In some Muslim versions, he is named as Ka'b al-Aḥbār, a Jewish convert to Islam; it may have been this tradition in the background of Petaḥyah's polemical remark.

48. Petaḥyah, *Sibbuv*, 1:33.

49. Here I am borrowing a phrase coined by B. Mann, *Space and Place*, 9.

50. *Toṣ'ot ereṣ yisra'el*, fol. 2, 55.

51. On Middot's description of the Temple, see Yaron Z. Eliav, *God's Mountain: The Temple Mount in Time, Place, and Memory* (Baltimore: Johns Hopkins University Press, 2005), 212–26.

52. *Toṣ'ot ereṣ yisra'el*, fol. 4, 56.

53. Hebrew: *le-havdil ben ṭum'ah le-ṭehara* (cf. Lev. 10:10); *Toṣ'ot ereṣ yisra'el*, fol. 4, 57.

54. On Islamic ritual as depicted in Jewish travel writings, see also Chapter 7 in this volume.

55. *Massa' meshullam*, 72.

56. See m. Yoma 3:3.

57. Meshullam's phrasing alludes to a purity ritual that the Bible associates with the epiphany at Sinai (Exod. 19:14–15): "Moses came down from the mountain to the people and warned the people to stay pure. . . . And he said to the people, 'Be ready for the third day: do not go near a woman.'"

58. *Massa' meshullam*, 72. Obadiah also refers to the same rumors about the lights going out on the Temple Mount, but he considers them to be "lies and deceits"; Letter B, *From Italy to Jerusalem*, 84.

59. The Hebrew text of the letter is to be found in David, *Reflections on Jewish Jerusalem*, 95.

60. As the mother of Ishmael, Hagar is considered the ancestress of all Ishmaelites, i.e., Arabs, and Muslims in general; but it seems unusual that she is called a sorceress here. Still, there are some midrashic traditions that attribute idol worship to Hagar, since she was an Egyptian (Gen. 16:1); e.g., see *Pirqe de Rabbi Eli'ezer* 30 (according to the editio princeps): *Pirke de-Rabbi Elieser nach der Edition Venedig 1544*, ed. Dagmar Börner-Klein (Berlin: Walter de Gruyter, 2004), 339; English translation: *Pirḳê de Rabbi Eliezer*, trans. Gerald Friedlander (New York: Hermon, 1965), 217.

61. Basola, *In Zion and Jerusalem*, Hebrew part, 33. I am quoting the translation in ibid., English part, 109. The turning of the crescent is similarly described in a letter from around 1520 by Abraham ben Eli'ezer ha-Levi, a kabbalist and messianic visionary; see Abraham David, "A Letter from Jerusalem from the Early Ottoman Period in Eretz Yisrael" (Hebrew), in *Jerusalem in the Early Ottoman Period* (Hebrew), ed. Amnon Cohen (Jerusalem: Ben-Zvi Institute, 1979), 59–60. Cf. Israel Ashkenazi's brief reference to the same miracle, David, "Letter of R. Israel Ashkenazi," 114–15.

62. Such a messianic interpretation of current Ottoman history can be found, inter alia, in the chronicle of Elijah Capsali, a leading rabbi of Venetian Crete; see my "Exposed to All the Currents of the Mediterranean: A Sixteenth-Century Venetian Rabbi on Muslim History," *AJS Review* 29 (2005): 43–46.

63. *Story of David Hareuveni*, 24.

64. Ibid., 25–26.

65. Re'uveni does not seem to have shared the belief according to which the Ottoman conquest of the Levant was part of a divine plan to repatriate all Jews to Palestine. Rather, he may have sought to promote the eschatological war between Gog and Magog (Christendom and Islam; see Chapter 1 n. 124), which would then lead to the "ingathering of the exiles."

66. On the gap between imagined and empirical space, see B. Mann, *Space and Place*, 23–24.

67. During the Byzantine period, the sepulchre of David was commonly believed to be in or around Bethlehem; see Ora Limor, "The Origins of a Tradition: King David's Tomb on Mount Zion," *Traditio* 44 (1988): 453–62. According to Limor, it was the liturgical tradition of a memorial service for King David, held annually at the church on Mount Zion, that may have led to the establishment of the burial chapel in its present location.

68. As medieval pilgrimage shrines often combined numerous sites of religious significance, the crusader church incorporated the Dormition where Mary was believed to have died, the tomb of David, and the Hall of the Last Supper, also known as the Cenacle; see (Louis) Hugues Vincent and F. M. Abel, *Jérusalem: Recherches de topographie, d'archéologie et d'histoire* (Paris: J. Cabalda, 1922), vol. 2, *Jérusalem nouvelle*, bk. 3, 459–64.

69. *Itinerary of Benjamin*, Hebrew part, 25.

70. Prawer (*History of the Jews*, 202) speculates that the tomb's "discovery" was related to a repair of the church after it had been struck by lightning in 1146.

71. *Itinerary of Benjamin*, Hebrew part, 25.

72. Ibid., Hebrew part, 25–26.

73. Josephus, *Antiquities* 16, 179–83.

74. *Itinerary of Benjamin*, Hebrew part, 26. Based on the Rome manuscript, Augustín Arce published a new critical edition of this chapter from Benjamin's *Massa'ot*; see Arce, "The Location of David's Tomb According to Benjamin of Tudela's Itinerary" (Hebrew), in *Jerusalem in the Middle Ages: Selected Papers* (Hebrew), ed. Benjamin Z. Kedar (Jerusalem: Ben-Zvi Institute, 1979), 112–21. Though this edition is superior to Adler's (*Itinerary of Benjamin*, Hebrew part, 25–26), the variants do not affect my interpretation.

75. Elchanan Reiner calls this figure a Jewish "adaptation" of the Christian concept of *veritas hebraica* (Jewish truth); here, "the Jew is the authentic transmitter of knowledge about the location of . . . biblical sites and holy places"; Reiner, "A Jewish Response to the Crusades," 219. On this topic, see also Ora Limor, "Christian Sacred Space and the Jew," in *From Witness to Witchcraft: Jews and Judaism in Medieval Christian Thought*, ed. Jeremy Cohen (Wiesbaden: Harrassowitz, 1996), 55–77.

76. *Itinerary of Benjamin*, Hebrew part, 26.

77. The oral origin of the narrative has been highlighted by Eli Yassif, "Legends and History: Historians Read Hebrew Legends of the Middle Ages" (Hebrew), *Zion* 64 (1999): 211–17. Even so, the narrative obviously had been redacted when it was integrated into Benjamin's book, as evidenced by the way it introduces R. Abraham al-Qūsṭanṭīnī, the source of the story; see Moshe Rosman's critique of Yassif's reading, *How Jewish Is Jewish History?* (Oxford: Littman Library of Jewish Civilization, 2007), 162–63.

78. Reiner, "A Jewish Response to the Crusades," 215.

79. What may have contributed to this uncertainty, it stands to reason, was the fact that, like most churches in crusader Palestine, the chapel was probably off-limits to Jews. Tellingly, Benjamin does not describe the actual chapel containing the cenotaph.

80. See Homi Bhabha, "Of Mimicry and Man: The Ambivalence of Colonial Discourse," *October 28* (1984): 125–33 (reprint in Bhabha, *The Location of Culture* [Abingdon, U.K.: Routledge, 1994; reprint, 2005], 121–31). On Bhabha's understanding of this critical concept, see also Loomba, *Colonialism/Postcolonialism*, 148–50.

81. On the Franciscan monastery of the fourteenth century, see Vincent and Abel, *Jérusalem*, vol. 2, bk. 3, 464–71. Even in its present state, this architectural conglomerate still offers visual testimony of how a sacred venue generated by Christianity has later been equally claimed by Jews and Muslims.

82. Obadiah, Letter A, *From Italy to Jerusalem*, 81.

83. Francesco Suriano, *Il Trattato di Terra Santa e dell' Oriente*, ed. Girolamo Golubovich (Milan: Artigianelli, 1900), 110–11. I here modify the English translation by Theophilus Bellorini and Eugene Hoade, *Treatise on the Holy Land* (Jerusalem: Franciscan, 1949), 123. As a result of this conflict, Venice barred Jews from traveling on its galleys to the Levant; see Chapter 3 in this volume.

84. According to Fabri's account, the otherwise locked door was left open during his stay in Jerusalem; Fabri, *Peregrinatio*, 1:253; *Wanderings of Felix Fabri*, 1:304. Similarly, the German nobleman Arnold von Harff (whose Near Eastern travels were in 1496–99) claims to have entered David's tomb in the company of a Mamluk; see Eberhard von Groote's

edition of the Middle German text, *Die Pilgerfahrt des Ritters Arnold von Harff* (Cologne: J. M. Heberle, 1860), 166.

85. *Massa' meshullam*, 74.

86. Basola, *In Zion and Jerusalem*, Hebrew part, 20. I slightly modify the translation in ibid., English part, 74.

87. See Chapter 7 in this volume.

88. See, further, Gen. 25:9, 49:31, and 50:13.

89. Petaḥyah, *Sibbuv*, 1:33. As per the twelfth-century pilgrim's fanciful estimates, the largest stones were 27, 28, and even 70 cubits long. With no regard to the fact that the length of a cubit varied historically, this would mean that single stones measured roughly 40.5, 42, and 105 feet (12.30, 12.80, and 32 meters). Obviously, Petaḥyah's account is part of a medieval tradition that considers holy places to be marvelous sites.

90. *Itinerary of Benjamin*, Hebrew part, 27.

91. The document (Cambridge, Or. 1080 22 J. 89) was published by Joseph Braslavi, "On the Appointment of R. Abiathar as Gaon During His Father's Lifetime and on the Cave of Machpelah" (Hebrew), *Eretz Israel* 5 (1958): 220–23; see also Gil, *History of Palestine*, 206–7.

92. A similar tendency characterizes their accounts of the Temple Mount; see above.

93. *Itinerary of Benjamin*, Hebrew part, 27. Reiner was first to draw attention to the polemical character of Benjamin's account of the Makhpelah; see Reiner, "A Jewish Response to the Crusades," 222–29.

94. Besides their polemics against the Christian occupation of the holy site, Benjamin's and Petaḥyah's accounts also echo a rich Jewish folklore that had developed around the sanctuary and its underworld—traces of which can already be found in the Babylonian Talmud. As the name Makhpelah often has been understood to mean "double cave," b. Bava Batra 58a (cf. b. 'Eruvin 53a) discusses whether its two parts consist of an inner and an outer cave or an upper and a lower one. In this context, a legend is told about a certain R. Bana'a who entered the cave, where he found Abraham lying in Sarah's arms.

95. *Itinerary of Benjamin*, Hebrew part, 27.

96. Petaḥyah, *Sibbuv*, 1:33.

97. See the account by Saewulf, an Anglo-Saxon who visited the Levant in 1101–03: "Every one of the three monuments is like a large church, and the sarcophaguses are reverently placed inside, that is to say, for the husband and his wife"; Latin text in Huygens, *Peregrinationes Tres*, 73; translation by Wilkinson, *Jerusalem Pilgrimage*, 110 (modified). The fact that a number of Jewish- and Christian-authored accounts speak of three shrines rather than six raises the question of whether they share a common (oral) source.

98. Petaḥyah, *Sibbuv*, 1:33–34.

99. Today, two accesses to an underground passage are known, both located in the southeastern part of the Ḥaram al-Khalīl's enclosure: one (point *i* on the plan by Vincent and Mackay) is near the outer wall, next to the *minbar* (pulpit of the mosque) and near the cenotaph of Isaac; yet it is blocked now. The other (marked by *j* in the same plan) is a narrow shaft next to the cenotaph of Abraham; see Louis H. Vincent and E. J. H. Mackay,

Hébron: Le Ḥaram El-Khalîl, Sépulture des Patriarches (Paris: Leroux, 1923), plate II. The only survey of the actual burial chamber beneath that passage was done by Doron Chen, "Measuring the Cave of Abraham in Hebron," *Liber Annuus* 37 (1987): 291–94. Entering through point *i* (on the plan by Vincent and Mackay), Chen descended sixteen steps leading to an underground corridor. He gives detailed measures of the subterranean area beneath the mosque, including the hypogeum (burial chamber), which he describes as including a smaller, second cavern.

100. On the poor state in which his *Sibbuv* has survived, see Chapter 1 in this volume.

101. Petaḥyah, *Sibbuv*, 1:34.

102. *Canonici Hebronensis Tractatus de inventione sanctorum Patriarcharum Abraham, Ysaac et Jacob (27 Jul. 1119)*, in *Recueil des historiens des Croisades, Historiens Occidentaux* (Paris: Imprimerie Nationale, 1895), 5:310.

103. Ibid., 5:312–13. In his Muslim pilgrimage guide, al-Harawī also refers to the crusader discovery of the cave. There al-Harawī tells of a Frankish knight named Bīran, who claimed to have descended into the cave, together with his father, at the age of thirteen; see al-Harawī, *Kitāb al-ziyārāt*, 31, and *Lonely Wayfarer's Guide*, 80. On Ibn al-Qalānisī's reference to the opening of the cave, see Meri, *Cult of Saints*, 162.

104. On the *rosh ha-golah* and the dynastic character of his office, see Chapter 6 in this volume.

105. Samuel ben Samson, *Mikhtav*, 7. It seems surprising that the dyer as a person of very low social standing would have been able to let the Jewish pilgrims in. Perhaps his introduction into the story is an echo of Benjamin's aforementioned account of Jerusalem that mentions some dyers as the only Jewish inhabitants of the city; see above.

106. Hebrew text in Ilan, *Tombs of the Righteous*, 135.

107. Obadiah, Letter A, *From Italy to Jerusalem*, 63. This hole may have been the reason for the draft coming out of the openings in the sanctuary's floor, mentioned in many descriptions. After 1967, the hole was sealed and the stairs removed.

108. Text in Ilan, *Tombs of the Righteous*, 135.

109. *Yiḥus ha-Ṣaddiqim*, ibid., 153.

110. Obadiah, Letter A, *From Italy to Jerusalem*, 63.

111. Ibid.

112. *Massa' meshullam*, 69.

113. *Story of David Hareuveni*, 23. According to Re'uveni's description, this blocked entrance was next to Isaac's cenotaph, which corresponds to one of the entrances known today; see above, n. 99.

114. *Story of David Hareuveni*, 24.

115. See Heribert Busse, "Die Patriarchengräber in Hebron und der Islam," *ZDPV* 114 (1998): 88.

116. Text in Ilan, *Tombs of the Righteous*, 135.

117. *Massa' meshullam*, 69. Basola speaks of 8,000 loaves of bread that were distributed daily; *In Zion and Jerusalem*, Hebrew part, 21; English part, 77.

118. According to b. Bava Meṣi'a 86b, R. Ḥanan ben Raba derived from Gen. 18:7

("Abraham . . . took a calf, tender and good") that Abraham offered each of the three angels "tongues in mustard."

119. Obadiah, Letter A, *From Italy to Jerusalem*, 63.

120. Text in Ilan, *Tombs of the Righteous*, 153. Not every pilgrim seems to have approved of the public jollity at the sacred shrine, as evidenced by the critical remarks by Abū 'Abdallāh Muḥammad al-'Abdarī. The Muslim jurist from North Africa particularly disapproved of the blaring of trumpets, drumming, and dancing that he witnessed on his visit to Hebron in 1289; see Ignaz Goldziher, "Das Patriarchengrab in Hebron nach Al-'Abdarī," *ZDPV* 17 (1894): 115–22 (reprint in Goldziher, *Gesammelte Schriften*, ed. Joseph Desomogyi [Hildesheim: Olms, 1969], 3:351–58).

CHAPTER 5. MEDIEVAL MINGLING AT HOLY TOMBS

1. On the various ways that pilgrimage sites might be shared among worshipers of various religious backgrounds, see Ora Limor, "Sharing Sacred Space: Holy Places in Jerusalem Between Christianity, Judaism and Islam," in *In Laudem Hierosolymitani: Studies in Crusades and Medieval Culture in Honour of Benjamin Z. Kedar*, ed. Iris Shagrir, Ronnie Ellenblum, and Jonathan Riley-Smith (Aldershot, U.K.: Ashgate, 2007), 219–31.

2. On pilgrimage as a "liminal" or "liminoid" experience that transcends social boundaries, see the Introduction to this volume, n. 53. On tomb veneration as a shared experience among women of different faiths, see Alexandra Cuffel, "From Practice to Polemic: Shared Saints and Festivals as 'Women's Religion' in the Medieval Mediterranean," *Bulletin of the School of Oriental and African Studies* 68 (2005): 401–19.

3. Pratt, *Imperial Eyes*, 7. In applying Pratt's definition to medieval times, I am aware that notions such as "domination" and "subordination" take on different meanings in a precolonial and an imperial context; the latter, of course, is the topic of Pratt's study.

4. Samuel's tomb has been mentioned in Chapter 4 of this volume, in its function as a major way station on the road to Jerusalem.

5. See Yoel Elitzur, *Ancient Place Names in the Holy Land: Preservation and History* (Jerusalem and Winona Lake, Ind.: Magnes and Eisenbrauns, 2004), 343.

6. While there seems to have been a Byzantine monastery on the site, it was not considered Samuel's burial place; see Yoel Elitzur, "Sources of the 'Nebi-Samuel' Tradition" (Hebrew), *Cathedra* 31 (1984): 75–90. On the Frankish church of Saint Samuel, see Pringle, *Churches of the Crusader Kingdom*, 2:86–87.

7. The identification of Ramah with the city of (al)-Ramla seems to be based on a (mistaken) popular etymology that goes back to the crusader period; it also occurs in the anonymous *Gesta Francorum Expugnantium Iherusalem* (1095–1108), chap. 28: "Ramatha which city is now called Ramula"; Latin text with Italian translation in *Itinera Hierosolymitana Crucesignatorum (saec. XII–XIII)*, ed. Sabino de Sandoli (Jerusalem: Franciscan, 1978), 1:146.

8. *Itinerary of Benjamin*, Hebrew part, 28.

9. Here *Massa'ot* may distantly echo a Christian tradition according to which Samuel's bones had been relocated by the Byzantines: according to Jerome, it was Emperor Arcadius who, at the turn of the fifth century, ordered the transfer of the prophet's relics to Thrace from an unknown place in Judea; Jerome, *Contra Vigilantium* 5, in *Patrologia Latina* 23, ed. Jean-Paul Migne (Paris: Vrayet, 1845), 348. Like Benjamin, Jerome calls this a sacrilege.

10. For a report on the extensive archaeological excavations at the site, see Yitzhak Magen and M. Dadon, "Nebi Samwil (Montjoie)," in *One Land—Many Cultures: Archaeological Studies in Honour of Stanislao Loffreda OFM*, ed. G. Claudio Bottini, Leah Di Segni, and L. Daniel Chrupcala (Jerusalem: Franciscan, 2003), 123–38.

11. *Toṣ'ot ereṣ yisra'el*, fol. 6, 58.

12. On Jewish pilgrimage to Nabī Ṣamwīl, see Reiner, "Pilgrims and Pilgrimage," 306–20. In the medieval conceptualization of sacred space, wells and sources are frequently associated with holy tombs; see Meri, *Cult of Saints*, 141. Apparently, they are part of the saint's aura of blessing.

13. *Yiḥus Avot*, 215.

14. In an (unintended) illustration of the pilgrimage's "liminal" character, Basola states that men and women used to get inebriated during this festival. This perceived abuse led Jewish community officials to issue a prohibition (*taqqanah*) against the consumption of alcohol during the celebrations; see *In Zion and Jerusalem*, Hebrew part, 30; English part, 101.

15. This again seems to be an echo of earlier traditions regarding David's tomb and Hebron; see Chapter 4 in this volume.

16. The Hebrew text of the letter was edited by David, *Reflections on Jewish Jerusalem*, 94.

17. On punitive miracles in the context of medieval Christian shrine veneration, see Benedicta Ward, *Miracles and the Medieval Mind: Theory, Record and Event, 1000–1215* (Philadelphia: University of Pennsylvania Press, 1982), 49, 65, 69, 115.

18. The conflict over access rights to and ownership of the site continued during Ottoman times. Besides Jewish-Muslim competition, there was a rivalry between Karaites and Rabbanites over the tomb; see A. Cohen, *Jewish Life Under Islam*, 101–4.

19. Long before Meshullam, Menaḥem ben Pereṣ, a twelfth-century French Jew and sometime resident of Hebron, claimed that Palestinian Jews preserved an unbroken tradition of local holy places that reached back to Second Temple times. The text of his Hebrew itinerary was first published by Adolf Neubauer (on the basis of MS Bodl. Or. 135), *Ha-Levanon* 5 (1868): 626–29, no. 40; reprint, Abraham M. Luncz, in *Ha-Me'amer* 3 (1920): 36–46. For the relevant passage, see ibid., 40; it was translated by Reiner, "Traditions of Holy Places," 9. See also Reiner's discussion in "Oral Versus Written," 308–10.

20. *Massa' meshullam*, 75.

21. Ibid.

22. Meshullam also speaks of an annual Jewish pilgrimage to Nabī Ṣamwīl on 28 Iyar (*Massa' meshullam*, 74), which would be a week before the date (Shavu'ot) mentioned in *Yiḥus Avot*; see above. Perhaps the pilgrimage season was more extended, while the major celebrations took place on 28 Iyar.

23. Obadiah, Letter B, *From Italy to Jerusalem*, 84.

24. Ibid., 84–85.

25. On Obadiah's criticism of the Jewish community elders, see Chapter 8 in this volume.

26. Basola, *In Zion and Jerusalem*, Hebrew part, 20; I am modifying the translation in ibid., English part, 75.

27. Though some traditions as to the location of venerated graves may hearken back to late antiquity, the authenticity of many of these sites is questionable, and there are frequently contradicting traditions as to their location. On the importance of holy tombs in kabbalah, see Pinchas Giller, "Recovering the Sanctity of the Galilee: The Veneration of Sacred Relics in Classical Kabbalah," *Journal of Jewish Thought and Philosophy* 4 (1994): 147–69.

28. E.g., *Elleh ha-Massa'ot*, 145 (Mount Carmel); ibid., 147 ('Avarta/'Awartā); ibid., 149 (Temple Mount); ibid., 152 (Nabī Ṣamwīl); ibid., 153 (Meron/Mīrūn); ibid., 156 (Kefar Ḥiṭṭim / Kafr Ḥiṭṭīn); ibid., 157 (Kefar Kana / Kafr Kanna); and ibid., 158 (Yavneh/Yibna). On this topic, see also Meri, *Cult of Saints*, 243–44, 246.

29. Samuel ben Samson's account preserves two traditions about this tomb: "Some say it is the tomb of Joshua, and others say it is the tomb of Jethro"; *Mikhtav*, 9. The tradition of locating Jethro's tomb in Galilee seems to have supplanted an earlier one concerning Joshua's burial site; see Elchanan Reiner, "From Joshua to Jesus—the Transformation of a Biblical Story to a Local Myth: A Chapter in the Religious Life of the Galilean Jew," in *Sharing the Sacred: Religious Contacts and Conflicts in the Holy Land: First–Fifteenth Centuries CE*, ed. Arieh Kofsky and Guy G. Stroumsa (Jerusalem: Ben-Zvi Institute, 1998), 232.

30. See Qur'an 15:78, 26:176–91; and *EI*, s.v. "Sh'ayb."

31. Al-Harawī, *Kitāb al-ziyārāt*, 20, and *Lonely Wayfarer's Guide*, 40. Today, Nabī Shu'ayb is the major pilgrimage site of the Druze.

32. *Toṣ'ot ereṣ yisra'el*, fols. 8–9, 61. Basola, by contrast, calls the mosque built at Jethro's tomb a "vexing" (*meragez*, or *margiz*) structure; *In Zion and Jerusalem*, Hebrew part, 17. Ordan's translation (ibid., English part, 70: "mosque") does not take into account the polemical tone. Basola uses the same derogatory term when speaking of the shrine built over the (alleged) tomb of R. 'Aqiva's wife; see bellow.

33. *Toṣ'ot ereṣ yisra'el*, fol. 9, 62; cf. al-Harawī, *Kitāb al-ziyārāt*, 20, and *Lonely Wayfarer's Guide*, 40. Over time, a separate village developed around the shrine that is known by the name of Mashhad—a common Arabic term for a saint's shrine. On the various sites venerated as Jonah's tomb, see Tewfik Canaan, *Mohammedan Saints and Sanctuaries in Palestine* (London: Luzac, 1927; reprint, Jerusalem: Ariel, 1980), 294; and Zeev Vilnay, *Maṣevot qodesh be-ereṣ yisra'el*, 2 vols., 3rd ed. (Jerusalem: Aḥi'avar, 1985), 1:390–98.

34. Basola, *In Zion and Jerusalem*, Hebrew part, 18. I slightly alter the translation in ibid., English part, 70. Basola reports the same about the tomb of the prophetess Hulda, which is situated on the Mount of Olives; ibid., Hebrew part, 20; English part, 73.

35. In his discussion of a Syrian pilgrimage place, Benjamin Z. Kedar differentiates among: a) spatial convergence of worshipers belonging to different religious communities; b) their convergence at the same service, "with the service officiated by members of one

religion"; and c) egalitarian convergence at a shared ceremony, such as a common prayer for rain; see Kedar, "Convergences of Oriental Christian, Muslim, and Frankish Worshipers: The Case of Saydnaya," in *De Sion Exibit Lex et Verbum Domini de Hierusalem: Essays on Medieval Law, Liturgy, and Literature in Honour of Amnon Linder*, ed. Yitzhak Hen (Turnhout: Brepols, 2001), 59–69. Medieval Jewish travel writings, to the best of my knowledge, reflect only the first type.

36. *Elleh ha-Massa'ot*, 158. In the Hebrew transcription, the name Abū Hurayra has been corrupted: *HDRYRH*. On the shrine that was expanded by the Mamluk sultan Baybars in 1274, see Hana Taragan, "Politics and Aesthetics: Sultan Baybars and the Abu Hurayra / Rabbi Gamliel Building in Yavneh," in *Milestones in the Art and Culture of Egypt*, ed. Asher Ovadiah (Tel Aviv: Tel Aviv University Press, 2000), 117–43. Even under the crusaders (who called the town Ibelin), the tomb attracted Muslim pilgrims, as reflected by al-Harawī's visit there in 1173; *Kitāb al-ziyārāt*, 33, and *Lonely Wayfarer's Guide*, 82. Since 1948, the shrine has exclusively served as a synagogue dedicated to the memory of Rabban Gamliel.

37. Al-Harawī, *Kitāb al-ziyārāt*, 19, and *Lonely Wayfarer's Guide*, 38. On the shrine, see Moshe Sharon, "The Cities of the Holy Land Under Islamic Rule" (Hebrew), *Cathedra* 40 (1986): 119, including a translation of its Arabic dedicatory inscription.

38. After 1948, the Islamic cemetery of Tiberias was neglected, and in 1995, the tomb of Sitt Sukayna was officially converted into a Jewish religious site; see Rivka Gonen, "How Is a New Saint's Tomb Created? The Case of the Tomb of Rachel, Wife of Rabbi Akiva," in *To the Tombs of the Righteous: Pilgrimage in Contemporary Israel*, ed. idem (Jerusalem: Israel Museum, 1999), 75–85; and Meron Benvenisti, *Sacred Landscape: The Buried History of the Holy Land Since 1948* (Berkeley: University of California Press, 2000), 280.

39. Basola, *In Zion and Jerusalem*, Hebrew part, 27; my translation. While R. 'Aqiva's wife bears no name in the best-known traditions about her life (b. Ketubbot 62b–63a, b. Nedarim 50), she is traditionally called "Rachel," based on *Avot de-Rabbi Natan*, version A, chap. 6; *Avoth de-Rabbi Nathan*, ed. Solomon Schechter, 2nd ed. (New York: Jewish Theological Seminary, 1997), 15a.

40. See Chapter 4 in this volume.

41. The anonymous traveler claims to have met the very same woman who gave him her personal recollections of the miracle; for the Hebrew text of the account, see David, *Reflections on Jewish Jerusalem*, 156.

42. Basola, *In Zion and Jerusalem*, Hebrew part, 15–16; English part, 65. See also Cuffel's suggestive interpretation of the story: "From Practice to Polemic," 407–8.

43. Basola, *In Zion and Jerusalem*, Hebrew part, 25. I slightly modify the translation in ibid., English part, 89.

44. On Iraq as an alternative Jewish Holy Land, see also my "The Sacred Text as a Mental Map," 401–5.

45. There is only a faint echo of local Christianity in Benjamin's account of Shūsh; see below.

46. See al-Harawī, *Kitāb al-ziyārāt*, 76–79, and *Lonely Wayfarer's Guide*, 196–204. See also the map of Iraqi pilgrimage sites, ibid., 175.

47. On Shiite pilgrimage, see Meri, *Cult of Saints*, 140–41.

48. Ibn Jubayr, *Riḥla*, 211–12; and *Travels of Ibn Jubayr*, 220. Ali's attacker was a Khārijite who struck him with a poisoned sword. Two days later, the caliph died.

49. Ibn Jubayr, *Riḥla*, 212. I slightly modify the translation by Broadhurst, *Travels of Ibn Jubayr*, 220.

50. Before leaving for his pilgrimage to Mecca in 1183, Ibn Jubayr was secretary to the Almohad governor of Granada; see Ian R. Netton, "Basic Structures and Signs of Alienation in the *Riḥla* of Ibn Jubayr," in *Golden Roads: Migration, Pilgrimage and Travel*, ed. idem (Richmond, U.K.: Curzon, 1993), 57.

51. *Itinerary of Benjamin*, Hebrew part, 45.

52. As in the case of the al-Mansūr Mosque in Baghdad or the Umayyad Mosque of Damascus; see Chapter 6 in this volume.

53. While in the Jewish context, "madman" refers to Hos. 9:7, this polemical term may have originated as an allusion to the Qur'anic tradition according to which some disbelievers compared the prophet of Islam to a "possessed poet" (*li-shā'irin majnūnin*); see Qur'an 7:184, 37:36.

54. For Benjamin's reference to the Holy Sepulchre, see Chapter 4 in this volume.

55. *Itinerary of Benjamin*, Hebrew part, 45.

56. Meri (*Cult of Saints*, 238) erroneously ascribes this tradition to Petaḥyah, though he is, in fact, quoting from Adler's translation of Benjamin's *Massa'ot*.

57. See Meri, *Cult of Saints*, 229–37.

58. See Qur'an 21:85, 28:48.

59. Al-Harawī, *Kitāb al-ziyārāt*, 76, and *Lonely Wayfarer's Guide*, 198. Cf. Yāqūt, *Mu'jam al-buldān*, as published by Ferdinand Wüstenfeld, *Jacut's Geographisches Wörterbuch* (Leipzig: Brockhaus, 1866), 1:594 (s.v. "Bar Malāḥa"). In fact, Yāqūt may here depend on the earlier work by al-Harawī.

60. The distance between Baghdad and Kifl is 77 miles (124 kilometers). For the present state of the shrine, see the photos and floor plan in Zvi Yehuda, "The Jews of Babylon Struggle for Control of the Tomb of the Prophet Ezekiel in Kifil in the Second Millennium CE" (Hebrew), in *Studies in the History and Culture of Iraqi Jewry* 6 (Hebrew), ed. Yitzhak Avishur (Or-Yehuda: Babylonian Jewry Heritage Center, 1991), 39–44, 74.

61. Petaḥyah, *Sibbuv*, 1:15.

62. In Arabic, such an intercessor-saint is called a *walī* ("friend" of God); see Olesen, *Culte de Saints*, 116–18. Apparently, Ezekiel's tomb was an especially popular pilgrimage site among Jewish merchants engaged in long-distance trade; see Shlomo D. Goitein, "Baderekh le-hishtaṭḥut 'al qever yeḥezqel," in *Studies on the History of the Iraqi Jewry and Their Culture* (Hebrew), ed. Shmuel Moreh (Tel Aviv: Center for the Heritage of Iraqi Jewry, 1981), 1:9–18.

63. *Itinerary of Benjamin*, Hebrew part, 44.

64. Petaḥyah, *Sibbuv*, 1:13.

65. *Itinerary of Benjamin*, Hebrew part, 44.

66. See Chapter 4 in this volume.

67. The Aramaic term originally designated a wedding feast.

68. Petaḥyah, *Sibbuv*, 1:13.

69. *Itinerary of Benjamin*, Hebrew part, 43–44.

70. Ibid. On the exilarch (*rosh ha-golah*) and the academy heads of Sura and Pumbedita, see Chapter 6 in this volume.

71. *Itinerary of Benjamin*, Hebrew part, 48. The precise distance to Basra is 60 miles (96 kilometers). The present shrine appears to go back to the eighteenth century; see Ben-Ya'aqov, *Qevarim qedoshim be-vavel* (Jerusalem: Mosad ha-Rav Kook, 1973), 146–47.

72. By contrast, Josephus (*Antiquities* 11:158) relates that Ezra died in Jerusalem.

73. *Itinerary of Benjamin*, Hebrew part, 48.

74. The earliest reference to Ezra's tomb in Mesopotamia is in the famous epistle of Sherira Ga'on from the late tenth century; see Solomon Schechter, *Saadyana: Geniza Fragments of Writings of R. Saadya Gaon and Others* (Cambridge: Deighton and Bell, 1903), 123; and *Iggeret r. sherira ga'on*, ed. Benjamin Lewin (Haifa: Goldah Ittskovski, 1921), 73.

75. Given Ezra's (Arabic: 'Uzayr's) less than superlative image in Islamic tradition—he is ordinarily cast in an adversarial role in polemics against Judaism—it is far from obvious that Muslims would venerate his tomb. According to Qur'an 9:30, the Jews believe 'Uzayr to be the son of God, which seems to be a distant echo of Christian doctrine. Medieval Muslim polemicists accused Ezra of having falsified the text of the Torah after its original vanished during the Babylonian exile; see Hava Lazarus-Yafeh, *Intertwined Worlds: Medieval Islam and Bible Criticism* (Princeton, N.J.: Princeton University Press, 1992), 50–74; and *EI*, s.v. "Uzayr." Other Islamic scholars considered the shrine under discussion to be the burial site of 'Azra Ibn Hārūn, a son of the biblical Aaron.

76. *Itinerary of Benjamin*, Hebrew part, 48–49. Petaḥyah similarly notes that "all the Ishmaelites prostrate themselves there"; *Sibbuv*, 1:20.

77. In Hebrew literature, the earliest source that places Daniel's tomb in Susa seems to be the *Yosippon*, a mid-tenth-century adaptation of the works by Josephus Flavius; see *The Jossipon* (Hebrew), ed. David Flusser, 2 vols. (Jerusalem: Bialik Institute, 1980–81), 1:36. The present shrine at Shūsh, which still attracts Muslim visitors, was built in the 1860s; see *Encyclopaedia Iranica*, ed. Ersan Yashater, 15 vols. (London: Routledge, 1982–2011), 6:658–60 (s.v. "Dānīāl-e Nabī," iii).

78. *Itinerary of Benjamin*, Hebrew part, 49.

79. In Arabic, the blessings associated with a saint's tomb are referred to as *baraka*; see Josef W. Meri, "Aspects of *Baraka* (Blessings) and Ritual Devotion Among Medieval Muslims and Jews," *Medieval Encounters* 5 (1999): 46–69; and idem, *Cult of Saints*, 101–8.

80. See Benjamin's reference to the various Christian communities living in crusader Jerusalem; *Itinerary of Benjamin*, Hebrew part, 23; discussed in Chapter 4 in this volume. In classical rabbinic literature, the terms *arami* and *arma'i* are used to refer to Romans—and, by extension, to Christians; see Marcus Jastrow, *A Dictionary of the Targumim, the Talmud Babli and Yerushalmi, and the Midrashic Literature*, 2 vols. (London: Luzac, 1903; reprint, New York: Judaica Press, 1985), 1:122–23.

81. Abū Iṣḥāq Ibraḥim al-Iṣṭakhrī, *Kitāb al-masālik wa'l-mamālik (Vitae Regnorum)*,

Bibliotheca Geographorum Arabicorum 1, ed. Michael J. de Goeje (Leiden: Brill, 1870; reprint, 1927), 92.

82. In a much shorter version of the story that was known to the tenth-century geographer al-Muqaddasī, the people fighting over Daniel's coffin are the inhabitants of Tustar and al-Sūs (Susa), both of them Muslims; Muḥammad bin Aḥmad al-Muqaddasī, *Descriptio imperii Moslemici* (Arabic), Bibliotheca Geographorum Arabicorum 3, ed. Michael J. de Goeje, 2nd ed. (Leiden: Brill, 1906), 417; and *The Best Divisions for Knowledge of the Regions*, trans. Basil A. Collins (Reading: Garnet, 1994; reprint, 2001), 370–71. On additional Muslim sources about Daniel's tomb, see Meri, *Cult of Saints*, 127 n. 21.

83. The legend also occurs in Petaḥyah's *Sibbuv*, 1:20–21, where it lacks any reference to the religion of the people living on either side of the river, and the decision to suspend the coffin from "iron pillars" erected in the middle of the river is attributed to some undetermined "elders."

84. On Sanjar's sultanate, see Clifford E. Bosworth, "The Political and Dynastic History of the Iranian World (AD 1000–1217)," in *The Cambridge History of Iran*, vol. 5, *The Saljuq and Mongol Periods*, ed. J. A. Boyle (Cambridge: Cambridge University Press, 1968), 135–57; and *EI*, s.v. "Sandjar."

85. *Itinerary of Benjamin*, Hebrew part, 50.

CHAPTER 6. MARVELS OF MUSLIM METROPOLISES

1. Benjamin's chapter on Baghdad encompasses eight pages in Adler's edition (*Itinerary of Benjamin*, Hebrew part, 35–42), while his account of Jerusalem covers only half that amount (ibid., 23–26). Regarding Benjamin's description of Baghdad, cf. my preliminary discussion in "From Lofty Caliphs to Uncivilized 'Orientals': Images of the Muslim in Medieval Jewish Travel Literature," *Jewish Studies Quarterly* 18 (2011): 72–82.

2. *Itinerary of Benjamin*, Hebrew part, 35.

3. It bears noting that there are not enough Arabic words in *Massa'ot* to determine the author's proficiency in Arabic; see Chapter 1 in this volume. I have frequently corrected the Arabic spelling of these loanwords, since a detailed discussion of their often corrupted Hebrew transliteration—and its variants in manuscripts and early print editions—would be too tiring.

4. *Itinerary of Benjamin*, Hebrew part, 35. Benjamin here reflects a Western Christian perspective on the Abbasids, for the German Jerusalem pilgrim Thietmar (1217–18) similarly says about Baghdad: "There resides the pope of the Saracens, who has the name of caliph" (translation by Pringle, *Pilgrimage to Jerusalem*, 106). Writing after the destruction of Baghdad by the Mongols (1258), Marco Polo (chap. 25) still makes a similar claim: "In Baghdad, which is a very large city, the caliph of all the Saracens in the world has his seat, just as the head of all the Christians in the world has his seat in Rome" (*Travels*, 51).

5. For a very readable introduction to the early Abbasid period, see Hugh N. Kennedy, *When Baghdad Ruled the Muslim World: The Rise and Fall of Islam's Greatest Dynasty* (Cambridge, Mass.: Da Capo, 2005), 1–84.

6. See Heribert Busse, *Chalif und Grosskönig: Die Buyiden im Iraq (945–1055)* (Beirut: Franz Steiner, 1969), 131–45.

7. Ibn Jubayr, *Riḥla*, 217. I am quoting the translation in *Travels of Ibn Jubayr*, 226 (insignificantly modified). On Ibn Jubayr and his travelogue, see, in this volume, Chapter 1 n. 19.

8. Ibn Jubayr, *Riḥla*, 225; and *Travels of Ibn Jubayr*, 234.

9. According to Netton, Ibn Jubayr describes "an Islamic world already divided upon itself by religious faction and suspicion"; Netton, "Basic Structures," 63.

10. *Itinerary of Benjamin*, Hebrew part, 35.

11. On the caliphal palaces, see Guy Le Strange, *Baghdad During the Abbasid Caliphate: From Contemporary Arabic and Persian Sources* (Oxford: Clarendon, 1924), 242–62; and Kennedy, *When Baghdad Ruled*, 150–59.

12. See Le Strange, *Baghdad During the Abbasid Caliphate*, 260.

13. Abū Bakr Aḥmad al-Khaṭīb al-Baghdādī, *Ta'rīkh Baghdād*, ed. Muṣṭafā A. 'Aṭā, 2 vols. (Beirut: Dār al-Kutub al-'Ilmiyya, 1997), 1:118. I am quoting the translation by Jacob Lassner, *The Topography of Baghdad in the Early Middle Ages* (Detroit: Wayne State University Press, 1970), 89–90.

14. Benjamin's description seems to be based on mere hearsay; but palace gardens, in the Islamic world, served as environmental representations of political power, as Fairchild D. Ruggles has shown in the case of Muslim Iberia; Ruggles, *Gardens, Landscape, and Vision in the Palaces of Islamic Spain* (University Park: Pennsylvania State University Press, 2000).

15. Similarly, Marco Polo offers a dazzling description of Kublai Khan's palace and its gardens; see *Travels*, 126 (chap. 84). According to Gaunt, Polo's description of Kublai Khan's court is part of his representation of "distant lands and cultures as significantly more sophisticated, powerful and opulent than Europe"—a characterization that applies just as well to Benjamin's portrayal of Baghdad; for the quoted passage, see Gaunt, *Marco Polo's Le Devisement*, 37; see also ibid., 125–26.

16. *Itinerary of Benjamin*, Hebrew part, 36. Illustrating medieval fantasies about distant rulers and their riches, the *Book of Mandeville*, 117 (chap. 21), offers a similar description of the royal palace at Java, including rooms that are "of alternating gold and silver." With regard to Baghdad, Marco Polo (chap. 25) tells of a gold-filled tower that was discovered when the Mongols captured the last caliph residing in the city. According to Polo, the Mongol leader (Hülegü Khan) incarcerated the caliph in the same tower, ordering that no food or drink should be given him. Unable to feed himself of his treasure, the caliph died of starvation, thereby offering a telling example for the uselessness of earthly wealth; Polo, *Travels*, 53.

17. *Itinerary of Benjamin*, Hebrew part, 36.

18. Ibn Jubayr, *Riḥla*, 227; and *Travels of Ibn Jubayr*, 236.

19. *Itinerary of Benjamin*, Hebrew part, 35–36.

20. On Benjamin's usage of the term *to'im* for Christian pilgrims, see Chapter 4 in this volume.

21. *Itinerary of Benjamin*, Hebrew part, 36.

22. See Patricia L. Baker, "Court Dress, Abbasid," in *Medieval Islamic Civilization: An Encyclopedia*, ed. Josef W. Meri (New York: Routledge, 2006), 1:178–89. Busse, *Chalif und Grosskönig*, 205, explains this choice of color as a symbol of mourning over the death of Ibrāhīm, brother of the first Abbasid caliph, who had been murdered by the Umayyads (in 749). However, the two explanations do not exclude each other. On public appearances of the caliph, see Busse, *Chalif und Grosskönig*, 209–11.

23. *Itinerary of Benjamin*, Hebrew part, 36–37. *Massa'ot*'s manuscript versions differ significantly with respect to the princes' countries of origin. Similar motifs can be found in "Mandeville's" portrait of the Great Khan of Cathay and his court; see chap. 25 of the *Book of Mandeville*, 140–45, which includes lavish descriptions of the Khan's public appearances at official celebrations, with his entourage and their robes.

24. *Itinerary of Benjamin*, Hebrew part, 37. Instead of *ḥozer* ("returns," MS London), I read *holekh* ("goes," with MS Rome and Asher's edition, *Itinerary of Rabbi Benjamin*, vol. 1, Hebrew part, 58).

25. See Le Strange, *Baghdad During the Abbasid Caliphate*, 103–5; Busse, *Chalif und Grosskönig*, 529–34; and Lassner, *Topography of Baghdad*, 278 n. 9.

26. Ibn Jubayr, *Riḥla*, 225; and *Travels of Ibn Jubayr*, 234–35.

27. *Itinerary of Benjamin*, ed. Adler, Hebrew part, 38.

28. Ibid.

29. Ibid., 35.

30. Ibid., 38.

31. See *Itinerary of Rabbi Benjamin*, ed. Asher, vol. 1, Hebrew part, 59. Within *Massa'ot* (MS London), the number of Baghdad's Jewish inhabitants is topped only by the clearly fanciful numbers that Benjamin gives for Jewish settlements in the Arabian Peninsula, e.g., Khaybar: 50,000; see Chapter 9 in this volume.

32. *Itinerary of Benjamin*, ed. Adler, Hebrew part, 42. Petaḥyah, who seems to draw on similar sources, mentions thirty synagogues; *Sibbuv*, 1:24.

33. *Itinerary of Benjamin*, Hebrew part, 42.

34. Ibid., 38–39.

35. Petaḥyah, *Sibbuv*, 1:9. On his reputed tomb at Nabī Ṣamwīl near Jerusalem, see Chapter 5 in this volume.

36. *Itinerary of Benjamin*, Hebrew part, 39.

37. See Chapter 4 in this volume.

38. Traditionally, the origins of the office have been traced back to the Babylonian captivity in the sixth century BCE, but the first named exilarch, Rav Huna—depicted in rabbinic sources as a rival of the Jewish patriarch (*nasi*) in Roman Palestine—is dated to the turn of the third century CE. In all likelihood, the institution has roots in Parthian, or Sasanian, times. More tangible evidence for its existence dates only to the Umayyad period. For scholarship on the earlier period, see Moshe Beer, *The Babylonian Exilarchate in the Arsacid and Sassanian Periods* (Hebrew) (Tel Aviv: Dvir, 1970); and David Goodblatt, *The Monarchic Principle: Studies in Jewish Self-Government in Antiquity* (Tübingen: Mohr Siebeck, 1994), 277–311.

39. For a discussion of the exilarchate during Abbasid times, see Robert Brody, *The Geonim of Babylonia and the Shaping of Medieval Jewish Culture* (New Haven, Conn.: Yale University Press, 1998), 67–82 (including more bibliography).

40. See Chapter 5 in this volume.

41. *Itinerary of Benjamin*, Hebrew part, 39–40. Daniel ben Ḥisdai was appointed *rosh ha-golah* before 1120 and seems to have served in this function until his death, in about 1175; see Moshe Gil, *In the Kingdom of Ishmael: Studies in Jewish History in Islamic Lands in the Early Middle Ages* (Hebrew), 4 vols. (Jerusalem: Tel Aviv University Press, 1997), 1:433–34.

42. Cf. Petaḥyah, *Sibbuv*, 1:9: "The king appoints a *rosh golah* over them only upon [recommendation by] the dignitaries [*sarim*] of the Jews."

43. See Moshe Gil, "The Exilarchate," in *The Jews of Medieval Islam: Community, Society, and Identity*, ed. Daniel Frank (Leiden: Brill, 1995), 33–65.

44. *Itinerary of Benjamin*, Hebrew part, 40.

45. In translating "chain," I follow Asher's reading (*Itinerary of Rabbi Benjamin*, vol. 1, Hebrew part, 62): *ravid*; whereas MS London has *redid*, "scarf," "veil" (*Itinerary of Benjamin*, ed. Adler, Hebrew part, 40). No substitute is used here for "Muhammad," which is probably a question of textual transmission.

46. *Itinerary of Benjamin*, Hebrew part, 40. In my translation of Gen. 49:10, I am deviating from the Jewish Publication Society's Bible translation that reads "So that tribute shall come to him": *The Jewish Study Bible*, ed. Adele Berlin and Marc Z. Brettler (Oxford: Oxford University Press, 2004), 97. The verse quoted here seems to predict the continuity of the Davidic dynasty that ultimately will achieve universal dominion. However, *'ad ki yavo shiloh* is obscure, and many emendations have been proposed. In both Jewish and Christian traditions, the phrase has been usually understood as a messianic prophecy in the sense of "until Shiloh comes"; see, e.g., *Bereshit Rabbah* 98, 8, ed. Julius Theodor and Chanoch Albeck, *Bereshit Rabbah*, 3 vols., 2nd ed. (Jerusalem: Wahrmann, 1965), 3:1259: "Until Shiloh comes—this is the king messiah"; yet the phrase could also mean "until he comes to Shiloh."

47. On the dress laws derived from the Pact of 'Umar and the prohibition to ride horses, see Mark R. Cohen, *Under Crescent and Cross: The Jews in the Middle Ages* (Princeton, N.J.: Princeton University Press, 1994), 61–64. Cohen, ibid., 63, points out: "The regimen of special clothing for non-Muslims did not arise from discriminatory or stigmatizing motives." On the specific restrictions issued by the Abbasid caliph al-Mutawakkil in the mid-ninth century and their enforcement, see Milka Levy-Rubin, *Non-Muslims in the Early Islamic Empire: From Surrender to Coexistence* (Cambridge: Cambridge University Press, 2011), 103–12.

48. See *Bereshit Rabbah* 97, 10 (3:1219); b. Sanhedrin 5a; and b. Horayot 11b.

49. For an Arabic document from the twelfth century, see Lawrence I. Conrad, "A Nestorian Diploma of Investiture from the *Taḏkira* of Ibn Ḥamdūn: The Text and Its Significance," in *Studia Arabica et Islamica: Festschrift for Iḥsān 'Abbās on His Sixtieth Birthday*, ed. Wadād al-Qāḍī (Beirut: American University of Beirut, 1981), 83–104. For an excerpt from an earlier document (roughly contemporary with Benjamin), see Brody, *Geonim of*

Babylonia, 68–69. More similar writs of appointment are mentioned in Gil, "Exilarchate," 35 n. 6.

50. *Itinerary of Benjamin*, Hebrew part, 41.

51. On Samuel ben ʻEli, who is otherwise known through his controversy with Maimonides, see Samuel Poznański, *Babylonische Geonim im nachgaonäischen Zeitalter* (Berlin: Mayer and Müller, 1914), 15–36, 54–61. His correspondence as preserved in the Cairo Genizah has been published by Simḥah Assaf, "Letters of R. Samuel ben Eli and His Contemporaries" (Hebrew), *Tarbiz* 1, no. 1 (1929–30): 102–30; *Tarbiz* 1, no. 2 (1929–30): 43–84; *Tarbiz* 1, no. 3 (1929–30): 15–80.

52. In addition, Samuel calls the institution of the *rosh ha-golah* superfluous; under diaspora conditions, there was no need for royalty but for teachers of the law. See letter no. 19, fol. 13b, in Assaf, "Letters of R. Samuel ben Eli," *Tarbiz* 1, no. 2: 66, as well as Assaf's remarks in *Tarbiz* 1, no. 1: 126. Undoubtedly, Samuel's opinion is not impartial but reflects the position of the academies in their power struggle with the exilarch.

53. *Itinerary of Benjamin*, Hebrew part, 41.

54. See Busse, *Chalif und Grosskönig*, 221.

55. See Goitein, *Mediterranean Society*, 1:275.

56. Nathan the Babylonian's account likewise has the exilarch riding in a "viceroyal carriage"; for the Hebrew text, see *Mediaeval Jewish Chronicles and Chronological Notes* (Hebrew), ed. Adolf Neubauer, 2 vols. (Oxford: Clarendon, 1887–95; reprint, Jerusalem, 1967), 2:83–84; trans. in Stillman, *Jews of Arab Lands*, 171–74. This, too, seems to be an echo of the Joseph narrative, for the relevant paragraph survives only in the Hebrew rendering of Nathan's account, which is of unknown provenance and time. It does not occur in its older Judeo-Arabic version from the mid-tenth century; see Israel Friedlaender, "The Arabic Original of the Report of R. Nathan Hababli," *JQR* 17 (1905): 747–61; and Menahem Ben-Sasson, "The Structure, Goals, and Content of the Story of Nathan Ha-Babli" (Hebrew), in *Culture and Society in Medieval Jewry: Studies Dedicated to the Memory of Haim Hillel Ben-Sasson* (Hebrew), ed. Ben-Sasson, Robert Bonfil, and Joseph R. Hacker (Jerusalem: Zalman Shazar Center, 1989), 137–96.

57. Abraham Ibn Da'ud, *Sefer ha-Qabbalah: The Book of Tradition*, ed. and trans. Gerson D. Cohen (Philadelphia: Jewish Publication Society, 1967), 49 (Hebrew); 67 (English).

58. My interpretation finds support in Esperanza Alfonso's reading of Ibn Da'ud's chronicle, in which "[n]ostalgia for al-Andalus is manifest"; Alfonso, *Islamic Culture Through Jewish Eyes*, 74.

59. *Itinerary of Benjamin*, Hebrew part, 40–41. The list given here is more extensive, but some of the country names as read by Adler have significant variants in manuscript and print versions; others may be later interpolations.

60. Ibid., 41.

61. Petaḥyah, *Sibbuv*, 1:10. It seems noteworthy that Maimonides considered Samuel ben ʻEli an ignoramus who freely dispensed honorific titles; see Marina Rustow, *Heresy and the Politics of Community: The Jews of the Fatimid Caliphate* (Ithaca, N.Y.: Cornell University Press, 2008), 84–85; and the sources cited therein, n. 37.

62. See Brody, *Geonim of Babylonia*, 71–80, 123–26; and Gil, "Exilarchate," 43–46.

63. See Brody, *Geonim of Babylonia*, 11–18; and Rustow, *Heresy and the Politics of Community*, 10–12.

64. In calling Baghdad "'Adinah," Alḥarizi is alluding to Isa. 48:9.

65. Alḥarizi, *Taḥkemoni*, ed. Yahalom and Katsumata, 457 (*maqāma* 39B). The same text can be found in Alḥarizi, *Wanderings of Judah*, 75. My translation leans on *Taḥkemoni of Judah al-Ḥarizi*, trans. Reichert, 2:327 (which is based on the received Hebrew text as published in *Taḥkemoni*, ed. Toporovsky, 365), which I am adapting to the manuscript version B. Alḥarizi expresses similarly negative opinions on Baghdad's Jewry in his Arabic *maqāmas*; see *Wanderings of Judah*, 159–62. Of course, Alḥarizi's satirical portrait of Baghdad's Jewish scholars is not to be taken at face value but reflects his own bias toward Near Eastern Jewish culture; for more on this question, see this volume's Chapter 8.

66. Cf. the full title of Ibn Baṭṭūṭa's work: *tuḥfat al-nuẓẓār fī gharā'ib al-amṣār wa-'ajā'ib al-asfār* ("Rare Insights into the Wonders of Metropolises and the Marvels of Travels").

67. Benjamin simply dubs him "the king of the *Togarmim* [Turks], who are called *Turcos*" in Romance language; *Itinerary of Benjamin*, Hebrew part, 30.

68. Petaḥyah, *Sibbuv*, 1:28.

69. *Itinerary of Benjamin*, Hebrew part, 30. While the biblical names Amana and Pharpar (2 Kings 5:12) cannot be associated with any specific waterway known today, Benjamin probably refers to the A'waj and Baradā Rivers, which flow through the Damascus oasis.

70. Petaḥyah, *Sibbuv*, 1:28–29.

71. Ibn Jubayr, *Riḥla*, 231. I am slightly modifying the translation in *Travels of Ibn Jubayr*, 272. The quoted saying alludes to Qur'an 47:12: "God shall surely admit those who believe and do righteous deeds into gardens underneath which rivers flow." Similarly, the Talmud mentions Damascus among the places where the gate to the Garden of Eden may be located (b. 'Eruvin 19a; the name of the city is corrupted, though).

72. *Itinerary of Benjamin*, Hebrew part, 30.

73. Ibid.

74. Still, Benjamin's misleading description might be explained by the fact that the clock was destroyed by fire in 1166–67, i.e., around the time when he may have traveled through the Levant. Ibn Jubayr, who visited Damascus in 1184, would have described the improved version in which the clock was rebuilt. It seems to have been finally destroyed by another fire in 1392; see Finbarr B. Flood, *The Congregational Mosque of Damascus: Studies on the Makings of an Umayyad Visual Culture* (Leiden: Brill, 2001), 114–18 (including more bibliographical references).

75. Ibn Jubayr, *Riḥla*, 270; I slightly modify the translation in *Travels of Ibn Jubayr*, 281.

76. *Itinerary of Benjamin*, Hebrew part, 30–31.

77. For a discussion of the courtyard mosaics and their iconographical program, see Flood, *Congregational Mosque*, 15–47.

78. *Itinerary of Benjamin*, Hebrew part, 31.

79. Ibn Jubayr, *Riḥla*, 273; I am quoting the translation in *Travels of Ibn Jubayr*, 284.

80. See Flood, *Congregational Mosque*, 108; and Meri, *Cult of Saints*, 200–201.

81. Nine spans equal about 6.75 feet (ca. 2 meters); two spans correspond to 1.5 feet (0.45 meter).

82. *Itinerary of Benjamin*, Hebrew part, 31. Cf. Josephus, *Antiquities* 1,159, who attributes to Nicolas of Damascus a tradition according to which Abrames reigned in Damascus after having invaded the city with an army "from the land of the Chaldeans." This Abrames is obviously the biblical Abraham, who originated from Ur of the Chaldeans (Gen. 11:31). A playful midrash on Josh. 14:15 likewise counts Abraham among the giants (*'anaqim*); see *Bereshit Rabbah* 14:6 (1:130).

83. Basola, *In Zion and Jerusalem*, Hebrew part, 24. I slightly modify the translation in ibid., English part, 87.

84. On Basola's negative view of Muslim shrines (especially those that were built over "Jewish" tombs), see Chapter 5 in this volume.

85. See Anne Wolff, "Merchants, Pilgrims, Naturalists: Alexandria Through European Eyes from the Fourteenth to the Sixteenth Century," in *Alexandria: Real and Imagined*, ed. Anthony Hirst and Michael Silk (Aldershot, U.K.: Ashgate, 2004), 185–98; and Wolff, *How Many Miles to Babylon? Travels and Adventures to Egypt and Beyond, from 1300 to 1640* (Liverpool: Liverpool University Press, 2003), 61–96. Wolff does not offer an analysis of the travel accounts that she presents but aims at a panoramic picture of Egypt in medieval and early modern times.

86. As noted in Chapter 2 of this volume, the ancient harbor had assumed the role of the principal maritime gateway to the Middle and Far East for people as well as goods. On Egypt as a site of Jewish Exodus pilgrimage, see my "The Sacred Text as a Mental Map," 407–12.

87. On Muslim and Jewish reflections on Alexandria's ancient history, see my "Alexandria oder Kairo: Die Metamorphose einer Stadtgründungslegende in der hellenistischen, islamischen und jüdischen Literatur," in *Jewish Studies Between the Disciplines—Judaistik zwischen den Disziplinen: Papers in Honor of Peter Schäfer on the Occasion of His Sixtieth Birthday*, ed. Klaus Herrmann, Margarete Schlüter, and Giuseppe Veltri (Leiden: Brill, 2003), 279–90.

88. *Itinerary of Benjamin*, Hebrew part, 66.

89. Ibid. One wonders how Benjamin was able to gain an unimpeded view from the "Gate of Rashīd" (Rosetta Gate) facing east to the "Sea Gate" (Bāb al-Baḥr) at the northern edge of the medieval city. Arguably, he confused the latter with the western gate because of its similar-sounding Arabic name (Bāb al-Bahār, Gate of the Spices). If this were the case, it would shed doubt on his proficiency in Arabic.

90. On further medieval descriptions of Alexandria, see the classic study by Hermann Thiersch, *Pharos: Antike, Islam und Occident: Ein Beitrag zur Architekturgeschichte* (Berlin: Teubner, 1909), 38–69. For more recent studies, see Saleh K. Hamarneh, "The Ancient Monuments of Alexandria According to the Accounts by Medieval Arab Authors

(IX–XV Century)," *Folia Orientalia* 13 (1971): 77–110; Faustina Doufikar-Aerts, "Alexander the Great and the Pharos of Alexandria in Arabic Literature," in *The Problematics of Power: Eastern and Western Representations of Alexander the Great*, ed. M. Bridges and J. Ch. Bürgel (Bern: Peter Lang, 1996), 191–202; and Frenkel, *The Compassionate and Benevolent*, 28–44.

91. Ibn Jubayr, *Riḥla*, 40–41; the translation follows *Travels of Ibn Jubayr*, 32.

92. *Massa' meshullam*, 48. Meshullam attributes the city's ruinous state to the attack on Alexandria by Peter I de Lusignan, ruler of Cyprus, which occurred more than a century (1365) before Meshullam's visit to Egypt; see Ya'ari's comments *ad loc.* What is more, the traveler seems to confuse some of the historical details related to the Cypriote expedition against Alexandria.

93. According to Anselmo Adorno (1470), Alexandria's fortifications looked impressive upon approach from the sea, while its ruins were visible only after one had entered the city; *Itinéraire d'Anselme Adorno*, 162–63. The Tuscan priest (and contemporary of Meshullam) Michele of Figline similarly states that at the time of his visit (1489), the once-magnificent city was hardly populated and its inner parts were totally in ruins ("dentro tutta rovinata"); *Da Figline a Gerusalemme: Viaggio del prete Michele in Egitto e in Terrasanta (1489–1490)*, ed. Marina Montesano (Rome: Viella, 2010), 63. On possible reasons for Alexandria's decay during the late Middle Ages, see Benjamin Arbel, "The Port Towns of the Levant in Sixteenth-Century Travel Literature," in *Mediterranean Urban Culture 1400–1700*, ed. Alexander Cowan (Exeter: University of Exeter, 2000), 161.

94. *Massa' meshullam*, 47.

95. Obadiah, Letter A, *From Italy to Jerusalem*, 50–51.

96. Ibid., 51.

97. *Itinerary of Benjamin*, Hebrew part, 66.

98. Jacob ben Nathanel, *Sippur Massa'ot*, 12. Probably, diameter and length should be switched in Jacob's following statement: "The middle [column] is thirty spans [roughly 22.5 feet (6.9 meters)] in diameter and four cubits [6 feet (1.83 meters)] long." Jacob ben Nathanel's description is also reminiscent of the sundial that Benjamin places in the Umayyad Mosque of Damascus; see above.The marvelous structure consisting of 365 elements seems to be a literary topos, as Adler (in his discussion of Benjamin's description of the Colosseum at Rome; *Itinerary of Benjamin,* Hebrew part, 7) observed: "Our author in the course of his narrative speaks more than once of buildings erected on a uniform plan corresponding with the days of the year"; *Itinerary of Benjamin*, English part, 6 n. 6.

99. Ibn Jubayr, *Riḥla*, 41; I am quoting the translation in *Travels of Ibn Jubayr*, 32.

100. As evidenced by an inscription on its base, the column was erected in 298 CE in honor of Diocletian.

101. 70 cubits are 105 feet (32 meters); 5 cubits are 7.5 feet (2.3 meters).

102. For 'Abd al-Laṭīf al Baghdādī's *Kitāb al-ifādah wa-'l-i'tibār*, I am using the bilingual edition, *The Eastern Key*, ed. and trans. Kamal H. Zand, John A. Videan, and E. Videan (London: George Allen and Unwin, 1965). For the quotation, see ibid., 129–33 (translation modified).

103. Jacob ben Nathanel, *Sippur Massa'ot*, 12. In medieval Christian art, these images

represent the authors of the four gospels. Perhaps it is Jacob ben Nathanel's French cultural background that (unconsciously) influences his account.

104. On medieval descriptions of the Pharos, see the bibliography mentioned above, n. 90. See also Miguel Asín Palacios, "Una descripción nueva del Faro de Alejandría," *Al-Andalus* 1 (1933): 241–92.

105. Jacob ben Nathanel, *Sippur Massa'ot,* 12. Jacob's mention of both Provence and Acre in this context reflects the sea route that he would have taken to crusader Palestine; see Chapter 2 in this volume. Benjamin also exaggerates the reach (100 miles) of the Pharos's beacon; *Itinerary of Benjamin,* Hebrew part, 67.

106. Ibn Jubayr, *Riḥla,* 41; the translation is from *Travels of Ibn Jubayr,* 33 (insignificantly modified).

107. *Itinerary of Benjamin,* Hebrew part, 67. In other versions, the device is believed to have served as a giant burning glass by the help of which foreign ships were set on fire; see, e.g., al-Harawī, *Kitāb al-ziyārāt,* 48, and *Lonely Wayfarer's Guide,* 118. Both theories—its use as a powerful spyglass and as a weapon—are combined in the geographical dictionary by Ibn 'Abd al-Mun'im al-Ḥimyarī, *Kitāb al-rawḍ al-mi'ṭār fī khabar al-aqṭār,* ed. Iḥsān 'Abbās (Beirut: Librairie du Liban, 1975), 54. For a translation, see Hamarneh, "Ancient Monuments," 104–5.

108. *Itinerary of Benjamin,* Hebrew part, 67; variant versions of the text have other Greek-sounding names, including Ṭordos or Ṭodros.

109. Indeed, a similar version is attested in Qazwīnī's geographical dictionary (*Kitāb āthār al-bilād,* in its 1276 recension). For the Arabic text, see *Zakarija Ben Muhammed Ben Mahmud el-Cazwini's Kosmographie,* 2 vols., ed. Ferdinand Wüstenfeld (Göttingen: Dieterichsche, 1848-49), 2:98.

110. Al-Ḥimyarī, *Kitāb al-rawḍ,* 54–55; I modify the translation by Hamarneh, "Ancient Monuments," 105–6.

111. *Massa' meshullam,* 45.

CHAPTER 7. ISHMAELITES AND EDOMITES

1. On Benjamin's account of the Holy Sepulchre, see Chapter 4 in this volume.

2. The reduction of political history to dynastic accounts is a common phenomenon of medieval historical writing, with little difference between Christian- and Muslim-authored works. Similarly, premodern Jewish accounts of Christian and Muslim history (few as there are) tend to focus on biographies of rulers and military events; for examples, see my *Islamische Geschichte in jüdischen Chroniken: Hebräische Historiographie des 16. und 17. Jahrhunderts* (Tübingen: Mohr Siebeck, 2004), 49–57, 63–65 (on Elijah Capsali), 88–91 (on Joseph ha-Kohen), 114–18 (on Joseph Sambari). See also my shorter remarks in "Joseph ha-Kohen," 70–71, 77; and "Exposed to All the Currents of the Mediterranean," 40–46, 59.

3. On this ban, see, in this volume, Chapter 2 n. 47.

4. Following his conquest of Babylon (539 BCE), Cyrus the Great authorized the

rebuilding of the Jerusalem Temple (a project to be realized much later) and permitted the Judean exiles in Mesopotamia to return to their homeland. On this background, the anonymous prophet known as Deutero-Isaiah idealizes the Persian ruler whom God is said to have "roused up" (Isa. 41:2 and 25) to defeat the Babylonians.

5. Based on the common anno mundi computation, this corresponds to 1190 CE; however, 1187 would be more exact.

6. Alḥarizi, *Taḥkemoni*, ed. Toporovsky, 248 (Gate 28), which corresponds to *Taḥkemoni*, ed. Yahalom and Katsumata, 264 (*maqāma* 16, with insignificant variants). I am quoting the translation by Segal, *Book of Taḥkemoni*, 240–41 (slightly modified).

7. According to Eliahu Ashtor (Strauss), Saladin adopted a stricter interpretation of the *dhimmī* laws than the Fatimids, his predecessors as rulers of Egypt; see Ashtor (Strauss), "Saladin and the Jews," *Hebrew Union College Annual* 27 (1956): 305–26. On Jewish hopes that the wars between Ayyubids and crusaders heralded the coming of the Messiah, see ibid., 317–23.

8. Alḥarizi, *Kitāb al-Durar*, 110, lines 35–37; the same text can be found in Alḥarizi's *Wanderings of Judah*, 107, lines 284–86. On the details of the protracted crusader expedition and their final defeat, see Runciman, *History of the Crusades*, 3:168.

9. Alḥarizi, *Kitāb al-Durar*, 110, lines 29–30; idem, *Wanderings of Judah*, 107, lines 275–77.

10. Alḥarizi, *Kitāb al-Durar*, 110, line 33; idem, *Wanderings of Judah*, 107, line 280.

11. Alḥarizi, *Kitāb al-Durar*, 110, lines 42–43; idem, *Wanderings of Judah*, 108, lines 290–92.

12. Cyrus's victory over the Babylonians would again be the closest case in comparison; see n. 4 above.

13. Petaḥyah, *Sibbuv*, 1:17, reads *MYLY* as the name of the place; but this must be a corruption because R. Meir's reputed tomb was in Ḥillah, as reflected by Benjamin's account; *Itinerary of Benjamin*, Hebrew part, 43. Though R. Meir is said to have died at an unspecified place in Asia (y. Kila'im 9:4 [32c]), other traditions place his grave in Palestine (Gush Ḥalav, Tiberias, Narbata, or Jerusalem).

14. On other stories about a punitive miracle, see Chapter 5 in this volume.

15. Petaḥyah, *Sibbuv*, 1:18.

16. The Muslim ruler's visit at Baruch ben Neriah's tomb and his near-conversion are told in two separate parts in Petaḥyah's *Sibbuv* but they are clearly related to one another. (A detailed discussion of the textual problems would go beyond the present scope.) In the first part (*Sibbuv*, 1:11), the ruler orders to uncover the tomb; Muslim workers drop dead (in a punitive miracle) when they try to open the tomb, whereas Jewish diggers stay unharmed. Only the second part (ibid., 1:26–27) includes the following negative comparison between the tomb of Baruch ben Neriah and that of Muhammad.

17. In the case of R. Judah the Patriarch, *Sibbuv* (1:29) speaks of a "pleasing odor" ascending from his tomb. In a Christian context, this kind of odor similarly serves to validate a relic's identity; see Susan Ashbrook Harvey, *Scenting Salvation: Ancient Christianity and the Olfactory Imagination* (Berkeley: University of California Press, 2006), 227. Also, the

Latin account of the Tomb of the Patriarchs' discovery tells of a sweet wind coming out of a crack in the floor; see Chapter 4 in this volume. Still other Jewish and Muslim pilgrimage accounts mention light miracles at holy tombs; see Meri, *Cult of Saints*, 21–24. Both topoi, then, seem to have been used interchangeably.

18. Petaḥyah, *Sibbuv,* 1:27. The base text of Grünhut's edition omits Muhammad's name, apparently for religious reasons.

19. On the Antoninus legends in rabbinic literature, see my *Die Institution des jüdischen Patriarchen: Eine quellen- und traditionskritische Studie zur Geschichte der Juden in der Spätantike* (Tübingen: Mohr Siebeck, 1995), 129–44; and Shaye J. D. Cohen, "The Conversion of Antoninus," in *The Talmud Yerushalmi and Graeco-Roman Culture 1,* ed. Peter Schäfer (Tübingen: Mohr Siebeck, 1998), 141–72. The Antoninus motif is also echoed in Benjamin's portrayal of the Abbasid caliph as a great supporter of Jews and Judaism; see Chapter 6 in this volume.

20. Within the account of his Holy Land journey (1217–18), the German pilgrim Thietmar, e.g., contends that Muhammad's tomb contains only his right foot "because the rest of his body was completely eaten by pigs of the Christians" (trans. Pringle, *Pilgrimage to Jerusalem*, 130); for additional Christian tales about Muhammad's death and burial, see Norman Daniel, *Islam and the West: The Making of an Image*, 2nd ed. (Oxford: Oneworld, 1993), 126–28.

21. On this topic, see C. A. Patrides, "'The Bloody and Cruell Turke': The Background of a Renaissance Commonplace," *Studies in the Renaissance* 10 (1963): 126–35; Steven Runciman, *The Fall of Constantinople, 1453* (Cambridge: Cambridge University Press, 1965), 160–63, 195–98; Robert Schwoebel, *The Shadow of the Crescent: The Renaissance Image of the Turk (1453–1517)* (Nieuwkoop: de Graaf, 1967), 8–10; and Yoko Miamoto, "The Influence of Medieval Prophecies on Views of the Turks: Islam and Apocalypticism in the Sixteenth Century," *Journal of Turkish Studies* 17 (1993): 125–45.

22. See the account by Pierre Barbatre, a Norman priest and Jerusalem pilgrim and one of the first foreign visitors to war-damaged Rhodes after the lifting of the siege; it has been published by Pierre Tucoo-Chala and Noel Pinzuti, "Le voyage de Pierre Barbatre à Jérusalem en 1480," *Annuaire Bulletin de la Société de l'Histoire de France, 1972–1973* (Paris: Klincksieck, 1974): 159–63. See also the brief discussion by Chareyron, *Pilgrims to Jerusalem*, 202–3. As a major nexus of trade and travel in the eastern Mediterranean, medieval Rhodes merited numerous descriptions by travelers of this period; see Michel Balard, "The Urban Landscape of Rhodes as Perceived by Fourteenth- and Fifteenth-Century Travellers," in *Intercultural Contacts in the Medieval Mediterranean: Studies in Honour of David Jacoby*, ed. Benjamin Arbel (London: Frank Cass, 1996), 24–34.

23. According to Franz Babinger, the reversal of the combat situation was caused by a proclamation of the Ottoman admiral that looting was forbidden and the booty of Rhodes belonged to the sultan's exchequer. As a result, the Janissaries lost their motivation to fight and rushed back to their camps; Babinger, *Mehmed the Conqueror and His Time*, trans. Ralph Manheim (Princeton, N.J.: Princeton University Press, 1978), 399.

24. *Massa' meshullam*, 44.

25. Ibid.; the quotation marks indicate an allusion to Exod. 32:27; cf. Isa. 19:2.

26. Obadiah, Letter A, *From Italy to Jerusalem*, 44–45.

27. In the early sixteenth century, the Cretan rabbi Elijah Capsali, by contrast, composed panegyrics on the Ottoman sultans, whose rule he associated with messianic expectations; see, in this volume, Chapter 4 n. 62.

28. *Massa' meshullam*, 60.

29. Ibid., 67.

30. Ibid., 60–61.

31. Obadiah, Letter A, *From Italy to Jerusalem*, 71.

32. Ibid.

33. *Massa' meshullam*, 58.

34. This claim echoes a much earlier derogatory statement from Marco Polo: the "Saracens" of Tabriz "would be great wrong-doers, if it were not for the government"; *Il Milione*, 338. I am quoting from *Travels*, 57.

35. *Massa' meshullam*, 58–59.

36. This accusation seems to respond to similar Muslim claims that Judaism represented a falsification (*taḥrīf*) of the true religion; see my "Interreligious Polemics in Medieval Spain: Biblical Interpretation Between Ibn Ḥazm, Shlomoh Ibn Adret, and Shim'on Ben Ṣemaḥ Duran," in *Gershom Scholem (1897–1982): In Memoriam*, vol. 2, Jerusalem Studies in Jewish Thought 21, ed. Joseph Dan (Jerusalem: Hebrew University, 2007), English part, 36, 52–53.

37. *Massa' meshullam*, 59.

38. Ibid.

39. See Ismar Elbogen, *Jewish Liturgy: A Comprehensive History*, trans. Raymond P. Scheindlin (Philadelphia: Jewish Publication Society, 1993), 71–72; and Stefan C. Reif, *New Perspectives on Jewish Liturgical History* (Cambridge: Cambridge University Press, 1993), 208–9, 240.

40. According to Israel J. Yuval, "This prayer served as an anti-Christian credo"; see Yuval, *Two Nations in Your Womb: Perceptions of Jews and Christians in Late Antiquity and the Middle Ages*, trans. Barbara Harshav and Jonathan Chipman (Berkeley: University of California Press, 2006), 119, 198–202.

41. The link that Meshullam draws between specific Islamic rituals and the *'Alenu* seems to be unique. Still, a number of medieval manuscript versions of the prayer interpret the contentious phrase "who bow to something vain and empty" as a numerological allusion to both Jesus and Muhammad; for "vain and empty" (Hebrew: *LHBL WLRYQ*) adds up to the same numerical value (413) as "Jesus, Muhammad" (here spelled *YShW MḤMT*); see Naphtali Wieder, *The Formation of Jewish Liturgy in the East and West* (Hebrew), 2 vols. (Jerusalem: Ben-Zvi Institute, 1998), 2:453–59. Such an interpretation obviously reflects a Western perception of Islam according to which Muslims are praying to Muhammad, much like Christians are praying to Jesus as the son of God.

42. On the following, cf. my preliminary discussion, "Lofty Caliphs," 83–85.

43. *Massa' meshullam*, 46–47. Ogier de Busbecq, by contrast, reveals a rather

nonjudgmental attitude when comparing the "Turkish" mode of sitting "with their legs crossed" to that of "tailors in our country." Ogier Ghislen de Busbecq was Viennese ambassador to Süleyman the Magnificent in 1554–62. The epistolary account of his time in Constantinople, originally written in Latin, is readily available in the translation by Edward S. Forster, *The Turkish Letters of Ogier Ghiselin de Busbecq, Imperial Ambassador at Constantinople 1554–1562* (Oxford: Clarendon, 1927; reprint, London: Sickle Moon, 2001). For the quotation, see ibid., 91.

44. *Massa' meshullam*, 47.

45. Ibid., 55.

46. On contemporaneous table manners, see the *Galateo*, one of the most important Italian courtesy guidebooks from the sixteenth century. Written by the Tuscan Giovanni della Casa, it has been translated by Konrad Eisenbichler and Kenneth R. Bartlett, *Galateo: A Renaissance Treatise on Manners* (Toronto: Centre for Reformation and Renaissance Studies, 1994). According to the *Galateo*, a gentleman should avoid sharing his plate (ibid., 92–95).

47. Obadiah, Letter A, *From Italy to Jerusalem*, 74.

48. Ibid., 55.

49. *Massa' meshullam*, 44.

50. Ibid., 78. *Sepulcro* is misspelled in the Hebrew transcription (*sepulo*). I do not find Ya'ari's comment (*ad locum*) convincing that this rendering might reveal the author's (or copyist's) polemical intention.

51. Basola, *In Zion and Jerusalem*, Hebrew part, 18; I am quoting the translation in ibid., English part, 70.

52. Ibid., Hebrew part, 20; my translation.

53. See Chapters 4 and 5 in this volume.

54. Obadiah, Letter A, *From Italy to Jerusalem*, 64.

55. Basola, *In Zion and Jerusalem*, Hebrew part, 21. I am slightly modifying the translation in ibid., English part, 76.

56. *Itinerary of Benjamin*, Hebrew part, 14–15.

57. Ibid., 23. On Benjamin's account of crusader Jerusalem, see Chapter 4 in this volume.

58. Obadiah, Letter A, *From Italy to Jerusalem*, 81.

59. Fabri, *Peregrinatio*, 1:345–53; and *Wanderings of Felix Fabri*, 1:428–38. On this passage, see Dorothea R. French, "Pilgrimage, Ritual, and Power Strategies: Felix Fabri's Pilgrimage to Jerusalem in 1483," in *Pilgrims and Travelers to the Holy Land*, Studies in Jewish Civilization 7, ed. Bryan F. Le Beau and Menachem Mor (Omaha, Neb.: Creighton University Press, 1996), 176–77.

60. As Meshullam (*Massa' meshullam*, 78) knew, Christians had to pay fourteen ducats to the Mamluk guards in order to visit the Holy Sepulchre, a sore point that is frequently lamented in contemporaneous Christian sources. On Christian pilgrimage to Mamluk Palestine as reflected in the account of Felix Fabri, see French, "Pilgrimage, Ritual, and Power Strategies," 169–79.

61. Obadiah, Letter A, *From Italy to Jerusalem*, 51.

62. Lit., "his blood will be on his head"; ibid. Regarding the restrictions imposed on Christians during Muslim Friday prayers, see also Symon Semeonis's travel account. In his description of a *funduq* in Alexandria, the Franciscan traveler similarly states that "during prayer-time Christians of all classes are absolutely forbidden to come forth from their houses, which the Saracens close and bolt from without. When their prayers are over, however, the Christians are free to move about the city and attend to their business"; *Itinerarium Symonis Semeonis*, 50 (Latin text); I am quoting the translation, ibid., 51.

63. Basola, *In Zion and Jerusalem*, Hebrew part, 21. I am editing the translation, ibid., English part, 76.

64. On the distinctive dress worn by Levantine Christians during the period under discussion, see Leo A. Mayer, *Mamluke Costume: A Survey* (Geneva: Albert Kundig, 1952), 65, 67–68.

65. The house (no longer in existence) seems to have been in Muslim ownership; however, Christian pilgrims such as Michele of Figline (1489) were let in for a fee to visit the site where Jesus was said to have been flagellated (*Da Figline a Gerusalemme*, 106). On other pilgrims' accounts mentioning the Casa di Pilato, see Nathan Schur, *Jerusalem in Pilgrims' and Travellers' Accounts: A Thematic Bibliography of Western Christian Itineraries, 1300–1917* (Jerusalem: Ariel, 1980), 25–26; Pringle, *Churches of the Crusader Kingdom*, 2:94; and Annabel J. Wharton, *Selling Jerusalem: Relics, Replicas, Theme Parks* (Chicago: University of Chicago Press, 2006), 116–17.

66. Basola, *In Zion and Jerusalem*, Hebrew part, 22. I am quoting the translation, ibid., English part, 79.

67. Not coincidentally, Postel embarked on a pair of journeys to the Levant. For more on this relationship, see David's introduction to his edition of Basola's travelogue, *In Zion and Jerusalem*, English part, 26–27; and Moshe Idel, "Italy in Safed, Safed in Italy: Toward an Interactive History of Sixteenth Century Kabbalah," in *Cultural Intermediaries: Jewish Intellectuals in Early Modern Italy*, ed. David B. Ruderman and Giuseppe Veltri (Philadelphia: University of Pennsylvania Press, 2004), 249.

68. *Massa' meshullam*, 78.

69. On Agostino Contarini, see Chapter 3 in this volume.

70. *Massa' meshullam*, 78.

71. In this case, Meshullam mainly wanted to avoid the higher tolls imposed on non-Muslim travelers; see Chapter 3 in this volume.

72. *Massa' meshullam*, 78–79.

CHAPTER 8. NEAR EASTERN JEWS

1. Similar questions are raised by Lehmann ("Levantinos," 4) in his discussion of Azulai's (Ḥida's) travel diary: "If Jews identified as Jews vis-à-vis their Gentile neighbors . . . , how did they identify when meeting other Jews? Was 'Jewishness' the only, or even the most important, lens through which they could perceive themselves?"

2. Here and in the chapter title, I am alluding to Steven Aschheim's *Brothers and Strangers: The East European Jew in German and German Jewish Consciousness, 1800–1923* (Madison: University of Wisconsin Press, 1982).

3. The enforcement of these rules greatly varied from period to period and region to region; see Ashtor (Strauss), *Toledot ha-yehudim*, 2:263–71; Antoine Fattal, *Le statut légal des non-Musulmans en pays d'Islam*, 2nd ed. (Beirut: Dar el-Machreq, 1995), 71–84; and M. Cohen, *Under Crescent and Cross*, 52–72.

4. Goitein, *Mediterranean Society*, 1:359. On various *jizya* payments mentioned in medieval sources, see Ashtor, *Toledot ha-yehudim*, 2:265–66. On the income-related graduated tax, see Fattal, *Statut légal des non-Musulmans*, 324; and M. Cohen, *Under Crescent and Cross*, 56.

5. Petaḥyah, *Sibbuv*, 1:5; see also ibid., 1:10. At the time, two cousins were contending over the position of exilarch, both of whom resided at Mosul. But Petaḥyah fails to explain how this might have affected the collection of fees.

6. Petaḥyah, *Sibbuv*, 1:10. Petaḥyah's account seems to reflect the decline in the power of the exilarch, who—in Baghdad, at least—had been overshadowed by the *ge'onim*; see Chapter 6 in this volume.

7. See Brody, *Geonim of Babylonia*, 71–73. The use of *dhimmī* representatives, rather than Muslim officials, to collect the *jizya* does seem to contradict the tax's religious nature as mandated by Islamic law.

8. Petaḥyah, *Sibbuv*, 1:10. Intensifying this statement, one manuscript version (MS Warsaw, fol. 129b) adds here that "they are not in a state of oppression [*galut*] at all" (David, "Sibbuv r. petaḥyah," 260), a phrasing that echoes similar statements by fifteenth-century Jewish travelers to the Levant; see below.

9. The *Āmirī* dinar was a coin issued in Fatimid Egypt and equaled one and a third Castilian *maravedi*, according to Benjamin; *Itinerary of Benjamin*, Hebrew part, 51.

10. See Chapter 6 in this volume.

11. Unlike their Baghdadi brethren, these Jews "live in [a state] of great oppression [*shi'abbud*] and great suffering," according to Petaḥyah (*Sibbuv*, 1:10). Persia thus appears to be an exception to both twelfth-century travelers' largely idealized depiction of the Islamic East.

12. *Itinerary of Benjamin*, Hebrew part, 51. As this remark is missing in MS London, the base text of Adler's edition, but included in the other textual versions, Adler considers it an omission and emendates the text accordingly.

13. Also, in the Mamluk and early Ottoman-ruled Middle East, local and foreign coins were simultaneously in circulation; see Jere L. Bacharach, "The Dinar Versus the Ducat," *International Journal of Middle East Studies* 4 (1973): 77–96.

14. Hebrew text in David, *Reflections on Jewish Jerusalem*, 151, 158.

15. Basola, *In Zion and Jerusalem*, Hebrew part, 12, calls this tax *kharga*, a loanword deriving from the Arabic *kharāj*, which was a land tax. However, he clearly has the poll tax in mind. As Shmuelevitz has pointed out, this kind of imprecise usage of Arabic tax terminology is not unusual in Hebrew sources from the period; see Shmuelevitz, *Jews of the Ottoman Empire*, 84.

16. Basola, *In Zion and Jerusalem*, Hebrew part, 12; I am slightly modifying the translation, in ibid., English part, 56.

17. See Shmuelevitz, *Jews of the Ottoman Empire*, 85–86.

18. Obadiah, Letter B, *From Italy to Jerusalem*, 88.

19. Hebrew text of the letter in David, *Reflections on Jewish Jerusalem*, 163–64.

20. Obadiah, Letter A, *From Italy to Jerusalem*, 80.

21. On this affair, see Abraham David, "The Historical Significance of the 'Elders' Mentioned in the Letters of R. Obadia of Bertinoro" (Hebrew), in *Jerusalem in the Middle Ages: Selected Papers* (Hebrew), ed. Benjamin Z. Kedar (Jerusalem: Ben-Zvi Institute, 1979), 221–43.

22. Obadiah, Letter A, *From Italy to Jerusalem*, 58. He furthermore accuses the elders of having sold Torah scrolls and other ceremonial items to Christians, which would have been a severe sacrilege.

23. Ibid., 65.

24. For a detailed and balanced discussion of dress codes in Islamic law, see M. Cohen, *Under Crescent and Cross*, 61–64. On the girdle as the distinguishing mark of indigenous Christians, see below.

25. For the dress code during the Mamluk period, see Ashtor, *Toledot ha-Yehudim*, 2:210–17; and Mayer, *Mamluke Costume*, 65–67. On early Ottoman rule, see Amnon Cohen, *Ottoman Documents on the Jewish Community of Jerusalem in the Sixteenth Century* (Hebrew) (Jerusalem: Ben-Zvi Institute, 1976), 22, 47.

26. On women's dress as reflected in the travelers' accounts, see Chapter 10 in this volume.

27. *Massa' meshullam*, 50.

28. Ibid., 58.

29. Here I follow Mark Cohen's interpretation of the *dhimmī* status as part of a social hierarchy that did not exclude but rather marginalized non-Muslim minorities; see M. Cohen, *Under Crescent and Cross*, 111–16.

30. See ibid., 58–60.

31. Obadiah, Letter A, *From Italy to Jerusalem*, 69–70.

32. Although founded in the early fifteenth century, this prayer house has been erroneously identified with the synagogue that Naḥmanides established some two hundred years earlier in a different location. In fact, Jews only moved into the present-day Jewish quarter under Mamluk rule; see Drory, "Jerusalem During the Mamluk Period," 213. On the history of the synagogue, see Elchanan Reiner, "The Courtyard of the Ashkenazim in Jerusalem: Early Days" (Hebrew), in *The Hurvah Synagogue: Six Centuries of Jewish Settlement in Jerusalem* (Hebrew), ed. Reuven Gafni, Arie Morgenstern, and David Cassuto (Jerusalem: Ben-Zvi Institute, 2010), 11–43.

33. Obadiah, Letter A, *From Italy to Jerusalem*, 68.

34. See Shlomo D. Goitein, "Ibn 'Ubayya's Book Concerning the Destruction of the Synagogue of Jerusalem" (Hebrew), *Zion* 13–14 (1948–49): 18–32; and Ashtor, *Toledot ha-yehudim*, 2:398–415.

35. This law is no Islamic innovation but has precedents in Byzantine legislation concerning synagogues; see M. Cohen, *Under Crescent and Cross*, 58–60. While numerous churches and synagogues are known to have been founded after the Muslim conquest, their status as ancient or new was sometimes subject to investigation.

36. The proximity between the synagogue and the mosque would lead to further conflicts and its eventual closure under Ottoman rule (1585); see A. Cohen, *Jewish Life Under Islam*, 77–84.

37. Obadiah, Letter A, *From Italy to Jerusalem*, 68.

38. See Chapter 7 in this volume.

39. Obadiah, Letter A, *From Italy to Jerusalem*, 71.

40. Ibid., 80; cf. Ashtor, *Toledot ha-yehudim*, 2:311–12. The Jewish community collected this tax by charging its members different prices on wine, depending on their economic standing, as evidenced by the letter of Obadiah's student; see David, *Reflections on Jewish Jerusalem*, 161.

41. See the documents published by Amnon Cohen and Elisheva Simon-Pikali, *Jews in the Moslem Court: Society, Economy and Communal Organization in the Sixteenth Century, Documents from Ottoman Jerusalem* (Hebrew) (Ben-Zvi Institute: Jerusalem, 1993), 173–76.

42. Joseph Sambari offers another example for how public opinion might infringe on the Jewish privilege of wine production. Written in Ottoman Egypt during the last third of the seventeenth century, his chronicle reflects how a puritanical tendency in contemporaneous Muslim society led to a temporary prohibition of wine production; see my "An Ex-Sabbatean's Remorse? Sambari's Polemics Against Islam," *JQR* 97, no. 3 (2007): 373.

43. Hebrew text in David, *Reflections on Jewish Jerusalem*, 166.

44. Basola, *In Zion and Jerusalem*, Hebrew part, 31; English part, 104–5.

45. Obadiah, Letter A, *From Italy to Jerusalem*, 65. In a missive to his brother, Obadiah expresses analogous observations; see Letter B, ibid., 85. A similar phrasing is used by the Moroccan rabbi Isaac ben Musa, in a letter that he sent to his father in 1541. With regard to the Upper Galilee, the author states that "there is not much *galut*, and the [Jewish] community there [lives] in peace and security" (the Judeo-Arabic letter includes the Hebrew word *galut*). For an edition of the text, see Jacob Mann, "Te'udot mi-kitve-yad," *Hebrew Union College Annual* 4 (1927): 458.

46. Ya'ari, *Iggerot ereṣ yisra'el*, 181.

47. On the "semantic field" that the term *galut* had acquired by the late Middle Ages, see M. Cohen, *Under Crescent and Cross*, 192–94, who includes in his discussion a number of the sources analyzed in this chapter. Here is not the place to discuss whether exile and diaspora are two opposing notions of Jewish identity, as Daniel Boyarin and Jonathan Boyarin have argued in "Diaspora: Generation and the Ground of Identity," *Critical Inquiry* 19 (1993): 693–725; and Jonathan Boyarin and Daniel Boyarin, *Powers of Diaspora: Two Essays on the Relevance of Jewish Culture* (Minneapolis: University of Minnesota Press, 2002). Such a distinction makes sense within a post-Emancipation context but seems artificial when applied to premodern Hebrew sources; see Erich S. Gruen, "Diaspora and Homeland," in *Diasporas and Exiles: Varieties of Jewish Identity*, ed. Howard Wettstein (Berkeley: University

of California Press, 2002), 20; Howard Wettstein, "Coming to Terms with Exile," in *Diasporas and Exiles*, ed. Wettstein, 49; and the recent critical remarks by Ra'anan S. Boustan, "The Dislocation of the Temple Vessels: Mobile Sanctity and Rabbinic Rhetorics of Space," in *Jewish Studies at the Crossroads of Anthropology and History: Tradition, Authority, Diaspora*, ed. Boustan, Oren Kosansky, and Marina Rustow (Philadelphia: University of Pennsylvania Press, 2011), 135–37.

48. Isaac ben Meir Latif, letter, in David, *Reflections on Jewish Jerusalem*, 93.

49. Joseph of Montagna, letter, in David, *Reflections on Jewish Jerusalem*, 116.

50. Letter by Obadiah's anonymous student, in David, *Reflections on Jewish Jerusalem*, 151–52. On the strained relations between European Christian pilgrims and the Levantine population, see also Chareyron, *Pilgrims to Jerusalem*, 75.

51. Letter by Obadiah's student, in David, *Reflections on Jewish Jerusalem*, 164.

52. Hebrew text in Hacker, "R. Elija of Massa Lombarda," 259; the same text can be found in David, *Reflections on Jewish Jerusalem*, 70.

53. Israel Ashkenazi, letter, 112.

54. Basola, *In Zion and Jerusalem*, Hebrew part, 15. I am slightly editing the translation in ibid., English part, 62–63. See also the largely positive statements of Italian Jewish travelers (discussed in Chapter 2 in this volume) concerning business opportunities in the Levant.

55. See b. Shabbat 11a: "Raba bar Meḥasia said in the name of Rav Hama bar Goria who said in the name of Rav: '[Let one be] under Ishmael rather than under a Gentile [*nokhri*]'"; variant readings of this passage have "Edom," meaning a Christian, instead of *nokhri*.

56. Israel Ashkenazi, letter, 117. On this passage, see also Bernard Septimus, "Better Under Edom than Under Ishmael: The History of a Saying" (Hebrew), *Zion* 47 (1982): 103–11. A revised English version of this essay has been published as "Hispano-Jewish Views of Christendom and Islam," in *In Iberia and Beyond: Hispanic Jews Between Cultures, Proceedings of a Symposium to Mark the 500th Anniversary of the Expulsion of Spanish Jewry*, ed. Bernard D. Cooperman (Newark: University of Delaware Press, 1998), 43–65. As Septimus argues, the version according to which it was "better under Edom than under Ishmael" originated in thirteenth-century Iberia when the Almohad invasion caused Jews to move to the Christian north (ibid., 45–46); apparently, this reading persisted in the Sephardic tradition even after the expulsion from Christian Spain.

57. Israel Ashkenazi, letter, 117.

58. Ibid.

59. For the Judeo-Arabic text and its Hebrew versions, see *Iggerot ha-RaMBaM*, ed. Yiṣḥaq Shailat, 3rd ed. (Jerusalem: Hoṣa'at Shailat, 1995), 1:108–9 (Judeo-Arabic), 160–61 (Hebrew translation). See also the related comments by M. Cohen, *Under Crescent and Cross*, 198–99. R. Israel's advice that a Jew should behave "as if he were blind and does not hear, and like a mute does not open his mouth" seems to be another allusion to Maimonides, who, in this context, quotes Ps. 38:14, "I am like a deaf man, unhearing, like a dumb man who cannot speak up."

60. Israel Ashkenazi, letter, 117.

61. Ibid., 117–18.

62. He actually speaks of a "green" turban, but this color would have been reserved for descendants of the Prophet Muhammad. In Christian Europe, the Fourth Lateran Council (1215) decreed that Jews had to wear distinctive clothing. While other European countries implemented distinguishing signs much earlier, it was only in the fifteenth century that a yellow badge became required for Jews in the northern Italian states; see Ariel Toaff, "The Jewish Badge in Italy during the Fifteenth Century," in *Die Juden in ihrer mittelalterlichen Umwelt*, ed. Alfred Ebenbauer and Klaus Zatloukal (Vienna: Bohlau, 1991), 275–80; idem, *Love, Work, and Death: Jewish Life in Medieval Umbria*, trans. Judith Landry (London: Littman Library of Jewish Civilization, 1996), 173–79; Flora Cassen, "From Iconic O to Yellow Hat: Anti-Jewish Distinctive Signs in Renaissance Italy," in *Fashioning Jews: Clothing, Culture, and Commerce*, Studies in Jewish Civilization 24, ed. Leonard J. Greenspoon (Omaha, Neb.: Purdue University Press, 2013), 29–48.

63. Israel Ashkenazi, letter, 117–18. These higher tolls caused Meshullam of Volterra to disguise himself as a Muslim when traveling through the Levant; see Chapter 3 in this volume. However, foreign Christian merchants had to pay twice as much at toll stations as Jews paid.

64. Petaḥyah, *Sibbuv*, 1:8.

65. Ibid., 1:23.

66. On the connection between this pietist movement and Petaḥyah of Regensburg, see Chapter 1 in this volume.

67. Petaḥyah, *Sibbuv*, 1:24.

68. Ibid., 1:8. In a thematically related passage (ibid., 1:24), *Sibbuv* makes contradictory statements: first, the text equally claims that the Jews of Baghdad have no *ḥazzan*; but a few lines down, it says that the prayer is divided between several *ḥazzanim*. This contradiction may be a question of the pilgrim account's complex process of editing and transmission; see Chapter 1 in this volume.

69. Petaḥyah, *Sibbuv*, 1:5–6.

70. Thus in the received version of Alḥarizi, *Taḥkemoni*, ed. Toporovsky, 224 (Gate 24); cf. *Taḥkemoni*, ed. Yahalom and Katsumata, 368 (*maqāma* 30).

71. Alḥarizi, *Taḥkemoni*, ed. Toporovsky, 224 (Gate 24); cf. *Taḥkemoni*, ed. Yahalom and Katsumata, 369 (*maqāma* 30B), apparatus to line 46.

72. Alḥarizi, *Taḥkemoni*, ed. Toporovsky, 224 (Gate 24); cf. *Taḥkemoni*, ed. Yahalom and Katsumata, 368 (*maqāma* 30). I am quoting here the translation by Segal, *Book of Taḥkemoni*, 215, which is based on the received version. In his Judeo-Arabic *Book of Pearls*, Alḥarizi similarly laments the intellectual decline of Baghdadi Jewry. Yet his major complaint there seems to be about a lack of generosity among the community's notables; see Alḥarizi, *Kitāb al-Durar*, 206 (Judeo-Arabic), 116* (English translation).

73. Cf. Ruth Langer, *To Worship God Properly: Tensions Between Liturgical Customs and Halakhah in Judaism* (Cincinnati: Hebrew Union College Press, 2005), 130–33. Though aware of the account's satirical character, Langer tends to read this *maqāma* as a source for the history of Hebrew liturgical poetry—an approach that seems questionable.

74. See Joachim Yeshaya, "Your Poems Are Like Rotten Figs: Judah al-Harīzī on Poets and Poetry in the Muslim East," in *Egypt and Syria in the Fatimid, Ayyubid and Mamluk Eras*, ed. U. Vermeulen and K. D'Hulster (Leuven: Peeters, 2010), 6:143–52.

75. Obadiah, Letter A, *From Italy to Jerusalem*, 70.

76. Ibid., 50.

77. Cf. Horowitz, "Towards a Social History," 142–43, who offers more examples for a lack of stringency among Italian Jews concerning non-kosher wine—to which the following may be added: according to Moses Basola, the Jews of Famagusta, who were of Sicilian origin, also consumed forbidden wine; see *In Zion and Jerusalem*, Hebrew part, 11; English part, 53.

78. Obadiah, Letter A, *From Italy to Jerusalem*, 55. Wine produced or touched by non-Jews is not to be consumed, according to common halakhic opinion, as it is considered wine used for idolatrous purposes (*yayn nesekh*). Unlike Christians, Muslims were not thought to be idolaters by most rabbinic authorities; even so, Maimonides prohibited in his responsa the consumption of wine produced or touched by Muslims (though a Jew may gain financial profit from such wine); *Teshuvot ha-RaMBaM*, ed. Joshua Blau, 2nd ed. (Jerusalem: Reuben Mas, 1986), 2:515–16, no. 269.

79. Israel Ashkenazi, letter, 110.

80. Ibid., 111.

81. Among the *taqqanot* (legal enactments) of the Jerusalem community listed by Basola in the appendix to his travelogue is a prohibition to summon a coreligionist to a non-Jewish court; see Basola, *In Zion and Jerusalem*, Hebrew part, 29; English part, 100. On this topic, see Jacob Katz, *Exclusiveness and Tolerance: Studies in Jewish-Gentile Relations in Medieval and Modern Times* (Oxford: Oxford University Press, 1961; reprint, Springfield, N.J.: Behrman, 1992), 51–55.

82. See A. Cohen, *Jewish Life Under Islam*, 115–19; the documents discussed by Cohen are later than 1522, the year that R. Israel wrote his letter.

83. Israel Ashkenazi, letter, 112.

84. The first official survey of Jerusalem's population, taken in 1525–26, indicates a relatively high number of Jews (1,194), i.e., about 20 percent of the overall population (5,607). This may reflect the immigration of Sephardic Jews but could also be a result of exceptional circumstances in the years after the Ottoman conquest. In the next survey, taken in 1538, Jews numbered only 15 percent; see Amnon Cohen and Bernard Lewis, *Population and Revenue in the Towns of Palestine in the Sixteenth Century* (Princeton, N.J.: Princeton University Press, 1978), 92–94; and A. Cohen, *Jewish Life Under Islam*, 14, 16.

85. Israel Ashkenazi, letter, 110–11. Moses Basola, who also wrote his travel account shortly after the Ottoman conquest of Palestine, appears to have had a particular awareness of Jewish diversity. Everywhere he visits, he mentions the ethnic background of the Jews living there, whether Sicilian, Sephardic, *maghrebi*, or *musta'rab* (he calls them *moriscos*); see Basola, *In Zion and Jerusalem*, Hebrew part, 13, 15, 18, 22, 24; English part, 58–59, 62, 71, 82, 87.

86. Israel Ashkenazi, letter, 116.

87. Ibid., 115.

88. Ibid., 113.

89. *Massa' meshullam*, 48. Obadiah likewise states that Near Eastern Jews removed their shoes when entering a synagogue or house, yet without implying any judgment with his description; see Letter A, *From Italy to Jerusalem*, 50.

90. Petaḥyah, *Sibbuv*, 1:24.

91. *Massa' meshullam*, 75.

92. Ibid., 47. In the eighteenth century, Azulai (Ḥida), a Sephardic rabbi from Ottoman Hebron, similarly ridiculed the way Tunisian Jews ate with their hands; see his *Ma'gal Ṭov*, 55; and Lehmann, "Levantinos," 17–18. In declaring table manners markers of cultural difference, Azulai may be revealing the extent to which he had adopted Italian cultural norms during his previous sojourn in Livorno.

93. *Massa' meshullam*, 55.

94. Therefore I have already cited parts of this passage in Chapter 7.

95. *Massa' meshullam*, 57–58. For an understanding of the term *nagid* as "lord," "leader," or "ruler," see 1 Kings 1:35; and Isa. 55:4.

96. Cf. my earlier discussion of this passage, "Lofty Caliphs," 86–88.

97. Obadiah, Letter A, *From Italy to Jerusalem*, 48–49. On this episode, see also Elliott Horowitz, "Sabbath Delights: Toward a Social History," in *Sabbath: Idea, History, Reality* (Hebrew), ed. Gerald L. Blidstein (Beersheva: Ben-Gurion University Press, 2004), 132–33.

98. Obadiah, Letter A, *From Italy to Jerusalem*, 49.

99. See Chapter 1 in this volume.

CHAPTER 9. KARAITES, SAMARITANS, AND LOST TRIBES

1. Obadiah, Letter A, *From Italy to Jerusalem*, 54.

2. Ibid., 55–56. On Karaite Bible interpretation, see Meira Polliack, "Major Trends in Karaite Biblical Exegesis in the Tenth and Eleventh Centuries," in *Karaite Judaism: A Guide to Its History and Literary Sources* (Leiden: Brill, 2003), 363–413.

3. The sociability between Rabbanite and Karaite Jews is best documented for the Fatimid Empire, where members of both communities jointly contributed to communal causes, formed business partnerships, and even intermarried; see Marina Rustow, "Karaites Real and Imagined: Three Cases of Jewish Heresy," *Past and Present* 197 (2007): 41–43.

4. The pre-calculated calendar, as it is in use in rabbinic Judaism today, goes back to ninth-century Babylonian yeshivot and was accepted by most rabbinic communities by the end of the eleventh century; see Sacha Stern, *Calendar and Community: A History of the Jewish Calendar, Second Century BCE–Tenth Century CE* (Oxford: Oxford University Press, 2001), 191–210.

5. See Zvi Ankori, *Karaites in Byzantium: The Formative Years, 970–1100* (New York: Columbia University Press, 1959), 292–95; and Rustow, *Heresy and the Politics of Community*, 57–65; Rustow, "The Qaraites as Sect: The Tyranny of a Construct," in *Sects and Sectarianism in Jewish History*, ed. Sacha Stern (Leiden: Brill, 2011), 169–76.

6. Obadiah, Letter A, *From Italy to Jerusalem*, 54–55. Despite Obadiah's claim to the contrary, calendar differences among the Karaite diaspora are known to have caused conflict; see Ankori, *Karaites in Byzantium*, 322–34.

7. Obadiah, Letter A, *From Italy to Jerusalem*, 55.

8. Ibid., 56. The fact that Karaite practice (and thought) over time accommodated to Rabbanite culture in many other ways is a much broader phenomenon that goes beyond the framework of the present discussion.

9. On the medieval history of the Samaritans, see Benjamin Z. Kedar, "The Frankish Period," in *The Samaritans*, ed. Alan D. Crown (Tübingen: Mohr Siebeck, 1989), 82–94. On early modern times, see Robert T. Anderson, "Samaritan History During the Renaissance," in *The Samaritans*, ed. Crown, 95–112. On references to Samaritans in Christian travel literature, see Nathan Schur, "The Samaritans, as Described in Christian Itineraries (14th–18th Centuries)," *Palestine Exploration Quarterly* 118 (1986): 144–55. However, Schur largely reads these accounts at face value and is mainly interested in the statistical data that they provide for the Samaritan community.

10. *Itinerary of Benjamin*, Hebrew part, 31. A textual variant has two hundred Karaites.

11. Ibid., 28–29.

12. Ibid., 21.

13. Ibid., 22. Asher's text speaks here of one hundred Samaritans only; *Itinerary of Rabbi Benjamin*, vol. 1, Hebrew part, 32.

14. *Itinerary of Benjamin*, ed. Adler, Hebrew part, 22.

15. Since the Hasmoneans destroyed the Samaritan Temple in the second century BCE, no proper sacrifices could be brought—a problem that Judaism similarly faced after 70 CE. For a detailed description of Samaritan ritual, see Reinhard Pummer, "Samaritan Rituals and Customs," in *The Samaritans*, ed. Crown, 678–81.

16. The Samaritan Torah adds to the Decalogue an additional commandment giving directions to build an altar on Mount Gerizim as the only legitimate place of sacrificial worship. For a translation of the Samaritan text and a detailed discussion of its variants from the Masoretic tradition, see Robert T. Anderson and Terry Giles, *Tradition Kept: The Literature of the Samaritans* (Peabody, Mass.: Hendrickson, 2005), 34–42.

17. Here I am emendating the text according to Asher's edition, *Itinerary of Rabbi Benjamin*, vol. 1, Hebrew part, 33; MS London (Adler's base text) reads *alef*, which makes no sense, given the continuation of the paragraph.

18. *Itinerary of Benjamin*, ed. Adler, Hebrew part, 22.

19. See Rudolf Macuch, "Samaritan Languages," in *The Samaritans*, ed. Crown, 543–46.

20. In Meshullam's view, the Samaritan script "lacks" even more letters, namely, *alef, heh, 'ayin, ṣadeh, bet, and ḥet*; *Massa' meshullam*, 57.

21. On the concept of *zekhut avot*, see Ephraim E. Urbach, *The Sages: Their Concepts and Beliefs*, trans. Israel Abrahams, 2 vols. (Jerusalem: Magnes, 1975), 1:496–508.

22. Obadiah, Letter A, *From Italy to Jerusalem*, 54. Cf. Maimonides' Commentary on m. Yadayim 4:5, in *Mishnah 'im perush rabbenu moshe ben maymon*, ed. Yosef Qāfiḥ, vol. 6, bk. 2 (Jerusalem: Mosad ha-Rav Kook, 1969), 716.

23. Basola, *In Zion and Jerusalem*, Hebrew part, 33; English part, 110.

24. De' Rossi, *Me'or 'enayim*, 394; *Light of the Eyes*, 666–67. In yet another sign of the topic's relevance to contemporaneous scholarship, Guillaume Postel, Basola's Christian friend, also reproduced the Samaritan alphabet (as well as a shekel coin) in his *Linguarum duodecim characteribus differentum alphabetum* (Paris: Lescuyer, 1538), 25 (no pagination). On this topic, see further Joanna Weinberg, "Azariah de' Rossi and LXX Traditions," *Italia* 5 (1985): 26–28.

25. Obadiah, Letter A, *From Italy to Jerusalem*, 54. In assuming that the Samaritan Pentateuch substitutes *ashima* for the tetragrammaton, Obadiah seems to depend on Abraham Ibn Ezra, who, in his introduction to the Book of Esther, claims that Gen. 1:1 reads in the Samaritan version "in the beginning, *ashima* created . . ."; see the critical edition by Mariano Gómez Aranda, *Dos commentarios de Abraham Ibn Ezra al libro de Ester* (Madrid: Consejo superior de investigaciones científicas, 2007), Hebrew part, 6*.

26. The "people of Kut" (*kutiim*) worshiped Nergal, according to 2 Kings 17:30, while it was the "people of Ḥamat" who created an image of Ashima.

27. Obadiah, Letter A, *From Italy to Jerusalem*, 54.

28. *Massa' meshullam*, 57. The reputed dove image is mentioned in both the Jerusalem and Babylonian Talmud; see y. 'Avodah Zarah 5:4(3) (44d), and b. Ḥullin 6a. According to Jarl Fossum, this claim originated as another way of accusing the Samaritans of worshiping Ashima—whom Fossum identifies with the Syrian Goddess that had a dove as an attribute; see Fossum, "Samaritan Demiurgical Traditions and the Alleged Dove Cult of the Samaritans," in *Studies in Gnosticism and Hellenistic Religions: Presented to Gilles Quispel on the Occasion of His 65th Birthday*, ed. R. van den Broek and Maarten J. Vermaseren (Leiden: Brill, 1981), 147–50. Basola likewise speaks of a dove image that was kept by the Samaritans on Mount Gerizim; *In Zion and Jerusalem*, Hebrew part, 18; English part, 71. So do some Christian travelers; see Schur, "Samaritans," 149.

29. Obadiah, Letter A, *From Italy to Jerusalem*, 54. Oscillating between inclusiveness and exclusiveness toward Samaritans, Obadiah seems to echo the variety of opinions expressed in classical rabbinic literature regarding the other group; see Moshe Lavee, "The Samaritan May Be Included: Another Look at the Samaritan in Talmudic Literature," in *Samaritans: Past and Present: Current Studies*, ed. Menachem Mor and Friedrich V. Reiterer (Berlin: de Gruyter, 2010), 147–73.

30. Obadiah, Letter A, *From Italy to Jerusalem*, 56.

31. Ibid.

32. Ibid.

33. See Ashtor, *Toledot ha-yehudim*, 2:106–10.

34. Obadiah, Letter A, *From Italy to Jerusalem*, 54.

35. Ibid.

36. The belief in the future reunification of the Israelite tribes was based on Ezek. 37:15–22; on this topic, see further David B. Ruderman, "Hope Against Hope: Jewish and Christian Messianic Expectations in the Late Middle Ages," in *Essential Papers on Jewish Culture in Renaissance and Baroque Italy*, ed. Ruderman (New York: New York University Press, 1992), 299–323.

37. It appears as though R. Elijah of La Massa had been sent to Egypt on a mission to obtain more information on this topic. This emerges from a letter sent in 1433 by the Jewish community of Bologna to the *nagid* 'Amram, who was then the highest Jewish official in Cairo; see Hacker, "R. Elija of Massa Lombarda," 245–49, 253–56.

38. For the literary range of this lore, see the sources surveyed by Neubauer, "Where Are the Ten Tribes?" including extensive English translations and paraphrases. Neubauer published the Hebrew sources in a separate article, "'Inyene 'aseret ha-shevaṭim." On the quest for the Lost Tribes through centuries and cultures, see the account by Zvi Ben-Dor Benite, *The Ten Lost Tribes: A World History* (Oxford: Oxford University Press, 2009).

39. Similar questions have been raised by Giuseppe Veltri, "'The East' in the Story of the Lost Tribes: Creation of Geographical and Political Utopias," in *Creation and Re-Creation in Jewish Thought: Festschrift in Honor of Joseph Dan*, ed. Rachel Elior and Peter Schäfer (Tübingen: Mohr Siebeck, 2005), 249–69 (reprint in Veltri, *Renaissance Philosophy in Jewish Garb* [Leiden: Brill, 2009], 144–68).

40. Epstein, *Eldad ha-Dani*, 25, §8.

41. Ibid., §9. Textual variants locate the tribes' place of residence at a distance of six months "from Jerusalem"; see Epstein's comments, ibid., 32 n. 13.

42. *Itinerary of Benjamin*, Hebrew part, 46.

43. An oasis and caravan town named Tema is mentioned in Isa. 21:14 and Job 6:19.

44. See *EI*, s.vv. "Khaybar" and "Taymā'in."

45. *Itinerary of Benjamin*, Hebrew part, 48.

46. Both biblical accounts, 2 Kings 17:6 and 1 Chron. 5:26, seem to confuse the geographic details. In any case, Ḥabur (this spelling) is a river—a tributary of the Euphrates—as well as an ancient district of the same name. For a disquisition on the facts and fantasies about the northern Israelites' fate, see Pamela Barmash, "At the Nexus of History and Memory: The Ten Lost Tribes," *AJS Review* 29 (2005): 207 36.

47. To confuse matters, *Massa'ot* also includes a tradition according to which four of the Lost Tribes live in the "mountains of Nishapur" (*Itinerary of Benjamin*, Hebrew part, 54), i.e., in Persia, and hence much nearer to the localities mentioned in 2 Kings 17:6. That said, the contradicting traditions concerning the tribes' location are somewhat reconciled by Benjamin's further claim that the tribes wage war from Persia up to "the land of Cush by way of the desert" (ibid.).

48. *Itinerary of Benjamin*, Hebrew part, 47.

49. Ibid., 46.

50. Ibid., 47.

51. Cf. Alanna E. Cooper, "Conceptualizing Diaspora: Tales of Jewish Travelers in Search of the Lost Tribes," *AJS Review* 30 (2006): 106–8.

52. *Story of David Hareuveni*, 7.

53. That even educated Italians were willing to believe Re'uveni's claims may appear less of a surprise, given that the Bolognese Ludovico di Varthema, who had traveled to the Hijāz in 1504, reported 5,000 Jews ("who go naked") living in the vicinity of Medina; *Itinerario di Ludovico de Varthema*, ed. Paolo Giudici (Milan: Istituto Editoriale Italiano, 1956),

58–59; for a translation (based on a different edition), see *The Travels of Ludovico di Varthema*, trans. John W. Jones, ed. George P. Badger (London: Hakluyt Society, 1863), 22–24.

54. Obadiah, Letter A, *From Italy to Jerusalem*, 76. According to 2 Kings 10:15–28 and Jer. 35:6–10, the Rechabites live in tents—which puts them into a desert setting. It seems to have been the divine promise that "there shall never cease to be a man of the line of Jonadab son of Rechab standing before Me" (Jer. 35:19) that gave rise to legends about their continued existence.

55. Obadiah, Letter A, *From Italy to Jerusalem*, 76.

56. On the Sambatyon lore and its origins in late antiquity, see Daniel Stein Kokin, "Toward the Source of the Sambatyon: Shabbat Discourse and the Origins of the Sabbatical River Legend," *AJS Review* 37 (2013): 1–28.

57. Obadiah, Letter A, *From Italy to Jerusalem*, 74.

58. See Robert Silverberg, *The Realm of Prester John* (Garden City, N.Y.: Doubleday, 1972), 163–64, 179–80; and the sources compiled by Ulrich Knefelkamp, *Die Suche nach dem Reich des Priesterkönigs Johannes: Dargestellt anhand von Reiseberichten und anderen ethnographischen Quellen des 12. bis 17. Jahrhunderts* (Gelsenkirchen: Andreas Müller, 1986), 74–85. During the age of exploration, the attraction of this phantasm was so great that it continued to appear in travel literature, geographical treatises, and notes that accompany maps; see ibid., 101–5.

59. Obadiah, Letter A, *From Italy to Jerusalem*, 74–75.

60. In fact, the Lost Tribes traditions have frequently moved between Jewish and Christian agencies, and their various versions are clearly conversant with one another; see Perry, "Imaginary War," 10.

61. Israel Ashkenazi, letter, 119.

62. On the Portuguese expeditions and their relation to the tribes' "discovery" in India or Ethiopia, see Gross, "Ten Tribes," 13–15, 32–33; and Fabrizio Lelli, "Messianic Expectations and Portuguese Geographical Discoveries: Yohanan Alemanno's Renaissance Curiosity," *Cadernos de Estudos Sefarditas* 7 (2007): 163–84. As Lelli shows, Yoḥanan Alemanno (1435–after 1506) compiled in his notebook all sorts of information about the tribes, going back to earlier sources as well as recent Portuguese expeditions.

63. Israel Ashkenazi, letter, 120.

64. On the concepts of exile and domicile in Jewish literature, see, in this volume, Introduction n. 5.

CHAPTER 10. ASSASSINS, BLACKS, AND VEILED WOMEN

1. *Itinerary of Benjamin*, Hebrew part, 18–19. The earliest Christian source to mention the Assassins is William of Tyre's Latin chronicle of the Crusades (written between 1170 and 1184); see Bernard Lewis, "The Sources for the History of the Syrian Assassins," *Speculum* 27 (1952): 475–89.

2. On the Nizaris, see Farhad Daftary, *The Ismāʿīlīs: Their History and Doctrines*

(Cambridge: Cambridge University Press, 1990), 324–548; and idem, *A Short History of the Ismailis: Traditions of a Muslim Community* (Edinburgh: Edinburgh University Press, 1998), 106–8, 120–58.

3. *Itinerary of Benjamin*, Hebrew part, 19. During Benjamin's time, Raymond III (1152–75) reigned as count of Tripoli.

4. See Farhad Daftary, *The Assassin Legends: Myths of the Isma'ilis* (London: I. B. Tauris, 1994), 88–128.

5. *Itinerary of Benjamin*, Hebrew part, 19.

6. Marco Polo, *Travels*, 70–73 (chap. 23); cf. the Mandeville author's version of this legend, *Book of John Mandeville*, 164–65 (chap. 30).

7. Ibn Jubayr, *Riḥla*, 255; and *Travels of Ibn Jubayr*, 264. On Rāshid al-Dīn Sinān, see Daftary, *Ismā'īlīs*, 396–402.

8. Ibn Jubayr, *Riḥla*, 255; and *Travels of Ibn Jubayr*, 264.

9. *Itinerary of Benjamin*, Hebrew part, 20.

10. On the origins of the Druze that are related to the reign of the Fatimid caliph al-Ḥākim (996–1021), see *EI*, s.v. "al-Ḥākim Bi-Amr Allāh"; Daftary, *Ismā'īlīs*, 195–200; Daftary, *Short History of the Ismailis*, 100–101; and Kais M. Firro, *A History of the Druze* (Leiden: Brill, 1992), 8–17. On their practice of dissimulation (*taqiyya*) and secrecy, see Firro, *History of the Druze*, 20–23.

11. *Itinerary of Benjamin*, Hebrew part, 20.

12. See Philip. K. Hitti, *The Origins of the Druze People and Religion* (New York: Columbia University Press, 1928), 52–53. Hitti (ibid., 49) also refers to the widespread claim that the Druze worship a calf.

13. See Campbell, *The Witness and the Other World*, 110. According to Marco Polo, the men in the northern Chinese city of Kamul are glad to offer their women to strangers (*Travels*, 87–88); he offers similarly tall tales about the people of the western Chinese province of Kaindu (ibid., 175). In Tibet, women who had frequent premarital sex with strangers are the most sought-after (ibid., 172).

14. *Itinerary of Benjamin*, Hebrew part, 20.

15. Ibid., 54; cf. ibid., 56.

16. Ibid., 55.

17. Ibid., 57.

18. See Paul Schwarz, *Iran im Mittelalter nach den arabischen Geographen* (Hildesheim: Georg Olms, 1969), 779; and *EI*, s.v. "al-Rayy."

19. See Bosworth, "Political and Dynastic History," 147–53; and Michal Biran, "True to Their Ways: Why the Qara Khitai Did Not Convert to Islam," in *Mongols, Turks, and Others: Eurasian Nomads and the Sedentary World*, ed. Reuven Amitai and Michal Biran (Leiden: Brill, 2005), 175–99. On the Oghuz rebellion against Sanjar bin Malik Shāh, see Biran, *The Empire of the Qara Khitai in Eurasian History: Between China and the Islamic World* (Cambridge: Cambridge University Press, 2005), 51. The Seljuk sultan is mentioned by Benjamin in his account of Daniel's tomb at Shūsh; see Chapter 5 in this volume.

20. *Itinerary of Benjamin*, Hebrew part, 54–55.

21. On these traditions and their classical roots, see Rudolf Wittkower, "Marvels of the East: A Study in the History of Monsters," *Journal of the Warburg and Courtauld Institutes* 5 (1942): 159–97; and Campbell, *The Witness and the Other World*, 47–75.

22. See John B. Friedman, *The Monstrous Races in Medieval Art and Thought* (Cambridge, Mass.: Harvard University Press, 1981), 1–25; Higgins, *Writing East*, 143–46; and Marina Münkler, "Experiencing Strangeness: Monstrous Peoples on the Edge of the Earth as Depicted on Medieval Mappae Mundi," *Medieval History Journal* 5, no. 2 (2002): 195–222.

23. I am here citing the Old French version as translated by Higgins, *Book of John Mandeville*, 124.

24. Petaḥyah, *Sibbuv*, 1:2.

25. I am quoting the translation by Israel J. Kazis, *The Book of the Gests of Alexander of Macedon* (Cambridge, Mass.: Mediaeval Academy of America, 1962), 114.

26. *Itinerary of Benjamin*, Hebrew part, 55.

27. Epstein, *Eldad ha-Dani*, 23.

28. On the etymological history, see Abraham Melamed, *The Image of the Black in Jewish Culture: A History of the Other*, trans. Betty Sigler Rozen (London: Routledge Curzon, 2003), 53–59.

29. As Adam Silverstein points out, the motif of the shipwrecked protagonist who miraculously escapes cannibals also occurs in Sindbad's tales (known to a Western audience through the *Tales from the Thousand and One Nights*); see Silverstein, "From Markets to Marvels: Jews on the Maritime Route to China ca. 850–ca. 950 CE," *Journal of Jewish Studies* 58 (2007): 100.

30. *Story of David Hareuveni*, 7.

31. Ibid., 8.

32. See S. Hillelson, "David Reubeni, an Early Visitor to Sennar," *Sudan Notes and Records* 16 (1933): 55–66, including a translation of the relevant passages from Re'uveni's travel tale; see also Hillelson, "David Reubeni's Route in Africa," *JQR* 28 (1937/38): 289–91. However, Hillelson's attempt to establish the credibility of Re'uveni's references to Sudan and Nubia seems naïve, given the novelistic character of the story. On King 'Amārah of the Funj, see *EI*, s.v. "Fundj."

33. *Story of David Hareuveni*, 8.

34. Ibid.

35. Ibid., 9. Here I read *nemarim*, "tigers," instead of *nemalim*, "ants."

36. Obviously, Eldad's and Re'uveni's narratives offer no evidence for the historical practice of anthropophagy. Here is not the place to discuss whether some accounts of cannibalism were based on actual observation or whether all of them should be considered mere projections of European fantasies; for a summary discussion of these questions, see Philip P. Boucher, *Cannibal Encounters: Europeans and Island Caribs, 1492–1763* (Baltimore: Johns Hopkins University Press, 1992; reprint, 2009), 6–8. On travel literature's role in the European construction of the savage cannibal, see Frank Lestringant, *Cannibals: The Discovery and Representation of the Cannibal from Columbus to Jules Verne*, trans. Rosemarie Morris (Berkeley: University of California Press, 1997); and Ted Motohashi, "The

Discourse of Cannibalism in Early Modern Travel Writing," in *Travel Writing and Empire*, ed. Clark, 84–99. On cannibalism as placed in Ethiopia, see Natalie Zemon Davis, *Trickster Travels: A Sixteenth-Century Muslim Between Worlds* (New York: Hill and Wang, 2006), 263.

37. *Itinerary of Benjamin*, Hebrew part, 62.

38. On the representation of blacks in premodern Jewish literature, see Melamed, *Image of the Black*, 62–121; David M. Goldenberg, *The Curse of Ham: Race and Slavery in Early Judaism, Christianity, and Islam* (Princeton, N.J.: Princeton University Press, 2003), 46–75; and Jonathan Schorsch, *Jews and Blacks in the Early Modern World* (New York: Cambridge University Press, 2003).

39. *Itinerary of Benjamin*, Hebrew part, 62.

40. See Bernard Lewis, *Race and Slavery in the Middle East: An Historical Inquiry* (New York: Oxford University Press, 1990). Muslim authors voice similar prejudices and stereotypes about black Africans; see ibid., 52–53. On Jewish slave ownership as reflected in Genizah documents, see Goitein, *Mediterranean Society*, 1:130–47; and Miriam Frenkel, "Slavery in Medieval Jewish Society Under Islam: A Gendered Perspective," in *Männlich und weiblich schuf Er sie: Studien zur Genderkonstruktion und zum Eherecht in den Mittelmeerreligionen*, ed. Matthias Morgenstern, Christian Boudignon, and Christiane Tietz (Göttingen: Vandenhoek and Ruprecht, 2011), 249–58.

41. *Itinerary of Benjamin*, Hebrew part, 62.

42. Ibid. On medieval theories about the climate's impact on human bodies and behavior, see Irina Metzler, "Perceptions of Hot Climate in Medieval Cosmography and Travel Literature," *Reading Medieval Studies* 23 (1997): 69–105 (reprint in *Medieval Ethnographies: European Perceptions of the World Beyond*, ed. Joan-Pau Rubiés [Farnham, U.K.: Ashgate, 2009], chap. 14); Robert Bartlett, "Medieval Concepts of Race and Ethnicity," *Journal of Medieval and Early Modern Studies* 31 (2001): 39–56; and Akbari, *Idols in the East*, 36–37, 140–47. Among Jewish authors, Judah Halevi, Maimonides, and Isaac Abarbanel made explicit use of such theories; see Melamed, *Image of the Black*, 137–39, 140–44, 181.

43. *Itinerary of Benjamin*, Hebrew part, 58. The association of Cush with India may be rooted in Esther 1:1; 8:9.

44. *Itinerary of Benjamin*, Hebrew part, 59.

45. Similar observations have been made by Akbari, *Idols in the East*, 147, with respect to medieval Christian sources: "Within the categories of climate theory, the Jews occupy a peculiar place. Belonging nowhere yet found everywhere, they inhabit no fixed climate. . . . As a result, texts that characterize the attributes of nations based upon their native climates face a conundrum in describing the Jews."

46. Hezser, *Jewish Travel*, 389–405, deals with Jewish women's mobility in late antiquity; certain gender-related restrictions discussed by Hezser in this context apply to later periods as well. Documents deposited in the Cairo Genizah show that medieval Jewish women (from the Islamic realm) traveled frequently and for a variety of reasons, including marriage, family visits, and pilgrimage; see Goitein, *Mediterranean Society*, 3:336–41; and Judith R. Baskin, "Mobility and Marriage in Two Medieval Jewish Societies," *Jewish History* 22 (2008): 223–43.

47. The letter by R. Joseph of Montagna (1480) is one of the few documents included in this study that refer to Jewish women pilgrims in some detail. The author mentions a Ms. Rebecca, who apparently had joined him and his wife on the journey from Italy to the Holy Land. Rebecca's health deteriorated en route. The travelers were forced to leave her in Damascus under the care of another woman, whom the letter merely refers to as Ms. Gerushah (lit., "the divorcée"); Hebrew text in David, *Reflections on Jewish Jerusalem*, 114.

48. Christian women travelers, such as Egeria, who left accounts of their journeys to the Holy Land belonged to a small elite of highly educated nuns. On Egeria, see Chapter 1 in this volume. On the widespread exclusion of women from the Hebrew "republic of letters," see Tova Rosen, *Unveiling Eve: Reading Gender in Medieval Hebrew Literature* (Philadelphia: University of Pennsylvania Press, 2003), 1–5.

49. The term "male gaze" was coined by Laura Mulvey in the context of film studies; see Mulvey, "Visual Pleasure and Narrative Cinema," *Screen* 16, no. 3 (1975): 6–18 (reprint in *Issues in Feminist Film Criticism*, ed. Patricia Erens [Bloomington: Indiana University Press, 1990], 28–40). For an example of how this interpretative model has been adopted by contemporary travel theory, see Geraldine Murphy, "Olaudah Equiano, Accidental Tourist," *Eighteenth-Century Studies* 27 (1994): 554.

50. Judah Halevi, *Dīwān*, 1:113; Yahalom, *Yehuda Halevi*, 148. Cf. Scheindlin, *Song of the Distant Dove*, 125.

51. Petaḥyah, *Sibbuv*, 1:23.

52. Ibid., 1:8.

53. As noted in Chapter 1 in this volume, Petaḥyah's account appears to have been edited by Judah he-Ḥasid, who is well-known for his radical socioreligious views; see Marcus, *Piety and Society*, 55–65.

54. On the *ga'on* Samuel ben 'Eli, see Chapter 6 in this volume.

55. Petaḥyah, *Sibbuv*, 1:9–10.

56. E.g., see m. Sotah 3:4; *Sifre Devarim* 46, in the edition by Louis Finkelstein, *Siphre ad Deuteronomium* (Berlin: Jüdischer Kulturbund, 1939; reprint, New York: Jewish Theological Seminary, 1969 and 1993), 106. On Torah-learned women during the classical rabbinic period, see Tal Ilan, "Women in Jewish Life and Law," in *The Cambridge History of Judaism*, vol. 4, *The Late Roman-Rabbinic Period*, ed. Steven Katz (Cambridge: Cambridge University Press, 2006), 643–44.

57. See Goitein, *Mediterranean Society*, 2:183–85.

58. On Jewish women teachers, see ibid., 2:185; 3:345–46, 355–56; and Judith R. Baskin, "The Education of Jewish Women in the Lands of Medieval Islam and Christendom" (Hebrew), *Pe'amim* 82 (2000): 36–37.

59. Based on a eulogy composed for the *ga'on*'s daughter, Avraham Grossman surmises that she was a learned woman; Grossman, *Pious and Rebellious: Jewish Women in Europe in the Middle Ages* (Hebrew) (Jerusalem: Zalman Shazar Center, 2001), 283–84. But that does not prove that she instructed male students, as Grossman believes.

60. Petaḥyah, *Sibbuv*, 1:10. The modest woman teaching from behind a screen or curtain appears to be a literary trope that occurs in both a Christian and an Islamic cultural

context; see the examples mentioned by Judith R. Baskin, "Some Parallels in the Education of Medieval Jewish and Christian Women," *Jewish History* 5 (1991): 46; and Ruth Roded, "Women as Intellectuals and Transmitters of Knowledge in Muslim History" (Hebrew), *Pe'amim* 82 (2000): 18–19. Roded, however, seems to interpret these instances as factual accounts.

61. On such illustrations, see Amanda Wunder, "Western Travelers, Eastern Antiquities, and the Image of the Turk in Early Modern Europe," *Journal of Early Modern History* 7 (2003): 115–17. On costume books, see Bronwen Wilson, "*Foggie diverse di vestire de' Turchi*: Turkish Costume Illustration and Cultural Translation," *Journal of Middle Eastern Studies* 37 (2007): 97–140.

62. *Massa' meshullam*, 46. A similar description of Alexandrian women can be found in the pilgrimage account by Symon Semeonis, the fourteenth-century Irish friar; see his *Itinerarium*, 60–61 (Latin text and English translation).

63. On the dress of Muslim women during the time under consideration, see Mayer, *Mamluke Costume*, 70–72.

64. See Jacqueline Herald, *Renaissance Dress in Italy: 1400–1500* (London: Bell and Hyman, 1981), 50; and Carole Collier Frick, *Dressing Renaissance Florence: Families, Fortunes, and Fine Clothing* (Baltimore: Johns Hopkins University Press, 2002), 154, 157.

65. On the varieties of veils (*miqna'a, qinā', niqāb*) known from Mamluk times, see Mayer, *Mamluke Costume*, 73; and Gillian Eastwood, "A Medieval Face-Veil from Egypt," *Costume* 17 (1983): 33–38 (reprint in *Patterns of Everyday Life: The Formation of the Classical Islamic World*, ed. David Waines [Aldershot, U.K.: Ashgate, 2002], 10:233–38).

66. *Massa' meshullam*, 69. Under the Mamluks, Jewish pilgrims had to pray at one of the compound's outer walls; see Chapter 4 in this volume. On the veiling of Jewish women as reflected in sources from the Cairo Genizah, see Mordechai A. Friedman, "Halakha as Evidence of Sexual Life Among Jews in Muslim Countries in the Middle Ages" (Hebrew), *Pe'amim* 45 (1990): 89–107. For the fifteenth and sixteenth centuries, see Ruth Lamdan, *A Separate People: Jewish Women in Palestine, Syria and Egypt in the Sixteenth Century* (Leiden: Brill, 2000), 101–4; and idem, "Communal Regulations as a Source for Jewish Women's Lives in the Ottoman Empire," *The Muslim World* 95 (2005): 252.

67. Hebrew text in David, *Reflections on Jewish Jerusalem*, 166. In an apparent echo of crusader terminology (*Templum Salomonis*), Hebrew travel accounts commonly call the al-Aqṣā Mosque the "Temple of Solomon," or his *bet midrash* (study house); see Chapter 4 in this volume.

68. Similar to Jewish men who donned yellow turbans, Jewish women, in the street, were required to wear a yellow cloth on their head (Mayer, *Mamluk Costume*, 67). But in order to be admitted to a mosque, these women would not have done so. Possibly, these rules were neglected with respect to women, anyway.

69. Here I am taking inspiration from Meyda Yeğenoğlu's analysis of Western representations of the veil; see Yeğenoğlu, *Colonial Fantasies: Towards a Feminist Reading of Orientalism* (Cambridge: Cambridge University Press, 1998), 39–67.

70. Israel Ashkenazi, letter, 116.

71. *Massa' meshullam*, 46.

72. Ibid., 55. While others perceived Oriental garb as a form of cross-dressing, R. Israel Ashkenazi describes it as a kind of unisex dress: "The garb of men and women is almost identical"; Israel Ashkenazi, letter, 116. He may be referring to the gowns worn by both men and women.

73. On Florentine men's legwear, see Herald, *Renaissance Dress*, 211; and Francesco Adorno, "Taste and Dignity in Dress," in *The World of Renaissance Florence*, ed. Adorno, trans. Walter Darwell (Florence: Giunti, 1999), 73–75.

74. Mayer, *Mamluke Costume*, 69–70.

75. Santo Brasca, *Viaggio in Terra Santa (1480) con l'itinerario di Gabriele Capodilista (1458)*, ed. Anna L. Momigliano Lepschy (Milan: Longanesi, 1966), 69. I am quoting the translation by Chareyron, *Pilgrims to Jerusalem*, 113. In a similar vein, Symon Semeonis compares the appearance of veiled women to "the fictitious devils which are customary in clerics' games"; *Itinerarium*, 60; trans. Hoade, *Western Pilgrims*, 20.

76. *Massa' meshullam*, 55.

77. Ibid.

78. See Chapter 2 in this volume.

79. According to Mamluk jurists, husbands were obliged to feed and *clothe* their wives but not to give them money. However, real life often differed from legal theory, for Mamluk women seem to have increasingly demanded monetary support from their husbands; see Yossef Rapoport, "The Monetization of Marriage," in *Marriage, Money and Divorce in Medieval Islamic Society* (Cambridge: Cambridge University Press, 2005), 52–53.

80. *Massa' meshullam*, 46. Meshullam repeats these statements almost verbatim, ibid., 75–76.

81. Ibid., 76.

82. Ibid. Von Harff, *Pilgerfahrt*, 94, similarly contends that Cairene women could easily file for divorce on grounds of nonmaintenance. This claim seems to have been a widespread rumor among European travelers to the Levant, most of whom were (Catholic) Christians and therefore abhorred the idea of divorce—especially when initiated by women.

83. *Massa' meshullam*, 46. Adorno, by contrast, knows that a Muslim man could not legally marry more than four women. But he might take additional concubines, if his financial means allowed him to do so. Even so, Adorno, too, claims that there are "many" Muslim men "who have ten, twenty, or thirty concubines"; *Itinéraire d'Anselme Adorno*, 84–85. On the Western stereotype of Islam as a licentious religion, see Daniel, *Islam and the West*, 158–63.

84. On polygamy in Jewish communities of the Levant, see Lamdan, *A Separate People*, 139–56.

85. *Massa' meshullam*, 46; similarly, ibid., 76. "To spill semen in vain" seems to be an allusion to the biblical story about Onan and Tamar (Gen. 38:9).

CONCLUSION

1. Petaḥyah, *Sibbuv*, 1:24.

2. See Chapters 3 and 10 in this volume.

3. See Fernand Braudel, *The Mediterranean and the Mediterranean World in the Age of Philip II*, trans. Siân Reynolds, 2 vols. (New York: Harper and Row: 1972–73). Here is not the place to engage with the burgeoning field of Mediterranean studies that developed in the aftermath of Braudel's seminal work. Still, directly relevant to the topic under discussion are two chapters by Horden and Purcell, titled "Connectivity" and "Territories of Grace," in *The Corrupting Sea*, 123–72, 403–60. For further bibliography, see Eric R. Dursteler's insightful review, "On Bazaars and Battlefields: Recent Scholarship on Mediterranean Cultural Contacts," *Journal of Early Modern History* 15 (2011): 413–34.

4. On the distinctive waist belt worn by Levantine Christians, see Chapter 7 in this volume.

5. Janet L. Abu-Lughod, *Before European Hegemony: The World System AD 1250–1350* (New York: Oxford University Press, 1989), 137; Abu-Lughod does not refer to Benjamin in this context. One factor that contributed to expanding European commerce with the Levant was the growth of medieval cities; see ibid., 43–134; and Robert Bartlett, *The Making of Europe: Conquest, Colonization and Cultural Change 950–1350* (Princeton, N.J.: Princeton University Press, 1993), 167–96.

6. Abu-Lughod, *Before European Hegemony*, 137; the third route described by Abu-Lughod was "the northern route from Constantinople across the land mass of Central Asia," but it is not reflected in the sources discussed here.

7. Incidentally, nineteenth-century Jewish scholarship was characterized by a similar tendency to idealize the medieval Jewish experience under Islam against a dark-painted background of Christian enmity toward Jews. Mark Cohen, who describes this historiographical paradigm as the "myth of an interfaith utopia," addresses the political agenda of Jewish *Wissenschaft* historians, such as Heinrich Graetz; see M. Cohen, *Under Crescent and Cross*, 3–5. On the romanticization of Sephardic history by German Jewish scholars of the post-Enlightenment era, see also Ismar Schorsch, "The Myth of Sephardic Supremacy," *Leo Baeck Institute Yearbook* 34 (1989): 47–66.

8. See Chapter 6 in this volume. The effects of the Almoravid and Almohad invasions into southern Iberia are not reflected in *Massaʿot.*

9. Ning Wang, *Tourism and Modernity: A Sociological Analysis* (Amsterdam: Pergamon, 2000), 19. See also Wang's following statement that tourism serves "to consolidate the everyday order at home"; ibid., 20.

10. See Introduction, n. 45, in this volume.

11. See Chapters 3, 7, and 10 in this volume.

12. See Chapter 7 in this volume.

Selected Bibliography

Whenever publications in Hebrew or Arabic include a title in a European language, I have cited it while indicating the original language; otherwise I have transliterated the title.

ʿAbd al-Laṭīf al-Baghdādī. *The Eastern Key: Kitāb al-ifādah wa-ʾl-iʿtibār*, ed. and trans. Kamal H. Zand, John A. Videan, and E. Videan. London: George Allen and Unwin, 1965.

Abu-Lughod, Janet L. *Before European Hegemony: The World System AD 1250–1350*. New York: Oxford University Press, 1989.

Adler, Elkan N., ed. *Jewish Travellers*. London: Routledge, 1930. Reprinted as *Jewish Travellers in the Middle Ages: 19 Firsthand Accounts*. New York: Dover, 1987.

Adorno, Anselmo, and Giovanni Adorno. *Itinéraire d'Anselme Adorno en Terre Sainte (1470–1471)*, ed. and trans. Jacques Heers and Georgette de Groer. Paris: Éditions du Centre national de la recherche scientifique, 1978.

Akbari, Suzanne Conklin. "The Diversity of Mankind in the Book of John Mandeville." In *Eastward Bound: Travel and Travellers, 1050–1550*, ed. Rosamund Allen, 156–76. Manchester: Manchester University Press, 2004.

———. "From Due East to True North: Orientalism and Orientation." In *The Postcolonial Middle Ages*, ed. Jeffrey J. Cohen, 19–34. New York: St. Martin's, 2000.

———. *Idols in the East: European Representations of Islam and the Orient, 1100–1450*. Ithaca, N.Y.: Cornell University Press, 2009.

Alfonso, Esperanza. *Islamic Culture Through Jewish Eyes: Al-Andalus from the Tenth to the Twelfth Century*. London: Routledge, 2008.

Alḥarizi, Judah. *The Book of Taḥkemoni: Jewish Tales from Medieval Spain*, trans. David S. Segal. London: Littman Library of Jewish Civilization, 2001.

———. *Kitāb al-Durar: A Book in Praise of God and the Israelite Communities*. Judeo-Arabic and Hebrew, ed. Joshua Blau, Paul Fenton, and Joseph Yahalom. Jerusalem: Ben-Zvi Institute, 2009.

———. *Taḥkemoni*, ed. Yisra'el Toporovsky. Tel Aviv: Maḥbarot la-Sifrut and Mosad ha-Rav Kook, 1952.

———. *The Taḥkemoni of Judah al-Ḥarizi*, trans. Victor E. Reichert. 2 vols. Jerusalem: R. H. Cohen's, 1965–73.

———. *Taḥkemoni: Or the Tales of Heman the Ezraḥite.* Hebrew, ed. Joseph Yahalom and Naoya Katsumata. Jerusalem: Ben-Zvi Institute, 2010.

———. *The Wanderings of Judah Alḥarizi: Five Accounts of His Travels.* Hebrew, ed. Joseph Yahalom and Joshua Blau. Jerusalem: Ben-Zvi Institute, 2002.

Altschul, Nadia R. "Postcolonialism and the Study of the Middle Ages." *History Compass* 6 (2008): 588–606.

Arbel, Benjamin. "The Port Towns of the Levant in Sixteenth-Century Travel Literature." In *Mediterranean Urban Culture 1400–1700*, ed. Alexander Cowan, 151–64. Exeter: University of Exeter, 2000.

Arce, Augustín. "The Location of David's Tomb According to Benjamin of Tudela's Itinerary." Hebrew. In *Jerusalem in the Middle Ages: Selected Papers.* Hebrew, ed. Benjamin Z. Kedar, 112–21. Jerusalem: Ben-Zvi Institute, 1979.

Ashtor (Strauss), Eliyahu. *Toledot ha-yehudim be-miṣrayim ve-suriyah taḥat shilṭon ha-mamlukim.* 3 vols. Jerusalem: Mosad ha-Rav Kook, 1944–70.

———. "Venezia e il Pellegrinaggio in Terrasanta nel Basso Medioevo." *Archivio Storico Italiano* 143 (1985): 197–223.

———. "The Volume of Levantine Trade in the Later Middle Ages (1370–1498)." *Journal of European Economic History* 4 (1975): 573–612. Reprint in Eliyahu Ashtor. *Studies on the Levantine Trade in the Middle Ages*, chap. 10. London: Variorum, 1978.

Assaf, Simḥah. "Toṣ'ot ereṣ yisra'el." In *Yerushalayim: Qoveṣ ha-ḥevrah ha-'ivrit le-ḥaqirat ereṣ yisra'el ve-'atiqoteha, muqdash le-zekher r. avraham moshe lunṣ*, ed. A. L. Sukenik and Y. Peres, 51–66. Jerusalem: Bet Misḥar and Derom, 1928. Reprint in Simḥah Assaf. *Texts and Studies in Jewish History.* Hebrew, 74–90. Jerusalem: Mosad ha-Rav Kook,1946.

Aune, M. G. "Early Modern European Travel Writing After Orientalism." *Journal for Early Modern Cultural Studies* 5, no. 2 (2005): 120–38.

Azulai, Ḥayim J. D. (Ḥida). *Sefer ma'gal ṭov ha-shalem*, ed. Aharon Freiman. Jerusalem: Meqiṣe Nirdamim, 1934.

Balard, Michel. "The Urban Landscape of Rhodes as Perceived by Fourteenth- and Fifteenth-Century Travellers." In *Intercultural Contacts in the Medieval Mediterranean: Studies in Honour of David Jacoby*, ed. Benjamin Arbel, 24–34. London: Frank Cass, 1996.

Barbour, Richmond. *Before Orientalism: London's Theatre of the East, 1576–1626.* Cambridge: Cambridge University Press, 2003.

Barmash, Pamela. "At the Nexus of History and Memory: The Ten Lost Tribes." *AJS Review* 29 (2005): 207–36.

Bartlett, Robert. *The Making of Europe: Conquest, Colonization and Cultural Change 950–1350.* Princeton, N.J.: Princeton University Press, 1993.

———. "Medieval Concepts of Race and Ethnicity." *Journal of Medieval and Early Modern Studies* 31 (2001): 39–56.

Baskin, Judith R. "Mobility and Marriage in Two Medieval Jewish Societies." *Jewish History* 22 (2008): 223–43.

Basola, Moses. *In Zion and Jerusalem: The Itinerary of Rabbi Moses Basola (1521–1523)*. Hebrew, ed. Abraham David and trans. Dena Ordan. Jerusalem: Bar-Ilan University Press, 1999.

Beckingham, C. W. "The Riḥla: Fact or Fiction?" In *Golden Roads: Migration, Pilgrimage and Travel*, ed. Ian R. Netton, 86–94. Richmond, U.K.: Curzon, 1993.

Benite, Zvi Ben-Dor. *The Ten Lost Tribes: A World History*. Oxford: Oxford University Press, 2009.

Benjamin of Tudela. *The Itinerary of Benjamin of Tudela*, ed. and trans. Marcus N. Adler. London: H. Frowde, 1907.

———. *The Itinerary of Benjamin of Tudela: Travels in the Middle Ages*. Introductions by Michael A. Signer, Marcus N. Adler, and A. Asher. Malibu: Joseph Simon / Pangloss, 1983. Reprint, 1993.

———. *The Itinerary of Rabbi Benjamin of Tudela*, ed. and trans. Adolf Asher. 2 vols. New York: Hakesheth, 1840–41.

———. *Die Reisebeschreibungen des R. Benjamin von Tudela: Nach drei Handschriften, aus dem 13. und 14. Jahrhundert stammend und ältern Druckwerken*, ed. and trans. Lazar (El'azar) Grünhut. Frankfurt am Main: J. Kauffmann, 1903.

———. *Syrien und Palaestina nach dem Reisebericht des Benjamin von Tudela*, trans. Hans Peter Rüger. Wiesbaden: Harrassowitz, 1990.

Benmelech, Moti. "History, Politics, and Messianism: David Ha-Reuveni's Origin and Mission." *AJS Review* 35 (2011): 35–60.

Bennett, Josephine W. *The Rediscovery of Sir John Mandeville*. New York: Modern Language Association, 1954.

Ben-Shalom, Ram. "The Unwritten Travel Journal to the East of Joseph ibn Caspi: Images and Orientalism." Hebrew. *Pe'amim* 124 (2011): 7–51.

Benvenisti, Meron. *Sacred Landscape: The Buried History of the Holy Land Since 1948*. Berkeley: University of California Press, 2000.

Ben-Ya'aqov, Avraham. *Qevarim qedoshim be-vavel*. Jerusalem: Mosad ha-Rav Kook, 1973.

Berger, Pamela. "Jewish-Muslim Veneration at Pilgrimage Places in the Holy Land." *Religion and the Arts* 15 (2011): 1–60.

Berliner, Abraham. "Mikhtav me-r. shmu'el bar shimshon." *Oṣar Ṭov* (1876): 35–38.

Bhabha, Homi K. "Of Mimicry and Man: The Ambivalence of Colonial Discourse." *October* 28 (1984): 125–33. Reprint in Homi Bhabha. *The Location of Culture*, 121–31. Abingdon, U.K.: Routledge, 1994; reprint, 2005.

Blau, Joshua, and Joseph Yahalom. "Kitab Aldurar: An Unpublished Work by Judah Alharizi." Hebrew. *Pe'amim* 108 (2006): 19–51.

Borm, Jan. "Defining Travel: On the Travel Book, Travel Writing and Terminology." In *Perspectives on Travel Writing*, ed. Glen Hooper and Tim Youngs, 13–26. Aldershot, U.K.: Ashgate, 2004.

Bosworth, Clifford E. "The Political and Dynastic History of the Iranian World (AD 1000–1217)." In *The Cambridge History of Iran*. Vol. 5, *The Saljuq and Mongol Periods*, ed. J. A. Boyle, 1–202. Cambridge: Cambridge University Press, 1968.

Boustan, Ra'anan S. "The Dislocation of the Temple Vessels: Mobile Sanctity and Rabbinic Rhetorics of Space." In *Jewish Studies at the Crossroads of Anthropology and History: Tradition, Authority, Diaspora*, ed. Ra'anan S. Boustan, Oren Kosansky, and Marina Rustow, 135–46. Philadelphia: University of Pennsylvania Press, 2011.

———. "The Spoils of the Jerusalem Temple at Rome and Constantinople: Jewish Counter-Geography in a Christianizing Empire." In *Antiquity in Antiquity: Jewish and Christian Pasts in the Greco-Roman World*, ed. Gregg Gardner and Kevin L. Osterloh, 327–72. Tübingen: Mohr Siebeck, 2008.

Boyarin, Daniel, and Jonathan Boyarin. "Diaspora: Generation and the Ground of Identity." *Critical Inquiry* 19 (1993): 693–725.

Boyarin, Jonathan, and Daniel Boyarin. *Powers of Diaspora: Two Essays on the Relevance of Jewish Culture*. Minneapolis: University of Minnesota Press, 2002.

Brasca, Santo. *Viaggio in Terrasanta (1480) con l'itinerario di Gabriele Capodilista (1458)*, ed. Anna L. Momigliano Lepschy. Milan: Longanesi, 1966.

Braudel, Fernand. *The Mediterranean and the Mediterranean World in the Age of Philip II*, trans. Siân Reynolds. 2 vols. New York: Harper and Row, 1972–73.

Brentjes, Sonja. "Early Modern Western Travellers in the Middle East and Their Reports About the Sciences." In *Sciences, techniques et instruments dans le monde iranien (Xe–XIXe siècle): Actes du colloque tenu à l'Université de Téhéran, 7–9 June 1998*, ed. N. Pourjavadi and Z. Vesel, 379–420. Louvain: Peeters, 2004. Reprint in Sonja Brentjes. *Travellers from Europe in the Ottoman and Safavid Empires: 16–17th Centuries*, chap. 5. Farnham, U.K.: Ashgate, 2010.

Brody, Robert. *The Geonim of Babylonia and the Shaping of Medieval Jewish Culture*. New Haven, Conn.: Yale University Press, 1998.

Busbecq, Ogier Ghislen de. *The Turkish Letters of Ogier Ghiselin de Busbecq, Imperial Ambassador at Constantinople, 1554–1562*, trans. Edward S. Forster. Oxford: Clarendon, 1927. Reprint, London: Sickle Moon, 2001.

Busse, Heribert. *Chalif und Grosskönig: Die Buyiden im Iraq (945–1055)*. Beirut: Franz Steiner, 1969.

———. "Die Patriarchengräber in Hebron und der Islam." *ZDPV* 114 (1998): 71–94.

———. "Vom Felsendom zum Templum Domini." In *Das Heilige Land im Mittelalter: Begegnungsraum zwischen Orient und Okzident*, ed. Wolfdietrich Fischer and Jürgen Schneider, 19–32. Neustadt an der Aisch: Degener, 1982.

Campbell, Mary Baine. "Travel Writing and Its Theory." In *The Cambridge Companion to Travel Writing*, ed. Peter Hulme and Tim Youngs, 261–78. Cambridge: Cambridge University Press, 2002.

———. *The Witness and the Other World: Exotic European Travel Writing, 400–1600*. Ithaca, N.Y.: Cornell University Press, 1988.

Canaan, Tewfik. *Mohammedan Saints and Sanctuaries in Palestine*. London: Luzac, 1927. Reprint, Jerusalem: Ariel, 1980.

Carmoly, Eliakim, trans. *Itinéraires de la Terre Sainte traduit de l'hébreu*. Brussels: A. Vandale, 1847.

Casale Pilgrim. *The Casale Pilgrim: A Sixteenth-Century Illustrated Guide to the Holy Places*, ed. and trans. Cecil Roth. London: Soncino, 1929.

Casola, Pietro. *Canon Pietro Casola's Pilgrimage to Jerusalem in the Year 1494*, trans. M. Margaret Newett. Manchester: Manchester University Press, 1907.

———. *Viaggio a Gerusalemme di Pietro Casola*, ed. Anna Paoletti. Alessandria: Edizioni dell'Orso, 2001.

Casson, Lionel. *Travel in the Ancient World*. London: George Allen and Unwin, 1974. Reprint, Baltimore: Johns Hopkins University Press, 1994.

Champagne, Marie Thérèse, and Ra'anan S. Boustan. "Walking in the Shadows of the Past: The Jewish Experience of Rome in the Twelfth Century." *Medieval Encounters* 17 (2011): 464–94.

Chareyron, Nicole. *Pilgrims to Jerusalem in the Middle Ages*, trans. Donald W. Wilson. New York: Columbia University Press, 2005.

Cippi Hebraici: Sive Hebraeorum, tam veterum, Prophetarum, Patriarcharum, quam recentiorum, Tannaeorum, Amoraeorum, Rabbinorum monumenta, ed. and trans. Johann Heinrich Hottinger. 2nd ed. Heidelberg: Samuel Broun, 1662.

Clark, Steve, ed. *Travel Writing and Empire: Postcolonial Theory in Transit*. London: Zed, 1999.

Cohen, Amnon. *Jewish Life Under Islam: Jerusalem in the Sixteenth Century*. Cambridge, Mass.: Harvard University Press, 1984.

———. *Ottoman Documents on the Jewish Community of Jerusalem in the Sixteenth Century*. Hebrew. Jerusalem: Ben-Zvi Institute, 1976.

———, and Bernard Lewis. *Population and Revenue in the Towns of Palestine in the Sixteenth Century*. Princeton, N.J.: Princeton University Press, 1978.

Cohen, Amnon, and Elisheva Simon-Pikali. *Jews in the Moslem Court: Society, Economy and Communal Organization in the Sixteenth Century: Documents from Ottoman Jerusalem*. Hebrew. Jerusalem: Ben-Zvi Institute, 1993.

Cohen, Mark R. *Under Crescent and Cross: The Jews in the Middle Ages*. Princeton, N.J.: Princeton University Press, 1994.

Constable, Olivia R. *Housing the Stranger in the Mediterranean World: Lodging, Trade, and Travel in Late Antiquity and the Middle Ages*. Cambridge: Cambridge University Press, 2003.

Crown, Alan D., ed. *The Samaritans*. Tübingen: Mohr Siebeck, 1989.

Cuffel, Alexandra. "Call and Response: European Jewish Emigration to Egypt and Palestine in the Middle Ages." *JQR* 90 (1999): 61–102.

———. "From Practice to Polemic: Shared Saints and Festivals as 'Women's Religion' in the Medieval Mediterranean." *Bulletin of the School of Oriental and African Studies* 68 (2005): 401–19.

Daniel, Norman. *Islam and the West: The Making of an Image*. 2nd ed. Oxford: Oneworld, 1993.

David, Abraham. "Benjamin ben Jonah of Tudela." *Encyclopedia of Jews in the Islamic World*, ed. Norman A. Stillman. Leiden: Brill Online, 2013. http://referenceworks.

brillonline.com/entries/encyclopedia-of-jews-in-the-islamic-world/benjamin-ben-jonah-of-tudela-COM_0003980 (accessed June 26, 2013).

———. "A Letter from Jerusalem from the Early Ottoman Period in Eretz Yisrael." Hebrew. In *Jerusalem in the Early Ottoman Period.* Hebrew, ed. Amnon Cohen, 39–60. Jerusalem: Ben-Zvi Institute, 1979.

———. "The Letter of R. Israel Ashkenazi of Jerusalem to R. Abraham of Perugia." Hebrew. *Alei Sefer* 16 (1990): 95–122.

———. "New Sources Describing Travel by Sea from Venice to the Orient and Eretz Israel (Palestine) in the Fifteenth to the Seventeenth Centuries." Hebrew. *Shalem* 6 (1992): 319–33.

———, ed. *Reflections on Jewish Jerusalem: An Anthology of Hebrew Letters from the Mamluk Age.* Hebrew. Tel Aviv: Hakibbutz Hameuchad, 2003.

———. "Sibbuv r. petaḥyah me-regensburg be-nusaḥ ḥadash." *Qoveṣ 'al Yad* 13 (1996): 237–69.

———. *To Come to the Land: Immigration and Settlement in Sixteenth-Century Eretz-Israel,* trans. Dena Ordan. Tuscaloosa: University of Alabama Press, 1999.

Davis, Natalie Zemon. *Trickster Travels: A Sixteenth-Century Muslim Between Worlds.* New York: Hill and Wang, 2006.

Delano-Smith, Catherine. "The Intelligent Pilgrim: Maps and Medieval Pilgrimage to the Holy Land." In *Eastward Bound: Travel and Travellers, 1050–1550,* ed. Rosamund Allen, 107–29. Manchester: Manchester University Press, 2004.

Dietz, Maribel. *Wandering Monks, Virgins, and Pilgrims: Ascetic Travel in the Mediterranean World, A.D. 300–800.* University Park: Pennsylvania State University Press, 2005.

Drory, Joseph. "Jerusalem During the Mamluk Period (1250–1517)." *Jerusalem Cathedra* 1 (1981): 190–213.

Dunn, Ross E. *The Adventures of Ibn Battuta: A Muslim Traveler of the 14th Century.* 2nd ed. Berkeley: University of California Press, 2005.

Dursteler, Eric R. "On Bazaars and Battlefields: Recent Scholarship on Mediterranean Cultural Contacts." *Journal of Early Modern History* 15 (2011): 413–34.

Eade, John, and Michael J. Sallnow, eds. *Contesting the Sacred: The Anthropology of Christian Pilgrimage.* London: Routledge, 1991.

Egeria. *Egeria's Travels to the Holy Land,* trans. John Wilkinson. Jerusalem: Ariel, 1981.

Eisenstein, Judah D., ed. *Ozar Massaoth: A Collection of Itineraries by Jewish Travelers to Palestine, Syria, Egypt, and Other Countries.* Hebrew. New York: Or Yom, 1926. Reprint, Tel Aviv, 1969.

Eliav-Feldon, Miriam. "Invented Identities: Credulity in the Age of Prophecy and Exploration." *Journal of Early Modern History* 3 (1999): 203–32.

Elleh ha-massa'ot. In *Die Reisebeschreibungen des R. Benjamin von Tudela: Nach drei Handschriften, aus dem 13. und 14. Jahrhundert stammend und ältern Druckwerken.* Hebrew, ed. Lazar (El'azar) Grünhut, 145–64. Frankfurt am Main: J. Kauffmann, 1903.

Elsner, John (Jaś). "Hagiographic Geography: Travel and Allegory in the *Life of Apollonius of Tyana.*" *Journal of Hellenic Studies* 117 (1997): 22–37.

Epstein, Abraham. *Eldad ha-Dani: Seine Berichte über die X Stämme und deren Ritus in verschiedenen Versionen nach Handschriften und alten Drucken.* Pressburg (Bratislava): Adolf Alkalay, 1891.

Euben, Roxanne L. *Journeys to the Other Shore: Muslim and Western Travelers in Search of Knowledge.* Princeton, N.J.: Princeton University Press, 2006.

Fabri, Felix. *Fratris Felicis Fabri Evagatorium in Terrae Sanctae, Arabiae et Aegypti peregrinatio*, ed. Conrad D. Hassler. 3 vols. Stuttgart: Literarischer Verein, 1843–49.

———. *The Wanderings of Felix Fabri*, trans. Aubrey Stewart. 4 vols. London: Palestine Pilgrims' Text Society, 1893–96.

Fattal, Antoine. *Le statut légal des non-Musulmans en pays d'Islam.* 2nd ed. Beirut: Dar el-Machreq, 1995.

French, Dorothea R. "Pilgrimage, Ritual, and Power Strategies: Felix Fabri's Pilgrimage to Jerusalem in 1483." In *Pilgrims and Travelers to the Holy Land.* Studies in Jewish Civilization 7, ed. Bryan F. Le Beau and Menachem Mor, 169–79. Omaha, Neb.: Creighton University Press, 1996.

Frenkel, Miriam. *"The Compassionate and Benevolent": The Leading Elite in the Jewish Community of Alexandria in the Middle Ages.* Hebrew. Jerusalem, Ben-Zvi Institute, 2006.

———. "'Yated ha-tequ'ah be-makom ne'eman': Poliṭiqah ve-koaḥ ba-'aliyah le-regel ha-yehudit l-irushalayim ba-tequfah ha-faṭimit." In *Ut Videant et Contigant: Essays on Pilgrimage and Sacred Space in Honor of Ora Limor.* Hebrew, ed. Yitzhak Hen and Iris Shagrir, 135–56. Raanana: Open University of Israel, 2011.

Friedman, John B. *The Monstrous Races in Medieval Art and Thought.* Cambridge, Mass.: Harvard University Press, 1981.

Games, Alison. *The Web of Empire: English Cosmopolitans in an Age of Expansion.* Oxford: Oxford University Press, 2008.

Gaunt, Simon. *Marco Polo's Le Devisement du Monde: Narrative Voice, Language and Diversity.* Cambridge, U.K.: D. S. Brewer, 2013.

Gellens, Sam I. "The Search for Knowledge in Medieval Muslim Societies: A Comparative Approach." In *Muslim Travelers: Pilgrimage, Migration and the Religious Imagination*, ed. Dale F. Eickelman and James Piscatori, 50–65. Berkeley: University of California Press, 1990.

Genette, Gérard. *Paratexts: Threshold of Interpretation*, trans. Jane E. Lewis. Cambridge: Cambridge University Press, 1997.

George-Tvrtković, Rita. *A Christian Pilgrim in Medieval Iraq: Riccoldo da Montecroce's Encounter with Islam.* Turnhout: Brepols, 2012.

Gil, Moshe. "Aliya and Pilgrimage in the Early Arab Period (634–1009)." *Jerusalem Cathedra* 3 (1983): 163–73.

———. "The Exilarchate." In *The Jews of Medieval Islam: Community, Society, and Identity*, ed. Daniel Frank, 33–65. Leiden: Brill, 1995.

———. *A History of Palestine, 634–1099.* Cambridge: Cambridge University Press, 1992.

———. *In the Kingdom of Ishmael: Studies in Jewish History in Islamic Lands in the Early Middle Ages.* Hebrew. 4 vols. Jerusalem: Tel Aviv University, 1997.

———. "The Jewish Merchants in the Light of Eleventh-Century Geniza Documents." *Journal of the Economic and Social History of the Orient* 46 (2003): 273–319.

———. *Palestine During the First Muslim Period (634–1099).* Hebrew. 3 vols. Tel Aviv: Tel Aviv University Press, 1983.

———, and Ezra Fleischer, eds. *Yehudah Ha-Levi and His Circle: Fifty-Five Geniza Documents.* Hebrew. Jerusalem: World Union of Jewish Studies: 2001.

Gildemeister, Johann. "Die arabischen Nachrichten zur Geschichte der Harambauten." *ZDPV* 13 (1890): 1–24.

———. "Beiträge zur Palästinakunde aus arabischen Quellen." *ZDPV* 8 (1885): 117–45.

Gingras, George E. "Travel." In *Dictionary of Literary Themes and Motifs*, ed. Jean-Charles Seigneuret, 2:1292–1331. Westport, Conn.: Greenwood, 1988.

Goitein, Shlomo D. "Ba-derekh le-hishtaṭḥut ʿal qever yeḥezqel." In *Studies on the History of the Iraqi Jewry and their Culture* 1. Hebrew, ed. Shmuel Moreh, 9–18. Tel Aviv: Center for the Heritage of Iraqi Jewry, 1981.

———. *Letters of Medieval Jewish Traders.* Princeton, N.J.: Princeton University Press, 1974.

———. *A Mediterranean Society: The Jewish Communities of the Arab World as Portrayed in the Documents of the Cairo Geniza.* 6 vols. Berkeley: University of California Press, 1967–93. Reprint, 1999.

———, and Mordechai A. Friedman. *India Traders of the Middle Ages: Documents from the Cairo Geniza: India Book.* Leiden: Brill, 2008.

Goldberg, Jessica L. *Trade and Institutions in the Medieval Mediterranean: The Geniza Merchants and Their Business World.* Cambridge: Cambridge University Press, 2012.

Goldenberg, David M. *The Curse of Ham: Race and Slavery in Early Judaism, Christianity, and Islam.* Princeton, N.J.: Princeton University Press, 2003.

Goldziher, Ignaz. "Das Patriarchengrab in Hebron nach Al-ʿAbdarī." *ZDPV* 17 (1894): 115–22. Reprint in Ignaz Goldziher. *Gesammelte Schriften*, ed. Joseph Desomogyi, 3:351–58. Hildesheim: Olms, 1969.

Greenblatt, Stephen. *Marvelous Possessions: The Wonder of the New World.* Chicago: University of Chicago Press, 1991.

Gross, Avraham. "The Ten Tribes and the Kingdom of Prester John: Rumors and Investigations Before and After the Expulsion from Spain." Hebrew. *Pe'amim* 48 (1991): 5–41.

Gruen, Erich S. "Diaspora and Homeland." In *Diasporas and Exiles: Varieties of Jewish Identity*, ed. Howard Wettstein, 1–17. Berkeley: University of California Press, 2002.

Hacker, Joseph R. "R. Elijah of Massa Lombarda in Jerusalem." Hebrew. *Zion* 50 (1985): 241–63.

Halevi, Judah. *Dîwân des Abû-l-Hasan Jehuda Halevi.* Hebrew, ed. Heinrich Brody. 4 vols. Berlin: Mekiṣe Nirdamim, 1894–1930.

———. *Selected Poems of Jehuda Halevi*, ed. Heinrich Brody and trans. Nina Salaman. Philadelphia: Jewish Publication Society, 1924. Reprint, 1974.

Hamarneh, Saleh K. "The Ancient Monuments of Alexandria According to the Accounts by Medieval Arab Authors (IX–XV Century)." *Folia Orientalia* 13 (1971): 77–110.

Hamilton, Bernard. "Continental Drift: Prester John's Progress Through the Indies." In *Prester John, the Mongols and the Ten Lost Tribes*, ed. Charles F. Beckingham and Bernard Hamilton, 237–69. Aldershot, U.K.: Ashgate, 1996. Reprint in *Medieval Ethnographies: European Perceptions of the World Beyond*, ed. Joan-Pau Rubiés, chap. 4. Farnham, U.K.: Ashgate, 2009.

al-Harawī, Abū l'Ḥasan 'Alī. *Kitāb al-ishārāt ilā ma'rifat al-ziyārāt*, ed. Janine Sourdel-Thomine. Damascus: al-Ma'had al-Faransiy li-'l-Dirāsāt al-'Arabiyya, 1953.

———. *A Lonely Wayfarer's Guide to Pilgrimage: 'Alī ibn Abī Bakr al-Harawī's Kitāb al-Ishārāt ilā Ma'rifat al-Ziyārāt*, ed. and trans. Josef W. Meri. Princeton, N.J.: Darwin, 2004.

Harbsmeier, Michael. "Reisen in der Diaspora: Eigenes in der Fremde in der jüdischen Reiseliteratur des Mittelalters." *Das Mittelalter: Perspektiven mediävistischer Forschung* 3, no. 2 (1998): 63–80.

Hartog, François. *The Mirror of Herodotus: The Representation of the Other in the Writing of History*, trans. Janet Lloyd. Berkeley: University of California Press, 1988.

Hasan-Rokem, Galit. "*Homo viator et narrans judaicus*—Medieval Jewish Voices in the European Narrative of the Wandering Jew." In *Europäische Ethnologie und Folklore im internationalen Kontext: Festschrift Leander Petzoldt*, ed. Ingo Schneider, 93–102. Frankfurt am Main: Peter Lang, 1999.

Hezser, Catherine. *Jewish Travel in Antiquity.* Tübingen: Mohr Siebeck, 2011.

———. "Travel and Mobility." In *The Oxford Handbook of Jewish Daily Life in Roman Palestine*, ed. Catherine Hezser, 210–26. Oxford: Oxford University Press, 2010.

Higgins, Iain Macleod. *Writing East: The "Travels" of Sir John Mandeville.* Philadelphia: University of Pennsylvania Press, 1997.

al-Ḥimyarī, Ibn 'Abd al-Mun'im. *Kitāb al-rawḍ al-mi'ṭār fī khabar al-aqṭār*, ed. Iḥsān 'Abbās. Beirut: Librairie du Liban, 1975.

Holsinger, Bruce W. "Medieval Studies, Postcolonial Studies, and the Genealogies of Critique." *Speculum* 77 (2002): 195–227.

Horden, Peregrine, and Nicholas Purcell. *The Corrupting Sea: A Study of Mediterranean History.* Oxford: Blackwell, 2000.

Horowitz, Elliott S. "Religious Practices Among the Jews in the Late Fifteenth Century According to Letters of R. Obadia of Bertinoro." Hebrew. *Pe'amim* 37 (1988): 31–40.

———. "Speaking to the Dead: Cemetery Prayer in Medieval and Early Modern Jewry." *Journal of Jewish Thought and Philosophy* 8 (1999): 303–17.

———. "Towards a Social History of Jewish Popular Religion: Obadiah of Bertinoro on the Jews of Palermo." *Journal of Religious History* 17 (1992): 138–51.

Howard, Deborah. "The Status of the Oriental Traveller in Renaissance Venice." In *Re-Orienting the Renaissance: Cultural Exchanges with the East*, ed. Gerald MacLean, 29–49. Houndsmills, U.K.: Palgrave Macmillan, 2005.

———. *Venice and the East: The Impact of the Islamic World on Venetian Architecture, 1100–1500.* New Haven, Conn.: Yale University Press, 2000.

Howard, Donald R. *Writers and Pilgrims: Medieval Pilgrimage Narratives and Their Posterity.*

Berkeley: University of California Press, 1980. Reprint in *Pilgrimage: Jews, Christians, Moslems: Collected Essays*. Hebrew and English, ed. Ora Limor and Elchanan Reiner, 95E–136E. Raanana: Open University of Israel, 2005.

Hyde, J. Kenneth. "Navigation of the Eastern Mediterranean in the Fourteenth and Fifteenth Centuries According to Pilgrims' Books." In *Literacy and Its Uses: Studies on Late Medieval Italy*, ed. J. Kenneth Hyde and Daniel P. Waley, 87–111. Manchester: Manchester University Press, 1993.

Ibn Baṭṭūṭa, Abū 'Abd Allah Muḥammad. *The Travels of Ibn Baṭṭūṭa (A.D. 1325–54)*, trans. H. A. R. Gibb. 4 vols. Cambridge, U.K.: Hakluyt Society, 1958–94. Index by A. D. H. Bivar. Aldershot, U.K.: Ashgate, 2001.

———. *Voyages d'Ibn Batoutah*. Arabic. ed. and trans. C. Defrémery and B. R. Sanguinetti. 4 vols. Paris: Imprimerie Nationale, 1853–59. Reprint, Paris: Vincent Monteil, 1979.

Ibn Da'ud, Abraham. *Sefer ha-Qabbalah: The Book of Tradition*, ed. and trans. Gerson D. Cohen. Philadelphia: Jewish Publication Society, 1967.

Ibn Jubayr, Abū al-Ḥusayn Muḥammad. *The Travels of Ibn Jubayr.* Arabic, ed. William Wright and Michael J. de Goeje. Leiden: Brill, 1907.

———. *The Travels of Ibn Jubayr*, trans. Roland J. C. Broadhurst. London: Jonathan Cape, 1952.

Ibn Yaḥia, Gedalyah. *Shalshelet ha-qabbalah.* Jerusalem: Ha-Dorot ha-rishonim ve-qorotam, 1962.

Ilan, Zvi. *Tombs of the Righteous in the Land of Israel.* Hebrew. Jerusalem: Kanah, 1997.

Islam, Syed Manzurul. *The Ethics of Travel: From Marco Polo to Kafka.* Manchester: Manchester University Press, 1996.

al-Iṣṭakhrī, Abū Iṣḥāq Ibrahīm. *Kitāb al-masālik wa'l-mamālik: Viae Regnorum.* Bibliotheca Geographorum Arabicorum 1, ed. Michael J. de Goeje. Leiden: Brill, 1870. Reprint, 1927.

Jacobs, Andrew S. *Remains of the Jews: Holy Land and Christian Empire in Late Antiquity.* Stanford, Calif.: Stanford University Press, 2004.

Jacobs, Martin. "Alexandria oder Kairo: Die Metamorphose einer Stadtgründungslegende in der hellenistischen, islamischen und jüdischen Literatur." In *Jewish Studies Between the Disciplines—Judaistik zwischen den Disziplinen: Papers in Honor of Peter Schäfer on the Occasion of His Sixtieth Birthday*, ed. Klaus Herrmann, Margarete Schlüter, and Giuseppe Veltri, 279–98 (Leiden: Brill, 2003).

———. "David ha-Re'uveni: Ein 'zionistisches Experiment' im Kontext der europäischen Expansion des 16. Jahrhunderts?" In *An der Schwelle zur Moderne: Juden in der Renaissance*, ed. Giuseppe Veltri and Annette Winkelmann, 191–206. Leiden: Brill, 2002.

———. "Exposed to All the Currents of the Mediterranean: A Sixteenth-Century Venetian Rabbi on Muslim History." *AJS Review* 29 (2005): 33–60.

———. "An Ex-Sabbatean's Remorse? Sambari's Polemics Against Islam." *JQR* 97, no. 3 (2007): 347–78.

———. "Flying Camels and Other Exotic Species: Natural Marvels in Medieval Jewish Travel Writing." (forthcoming).

———. "From Lofty Caliphs to Uncivilized 'Orientals': Images of the Muslim in Medieval Jewish Travel Literature." *Jewish Studies Quarterly* 18 (2011): 64–90.

———. *Islamische Geschichte in jüdischen Chroniken: Hebräische Historiographie des 16. und 17. Jahrhunderts.* Tübingen: Mohr Siebeck, 2004.

———. "Joseph ha-Kohen, Paolo Giovio, and Sixteenth-Century Historiography." In *Cultural Intermediaries: Jewish Intellectuals in Early Modern Italy*, ed. David B. Ruderman and Giuseppe Veltri, 67–85. Philadelphia: University of Pennsylvania Press, 2004.

———. "The Sacred Text as a Mental Map: Biblical and Rabbinic 'Place' in Medieval Jewish Travel Writing." In *Envisioning Judaism: Studies in Honor of Peter Schäfer on the Occasion of His Seventieth Birthday*, ed. Ra'anan S. Boustan et al., 1:395–417. Tübingen: Mohr Siebeck, 2013.

Jacoby, David. "Benjamin of Tudela and His 'Book of Travels.'" In *Venezia incrocio di culture: Percezioni di viaggiatori europei e non europei a confronto: Atti del convegno Venezia, 26–27 gennaio 2006*, ed. Klaus Herbers and Felicitas Schmieder, 135–64. Rome: Centro Tedesco di Studi Veneziani, 2008.

John of Würzburg. *Descriptiones Terrae Sanctae.* In *Peregrinationes Tres: Saewulf, John of Würzburg, Theodericus.* CCCM 139, ed. R. B. C. Huygens, 79–138. Turnhout: Brepols, 1994.

Kanarfogel, Ephraim. "The *'Aliyah* of 'Three Hundred Rabbis' in 1211: Tosafist Attitudes Toward Settling in the Land of Israel." *JQR* 76 (1985): 191–215.

Kedar, Benjamin Z. "Convergences of Oriental Christian, Muslim, and Frankish Worshippers: The Case of Saydnaya." In *De Sion Exibit Lex et Verbum Domini de Hierusalem: Essays on Medieval Law, Liturgy, and Literature in Honour of Amnon Linder*, ed. Yitzhak Hen, 59–69. Turnhout: Brepols, 2001.

———. "The Jerusalem Massacre of July 1099 in the Western Historiography of the Crusades." *Crusades* 3 (2004): 15–75.

———. "The Jewish Community of Jerusalem in the Thirteenth Century." Hebrew. *Tarbiz* 41 (1972): 82–94.

———. "The Jews of Jerusalem, 1187–1267, and the Role of Naḥmanides in the Re-Establishment of Their Community." Hebrew. In *Jerusalem in the Middle Ages: Selected Papers.* Hebrew, ed. Benjamin Z. Kedar, 122–36. Jerusalem: Ben-Zvi Institute, 1979.

———. "Rashi's Map of the Land of Canaan, ca. 1100, and Its Cartographical Background." In *Cartography in Antiquity and the Middle Ages: Fresh Perspectives, New Methods*, ed. Richard J. A. Talber and Richard W. Unger, 155–68. Leiden: Brill, 2008.

Kennedy, Hugh N. *When Baghdad Ruled the Muslim World: The Rise and Fall of Islam's Greatest Dynasty.* Cambridge, Mass.: Da Capo, 2005.

al-Khaṭīb al-Baghdādī, Abū Bakr Aḥmad. *Ta'rīkh Baghdād.* Vol. 1, ed. Muṣṭafā A. 'Aṭā. Beirut: Dār al-Kutub al-'Ilmiyya, 1997.

Knefelkamp, Ulrich. *Die Suche nach dem Reich des Priesterkönigs Johannes: Dargestellt anhand von Reiseberichten und anderen ethnographischen Quellen des 12. bis 17. Jahrhunderts.* Gelsenkirchen: Andreas Müller, 1986.

ha-Kohen, Jacob ben Nathanel. *Sippur massa'ot.* In *Die Rundreise des R. Petachjah aus Regensburg.* Hebrew, ed. Lazar (El'azar) Grünhut, 1:4–14. Jerusalem: J. Kauffmann, 1905.

Kokin, Daniel Stein. "Toward the Source of the Sambatyon: Shabbat Discourse and the Origins of the Sabbatical River Legend." *AJS Review* 37 (2013): 1–28.

Lane, Frederic C. *Venetian Ships and Shipbuilders of the Renaissance.* Baltimore: Johns Hopkins University Press, 1934. Reprint, New York: Arno, 1979.

———. *Venice: A Maritime Republic.* Baltimore: Johns Hopkins University Press, 1973.

Larner, John. *Marco Polo and the Discovery of the World.* New Haven, Conn.: Yale University Press, 1999.

Lassner, Jacob. *The Topography of Baghdad in the Early Middle Ages.* Detroit: Wayne State University Press, 1970.

Lehmann, Matthias B. "Levantinos and Other Jews: Reading H. Y. D. Azulai's Travel Diary." *Journal of Jewish Studies* 13, no. 3 (2007): 1–34.

Le Strange, Guy. *Baghdad During the Abbasid Caliphate: From Contemporary Arabic and Persian Sources.* Oxford: Clarendon, 1924.

———. *The Lands of the Eastern Caliphate.* Cambridge: Cambridge University Press, 1905.

Levanon, Yosef. "The Holy Place in Jewish Piety: Evidence of Two Twelfth-Century Jewish Itineraries." *Annual of Rabbinic Judaism* 1 (1998): 103–18.

Levy-Rubin, Milka. *Non-Muslims in the Early Islamic Empire: From Surrender to Coexistence.* Cambridge: Cambridge University Press, 2011.

Lewis, Bernard. *Race and Slavery in the Middle East: An Historical Inquiry.* New York: Oxford University Press, 1990.

Limor, Ora. "Christian Sacred Space and the Jew." In *From Witness to Witchcraft: Jews and Judaism in Medieval Christian Thought*, ed. Jeremy Cohen, 55–77. Wiesbaden: Harrassowitz, 1996.

———. *Holy Land Travels: Christian Pilgrims in Late Antiquity.* Hebrew. Jerusalem: Ben-Zvi Institute, 1998.

———. "The Origins of a Tradition: King David's Tomb on Mount Zion." *Traditio* 44 (1988): 453–62.

———. "Pilgrims and Authors: Adomnán's *De locis sanctis* and Hugeburc's *Hodoeporicon Sancti Willibaldi.*" *Revue Bénédictine* 114 (2004): 253–75.

———. "Sharing Sacred Space: Holy Places in Jerusalem Between Christianity, Judaism and Islam." In *In Laudem Hierosolymitani: Studies in Crusades and Medieval Culture in Honour of Benjamin Z. Kedar*, ed. Iris Shagrir, Ronnie Ellenblum, and Jonathan Riley-Smith, 219–31. Aldershot, U.K.: Ashgate, 2007.

Lockman, Zachary. *Contending Visions of the Middle East: The History and Politics of Orientalism.* Cambridge: Cambridge University Press, 2004.

Loomba, Ania. *Colonialism/Postcolonialism.* 2nd ed. London: Routledge, 2005.

Luncz, Moshe. "Yiḥus Avot." *Ha-Me'amer* 3 (1920): 209–23.

Malkiel, David J. "Three Perspectives on Judah Halevi's Voyage to Palestine." *Mediterranean Historical Review* 25, no. 1 (2010): 1–15.

"Mandeville, John." *The Book of John Mandeville with Related Texts*, ed. and trans. Iain Macleod Higgins. Indianapolis: Hackett, 2011.

———. *Le livre des merveilles du monde*, ed. Christiane Deluze. Paris: Centre national de la recherche scientifique, 2000.

Mann, Barbara E. *Space and Place in Jewish Studies.* New Brunswick, N.J.: Rutgers University Press, 2012.

Mann, Jacob. *The Jews in Egypt and in Palestine Under the Fāṭimid Caliphs.* 2 vols. London: Oxford University Press, 1920–22. Reprint, 1969.

Marcus, Ivan G. "History, Story, and Collective Memory: Narrativity in Early Ashkenazic Culture." *Prooftexts* 10 (1990): 365–88.

———. *Piety and Society: The Jewish Pietists of Medieval Germany.* Leiden: Brill, 1981.

Margariti, Roxani E. *Aden and the Indian Ocean Trade: 150 Years in the Life of a Medieval Arabian Port.* Chapel Hill: University of North Carolina Press, 2007.

Marmorstein, Arthur. "Qivre Avot." *Measef Zion* 1 (1926): 31–39.

Matar, Nabil I. "Arab Views of Europeans, 1578–1727: The Western Mediterranean." In *Re-Orienting the Renaissance: Cultural Exchanges with the East*, ed. Gerald MacLean, 126–47. Houndsmills, U.K.: Palgrave Macmillan, 2005.

———. *In the Lands of the Christians: Arab Travel Writing in the Seventeenth Century.* New York: Routledge, 2003.

———. "Two Journeys to Seventeenth-Century Palestine." *Journal of Palestine Studies* 29, no. 4 (2000): 37–50.

Mayer, Leo A. *Mamluke Costume: A Survey.* Geneva: Albert Kundig, 1952.

Melamed, Abraham. *The Image of the Black in Jewish Culture: A History of the Other*, trans. Betty Sigler Rozen. London: Routledge Curzon, 2003.

Meri, Josef W. "Aspects of Baraka (Blessings) and Ritual Devotion Among Medieval Muslims and Jews." *Medieval Encounters* 5 (1999): 46–69.

———. *The Cult of Saints Among Muslims and Jews in Medieval Syria.* Oxford: Oxford University Press, 2002.

———. "The Etiquette of Devotion in the Islamic Cult of Saints." In *The Cult of Saints in Late Antiquity and the Middle Ages: Essays on the Contribution of Peter Brown*, ed. James Howard-Johnston and Paul A. Hayward, 263–86. Oxford: Oxford University Press, 1999. Reprint in *Pilgrimage: Jews, Christians, Moslems: Collected Essays.* Hebrew and English, ed. Ora Limor and Elchanan Reiner, 45E–68E. Raanana: Open University of Israel, 2005.

Meshullam of Volterra. *Massa' meshullam me-volṭera be-ereṣ yisra'el*, ed. Avraham Ya'ari. Jerusalem: Bialik Institute, 1949.

———. *Viaggio in Terra d'Israele*, trans. Alessandra Veronese. Rimini: Luisè, 1989.

———. *Von der Toskana in den Orient: Ein Renaissance-Kaufmann auf Reisen*, trans. Daniel Jütte. Göttingen: Vandenhoek and Ruprecht, 2012.

Metzler, Irina. "Perceptions of Hot Climate in Medieval Cosmography and Travel Literature." *Reading Medieval Studies* 23 (1997): 69–105. Reprint in *Medieval Ethnographies: European Perceptions of the World Beyond*, ed. Joan-Pau Rubiés, chap. 14. Farnham, U.K.: Ashgate, 2009.

Michele of Figline. *Da Figline a Gerusalemme: Viaggio del prete Michele in Egitto e in Terrasanta (1489–1490)*, ed. Marina Montesano. Rome: Viella, 2010.

Müller, David H. *Die Recensionen und Versionen des Eldad had-Dânî.* Denkschriften der

Kaiserlichen Akademie der Wissenschaften in Wien, Philosophisch-Historische Classe 41. Vienna: Tempsky, 1892.

Münkler, Marina. "Experiencing Strangeness: Monstrous Peoples on the Edge of the Earth as Depicted on Medieval Mappae Mundi." *Medieval History Journal* 5, no. 2 (2002): 195–222.

al-Muqaddasī, Muḥammad bin Aḥmad. *Descriptio imperii Moslemici.* Arabic. Bibliotheca Geographorum Arabicorum 3, ed. Michael J. de Goeje. 2nd ed. Leiden: Brill, 1906.

Naḥmanides, Moses (Ramban). *Kitve rabbenu moshe ben naḥman*, ed. Ḥayim (Charles) Chavel. 2 vols. Jerusalem: Mosad ha-Rav Kook, 1963–64. Reprint, 1982.

———. *Writings and Discourses*, trans. Charles B. Chavel. 2 vols. New York: Shilo, 1978.

Nathan the Babylonian. *Sippur.* In *Mediaeval Jewish Chronicles and Chronological Notes, Edited from Printed Books and Manuscripts.* Hebrew, ed. Adolf Neubauer, 2:77–88. Oxford: Clarendon, 1887–95. Reprint, Jerusalem, 1967.

Netton, Ian R. "Basic Structures and Signs of Alienation in the *Riḥla* of Ibn Jubayr." In *Golden Roads: Migration, Pilgrimage and Travel*, ed. Ian R. Netton, 57–74. Richmond, U.K.: Curzon, 1993. Reprint in Ian R. Netton. *Seek Knowledge: Thought and Travel in the House of Islam.* Richmond, U.K.: Curzon, 1996, 127–44.

Neubauer, Adolf. "'Inyene 'aseret ha-shevaṭim." *Qoveṣ 'al Yad* 4 (1888): 9–74.

———. "Where Are the Ten Tribes?" *JQR* 1, no 1 (1888): 14–28, no. 2 (1889), 95–114, no. 3 (1889), 185–201, no. 4 (1889), 408–23.

Noonan, F. Thomas. *The Road to Jerusalem: Pilgrimage and Travel in the Age of Discovery.* Philadelphia: University of Pennsylvania Press, 2007.

Obadiah of Bertinoro. *From Italy to Jerusalem: The Letters of Rabbi Obadiah of Bertinoro from the Land of Israel.* Hebrew, ed. Menahem E. Artom and Abraham David. Ramat Gan: Bar-Ilan University, 1997.

Ohler, Norbert. *The Medieval Traveller*, trans. Caroline Hillier. Woodbridge, U.K.: Boydell, 1989.

Olesen, Niels H. *Culte des saints et pèlerinage chez Ibn Taymiyya (661/1263–728/1328).* Paris: Paul Geuthner, 1991.

O'Loughlin, Thomas. "Adomnan and Arculf: The Case of an Expert Witness." *Journal of Medieval Latin* 7 (1997): 127–46.

Olschki, Leonardo. *Marco Polo's Asia: An Introduction to His "Description of the World" Called "Il Milione."* Berkeley: University of California Press, 1960.

Perry, Micha. "The Imaginary War Between Prester John and Eldad the Danite and Its Real Implications." *Viator* 41 (2010): 1–23.

Petaḥyah of Regensburg. *Die Rundreise des R. Petachjah aus Regensburg.* Hebrew, ed. Lazar (El'azar) Grünhut. 2 vols. Jerusalem: J. Kauffmann, 1904–5.

———. *Travels of Rabbi Petachia of Ratisbon*, ed. and trans. Abraham Benisch. London: Trubner, 1856.

Peters, F. E. *Jerusalem: The Holy City in the Eyes of Chroniclers, Visitors, Pilgrims, and Prophets from the Days of Abraham to the Beginnings of Modern Times.* Princeton, N.J.: Princeton University Press, 1985.

Pfister, Manfred. "Intertextuelles Reisen, oder: Der Reisebericht als Intertext." In *Tales and "Their Telling Difference": Zur Theorie und Geschichte der Narrativik, Festschrift für Franz K. Stanzel*, ed. Herbert Foltinek, Wolfgang Riehle, and Waldemar Zacharasiewicz, 109–32. Heidelberg: Carl Winter, 1993.

Polo, Marco. *Milione: Le Divisament dou monde: Il Milione nelle redazioni toscana e franco-italiana*, ed. Gabriella Ronchi. Milan: Mondadori, 1982.

———. *The Travels*, trans. Ronald Latham. Harmondsworth, U.K.: Penguin, 1958.

Pratt, Mary Louise. *Imperial Eyes: Travel Writing and Transculturation*. London: Routledge, 1992.

Prawer, Joshua. "Gefälschte hebräische Itinerarien des Heiligen Landes aus dem Mittelalter." In *Fälschungen im Mittelalter: Internationaler Kongreß der Monumenta Germaniae Historica, München, 16.–19. September 1986*. Monumenta Germaniae Historica 33, no. 5, 505–18. Hanover: Hahnsche, 1988.

———. *The History of the Jews in the Latin Kingdom of Jerusalem*. Oxford: Clarendon, 1988.

Prescott, Hilda F. M. *Jerusalem Journey: Pilgrimage to the Holy Land in the Fifteenth Century*. London: Eyre and Spottiswoode, 1954.

Pringle, Denys. *The Churches of the Crusader Kingdom of Jerusalem: A Corpus*. 2 vols. Cambridge: Cambridge University Press, 1993.

———. *Pilgrimage to Jerusalem and the Holy Land: 1187–1291*. Farnham, U.K.: Ashgate, 2012.

al-Qazwīnī, Zakariyyā'. *'Ajā'ib al-makhlūqāt: Zakarija Ben Muhammed Ben Mahmud el-Cazwini's Kosmographie*. 2 vols., ed. Ferdinand Wüstenfeld. Göttingen: Dieterichsche, 1848–49.

Raspe, Lucia. "Sacred Space, Local History, and Diasporic Identity: The Graves of the Righteous in Medieval and Early Modern Ashkenaz." In *Jewish Studies at the Crossroads of Anthropology and History: Tradition, Authority, Diaspora*, ed. Ra'anan S. Boustan, Oren Kosansky, and Marina Rustow, 147–63. Philadelphia: University of Pennsylvania Press, 2011.

Reiner, Elchanan. "From Joshua to Jesus—the Transformation of a Biblical Story to a Local Myth: A Chapter in the Religious Life of the Galilean Jew." In *Sharing the Sacred: Religious Contacts and Conflicts in the Holy Land: First–Fifteenth Centuries CE*, ed. Arieh Kofsky and Guy G. Stroumsa, 223–71. Jerusalem: Ben-Zvi Institute, 1998.

———. "A Jewish Response to the Crusades: The Dispute over Sacred Places in the Holy Land." In *Juden und Christen zur Zeit der Kreuzzüge*, ed. Alfred Haverkamp, 209–31. Sigmaringen: J. Thorbecke, 1999.

———. "'Oral Versus Written': The Shaping of Traditions of Holy Places in the Middle Ages." Hebrew. In *Studies in the History of Eretz Israel: Presented to Yehuda Ben-Porat*. Hebrew, ed. Yehoshua Ben-Arieh and Elchanan Reiner, 308–45. Jerusalem: Ben-Zvi Institute, 2003.

———. "Pilgrims and Pilgrimage to Eretz Yisrael, 1099–1517." Hebrew. Ph.D. diss., Hebrew University of Jerusalem, 1988.

———. "Traditions of Holy Places in Medieval Palestine—Oral Versus Written." In

Offerings from Jerusalem: Portrayals of Holy Places by Jewish Artists. Hebrew and English, ed. Rachel Sarfati. English part, 9–19. Jerusalem: Israel Museum, 2002.

Re'uveni, David. *The Story of David Hareuveni*. Hebrew, ed. Aaron Z. Aescoly. 2nd ed., with new introductions by Moshe Idel and Eliahu Lipiner. Jerusalem: Bialik Institute, 1993.

Richard, Jean. *Les récits de voyage et de pèlerinage*. Turnhout: Brepols, 1981.

Romanelli, Samuel. *Ketavim nivḥarim: Massa' ba-'rav, leqeṭ shirim, qeṭa'im mit-tokh maḥazot*, ed. Ḥayyim Schirmann. Jerusalem: Mosad Bialik, 1968.

———. *Travail in an Arab Land*, trans. Yedida K. Stillman and Norman A. Stillman. Tuscaloosa: University of Alabama Press, 1989.

Rossi, 'Azariah de'. *The Light of the Eyes*, trans. Joanna Weinberg. New Haven, Conn.: Yale University Press, 2001.

———. *Sefer me'or 'enayim*, ed. David Cassel. 2nd ed. Warsaw: Alapin, 1899.

Rubiés, Joan-Pau. *Travel and Ethnology in the Renaissance: South India Through European Eyes, 1250–1625*. Cambridge: Cambridge University Press, 2000.

———. "Travel Writing and Ethnography." In *The Cambridge Companion to Travel Writing*, ed. Peter Hulme and Tim Youngs, 242–60. Cambridge: Cambridge University Press, 2002. Reprint in *Travellers and Cosmographers: Studies in the History of Early Modern Travel and Ethnology*, ed. Joan-Pau Rubiés, chap. 4. Aldershot, U.K.: Ashgate, 2007.

———. "Travel Writing as a Genre: Facts, Fictions and the Invention of a Scientific Discourse in Early Modern Europe." *Journeys* 1 (2000): 5–35. Reprint in *Travellers and Cosmographers: Studies in the History of Early Modern Travel and Ethnology*, ed. Joan-Pau Rubiés, chap. 1. Aldershot, U.K.: Ashgate, 2007.

Ruderman, David B. *Early Modern Jewry: A New Cultural History*. Princeton, N.J.: Princeton University Press, 2010.

———. *The World of a Renaissance Jew: The Life and Thought of Abraham ben Mordecai Farissol*. Cincinnati: Hebrew Union College Press, 1981.

Runciman, Steven. *A History of the Crusades*. 3 vols. Cambridge: Cambridge University Press, 1951–54.

Rustow, Marina. *Heresy and the Politics of Community: The Jews of the Fatimid Caliphate*. Ithaca, N.Y.: Cornell University Press, 2008.

Saewulf. *Relatio de situ Ierusalem*. In *Peregrinationes Tres: Saewulf, John of Würzburg, Theodericus*. CCCM 139, ed. R. B. C. Huygens, 59–77. Turnhout: Brepols, 1994.

Safrai, Shmuel. *Pilgrimage at the Time of the Second Temple*. Hebrew. Tel Aviv: 'Am ha-Sefer, 1965.

Said, Edward W. *Orientalism*. New York: Pantheon, 1978. Reprint, New York: Vintage, 2003.

Salah, Asher. "The Otherness of the Self: On Romanelli's Travelogue." *European Journal of Jewish Studies* 5 (2011): 219–40.

Samuel ben Samson. *Itinerarium Palestinae*. Hebrew, ed. Fülöp Schulcz. Vác: Kohn, 1929.

Sarfati, Rachel. "The Illustrations of *Yiḥus ha-Avot*." In *Offerings from Jerusalem: Portrayals of Holy Places by Jewish Artists*. Hebrew and English, ed. Rachel Sarfati. English part, 21–29. Jerusalem: Israel Museum, 2002.

Schatz, Andrea. "Detours in a 'Hidden Land': Samuel Romanelli's *Masa ba'rav*." In *Jewish Studies at the Crossroads of Anthropology and History: Tradition, Authority, Diaspora*, ed. Ra'anan S. Boustan, Oren Kosansky, and Marina Rustow, 164–84. Philadelphia: University of Pennsylvania Press, 2011.

Scheindlin, Raymond P. *The Song of the Distant Dove: Judah Halevi's Pilgrimage*. Oxford: Oxford University Press, 2008.

Schorsch, Jonathan. *Jews and Blacks in the Early Modern World*. New York: Cambridge University Press, 2003.

Schroeter, Daniel. "Orientalism and the Jews of the Mediterranean." *Journal of Mediterranean Studies* 4 (1994): 183–96.

Semeonis, Symon. *Itinerarium Symonis Semeonis ab Hybernia ad Terram Sanctam*. Scriptores Latini Hiberniae 4, ed. and trans. Mario Esposito. Dublin: Dublin Institute for Advanced Studies, 1960.

Shalev, Zur. "Benjamin of Tudela, Spanish Explorer." *Mediterranean Historical Review* 25, no. 1 (2010): 17–33.

Shatzmiller, Joseph. "Jews, Pilgrimage, and the Christian Cult of Saints: Benjamin of Tudela and His Contemporaries." In *After Rome's Fall: Narrators and Sources of Early Medieval History: Essays Presented to Walter Goffart*, ed. Alexander Callander Murray, 337–47. Toronto: University of Toronto Press, 1998.

Shaw, Ezel K. "The Double Veil: Travelers' Views of the Ottoman Empire, Sixteenth Through Eighteenth Centuries." In *English and Continental Views of the Ottoman Empire, 1500–1800*, ed. Ezel K. Shaw and C. J. Heywood, 3–29. Los Angeles: W. A. Clark Memorial Library, 1972.

Shmuelevitz, Aryeh. *The Jews of the Ottoman Empire in the Fifteenth and Sixteenth Centuries: Administrative, Economic, Legal, and Social Relations as Reflected in the Responsa*. Leiden: Brill, 1984.

Silverberg, Robert. *The Realm of Prester John*. Garden City, N.Y.: Doubleday, 1972.

Sittig, C. "Reiseliteratur." In *Historisches Wörterbuch der Rhetorik*, ed. Gert Ueding, 7:1144–56. Tübingen: Max Niemeyer, 2005.

Stillman, Norman A. *The Jews of Arab Lands: A History and Source Book*. Philadelphia: Jewish Publication Society, 1979.

Stones, M. Alison. "Medieval Pilgrimage Writing and Its Manuscript Sources." In *Encyclopedia of Medieval Pilgrimage*, ed. Larissa J. Taylor et al., 395–413. Leiden: Brill, 2010.

Suriano, Francesco. *Il Trattato di Terra Santa e dell' Oriente*, ed. Girolamo Golubovich. Milan: Artigianelli, 1900.

———. *Treatise on the Holy Land*, trans. Theophilus Bellorini and Eugene Hoade. Jerusalem: Franciscan, 1949.

Taylor, Christopher S. *In the Vicinity of the Righteous:* Ziyāra *and the Veneration of Muslim Saints in Late Medieval Egypt*. Leiden: Brill, 1999.

Theoderic. *Libellus de Locis Sanctis*. In *Peregrinationes Tres: Saewulf, John of Würzburg, Theodericus*. CCCM 139, ed. R. B. C. Huygens, 143–97. Turnhout: Brepols, 1994.

Thompson, Carl. *Travel Writing*. London: Routledge, 2011.

Toledot Aleksandros ha-Maqdon: The Book of the Gests of Alexander of Macedon, trans. Israel J. Kazis. Cambridge, Mass.: Mediaeval Academy of America, 1962.

Turner, Victor. "The Center Out There: Pilgrim's Goal." *History of Religions* 12 (1973): 191–230.

———, and Edith L. B. Turner. *Image and Pilgrimage in Christian Culture: Anthropological Perspectives.* New York: Columbia University Press, 1978. Reprint, 1995.

Ullendorff, Edward, and Charles F. Beckingham. *The Hebrew Letters of Prester John.* Oxford: Oxford University Press, 1982.

Varthema, Ludovico. *Itinerario di Ludovico de Varthema*, ed. Paolo Giudici. Milan: Istituto Editoriale Italiano, 1956.

———. *The Travels of Ludovico di Varthema*, trans. John W. Jones. London: Hakluyt Society, 1863.

Veronese, Alessandra. *Una famiglia di banchieri ebrei tra XIV e XVI secolo: I da Volterra.* Pisa: Edizione ETS, 1998.

Vilnay, Zeev. *Maṣevot qodesh be-ereṣ yisra'el.* 2 vols. 3rd ed. Jerusalem: Aḥi'avar, 1985.

Vincent, Louis-Hugues, and E. J. H. Mackay. *Hébron: Le Ḥaram El-Khalîl, sépulture des Patriarches.* Paris: Leroux, 1923.

Vincent, (Louis)-Hugues, and F. M. Abel. *Jérusalem: Recherches de topographie, d'archéologie et d'histoire.* Vol. 2, *Jérusalem nouvelle*, bk. 3. Paris: J. Cabalda, 1922.

Vitkus, Daniel, J. "Early Modern Orientalism: Representations of Islam in Sixteenth- and Seventeenth-Century Europe." In *Western Views of Islam in Medieval and Early Modern Europe: Perception of Other*, ed. David R. Blanks and Michael Frassetto, 207–30. New York: St. Martin's, 1999.

von Harff, Arnold. *Die Pilgerfahrt des Ritters Arnold von Harff*, ed. Eberhard von Groote. Cologne: J. M. Heberle, 1860.

von Martels, Zweder. "Introduction: The Eye and the Mind's Eye." In *Travel Fact and Travel Fiction: Studies on Fiction, Literary Tradition, Scholarly Discovery and Observation in Travel Writing*, ed. Zweder von Martels, xi–xviii. Leiden: Brill, 1994.

Wang, Ning. *Tourism and Modernity: A Sociological Analysis.* Amsterdam: Pergamon, 2000.

Wasserstein, David J. "Eldad ha-Dani and Prester John." In *Prester John, the Mongols and the Ten Lost Tribes*, ed. Charles F. Beckingham and Bernard Hamilton, 213–36. Aldershot, U.K.: Ashgate, 1996.

Weber, Elka. "Sharing the Sites: Medieval Jewish Travellers to the Land of Israel." In *Eastward Bound: Travel and Travellers, 1050–1550*, ed. Rosamund Allen, 35–52. Manchester: Manchester University Press, 2004.

———. *Traveling Through Text: Message and Method in Late Medieval Pilgrimage Accounts.* New York: Routledge, 2005.

Weingrod, Alex, and André Levy. "On Homelands and Diasporas: An Introduction." In *Homelands and Diasporas, Holy Lands and Other Places*, ed. Alex Weingrod and André Levy, 3–26. Stanford, Calif.: Stanford University Press, 2005.

Wettstein, Howard. "Coming to Terms with Exile." In *Diasporas and Exiles: Varieties of Jewish Identity*, ed. Howard Wettstein, 47–59. Berkeley: University of California Press, 2002.

Wharton, Annabel J. *Selling Jerusalem: Relics, Replicas, Theme Parks.* Chicago: University of Chicago Press, 2006.

Wilhelm, Kurt, ed. *Roads to Zion: Four Centuries of Traveler's Reports.* New York: Schocken, 1948.

Wilkinson, John. "Jewish Holy Places and the Origins of Christian Pilgrimage." In *The Blessings of Pilgrimage*, ed. Robert Ousterhout, 41–53. Urbana: University of Illinois Press, 1990.

———, Joyce Hill, and W. F. Ryan, eds. *Jerusalem Pilgrimage, 1099–1185.* London: Hakluyt Society, 1988.

Wittkower, Rudolf. "Marvels of the East: A Study in the History of Monsters." *Journal of the Warburg and Courtauld Institutes* 5 (1942): 159–97.

Ya'ari, Avraham, ed. *Iggerot ereṣ yisra'el.* Ramat Gan: Masada, 1971.

Yahalom, Joseph. *Yehuda Halevi: Poetry and Pilgrimage*, trans. Gabriel Levin. Jerusalem: Magnes, 2009.

Yāqūt al-Rūmī. *Mu'jam al-buldān: Jacut's Geographisches Wörterbuch*, ed. Ferdinand Wüstenfeld. 6 vols. Leipzig: Brockhaus, 1866–70.

Yérasimos, Stéphane. *Les voyageurs dans l'empire ottoman (XIVe–XVIe siècles): Bibliographie, itinéraires et inventaire des lieux habités.* Ankara: Türk Tarih Kurumu, 1991.

Yerushalmi, Yosef H. "Exile and Expulsion in Jewish History." In *Crisis and Creativity in the Sephardic World, 1391–1648*, ed. Benjamin R. Gampel, 3–22. New York: Columbia University Press, 1997.

Zunz, Leopold. "An Essay on the Geographical Literature of the Jews, from the Remotest Times to the Year 1841." In *The Itinerary of Rabbi Benjamin of Tudela.* 2 vols., ed. Adolf Asher, 2:230–317. New York: Hakesheth, 1840–41.

———. "Geographische Literatur der Juden von den ältesten Zeiten bis zum Jahre 1841." In Leopold Zunz. *Gesammelte Schriften.* 1:146–216. Berlin: Louis Gerschel, 1875. Reprint, Hildesheim: Olms, 1976.

Index

Samaritans, 160, 180, 182–86, 209, 291*n*9, 292*n*24, 292*n*28, 292*n*29
Sambatyon, 189, 295*n*56
Samuel, tomb of. *See* Nabī Ṣamwīl
Samuel ben 'Eli, 131, 135, 136, 200, 274*n*51, 274*n*52, 274*n*61
Samuel ben Samson, 26, 47, 104, 215, 230*n*25
Sanjar bin Malik Shāh, 123, 194, 270*n*84, 295*n*29
Santo Brasca, 204, 300*n*74
sea travel, 26, 34, 39–41, 43, 46, 47, 49, 61, 64–70, 75–78, 141, 196, 208, 243*n*1, 250*n*12, 253*n*64
Seljuks, 123, 126, 192, 194
Semeonis, Symon, 255*n*87, 283*n*62, 299*n*62, 300*n*75
Sephardic Jews, as immigrants to the Ottoman Empire, 6, 96, 171, 289*n*85; as readership, 233*n*46; as residents of Jerusalem, 39, 176, 289*n*84; as travelers, 38, 49, 64, 290*n*92. *See also* Alḥarizi, Judah; Benjamin of Tudela; Judah Halevi
sexual practices, 193, 197, 205, 212, 295*n*13
Shabbat and holiday observance, 12, 57, 70, 75, 76, 156, 174, 175, 178, 189, 253*n*64, 254*n*72
Shiites, 118, 126, 191–93
Shūsh, vii, 121–23, 269*n*77, 270*n*82
Sicily, 34, 64, 65, 69. *See also* Palermo; Syracuse
Sidon, viii, 74, 84, 193
Sinai, Mount, 74; Peninsula, 26, 63, 64, 67, 68, 76, 78
slavery, 158, 197, 198, 297*n*40
Sudan, 196–98, 296*n*32
Sukayna bint al-Ḥusayn, tomb of, 115, 267*n*38
supersession, 3, 91, 114, 247*n*47
Suriano, Francesco, 99, 261*n*83
Susa. *See* Shūsh
Syracuse, vii, 64

table manners, ridiculed, 16, 157, 158, 177, 178, 282*n*46, 290*n*92
Tarragona, vii, 33
Theoderic, 87, 257*n*22
Thietmar, 270*n*4, 280*n*20
Thompson, Carl, 24, 229*n*15
Tiberias, viii; cemetery of, 115, 248*n*57, 267*n*38, 279*n*13
Tigris, vii, 64, 68, 121, 127, 130, 131
to'eh, *to'im*, 84, 90, 102, 255*n*8, 256*n*10
Toledo, vii, 1, 47, 136
tolls, 73, 74, 79, 172, 255*n*89
Tosafists, 35, 59, 176, 248*n*50
Toṣ'ot Ereṣ Yisra'el, 26, 27, 86, 93–95, 110, 114, 215, 231*n*28, 231*n*31
trade, 4, 5, 14, 39, 51–56, 99, 182, 198, 204, 209, 222*n*10, 244*n*9, 245*n*19, 245*n*32, 245*n*34
transportation, 53, 58, 64– 66, 72, 74, 84, 210. *See also* caravan
Tripoli, vii, viii, 55, 65, 66, 71, 165, 192
Tudela, vii, 29, 32
Turner, Victor, 15, 227*n*15
Tyre, viii, 51, 84

Uri ben Simeon of Biella, 232*n*37, 232*n*40
Usque, Abraham, 29, 30, 33
'Uzayr, place, vii, 121; person (Ezra), 269*n*75. *See also* Ezra, tomb of

Varthema, Ludovico di, 293*n*53
veil, 199–205, 299*n*65, 299*n*66, 299*n*69
Venice, vii, 5, 42–45, 53, 55, 56, 63, 65, 66, 75–78, 141, 162, 245*n*19, 250*n*3, 252*n*48
von Breydenbach, Bernhard, 202
von Harff, Arnold, 261*n*84, 300*n*82

wine, 39, 78, 103, 145, 169, 175, 177–79, 182, 195, 286*n*42, 289*n*77, 289*n*78
Wissenschaft des Judentums, 7, 301*n*7
women and gender, 12, 17, 63, 71, 197, 199–205, 212, 264*n*2, 265*n*14, 297*n*46, 298*n*47

Yāqūt al-Rūmī, 119, 268*n*59
Yiḥus Avot, 28, 43, 54, 92, 110, 111, 216, 232*n*37, 232*n*39, 245*n*25
Yiḥus ha-Ṣaddiqim, 28, 54, 105, 106, 216, 232*n*36
Yitgaddal the Scribe, 27, 104–6, 215, 232*n*34

ziyāra, 57, 58, 91, 106, 113, 115, 118, 120, 246*n*40, 247*n*41. *See also* pilgrimage, Jewish pilgrimage; pilgrimage, Muslim pilgrimage
Zunz, Leopold, 7, 8, 225*n*27

Acknowledgments

With this intellectual journey, I have continued to pursue several interests that I have had over the years, but it also breaks new paths. A general issue that has engaged me for some time is Jewish encounters—real as well as purely literary—with medieval Islam, Muslims, and Islamicate culture; another is my interest in premodern Jewish historical narratives, which were the specific topic of my book *Islamische Geschichte in jüdischen Chroniken: Hebräische Historiographie des 16. und 17. Jahrhunderts* (Tübingen: Mohr Siebeck, 2004). While working on the chronicles, I discovered that medieval Jewish travel narratives are an equally fascinating and understudied field. I was also drawn to the topic because I am an avid traveler who has visited many of the places described in the travel accounts that are analyzed in this study.

As is often the case, the research process involved significant travels. A year of leave granted me by Washington University in St. Louis in 2006–7, which I spent at the Hebrew University of Jerusalem, enabled me to begin the work. During this time, I collected most of my source material at the National Library of Israel, where I returned during the summer of 2008—this time supported by a research grant from Washington University's Graduate School. I was fortunate to have extensive access to the National Library's Judaica and Oriental Reading Rooms and am particularly indebted to its staff for their helpfulness over the years. The final draft of this book was written in Philadelphia during a fellowship year (2011–12) at the Herbert D. Katz Center for Advanced Judaic Studies, University of Pennsylvania. The fellowship program's annual theme (Travel Facts, Travel Fictions, and the Performance of Jewish Identity) so closely aligned with my own project that there could hardly have been a more inspiring environment in which to complete this study. I owe a vast debt of gratitude to David Ruderman for his gracious hospitality and for his enthusiastic interest in and support for the book. I am grateful to the center's librarians and staff—Josef Gulka, Arthur Kiron, Etty Lassman, Judith Leifer, and Bruce Nielsen—for their unfailing assistance and good humor. I also want to thank the other fellows in residence for the stimulating discussions we had, the questions they raised, and the camaraderie we shared. They surely will recognize an echo of our conversations within these pages.

Colleagues and friends from various places and institutions were liberal with their time and advice. I am particularly grateful to Miriam Frenkel, Beata Grant, Christine Johnson, Daniel Stein Kokin, and Joshua Levinson, who read specific chapters of the manuscript at different stages and made valuable suggestions concerning its content and style. Likewise, the comments provided by the two anonymous University of Pennsylvania Press readers proved to be highly beneficial, and I am very grateful for their careful reading and enthusiastic support. Many others deserve special thanks: I have drawn much insight and pleasure from conversations with Ora Limor, Elchanan Reiner, Joan-Pau Rubiés, David Wasserstein, and Yosef Yahalom. My debt to Avraham David's editions and source studies is clearly visible throughout this book; he provided me with a whole pile of his numerous publications. Additional thanks go to Micha Perry and Andrea Schatz, who shared some of their then-unpublished research with me. Thanks also to Daniel Bornstein and Liran Yadgar for providing me with valuable bibliographic references.

Studying a number of the travel writings with my students was not only a stimulating experience but helped clarify some of my arguments. I have profited from the questions, comments, and discussions that followed my presentation of work-in-progress at two annual meetings of the Association for Jewish Studies (Toronto, 2007; and Los Angeles, 2009); conferences and workshops at Saint Louis University (2010), Washington University in St. Louis (2011), and the University of Pennsylvania (2011 and 2012); and speaking opportunities at Princeton University (2012) and Columbia University (2012).

I owe special thanks to Avi Aronsky, who tirelessly copyedited an earlier draft and found a tactful way to improve the readability of my nonidiomatic English. Given that I later made extensive revisions to the book, I alone am responsible for any flaws and imperfections. My appreciation goes to Jennifer Moore, GIS Librarian at Washington University in St. Louis, who—supported by Deborah Katz, the Jewish and Near Eastern studies librarian—produced the maps that accompany this book. At the University of Pennsylvania Press, I would like to thank Jerome Singerman for his editorial guidance, Caroline Hayes, Noreen O'Connor-Abel, and Janice Meyerson, the copyeditor, for their great care in bringing this study to publication.

Some early fruits of my research on the travel accounts have been published as "From Lofty Caliphs to Uncivilized 'Orientals': Images of the Muslim in Medieval Jewish Travel Literature," *Jewish Studies Quarterly* 18 (2011): 64–90. The arguments I made there are spread over different parts of this volume (including the Introduction and Chapters 6 and 8) and have been significantly revised.

The title page of the 1556 Ferrara edition of Benjamin of Tudela's *Massa'ot* (Figure 1) is reproduced here with kind permission of the British Library Board, while all the other images are of early print editions held at the University of Pennsylvania's Herbert D. Katz Center for Advanced Judaic Studies (Figures 2–4) and Penn's Van Pelt–Dietrich Library (Figure 5); I am particularly grateful for the permissions to reproduce them here.